The Privy Councillors in the House of Commons, 1604–1629

THE PRIVY COUNCILLORS
in the
HOUSE OF COMMONS
1604–1629

by

DAVID HARRIS WILLSON
Assistant Professor of History
University of Minnesota

THE UNIVERSITY OF MINNESOTA PRESS
Minneapolis

Printed at The Lund Press, Inc., Minneapolis

Acknowledgments

I wish to acknowledge indebtedness of varying kinds and degrees to a number of persons and institutions. Much of the material for this book was collected when I was a fellow of the Social Science Research Council in 1932–33; and I must express my gratitude for this fellowship as well as for smaller supplementary grants. I am also grateful to the University of Minnesota Press for assuming the responsibility of publication and for the efficient aid of its editorial staff. To Professor Wallace Notestein, of Yale University, who first introduced me to the study of seventeenth-century parliaments, I am deeply indebted for constant friendship and assistance. His brilliant essay, *The Winning of the Initiative by the House of Commons,* confirmed the trend of my own studies and supplied me with fresh ideas and illustrations. I am also indebted to Mr. Hartley Simpson, whose knowledge of the early Stuart period is deep and profound, for a number of helpful suggestions. For errors of fact or judgment, I am, of course, solely responsible.

My thanks are due to the Marquis of Salisbury, Lord Sackville, the Benchers of the Inner Temple, London, and the Huntington Library, San Marino, California, for permission to use manuscripts and for the right to quote from them. To the libraries in which I have done the bulk of my work — the libraries of the University of Minnesota and of Cornell University, the Institute of Historical Research, London, the Bodleian Library, the British Museum, and the Public Record Office — I must return thanks for courtesy and cooperation. I also wish to thank the *American Historical Review* for permission to use material from two articles of mine published there.

Large portions of this book are based upon unpublished parliamentary diaries not easily accessible; and I should perhaps explain the forms in which I have used them. For the bulk of this material I have been dependent upon typed transcriptions kindly lent me by Professor Notestein. I have also used photostats in the rich

v

collection of the University of Minnesota Library and have read the originals of those diaries obtainable in the Bodleian Library, in the British Museum, and in the Public Record Office.

To illustrate one point (page 238), I have used data collected by Miss Dorothy A. Keane in an M.A. thesis (University of London) which deals with the subject of my book.

In conclusion, I wish to mention Thomas Harris Willson, a loyal and generous father; I would wish this book to stand as a tribute to him.

D. H. W.

Minneapolis, January, 1940

Abbreviations

Add. MSS. Additional Manuscripts, British Museum.

Borlase. Stowe MSS 366. An account of the session of 1628, probably a daily newsletter. The name on the title page, William Borlase, does not indicate the author but merely a former owner of the manuscript.

Bowyer. D. H. Willson (ed.), *The Parliamentary Diary of Robert Bowyer, 1606–1607.* Minneapolis, 1931.

C. J. Journals of the House of Commons, Vol. I, 1547–1629.

Cabala. Cabala, Mysteries of State, in Letters of the Great Ministers of King James and King Charles. London, 1654.

Cal. St. P. Calendar of State Papers. Various series: Domestic, Foreign, Venetian.

Clarendon. W. D. Macray (ed.), Edward Hyde, earl of Clarendon, *The History of the Rebellion and Civil Wars in England.* Oxford, 1888. 6 vols.

Commons Debates 1621. W. Notestein, F. H. Relf, and H. Simpson (eds.), *Commons Debates 1621.* New Haven, 1935. 7 vols.

Commons Debates in 1625. S. R. Gardiner (ed.), *Debates in the House of Commons in 1625.* Camden Society, 1873.

Commons Debates for 1629. W. Notestein and F. H. Relf (eds.), *Commons Debates for 1629.* Minneapolis, 1921.

Cott. MSS. Cottonian Manuscripts, British Museum.

Court and Times, James I. Robert F. Williams (ed.), Thomas Birch, *Court and Times of James I.* London, 1849. 2 vols.

Court and Times, Charles I. Robert F. Williams (ed.), Thomas Birch, *Court and Times of Charles I.* London, 1848. 2 vols.

D'Ewes (Elizabeth). Sir Simonds D'Ewes, *The Journals of All the Parliaments during the Reign of Queen Elizabeth.* London, 1682.

D'Ewes (Long Parl.). W. Notestein (ed.), *The Journal of Sir Simonds D'Ewes.* New Haven, 1923.

Erle. Additional MSS 18597. Diary of Sir Walter Erle for the parliament of 1624.

Gardiner. S. R. Gardiner, *History of England from the Accession of James I to the Outbreak of the Civil War.* London, 1883–84. 10 vols.

Goodman. John S. Brewer (ed.), Dr. Godfrey Goodman, *The Court of King James I.* London, 1839. 2 vols.

Grosvenor. MS 611, library of Trinity College, Dublin. Diary of Sir Richard Grosvenor for the parliaments of 1626 and 1628.

. Gurney. Gurney MS, at Keswick Hall, near Norwich. Anonymous diary for the parliament of 1624.

H. M. C. Publications of the Historical Manuscripts Commission.

Hacket, *Williams.* John Hacket, *A Memorial of John Williams, D. D.* London, 1693. Two parts in one volume.

Harl. MSS. Harleian Manuscripts, British Museum.

Harl. MSS 159. Harleian MSS 159. Anonymous diary for the parliament of 1624.

Harl. MSS 1601. Harleian MSS 1601. Parliamentary notes for the session of 1628.

Harl. MSS 4771. Harleian MSS 4771. A newsletter dealing with the session of 1628. This is one of many copies. Often called "The True Relation."

Holles. Harleian MSS 6383. Diary of John Holles for the parliament of 1624. Harleian MSS 2313 and 5324. Diary, probably by Denzil Holles, for the parliament of 1628.

L. J. Journals of the House of Lords.

Lansd. MSS. Lansdowne Manuscripts, British Museum.

Lowther. Historical Manuscripts Commission, Thirteenth Report, Part 7. Notes for the parliaments of 1626 and 1628 by a "Mr. Lowther."

Mass. Manuscript in the Massachusetts Historical Society Library. Copy of "The True Relation." See under Harl. MSS 4771.

Negotium Posterorum. Alexander B. Grosart (ed.), Sir John Eliot, *Negotium Posterorum.* London, 1881. 2 vols.

Nicholas. St. P. Domestic, 14/166 and 16/97. Diary of Edward Nicholas for the parliaments of 1624 and 1628. The diary for 1628 has been edited by Miss Louise M. Sumner (M. A. thesis, University of Minnesota); references to this are by page.

P. and D. Edward Nicholas, *Proceedings and Debates in the House of Commons in 1620 and 1621.* Oxford, 1766. 2 vols.

Paris Trans. Paris Transcripts, Public Record Office.

Parl. Debates in 1610. S. R. Gardiner (ed.), *Parliamentary Debates in 1610.* Camden Society, 1862.

Parl. Hist. The Parliamentary or Constitutional History of England from the Earliest Times to the Restoration of King Charles II. London, 1751–62. 24 vols.

ABBREVIATIONS

Rich. Manuscript in the possession of the duke of Manchester at Kimbolton Castle, St. Neots, Huntingdonshire. Diary of Sir Nathaniel Rich for the parliaments of 1624 and 1626. See *Commons Debates 1621*, I, 88–90.

Rushworth. John Rushworth, *Historical Collections*. London, 1721–22. 8 vols.

Sloane MSS. Sloane Manuscripts, British Museum.

Spanish Trans. Spanish Transcripts, Public Record Office.

Spedding. James Spedding, *The Letters and Life of Francis Bacon*. London, 1861–74. 7 vols.

St. P. State Papers, Public Record Office. Various series: Domestic, Spanish, German, Holland, Venice.

Stowe MSS. Stowe Manuscripts, British Museum.

Strafford's Letters. W. Knowler (ed.), *The Earl of Strafforde's Letters and Despatches with an Essay towards his Life by Sir George Radcliffe*. London, 1739. 2 vols.

Whitelocke. MS D. D. 12, 20–22, Cambridge University Library. Diary by Bulstrode Whitelocke for the parliament of 1626.

Winchilsea. Manuscript in the possession of the earl of Winchilsea. Diary of John Pym for the parliament of 1624. See *Commons Debates 1621*, I, 26–27.

Winwood. Edmund Sawyer (ed.), Sir Ralph Winwood, *Memorials of Affairs of State in the Reigns of Queen Elizabeth and King James I*. London, 1725. 3 vols.

Table of Contents

*The Privy Councillors in the House
of Commons, 1604–1629*

1

The Tudor and Stuart Background

The Tudor genius for government, which remains the admiration of posterity, evolved a form of absolutism that was not incompatible with the growth of the house of commons. That growth was, in fact, astonishingly rapid under the Tudors. When Henry VII secured the throne, the commons were still in the medieval stage of their development, with little organization or influence. When Elizabeth died in 1603, they had secured an established place in the counsels of the nation, their house was on an equality with that of the lords, their privileges were becoming realities, and they were ready, though they would have been the first to deny it, to make a successful bid for sovereignty in the decades ahead. But if Henry VIII and Elizabeth tolerated and at times encouraged this development, it was because they were able to direct and control it to a large extent. They did this chiefly through the force of their own dominant personalities and through their skill and adroitness in dealing with the commons. But they relied also upon their councillors and other officials who were members of the house. The sovereign remained in the background and left the details of parliamentary management to the more invisible guidance of his ministers. These men, clustered in a group close to the speaker, formed a sort of ministerial bench and were, in fact, the leaders of the house. They initiated the most important legislation, they made clear the need for subsidies, and under Elizabeth they formed a breakwater against the increasing demands of the commons for more liberty in the house and for less autocratic methods of government in church and state.

James and Charles, however, conjured into the Tudor period an absolutism more complete than the reality and utterly misunderstood the transformation that was taking place in the house of commons. The commons, on their side, highly sensitive to their position and privileges and goaded by grievances and abuses in the government, became increasingly aggressive. A clash was thus inevitable. The impact of that clash fell heavily upon the councillors in the house. Their preparations for a session dwindled into a search for grievances that could be redressed without loss to the crown. They could no longer obtain election from popular constituencies. Their parliamentary tactics ceased to be efficacious. Their defense of government policy became mere pleading for moderation. New procedures arose that robbed them of their influence. New leaders, drawn from the opposition, usurped their function of initiating legislation and won the support of the majority of members. Even in their more formal functions councillors were regarded with suspicion and hostility. They were reduced to impotent spokesmen of the crown in an assembly that had slipped from their control. It is with this decline in the position of councillors that this study is concerned.

An attempt has also been made to look behind the councillors to the forces at court that were directing parliamentary policy and to the elements in the commons from which the councillors might reasonably expect support. Two points stand out. The parliamentary tactics of the crown were, generally speaking, so ill advised that they became a major cause of discontent, and opposition was swollen by resentment at the awkward and unsuitable methods of the government in dealing with the commons. In the second place, the crown was constantly losing the support of members who were connected in one way or another with the government, and the opposition was constantly recruited by deserters from the royal cause. The spirit of opposition abroad in the land was highly contagious. But here again the tactlessness of the crown was responsible for the dissidence of many former adherents.

This study is not merely a story of retreat. Parliamentary procedures were developing that remain in use today in every legislative assembly. The faint foreshadowings of later political parties were beginning to emerge. The commons were learning to achieve results and not merely to indulge in captious criticism. Their opposition to councillors pointed clearly to the later theory and practice of ministerial responsibility.

The appearance of councillors as elected members of the commons in the early Tudor period was an event of fundamental importance. Councillors had been the core of the medieval parliament, which was in essence an expanded meeting of the council for certain kinds of business. The councillors had sat in the middle of the parliament chamber surrounded by the magnates; and the commons appeared before them only occasionally during the session, standing bareheaded and deferential at the lower end of the chamber. But slowly the position of the council in parliament had grown precarious. As the lords evolved the idea of a peerage and moved toward a house with hardened rules of membership, they gradually reduced the position of councillors to that of other lords and threatened with exclusion those councillors who were not members of the nobility. In 1539 Henry passed an act giving the great officers of state the right to attend the lords whether they were peers or not; but if they were not peers they could not vote and the measure applied only to a small group of councillors. The situation was aggravated by the Tudor practice of placing in the council men of humble origin, selected for their ability rather than for their family connections. These councillors now sought election to the commons. This step was an indication that the commons were worth controlling and that councillors could do the crown good service by becoming members.[1]

The commons advanced rapidly during the reign of Henry VIII. They obtained some control over their own members and assumed something of the aspect of a court in punishing offenders against their privileges. Their self-respect and self-confidence were increased by the attitude of the king. Henry had a parliamentary policy in a new sense of the word; and in the great Reformation Parliament he took the commons into partnership and brought about the break with Rome through parliamentary action when he might have done so by other means. He was ready to persuade rather than coerce the commons. He tolerated occasional criticism of his policy, thus providing us with the Tudor definition of what free speech in the commons should comprise. If foreign envoys were told that in England the commons were free and that therefore antipapal legislation could not be prevented, members might take comfort from the suggestion even though they knew it to be false. Above all, Henry gave the commons a thorough schooling in the art of legislation; and the statutes of his reign equal in bulk the statutes of all the medieval kings. But if Henry thus accorded

---

[1] In a larger sense, it embedded the executive in the commons as well as in the lords, it added responsibility to debate, and it facilitated the evolution of the cabinet system. See A. F. Pollard, *The Evolution of Parliament* (London, 1926), 268–69, 278–98.

the commons an outward tolerance and recognition, he had his way with them nevertheless. There was occasional coercion; and there were threats which could not safely be ignored. Henry also had his councillors in the commons to see that his will was done.

Parliament was under the general supervision of councillors. Cromwell and other ministers prepared public opinion before sessions began and influenced elections through letters to nobles and country gentry. Cromwell wrote Henry in 1539 that he anticipated no opposition in a coming session "forasmoche as I and other your dedicate conseillers be aboutes to bring all thinges so to passe that your Maiestie had never more tractable parlement." Laws were drafted or sketched out before parliament met and councillors supervised their passage through the house. At times bills were introduced in the lords and then brought to the commons with the added prestige of the approval of leading peers; though normally, as the reign progressed, important legislation was introduced first in the commons. Criticism was answered or dragooned into silence. Cromwell wrote Henry in 1539 that he had taken the precaution of placing in the commons "your Maiesties seruaunt Mr. Morisson," who "shalbe redy to answer and take vp suche as wold crake or face with literature of lernyng." Supporters of the government were encouraged to remain until the end of the session and opponents encouraged to leave early. The speaker was the servant of the crown and could do much. Thus Henry secured the legislation he desired without playing the dictator too openly. And it must be remembered that management of this sort placed the commons on a far higher plane than they might have expected from the power of the king.[2]

Elizabeth was faced with a far more difficult task than her father. The commons were more independent and aggressive, they broadened the crown's definition of free speech to something like its modern meaning, and they showed a propensity to initiate legislation on delicate questions which was most embarrassing to the crown. The same members were elected to parliament after parliament and gained more of a corporate spirit. Puritanism inculcated a fearless determination to follow conscience with little regard for the wishes of earthly kings. There was not one session in Eliza-

---

[2] R. B. Merriman, *Life and Letters of Thomas Cromwell* (2 vols., Oxford, 1902), II, 199. W. Notestein, *The Winning of the Initiative by the House of Commons* (London, 1925), 4–10, and sources therein cited.

beth's long reign in which some point of dispute did not arise between her and the commons. The power of the crown, moreover, had diminished. Elizabeth could not alter bills once they were passed. She could not use her veto without caution. Yet there were certain things — notably the succession and her religious settlement — which by necessity she placed above parliamentary interference. She could not allow laws concerning these matters to be introduced for fear they would gain momentum and force her to use the veto against the wishes of large numbers of her people. Hence if her councillors could not stop these measures at their inception, Elizabeth was forced to intervene and thus raise questions of parliamentary privilege.

Elizabeth acted with consummate skill, following the lead of her father in combining outward tolerance with quiet manipulation through her ministers. By playing upon the chivalry of her parliaments, by able and flattering speeches, by her regal bearing and tactful management, she obtained most of what she wanted from the commons without sacrificing those points on which she knew she must stand firm. Yet she made concessions and allowed constitutional questions to go unsettled if only she won the practical point at issue. Occasionally she sent an imperious command which the house could not but obey. But she avoided extreme measures where she could, preferring to remain in the background, a slightly mystic figure, whose swift alternation of gracious affability and tart reproof created an atmosphere of loyalty tinged with awe. Elizabeth thus created for the sovereign a role which she could play but which in all probability could not be played by anyone else; and won immediate results at the cost of embarrassing her successor.[3]

The councillors in the house formed an essential feature of Elizabeth's policy. There were more of them in the commons than before and they worked together with method and precision. They influenced elections where they could. The great mass of elections were in the hands of the nobility and gentry, and Elizabeth, of course, gained many more adherents in the commons through her cultivation of the upper classes than by any interference of the council. To say that her parliaments were packed would be absurd. Nevertheless, an impressive amount of evidence shows the efforts

[3] See J. E. Neale, "The Commons' Privilege of Free Speech in Parliament," *Tudor Studies* (London, 1924), 257–86.

7

of councillors, as a group and as individuals, to influence elections wherever possible. Letters to sheriffs declaring that candidates must be well affected to the government, letters to local magnates supporting certain candidates and deprecating others, letters to town corporations, letters to troublesome persons suggesting that they withdraw from election contests — these are found in abundance. Elizabeth increased the size of the commons by fifty-nine members. And though this is pictured as evidence of the growing interest of the country in parliament, it is obvious that many newly enfranchised boroughs were located in districts where the influence of the crown was paramount. Interference in elections, though it touched but a small percentage of the total membership of the commons, at least provided the government with a nucleus of members more or less pledged to support the existing regime. It enabled the government to place certain persons, the speaker-elect, minor officials with a gift for debate; while troublemakers might perhaps be excluded.

Councillors prepared a program of legislation to be laid before the commons. In 1558 the council appointed a committee of its members "for consideration of all things necessary for the Parlyamente"; and earlier, in 1554, a committee "to consider what laws shalbe established in this parliament and to name the men that shall make the books thereof." The state papers and Cecil manuscripts contain a mass of evidence showing that the Cecils and other councillors sketched out legislation for the commons. Lists of matters "considerable in parliament"; memorials "of things fit to be considered by the parliament"; "business to be moved in parliament"; extracts of "acts to be made this parliament"; "articles whereupon an act of parliament may be made"; "proposed bills to be introduced into parliament; new laws to be offered to the lower house; . . . bills that were dealt with in the last session but proceeded no further than the lower house for want of time" — entries such as these are found in large numbers and demonstrate the amount of paternalistic legislation put forward by the government. They give point to the Tudor conception of the commons as an assembly whose function was to examine and criticize the legislation proposed by the government.

The advantages of preparing a program for the commons are quite obvious. Parliamentary sessions were shortened. A member named Tate, writing in the reign of Elizabeth, remarked, "One meane to shorten the Session, is to have those matters thoroughlie provided afore as the Subsidie taske, readdie written both in paper and parchment. If any alteracion happen, a peece of parchment is soone cutt out, and a new put in amended. If it be any other matter, that then it be well prepared by the Queenes Lerned Counsell and if it be not a matter too secret, it were well that some other were privie of it afore." [4] The councillors had the advantage of taking the initiative, and the commons were soon at work on matters other than their grievances. Ordinary members, coming up from their isolated countrysides, were usually ready to adopt the program laid before them.

The councillors worked together to push their program through the commons. They introduced many bills and supported one another in securing legislative action. Their control was greatly facilitated in the early part of the reign by the committee system. Councillors were members of all important committees; and the clerk fell into the habit of beginning lists of committee members with the words, "All the Privy Councillors of the House." Committees were small and could be controlled more easily than the house. They could alter bills drastically and, if they wished, bring in an entirely new bill. Occasionally they were asked to frame a bill upon propositions offered in debate. Their power gives point to the many notes of amendments and provisos found in the papers of the Cecils and other councillors. Certainly the committee system gave councillors added control over legislation.

Councillors could also guide the commons in selecting the bills to be pushed and in discarding others. In the early part of the reign bills were sometimes referred to a councillor for consideration before the house proceeded with them. As late as 1593 the speaker was instructed not to receive bills dealing with the church or commonwealth "until they be viewed and considered by those who it is fitter should consider of such things, and can better judge of them." Bills might be dropped in the house if the council spoke against them. In 1584 a member asked the house to read a bill concerning the church, "against which Sir Francis Knolles Knight, Treasurer of her Majesties Household, spake first, but in a few words; and after him Sir Christopher Hatton Knight her Maj-

---

[4] Harl. MSS 253, f. 35. The learned counsel were not, of course, privy councillors.

9

esties Vice-Chamberlain more largely, who pressed and moved the House so far therein, that it was at length resolved, that the said Book and Bill should not be read." A bill was withdrawn from the house in 1593 on the motion of Sir Robert Cecil. Bills could be stopped by commands from the queen, but commands had disadvantages. "I thinke good that a choise be made of Billes," wrote Tate, "wherein this I note, that it is not good in any that any thinge for choise of admittinge or reiectinge of bills be delivered by the Speaker, or any Counselor or other, as by her Majesties Commaundement, for soe would by and by be raised by some humerous bodie some question of the libertie of the Howse, and of restraininge their free consultacion perhaps offensive to her Majestie and assuredlie with longe speeches to the troublesome prolonginge of the Session." Tate preferred a royal message warning the house that the session must shortly end and that the commons must husband their time; followed by a motion — preferably not by a councillor, who might cause some jealousy if it was suspected that he spoke by command — that "there maie be committees of the Howse to consider of Billes offered, to prefer the forwardinge of the most necessarie, before the other, but in noe wise to make mencion of reiectinge any (although indeed it amounteth to a reiecting of those that be of small importance) for private billes ever be eagerlie followed and make factions." [5]

In guiding legislation through the commons the speaker could be useful. Details of the order of business were largely in his hands. He could determine almost at will the moment at which a bill should be read, committed, or passed; and could thus push certain bills and retard others. He gave the floor to members wishing to speak; he decided whether the aye or no sounded the louder at a time when divisions were still exceptional; he adjourned the house at the end of the day's business. He explained the contents of bills and framed the questions put in the house. In 1597 the speaker apologized to Cecil for the failure of a bill in which Cecil was interested. "I did all the good I could for the furthering of it and made two questions, whether it should be committed, which

[5] Examples of bills being referred to councillors in *D'Ewes (Elizabeth)*, 52, 83, 86, 126. *D'Ewes (Elizabeth)*, 460, 339, 513–14. Harl. MSS 253, f. 33–34. In 1571 a committee was named "for appointing such Bills for the Common-Weal as shall be first proceeded in, preferred before the residue, but not to reject any." *D'Ewes (Elizabeth)*, 179. See also Notestein, *Winning of the Initiative*, 13–22.

being denied, I moved whether it should be engrossed, which was also denied, so as now no more questions be to be made of it. I did favour it as much as, with the dignity of my place, I could, and I am sorry, if you did anything affect it, that it succeeded no better." The speaker could push the subsidy by forcing a vote and could word questions in such a way that members disliked voting in the negative. The speaker was equally useful in stopping debate. Tate wrote concerning long speeches and the speaker's power to stop them: "Lett them not be moved in the beginninge or middest of the forenoone, but neere towards the risinge of the Howse; here is the great difficultie of the speakers whole servise to give some temper, and yet to avoid opinion of overrulinge or straiteninge the liberties of the House, heere must be discreet interposinge of Committies, and such good meanes, and amonge other, not to be too hastie with eftsones readinge of those Billes that have bene found upon a first or seconde reading to be soe large walkinge feildes." When Peter Wentworth gave the speaker some leading questions about the liberties of the house and wished them read to the commons, the speaker "pocketted them up" and showed them to the council, which so handled the matter that Wentworth went to the Tower and the questions were never read.[6]

In his paper on parliament Tate raised the question whether a councillor should be selected as speaker, but concluded that it was not necessary. Since the election was controlled by the crown, the speaker would always be a person acceptable to the queen. If a councillor was nominated, the commons might imagine their privileges invaded; and if this difficulty arose, it would occur at the very opening of the session, which would be doubly unfortunate. The speaker, though not a councillor, would "without doubt be such as her Majesties services wilbe well advanced, and the speaker both maie of the Counsell receave directions for deliverance and assistance for furtherance, and one Counsellors voice the more saved, besides his travill as a Committie which the Speaker cannot be." The speaker must know the common law "and of that sort I thinke amongst the Counselle there is no great choise. . . . A Counsellor beinge speaker looseth his voice which would be no small hinderance to her highness service." Finally, if the speaker was a councillor, other members would not have easy access to

[6] Speaker Yelverton to Cecil, November 14, 1597, *Cal. Hatfield House MSS*, VII, 482. Harl. MSS 253, f. 35. *D'Ewes (Elizabeth)*, 411.

him, although out of courtesy he would offer it; and hence the speaker could not "find and disolve the humors of the howse as another shall." [7]

Elizabeth, as we know, hesitated to use violent methods. No one during her reign was imprisoned for his speeches in the commons. But members were called before the council and sharply rebuked. In 1572 Mr. Bell, after a reprimand of this sort, "came into the House with such an amazed Countenance, that it daunted all the House in such sort, that for ten, twelve, or sixteen days, there was not one in the House that durst deal in any matter of importance. And in those simple matters that they dealt in, they spent more words and time in their preamble, requiring that they might not be mistaken, than they did in the matter they spake unto." Peter Wentworth denounced the way in which rumors and whispered words about the wishes of the queen passed quietly from member to member and influenced their actions. He was also shocked to find that members watched the way in which councillors voted and then voted with them. In close divisions members were pulled by the sleeve to induce them to vote with one side rather than the other. And if none of the commons were imprisoned for what they said, they were imprisoned for introducing bills distasteful to the queen, for discussing parliamentary affairs in private meetings, and for planning with other members for joint action in the house. Thus means were found to overawe the commons and to restrain bold spirits.[8]

As the end of the reign approached, opposition became more open and the commons more difficult to control. Councillors were treated with disrespect. Disorderly scenes took place in the commons during the parliament of 1601. Members protested when they were told that there were topics they must not discuss. "When any great or weighty matter or Bill is here handled," the council was told, "we streight say it toucheth the Prerogative and must not be medled withal." [9] Committees were growing larger in membership and thus more difficult to handle; they also dealt with larger topics than the details of single measures. Once the great figure of the queen was removed and the commons found themselves in the altered atmosphere of a new dynasty to which

[7] Harl. MSS 253, f. 32–33.
[8] D'Ewes (Elizabeth), 237–42, 683–84.
[9] Ibid., 671.

they were not bound by long-established ties of affection and loyalty, opposition might well flare up with unexpected violence.

Precisely at the moment when the crown faced dangerous opposition in parliament and was forced to do battle for its place in the constitution, its position was undermined by the weaknesses and errors of the new ruler and by the rapid decline of the council as an instrument of government.

James, as everybody knows, was quite unfit to guide the commons at a most delicate moment of their history; and his personal relations with parliament were disastrous. He was not the fool that the scandalmongers of the court would have us believe. He was not without flashes of political insight and a sense of reality. "He needs no spectacles," wrote the Venetian ambassador, "and when he wishes to see he is like an Argus." [10] His faults were less those of unintelligence than of bad training and of basic weaknesses of character.

His struggle with the Presbyterian clergy in Scotland inculcated in him an exaggerated suspicion and dislike of puritanism; and blinded him to the distinction between radical forms of dissent and the moderate puritan tendencies of many members of the house of commons. All puritans were suspect because their conceptions of church government undermined the power of the bishops and hence the power of the king. There was thus no place for a larger comprehension in the English church. James, of very necessity, had parried the claims of the Scottish divines by a corresponding exaltation, in theory at least, of the position of the crown. Monarchy became the supremest thing on earth, kings little gods, and "the laws were but craved by his subjects and only made by him." Such theories fitted nicely with James's high opinion of himself. But they rendered unnecessary and ridiculous the caution and restraint of Elizabeth in dealing with the commons. To James the veto was a prerogative to be employed at will; the privileges of the commons mere examples of royal indulgence; and the demand for change mere clamor. Thus he presented a blind conservatism to the aspirations of the commons; all novelties are dangerous, he told them; and his answer was purely negative at all points. In these conceptions the adroit Tudor combination of outward toleration and quiet conciliar control could find no place.

[10] *Cal. St. P. Venetian, 1621–1623*, 441.

In Scotland James had governed by canny manipulation of rival factions, by sowing dissensions among his adversaries, by combining intrigue and sharp practices with a show of force. In England these methods produced chaos and stalemate at court and mere meddling in dealings with the commons.

James took a deep interest in parliament, following day by day and even hour by hour the fortunes of measures he desired. He demanded from his ministers long reports of parliamentary business. He interfered far too much, often without just cause, in the work of the commons, emphasizing the intrusion of the crown where Elizabeth had sought to minimize it. His meddling raised minor disputes to the dignity of constitutional issues and provoked heated rejoinders. He cheapened his speeches by their frequency, their scolding and didactic tone, and their references to the divine right of kings. His bearing was awkward and undignified, in striking contrast to that of the stately Elizabeth. "When he wishes to speak like a king," wrote Tillières, the French ambassador, "he rails like a tyrant and when he wishes to yield he does so with indecency." He could be astonishingly tactless. He told the commons, as an argument in favor of union with Scotland, that England had often been conquered in the past but Scotland never. As the Venetian ambassador once remarked, James had a wonderful faculty for doing himself harm.[11]

He was a very lazy person. He loved to make a speech or preside over a disputation and did both quite well. But the daily routine of attention to business, no small part of Tudor success, was abhorrent to him, and he lacked the power of will to follow it through. In 1605 he seriously proposed to the council that all business be placed in their hands and that he be left free to enjoy a quiet country life. For a time after Salisbury's death he attempted to be his own secretary and "took delight to show his readiness and ability in those causes"; but very soon "that vigour began to relent and he must daily more and more attend to his own health and quiet." The Venetian ambassador wrote in 1620 that James "seemed utterly weary of the affairs that were taking place all over

---

[11] Tillières to Puisieux, January 6, 1622, Paris Trans., 3/56. *C. J.*, I, 953. *Cal. St. P. Venetian, 1623–1625*, 78. Bacon suggested to James that he should speak less often to the commons. *Spedding*, V, 190. "Wearied with the long orations of King James, that did inherit but the winde," the commons liked the brevity of Charles's first speech to parliament in 1625. *Negotium Posterorum*, I, 44–45.

the world at this time, and hated being obliged every day to spend time over unpleasant matters and listen to nothing but requests and incitements to move in every direction and to meddle with everything. He remarked: I am not God Almighty."[12] His dependence upon favorites was in part the result of indolence; it was so easy to settle affairs by doing as the favorite wished. But government in England still required the close and constant scrutiny of the sovereign. Without it, honesty and efficiency quickly declined and money went like water. A session of parliament, moreover, greatly increased the need for attention to affairs.

The demands of business combined with minor physical ailments to aggravate James's natural petulance and irritability. He easily flew into petty fits of rage that could do great harm. The commons were extremely irritating; but caution, temper, and self-restraint were absolutely essential if the king was to deal with them successfully. Three of James's four parliaments were dissolved by the king in fits of anger. Whitehall was a hectic place at best, and James made matters worse by relaxing the rules governing access to the sovereign. He found himself confused by the diversity of counsel and harassed by the importunity of suitors. Calvert wrote in 1610 that the king was "so distracted with variety of Opinions, from a Number about him, especially Scots, that though he would, he cannot resolve that which he desires; which is the Cause that as often as he can he absents himself from the Town, yet is quickly fetched again on every Occasion, which much troubles him." He spent long periods in the country not only because he hated London and loved hunting but because he sought escape from the irritations and worries of the court. The Venetian ambassador wrote in 1621 that James gladly went on progress to free himself from the annoyance of ministers and ambassadors and to get as far away from them as possible.

But such absences interfered with business. "The Lords of the Council," wrote the Venetian ambassador in 1607, "have with great justice pointed out to his Majesty that his continued absence from the city, especially while the question of the Union is on, is very injurious to the negotiations." Two of the most serious parlia-

---

[12] John Chamberlain to Sir Dudley Carleton, January 28, 1613, *Court and Times, James I*, I, 157. *Cal. St. P. Venetian, 1619–1621*, 363, 475.

mentary crises of the reign found James loitering in the country. "It is much marvelled," wrote Chamberlain in 1621, "that so much business being now on foot, both at home and abroad, the king should keep still at Newmarket." [13]

As James grew older his weaknesses grew upon him; and he became irresolute and timid. "It seems to me that the intelligence of this king has diminished," wrote Tillières in 1621; "not that he cannot act firmly and well at times and particularly when the peace of the kingdom is involved, but such efforts are not so continual as they once were. His mind uses its powers only for a short time, but in the long run he is cowardly." His timidity, wrote Tillières again, "has increased day by day as old age carries him into apprehensions and vices diminish his intelligence." "The king seems very anxious and perplexed," wrote the Venetian ambassador; "as a matter of fact his Majesty is vexed by great irresolution and does not know what to do." These tendencies reached their climax during the journey of Charles and Buckingham to Madrid. To James this was a period of mental agony, in which he "spent some nights in unbroken fury," a prey to the darkest fears and apprehensions. It left him an old man too weak in will to resist his son and his favorite. When they urged him to call parliament in 1624, he could resist only by sinking into a state of distracted inaction, "sometimes swearing and calling upon God, heaven, and the angels, at other times weeping, then laughing, and finally pretending illness in order to play upon the pity of those who urge him to generous actions and to show them that sickness renders him incapable of deciding anything, demanding only repose and, indeed, the tomb." [14] These things are well known; yet they cannot be forgotten in a study of the house of commons.

As the quality of the ruler declined, so did that of his council. This was not noticeable, however, during the first ten years of the reign. James inherited from Elizabeth her chief minister, Robert

[13] Samuel Calvert to William Trumbull, June 10, 1610, *Winwood*, III, 182. *Cal. St. P. Venetian, 1619–1621*, 327; *1603–1607*, 479, 147. Chamberlain to Carleton, December 1, 1621, *Court and Times, James I*, II, 278. See also Thomas Locke to Carleton, November 29, 1621, St. P. Domestic, 14/123:135. James turned fiercely upon a suitor in 1623: "You will never let me alone. I would to God you had, first my doublett, and then my shirt, and when I were naked, I think you would give me leave to be quiett." Tobie Matthew to Buckingham, March 29, 1623, Harl. MSS 1581, f. 78.

[14] Tillières to Puisieux, July 3, 1620, September 28, October 18, 1621, January 6, 24, 1622, December 29, 1623, Paris Trans., 3/54, 55, 56, 57. *Cal. St. P. Venetian, 1619–1621*, 615, 264–65, 575; *1623–1625*, 50, 22–23.

Cecil, now earl of Salisbury, who made himself the pivot about which the entire machinery of government revolved and whose position resembled that of a modern prime minister, responsible for administration and legislation alike. But if he, more than a president, was alpha and omega in council, he nevertheless, as he said, did not like to carry great things alone. He constantly consulted his colleagues and was merely the first among the councillors of the king. The council was active during these years, and James left affairs very largely in its hands. Foreign observers came to the conclusion that it was the council that ruled the country. "The Council spares the King the trouble of governing," wrote the Venetian ambassador, "and not only do all subjects transact their business with it, but foreign representatives as well, and one might say it was the very ears, body, and voice of the King." Again he wrote that James "remits everything to the Council" and "has virtually given it full and absolute authority." Such statements, while overcharged, indicate the high place that the council, dominated by Salisbury, occupied at this time. As long as he lived it retained its Tudor characteristics.[15]

After his death in 1612 the council entered upon a rapid decline. Of many causes, two are pre-eminent: the factional strife of contending groups and the rise of government through favorites to the neglect of the council as a whole. Once Salisbury was removed, new opinions and influences, which he had suppressed or excluded, quickly emerged, and we enter upon a new phase of the reign. The Howards, with their Spanish and pro-Catholic sympathies, were already entrenched in the favor of the king before Salisbury's death, and now their influence was greatly increased. The mainspring of the Spanish faction was Henry Howard, earl of Northampton. He was supported by the other Howards, Suffolk, who became lord treasurer, and Nottingham, the lord admiral. The Howards placed many of their dependents, such as Sir Thomas Lake and Sir Charles Cornwallis, in places of trust; and eventually they joined forces with the favorite, Robert Carr, who became earl of Somerset. They formed but a fraction of the council, but they held many of the most important offices, had the aid of Sarmiento (later Count Gondomar) who came to England

[15] Harold S. Scott (ed.), *Journal of Sir Roger Wilbraham (Camden Miscellany*, X), 106. Salisbury to Cornwallis, August 17, 1606, *Winwood*, II, 249. *Cal. St. P. Venetian, 1603–1607*, 508, 90, 218–19.

in 1613, and could rely upon James's obsession for a Spanish marriage alliance. The Howards were a worthless and treacherous lot, ready to sacrifice the interests of the nation for their own ends. An anti-Spanish group of ministers was led by Ellesmere, the lord chancellor, Abbot, the austere archbishop of Canterbury, Pembroke, "always the mortal enemy of Spain," Southampton, whose impetuosity did as much harm as good, and the ultra-Protestant secretaries, Winwood and Naunton. Faction in the council was, of course, nothing new. But the Spanish and anti-Spanish groups opposed each other on fundamentals: on parliament, religion, and foreign policy. Their animosities had a deep and disastrous effect upon the relations of king and commons.

The Spanish party was momentarily weakened in 1618, when the Howards fell from power, Gondomar returned to Spain, and the Thirty Years' War began in Germany. The war caused Protestant and anti-Spanish sentiment to flare up at court and in the council. Abbot, Southampton, Pembroke, and Naunton urged James to intervene; other councillors—Mandeville, Bacon, Hamilton, Coke, Edmondes—were ready for a strong anti-Spanish policy; and Buckingham, now the arbiter of patronage, joined the war party. Gondomar wrote that everything was spoiled in England since his departure, and James complained almost in tears that he was surrounded by three hundred Winwoods. But with Gondomar's return in March, 1620, and Buckingham's defection from the war party in the following summer, former divisions reappeared in the council. Buckingham carried a number of other councillors with him; Gondomar regained his old ascendancy over the king; and the Spanish faction seemed stronger than ever. It remained in the ascendant until Charles and Buckingham returned from Madrid in 1623 with a new policy and a determination to crush pro-Spanish sentiment in their ministers.

It was the tragedy of James that he turned for advice to favorites and ministers connected with the Spanish faction and neglected the council as a whole. As early as 1612 the Spanish ambassador noted that James "maketh little or noe account att all of his Councillors and scarcely communicateth with them anything of importance." In 1613 Gondomar wrote of the sudden importance attained by Carr, then Viscount Rochester: "The Viscount Rochester at the Council Table showeth much temper and modesty, without seeming to press and sway anything. But afterward the King resolveth all business with him alone, both those that pass by Council, and many others, wherewith he never maketh them acquainted." Commissioners were appointed in 1617 to deal with the Spanish match and thus remove it from the hands of the council. This exclusion of councillors from important affairs tended to increase. By 1620 Buckingham had risen from an amanuensis and boon companion of the king to a counsellor of the greatest importance. During his early years at court he had cared little about affairs of state, and Gondomar had written in 1615 that "nothing of importance had appeared as yet to pass through his hands." But now he advised the king to the exclusion of older and more experienced men. Gondomar's influence was even more astonishing. "His proceedings pass with great secrecy," wrote the Venetian ambassador in 1620, "for the most part alone with the king, as he once intimated that he hated even the presence of the Secretaries of State, so they are politely requested to leave the room. Many of the leading Lords of the Council doubt whether his Majesty communicates to them all the things he treats of with the said ambassador." "He is not only an ambassador," wrote Tillières, who, it must be confessed, was consumed with jealousy, "but one of the first councillors of state of this kingdom, being day and night at the palace of Whitehall, where the most secret counsels are not only communicated to him, but where they listen to his own advises and follow them almost to the letter." "Some of the ministers here call him a new councillor to his Majesty." [16]

Thus private advisers took the place of government by council. The Venetian ambassador wrote in 1622, "The old ministers and those who look upon matters otherwise than the king desires, know little or nothing of the king's proceedings, as he avoids all except two or three strong partisans of Spain." The actual direction of affairs was in the hands of the king, the favorite, the prince, "and four or five of the cabinet, all well disposed to Spain." When Charles was in Madrid, negotiating the Spanish match, he wrote his father, "I beseech your Majestie advyse as littel with your Counsell in these businesses as you can"; and James replied, "Ye

[16] Pedro de Caunega to Philip III, July 10, 1612, St. P. Spanish, 94/19. Account of the English court, 1613, *ibid.*, 94/20. Sarmiento to the duke of Lerma, October 30, 1615, Spanish Trans., 12/36. *Cal. St. P. Venetian, 1619–1621*, 231, 517, 597–98; *1621–1623*, 442. Tillières to Puisieux, March 9, 1621, Paris Trans., 3/54.

neede not doubte but I will be warrie enough in not acquainting my counsell with any secreate in youre letres." When Charles and Buckingham came to power, the council was neglected more than ever. By 1626 the Venetian ambassador wrote that "there is no longer any council, as Buckingham alone with three or four of his creatures for show constitute it." "They have introduced a privy council," said Wentworth in the commons. A leading minister told the Venetian ambassador in 1626 that no council meeting had been summoned for a long time in any matter of importance.[17]

The council was abused as well as neglected. Councillors who differed from the king were browbeaten into silence, and divergence of opinion was regarded as factiousness and stupidity. When certain councillors defended Ralegh in 1618, James declared heatedly that he would do as he saw fit "without following the advice of fools and badly disposed persons." Opposition to the dissolution of parliament in 1621 was treated with insolence and bullied into silence. James told the council that the pope approved the Spanish match, not to impart information, but "to render everyone dumb." In 1623 councillors were forced to pledge their support to the Spanish marriage treaty and then to denounce it. Treatment of this kind, along with constant fear of dismissal, crushed all independence of judgment. When in 1628, in a meeting of the council, Buckingham suddenly asked the king to summon parliament, it was thought a piece of acting to induce other councillors to express their opinions. But no one said a word. The council had learned too well its lesson of silent obedience.[18] It was also abused in other ways. It was told of plans and policies merely to force it to share the opprobrium with which those plans and policies were regarded by the public. Its opinion was sought to give a semblance of sobriety to fantastic schemes. Its authority was abused in collecting the forced loan of 1627.

[17] *Cal. St. P. Venetian, 1621–1623,* 210, 229, 441–42, 510–11; *1625–1626,* 603. Charles and Buckingham to the king, Madrid, March 17, 1623, James to Charles in reply, Harl. MSS 6987, f. 34, 50. For Wentworth's speech, see March 22, 1628, Harl. MSS 4771, f. 18v–19. Procedure in summoning meetings of the council lent itself to these tendencies. "None of the Privy Council may come to sit in Council unless they be sent for or warned by the Lord President of the Council or the Principall Secretary, and every Council Day they are so warned specially." Add. MSS 36856, f. 58–59. The use of committees of the council and the frequent appointment of special commissioners for many kinds of business could easily exclude the majority of councillors from matters of importance.

[18] Gondomar to Philip III, July 15, 1618, Spanish Trans., 12/39; Gondomar to Philip IV, January 31, 1622, *ibid.,* 12/26. *Cal. St. P. Venetian, 1621–1623,* 149; *1626–1628,* 558–59.

Thus "the king used his council merely for show"; and it became "a mere shadow for ordinary affairs, to toil about providing money and to edit matters which are intended for publication." The council, excluded from a share in shaping national policy, devoted itself to administrative routine: the supervision and repair of public works, forts, and bridges; musters and military matters; Ireland, the Channel Islands, and the colonies; innumerable details of local government; much judicial work; and the regulation of commerce and industry. But all these things belonged to the details of government.

This development was emphasized by the increasing number of members who were essentially bureaucrats rather than statesmen. Councillors such as Sir George Calvert, Sir Robert Naunton, Sir Thomas Lake, Sir Lionel Cranfield, Sir Richard Weston, Sir John Coke, and later Sir Francis Windebank, many of whom rose to power with Buckingham, owed their places primarily to their industry and efficiency in detailed administration. To place administration in their hands was in many ways fortunate. They raised the standard of official honesty and saw to it that the crown was not cheated by every tradesman with whom it did business. But with the exception of Cranfield, none of these men had the making of statesmen. They were capable clerks who could take care of wearisome details and carry out instructions. They were content with routine matters and made no pretense to statesmanship on any higher plane. They paid abject homage to the favorite; and their letters breathe an atmosphere of submissive acceptance of their subordinate role. In a word, the king and Buckingham were not looking for advisers in the council, but for men who would do as they were told. And this was what they were getting. Personal government was replacing statesmen with bureaucrats, men who could work efficiently but without initiative or imagination. It was from their number that the councillors who served in the commons were largely drawn.

Other causes contributed to the council's decline. Many appointments to the council were open to question and aimed at other things than building an able body of advisers. James regarded membership somewhat as a mark of royal favor, as if it were another rank in the nobility; and Charles and Buckingham filled the council with their creatures. Many councillors, wrote the Venetian ambassador, were frivolous courtiers, better fitted to manipulate goblets than to deal with affairs. In an attempt to balance factions, James appointed men of radically different points of view. Thus Winwood, the ultra-Protestant, balanced Lake, the Catholic; and Naunton balanced Calvert in the same way. Gardiner has analyzed the council's membership about 1617 and finds it very heterogeneous. The churchmen represented different schools of theology; the secretaries supported different policies; some councillors urged a French and some a Spanish marriage for the prince.[19] Another ruler might have found such a council an admirable basis upon which to form an independent judgment; to James it was a babble of voices, and he turned to his intimates for advice he could understand.

The size of the council was greatly increased, and this proved detrimental in certain ways. The council under the Tudors had averaged about twenty members, and certainly its increase under Edward VI and Mary had been coeval with a decline in strength. James at his accession retained Elizabeth's council, which numbered fifteen, and increased it somewhat, partly by the inclusion of several Scots. In May, 1603, the council's membership stood at twenty-four. James said that he regarded this number as too large and gradually reduced it to nineteen or twenty members in 1610. But by 1615 membership had again risen to twenty-four and henceforth it steadily increased. It stood at thirty-one in 1618 and at approximately thirty-five in the period from 1620 to 1625. Charles at his accession reduced the council to some thirty members, but then increased it until in 1630 membership reached forty or just below. It was later reduced somewhat, decreasing to thirty-two in 1635 but rising again to thirty-seven in 1639.[20] Increased membership doubtless did something to lower efficiency. But this may easily be exaggerated. It was a rare occasion indeed when the entire council met together; a meeting with half the council present was a well-attended session, and the average attendance fell far below that figure. Efficiency suffered less from the size of the council than from fluctuations in attendance; for often the mem-

[19] *Gardiner*, III, 72–83.

[20] Declaration of the king in council, May 10, 1603, St. P. Domestic, 14/1:73. Registers of the Privy Council, *passim*. See also E. R. Turner, *The Privy Council of England in the Seventeenth and Eighteenth Centuries* (2 vols., Baltimore, 1927–28), I, 73–82. It is not an easy matter to determine the exact membership at a given date. The clerks inserted the names of new members in old lists and kept names on the lists after members had been dismissed or had ceased to attend.

bers attending one meeting differed radically in personnel from those attending the next. A much graver result of enlarging the council was the increased difficulty of maintaining secrecy. There was a disastrous leakage of important information from the council under James. The Spanish faction kept Gondomar informed of what went on; and the Venetian ambassador wrote in 1622 that "the king could not utter a thing without the Spanish ambassador, Gondomar, knowing, who was undoubtedly more minutely and profoundly advised than his Majesty." But if James was betrayed by his councillors, he set them a very bad example: it was said that he told Gondomar things he heard from other ambassadors, with the result that foreign princes withheld information from him.[21]

This difficulty in keeping official secrets illustrates the lowered tone of political morality in the early Stuart period. The atmosphere of James's court was venal and mercenary; and as a result the council suffered in both efficiency and reputation. It is not surprising that rapacious courtiers abused James's indulgence to bleed the public or that the Howards accepted Spanish pensions. But one is startled to find that Salisbury also accepted Spanish money and that Bacon received presents from litigants whose cases were pending in his court. The whole system of remuneration for high office was bad. In the middle ages ministers had been rewarded by gifts and grants from the crown; now they received comparatively little from that source and were expected to derive an income from those individuals with whom they dealt in the course of their official duties. But it was often difficult to distinguish a legitimate gift from a payment that was of the nature of a bribe. James accepted the situation with surprising equanimity. He was shaken by the discovery of the Spanish pensions, but the storm blew over without the thorough housecleaning that was called for. He apparently assumed that the more his ministers got from other sources, the less he would have to give them himself; and when they asked him whether they might accept presents offered to them, he told them to do so.

These things cannot be dissociated from the position of the council in the house of commons. Councillors represented kings who were failures and an institution that was falling into rapid decay.

[21] *Cal. St. P. Venetian, 1621–1623*, 442, 510, 65; *1619–1621*, 587, 597–98.

2

Preparations by the Council for a Meeting of the Commons

The prerogative of calling and dissolving parliament at will gave the crown an enormous advantage in dealing with the house of commons. Parliament could be summoned at auspicious moments, when the necessities of the country or the temper of the electors augured well for the success of the government. Public opinion could be prepared and grievances redressed. But what was far more important, the government had the opportunity of preparing business for the coming session, of framing a program of legislation or devising some other line of action which could at once be placed before the commons. The Tudors had taken full advantage of this opportunity. But in the reign of James it was not used as skillfully or as effectively as it might have been. Except for the union with Scotland, James had, broadly speaking, no program of importance to lay before the commons; his chief aim was to obtain supply. Adequate preparations, moreover, were seriously handicapped and disrupted by divisions and antagonisms in the council. And finally, the government was thrown so completely upon the defensive that it was forced to consider the grievances of the commons rather than a program of its own. This was a fundamental change. Preparations ceased to be an attempt to improve the condition of the country through beneficial legislation and became a desperate search for concessions that might appease the commons without diminishing appreciably the prerogatives or the revenues of the crown. In the reign of Charles preparations of any kind all but ceased. This was due in part to the reckless improvidence and confusion of Buckingham's administration. But it was due also to the fact that king and commons were now in such hopeless opposition, meeting with swords half drawn, that such concessions as the crown was willing to offer appeared a hollow mockery in the eyes of an alienated people. Preparations ceased because they were hopeless.

There is thus a clear though gradual evolution in the nature of the council's preparations for a meeting of the commons. In the Tudor period, as we have seen, preparations had largely taken the form of building a program of legislation, a program that could be presented to the commons with the assurance that it would, for the most part, be enacted into law. There was little attempt to cultivate public opinion before a session opened. Thomas Cromwell, indeed, used preachers and pamphleteers to clear the way for a session of the commons. The council told Elizabeth in 1579 that if she married Alençon parliament would have to be postponed until the people could be persuaded to accept the marriage with some equanimity.[1] But such instances were rare. Public opinion was already prepared, generally speaking, by the approval it gave to the government of the Tudors. The legislation proposed by the council often met grievances halfway and kept them from dangerous accumulation.

The first parliament of James, when Salisbury was parliamentary manager for the crown, is in this, as in many other matters, a period of transition. Salisbury continued the Tudor tradition of preparing legislation to be placed before the commons. The state papers and Cecil manuscripts contain drafts of many bills and notes upon which bills could be framed, obviously the work of Salisbury and other officials. There are many corrections and marginal notes in Salisbury's hand which testify to his care and thoroughness. A paper of 1604 contains sixty-one "acts to be considered of against next Parliament." Certain acts are checked as if the list had been submitted to Salisbury or some other councillor who chose the more significant bills for closer consideration. Before the session of 1610 the council surveyed the statutes. A paper, dated February, 1610, contains "notes of statute laws, the repeal of which is desirable, with reasons therefor"; and the commons were told that the council "had considered penal Laws" and compiled a list of those that should be repealed.[2] Salisbury carefully prepared the legislation necessary for the proposed union with Scotland. Corrections in his hand are found in a draft of the act of 1604 appointing commissioners to consider the union. A number of officials were set to work on the probable effect of the union upon

[1] Notestein, *Winning of the Initiative*, 5–6. *Cal. St. P. Spanish, 1568–1579*, 703. See also *Cal. St. P. Domestic, 1595–1597*, 448–49, 482; *Cal. Hatfield House MSS*, VII, 352.
[2] St. P. Domestic, 14/6:99; *ibid.*, 14/52:72. *C. J.*, I, 396; *L. J.*, II, 551.

trade, justice, and other aspects of national life.[3] To draft this legislation was a most difficult matter, in which the recommendations of the commissioners as well as the susceptibilities of both James and the commons had to be considered. James was severely critical of Salisbury's work and on one occasion threatened to attack the act of union before the commons unless alterations were made. Salisbury also planned and revised with great care the legislation of 1610 by which he hoped to put the Great Contract into effect. In 1606 Bacon sent him a draft of the preamble to the act of subsidy with a request for any alterations he might see fit to make.[4]

Objections likely to be raised by the commons were anticipated where that was possible. In 1606 Thomas Wilson prepared for Salisbury "a collection of objections against the Union, likely to be discussed at the approaching Parliament; with answers thereto." Before the same session Salisbury wrote the council outlining the measures which the king desired to have passed; and asked councillors to deliberate upon ways and means to facilitate their passage through the house. Members of the house, he wrote, would come prepared with many arguments; and it was essential that the council meet to discuss how they should be answered and how affairs could be presented to parliament so as to give satisfaction both to the king and to his subjects. There were many minor points regarding the union, Salisbury confessed, upon which he felt himself doubtful; and if success was to be obtained in the house, councillors must prepare themselves in advance.[5]

But if Salisbury mapped a legislative program for parliament, he also found himself forced to pay a vast amount of attention to the grievances of the commons. Twice during the parliament, in 1606 and 1610, the commons presented long formal petitions of grievances to the king. These petitions were thoroughly debated in the council, where answers were prepared. James wrote Salisbury in August, 1606, commending the care taken by the council

[3] St. P. Domestic, 14/8:6, 61, 63; 14/23:60, 61; 14/26:80. Earl of Shrewsbury to Cranborne, December 14, 1604, James to Cranborne, 1604, *Cal. Hatfield House MSS,* XVI, 382, 395; James to Salisbury, 1606, Hatfield House MSS. Lord Fyvie to Cranborne, November 22, 1604, St. P. Domestic, 14/10:39. Sir Thomas Fleming, Robert Clark, John Savile, and George Snigg to the earl of Dorset, November 20, 1604, *Cal. Hatfield House MSS,* XVI, 359.

[4] St. P. Domestic, 14/24:65; 14/52:86, 87, 88; 14/55:56, 57, 60. *Spedding,* III, 277.

[5] St. P. Domestic, 14/23:61. Salisbury to the council, 1605, *Cal. Hatfield House MSS,* XVI, 425–26 (where letter is misdated 1604).

in answering certain of these grievances. James hoped that "for the other matter of grievances your resolution may be hastened as much as may be, and likewise for the form of publishing his Majesties determination therein to the people. And in all other things that may concern the Parliament he hopeth that you will be ready against his return." [6] In 1610 James wrote Salisbury, "My last desire is that according to the order I gave before my parting, the Council would now in my absence meet and maturely deliberate upon my answer to the grievances, and that they may be ready to give me their advice therein against my return." [7]

Before the session of 1606 councillors were busy with grievances arising from purveyance. "Above all," James wrote Salisbury and the council, "be earnest in trying and severe in punishing the thievish purveyors." "At this instant," Northampton wrote in October, "we sitte harde about the preparation of matters for the parliament. . . . We are about to take awaie the scandales raised upon purveyors and such prolinge officers which were the subjecte of exception the last time." Before the commons met in 1610 James wrote the council "to be extremely careful . . . to sound and prevent all occasions of scandal or grudge that may trouble the Parliament and that before their meeting, which is the ground of all your consultations at this time." That members might assemble "prepared for good and purged of evil," the council should "sound and try the bottoms of their mindes and intentions beforehand" where that was possible.[8] The sessions of 1610 show clearly how seriously Salisbury had meditated upon the grievances of the commons. His scheme known as the Great Contract was an offer of redress of certain grievances in return for financial support; and when the contract came to nothing, he continued to outline points upon which the crown would yield if subsidies were granted in the ordinary way.

[6] Sir Thomas Lake to Salisbury, August 24, 1606, Hatfield House MSS. See also Sir Robert Johnson to Salisbury, October 31, 1606, *ibid.* Josias Kirton wrote Salisbury asking protection, since "the office of muster-master is to be questioned at the council-table." Undated letter, 1606, *ibid.* St. P. Domestic, 14/23:66 contains "the Judgement of the Lords of the Privie Council and others, what answers were fit to be given and what course to be holden concerning the several grievances presented to his Majesty by the Common House of Parliament." St. P. Domestic, 14/23:67 contains the answer presented to the commons. Two other drafts of this document are corrected by Salisbury, *ibid.*, 14/23:69, 70.

[7] James to Salisbury, undated, 1610, Hatfield House MSS.

[8] James to Salisbury, October 7, 1605, *Cal. Hatfield House MSS*, XVI, 326 (where letter is misdated 1604). Northampton to Sir Thomas Edmondes, October 10, 1605, Stowe MSS 168, f. 169v. James to Salisbury (two letters), undated, 1610, Hatfield House MSS.

But already in this parliament the fundamental futility of these deliberations of the council was making itself apparent. The council had no wish, and would not have dared had it had the wish, to touch the fundamental difficulties of the situation. It offered mere palliatives and the superficial appearance of redress of grievances. The grievances that were redressed were but minor in character. "Theise matters offred by the Lords," said a member in 1610, "are not the principall, no matters ecclesiasticall, proclamations, or such like." James's policy was essentially negative, a determination to keep intact the Tudor inheritance. When the commons complained of the jurisdiction of the council of Wales, James merely wrote councillors to prevent, if possible, the recurrence of the matter in future debates.[9] Salisbury, though more tactful and conciliatory, was equally conservative; the Howards regarded the aspirations of the commons with mingled hatred and horror; and Ellesmere, while he became a bitter opponent of the Howard faction, was rigidly conservative in matters concerning parliament.

There was thus too wide a gulf between the demands of the commons and the concessions which the crown was willing to make. Purveyance may serve as an example. Parliament had complained of it bitterly in 1604. Between 1604 and 1606 the council debated its abuses, although Salisbury confessed that the reforms that resulted were "but shadows and colours without substance." By 1606 the commons were demanding that purveyance be done away with altogether. But this the government opposed, its policy being, as Salisbury wrote Mar, to put down abuses but in no way to end purveyance itself.[10] Salisbury allowed a law to pass against it in the commons because they were at that moment also discussing supply. But he saw to it that the law was smothered in the lords. It is small wonder if the commons came to the conclusion that offers of the government were insincere and were baits cunningly set out to entice them into voting supply.

Finally it may be noted that Salisbury, by offering concessions openly and directly in return for a money grant, as he did in the Great Contract, taught the commons to weigh carefully the monetary value of concessions offered by the crown. In the end, the

[9] *Parl. Debates in 1610*, 136. James to Salisbury, October 7, 1605, *Cal. Hatfield House MSS*, XVI, 325.

[10] Salisbury to the council, 1605, *Cal. Hatfield House MSS*, XVI, 426. Salisbury to the earl of Mar, March 9, 1606, St. P. Domestic, 14/19:27.

commons concluded that the crown placed too high a value upon its concessions, which came to be despised as inconsequential in comparison with others desired by the house. It was for these reasons that Bacon regarded the Great Contract as a gross and unpardonable blunder.

Preparations for the parliament of 1614 center almost exclusively in the search for concessions sufficiently attractive to induce the commons to grant supply. Parliament was summoned because of the desperate need of money, and beyond obtaining that money the government had little business to place before the house. What little legislation was prepared by the council grew as an afterthought from the search for concessions. And this search induced the government to consider a plan of Sir Henry Neville, which, in the event, proved utterly disastrous.

In an important debate lasting three entire days in February, 1614, the council considered the whole subject of calling and preparing for a parliament. Its advice to the king was that parliament should be summoned, in spite of obvious difficulties. Concerning preparations, it reported: "In the second day we ran over such Presidents, as well of grievances as of desires, as seemed to affect the Lower House at their last breaking up, being very careful of the better incouragement of their affections at this time to cull out such particularities as without any great offence or prejudice to his Majesties prerogative might yield them satisfaction to their own desires." And Northampton wrote of this debate, "We have resolved among ourselves that every one of us shall consider of the best means whereby the subject shall receive comfort without prejudice. Besides we have taken order that all the requests and aggreviances which were given in at the breaking up of the last parliament may be brought in the same day to be scanned by the Lords." [11] Thus the council concentrated upon concessions that might be offered to the commons.

At the same time it considered "certain Propositions" that came originally from Sir Henry Neville. He was a courtier and diplomat who nevertheless had supported the popular cause in James's

[11] The council to the king, February 16, 1614, St. P. Domestic, 14/76:22. Northampton to Somerset, February, 1614, Cott. MSS Titus F IV, f. 329. The conciliatory attitude of the government may be seen in a letter of Ellesmere in which he wishes to consult some of the council about the wording of a bill for the preservation of woods. He feared the bill, as drawn, might disturb "the fayre and quiett passage" of the king's affairs in this "hopefull Parlement." Ellesmere to Lake, February 23, 1614, St. P. Domestic, 14/76:31.

first parliament. Yet he retained close connections with the court and still hoped for important employment under the crown. Prompted by patriotism and self-interest, he urged upon James in 1612 and now again in 1614 a plan whereby he hoped to reconcile king and commons and win advancement for himself. Out of his plan grew the famous episode of the undertakers.

James was not at all certain that he wished to call another parliament, and there were many at court who tried to dissuade him from doing so. Neville began, therefore, by pointing out that extraparliamentary methods for raising money had failed and that no way was "so fit, so honourable, and so necessary as by a parliament." The "distaste and acrimony" of the last session could be removed only by summoning the commons once more, "for there the error grew and there and nowhere else it must be repaired." Neville also insisted that another parliament, if properly managed and offered attractive concessions, would prove tractable and grant the king supply. Neville claimed to know the commons and did not believe that they would make unreasonable demands. He had "lived and conversed inwardly with the chief of them, that were noted to be most backward and knew their inwardest thoughts in this business. And so he dared undertake for the most of them, that the king's majesty proceeding in a gracious course towards his people, should find those gentlemen exceeding willing to do him service." Unless the king would make concessions Neville "dared promise nothing"; for "some things would be desired and expected of the king by grace." Yet matters "of small moment and loss to his Majesty" might nevertheless be highly valued by the people. Neville therefore compiled a list of possible concessions which he had "collected out of the desires of sundry of the principal and most understanding gentlemen that were of the last Parliament and were like to be of this." [12]

These concessions sought chiefly to protect the subject from the technicalities of the law through which unscrupulous royal agents constantly fleeced the public. The law of treason should be more

[12] Neville also suggested ways of preparing public opinion before parliament began. James should "forbear to use any speech of the parliament that may irritate" and should "seem rather confident than diffident of their affections"; he should "speak graciously and benignly to the people" as he went on progress and "take notice of the principal gentlemen and let them kiss his hand." He should "prohibit all books and invective sermons against the parliament." Promises made in 1610 should be fulfilled and grievances then complained of redressed where possible.

clearly defined; subjects should be treated more justly in legal actions brought against them by the crown; fines and forfeitures should not be levied for small offenses or for technical omissions in dealings over revenue; forfeitures upon penal statutes should be turned into some other form of correction; patents, licenses, and royal grants (including crown lands held for sixty years), if not already questioned, should stand good against the crown, and lands rented from the king should not be forfeited upon technicalities; respite of homage should be taken away; old and useless laws repealed. A liberal general pardon should be granted, forgiving old debts, fines and amercements, concealed wards, and trespasses in royal parks and chases. These concessions included some offered in 1610, which, Neville assumed, would now be offered again.[13]

As to the thorny question of impositions, Neville proposed that parliament grant the king for life those impositions already in existence in return for a promise that no more be levied. This, Neville claimed, would not affect the king's right to levy impositions, a point which need not appear in the agreement, nor would James's promise bind his successors. Much would be gained if existing impositions were paid without further question; and the nation would thus become accustomed to these imposts.[14]

There were many points in these suggestions upon which the crown might well give way. But with the exception of impositions (and here Neville offered a solution which parliament might reject), he did not deal with any of the deeper causes of division between James and the commons. He had nothing to say about religion or the extravagance of the king, nothing about royal favorites or the pro-Spanish and Catholic leanings of certain ministers. But his cardinal error was to give a half promise that the commons would respond to the concessions he proposed. It was one thing to advise yielding to the commons. It was quite another

[13] Neville to James, 1612, St. P. Domestic, 14/74:44; *ibid.,* 14/74:46; Lansd. MSS 486, f. 17–20; Harl. MSS 4289, f. 231v–33; Cott. MSS Titus F IV, f. 346. He suggests a liberal general pardon in *ibid.,* f. 344. He also wrote Somerset (*ibid.,* f. 349) asking him to remind the king that these concessions might diminish the revenue of the crown but did not touch its prerogatives. They gave the king an opportunity to blame the failure of 1610 upon Salisbury. Neville urged that new projects for raising money be abandoned. The men who proposed these projects spent "their time in Court or about London only" and did not understand the temper of the people. But the king's rights should be carefully examined before parliament met so that the king might realize upon them where his title was beyond question.

[14] Cott. MSS Titus F IV, f. 350, in Neville's hand.

to make a sort of guarantee that concessions on certain points would produce a fundamental alteration in the attitude of the commons toward the crown. This aspect of his plan, distorted by popular rumor into a widespread interference with elections — about which Neville said absolutely nothing — did irretrievable harm both in and out of parliament.

Neville had powerful friends and his scheme received a hearing. It was placed before the council in February, as we have seen. Again at the end of March both Pembroke and Suffolk, though actuated by quite different motives, promised Neville to urge his plan once more upon the council. Neville was also in touch with Somerset and begged him to influence James in favor of his plan. James allowed the council to consider it and asked the learned counsel for a legal opinion of its worth.[15]

Most members of the government, however, did not approve of Neville's scheme. Bacon certainly did not. His report as learned counsel was a plea for time to consider the matter further, since Neville's suggestions could only be accepted with many "differences and limitations." Bacon's private advice to James on the matter was extremely conservative. Let the undertakers be given a hearing, but let the government hold itself completely free to adopt only such portions of the plan as should appear desirable. If the concessions of the undertakers were based on the assumption that the commons must be bought by matters of substance and profit, if the undertakers were but brokers for bargains, their advice should be discarded as worse than useless. If they proposed a program which the government considered fit, let it be followed, "because they are likest to be in love with their own child, and to nurish it." If their propositions were useless, the undertakers might still be induced to fall in line with other suggestions put forward by the crown. Northampton, as Bacon wrote later, hated the very name of the undertakers and sought all means to ruin their scheme.[16] One document among his papers in the Cottonian collection is a bitter attack upon the undertakers as preposterous

[15] Suffolk and Pembroke promised "to bring to my Lords the demands that will be asked of the king this parliament, and that they will be moderate for the king, and yet pleasing to them [the commons]. Which we affirm to my Lords we conceive will be attractive inducements to get the good we look for." Suffolk to Somerset, end of March, 1614, Cott. MSS Titus F IV, f. 340. "A memoriall for my Lord of Rochester," in Neville's hand, 1614, *ibid.*, f. 349. Bacon to Somerset, February 17, 1614, *Spedding,* V, 13.

[16] Bacon to the king, soon after January 9, Bacon to Somerset, February 17, 1614, *Spedding,* V, 1-2, 13.

and absurd in thinking they could sway a house of commons before it was elected.[17] And other councillors were doubtful. Late in March Suffolk wrote that Pembroke had come to him and confessed "that he could not tell what would come of this Parliament, because he found by the consultation the last day [in the council] that my Lords had no great conceit that there would be any great good affected for our master: divers of my Lords having spoken with many wise parliament men, who do generally decline from the Undertakers, only Pembroke and myself were the hopefull believers of good success, two or three petty Councillors more seemed to be indifferently conceited, but so as my Lord of Pembroke was much unsatisfied that they are no more confident in his friends." Northampton wrote that the council, having debated Neville's suggestions, came to the conclusion that the king could attain success in parliament only by convincing the commons of the desperate need of money, by "gracious favours in giving satisfaction so far as the prerogative smart not," and "by the industry of the king's own faithful servants and councillors." The "pragmatic invention" and "hasty prosecution" of the undertakers would not serve the purpose.

Nor were those ministers who appeared to support the plan entirely sincere. Pembroke, indeed, was ready to welcome any scheme that might improve the relations of king and parliament. But Suffolk and Somerset wished only to secure the support of Neville and his friends during the parliament and cared little whether his plan succeeded or not. When Neville told Suffolk

[17] "It is bruted abroad that some few gentlemen that were most opposett to his Majestie the last Parliament, for particular promotions, will undertake to carrie this Parliament for his Majesties profitt, and ends, which other men of their like Rancke and quality doth so much conteme and scorne, and takes for so great an Iniurie to themselves, and the Parliament house, as that they begin to bandy, and to make a faction which is like to break forth to open discontent at their sitting.

"If theis few gentlemens estates, their callings, their deserts in the Common Wealthe, and peoples estimation of them, be truely examined, I think they can assume little to themselves, to challenge such prerogative above others of better Ranke and quallitie. But especially when they think to Commaund the tonge, harte, and Consciences, of those that are strangers to them, dwelling in farr shires, and remote places, where perhaps their names have not been so much as heard of amongst them. And therefore it is strange to me, that men will so undertake to carry a Parliament, before they shall knowe whoe shalbe elected into the house, or whether their propositions wilbe acceptable unto them yea, or no. Though I confesse considering the factousnes of the tyme, it maie be in their power to doe hurt in speaking against the King, but not in their abilities to doe good for the king, by example of the King's Solicitor [Yelverton] in the last Parliament. And therefore I pray God this presumption of theirs do not hinder other good descines that may be propounded for his Majesties benefit." Cott. MSS Titus F IV, f. 351–52v.

that he hoped his efforts would bring him the secretaryship, Suffolk replied that he must support the king in parliament before he could hope for favor. At the same time Suffolk wrote to Somerset, "I must make you laugh to tell you that my Lord Privy Seal [Northampton] soberly says to me, 'My Lord, you incline before the Council too much to these Undertakers.' This troubles me nothing, for if we may do our master the service we wish by our dissembling, I am well content to play the knave a little with them, [for] which you must give me dispensation for following your direction." [18]

Nevertheless the privy council (or perhaps the learned counsel) drew up two lists of bills for possible presentation to the commons. They are printed in Spedding. The bills in the first list, eleven in number, were drawn by the king's command from "propositions exhibited to his Majesty"; and their contents correspond roughly with Neville's suggestions, although none of them deal with impositions. They correspond also with a number of bills of grace offered by James to the commons in the first days of the session. Thus the government followed Neville's plan so far as to introduce in parliament a number of measures embodying the minor concessions he proposed. The bills in the second list, forty-seven in number, based "upon other heads besides those that were propounded," represent further suggestions of the council for possible legislation. They concern a great variety of subjects, abuses needing reform, projects for the improvement of the country, many private bills for the benefit of individuals or localities. But it seems clear that these headings were jotted down without full consideration and never got beyond the exploratory stage. Some are marked "bills to be propounded, not yet consulted upon." So far as I know, they were never introduced in parliament. The one attempt of the council to initiate legislation was confined to the bills of grace which, it was hoped, the commons would find attractive.[19]

But rumors about undertaking raised such a violent storm in the house that all gratitude for the bills of grace was swept away.

[18] Suffolk to Somerset, end of March, 1614, Cott. MSS Titus F IV, f. 340 (partly printed in *Gardiner*, II, 229). Northampton to Somerset, February, 1614, Cott. MSS Titus F IV, f. 329.

[19] *Spedding*, V, 14–18. Of the bills in the first list which incorporated Neville's suggestions, some were "to be offered to the parliament" and others "to be ready if they be sued for by the Commons."

They were regarded, as Bacon feared, as a sort of valued gift to induce the commons to vote supply, and as such they came to be despised. The net result of Neville's plan was to breed such deep suspicion that the government was feared even while bearing gifts.[20] The dangers inherent in his proposals were thus apparent. The government had injured its chances of success by listening to a plan which, however well intended, was faulty, superficial, and easily misunderstood. The government, moreover, had not followed Neville in seeking to end the difficult question of impositions. There were no concessions of real importance offered to the commons; and thus the mistake of James's first parliament was repeated. Finally, divisions and disagreements among important councillors did much harm. All in all, the government's preparations for the parliament of 1614 were badly conceived and badly executed.

The question of a parliament was again under discussion in the autumn of 1615; and we are fortunate in possessing a very full account of a debate in the council upon preparations for parliament if one was called at that time. The crown's finances were now in a desperate condition; and as a last expedient for obtaining funds the council "insinuated" to the king the necessity of calling parliament. James at first demurred but finally instructed the council, if it could find no other means of supplying money, to consider what preparations for parliament might give hope of success. The council quickly appointed a day (September 28) when each member in turn should offer his opinion on preparations to the board.

Sir Thomas Lake began the discussion. A parliament was necessary, he said, not only to grant money but to mend the harm done the king's reputation by the quarrels of the last two sessions. Preparations, however, were absolutely essential. Grievances and false impressions which alienated the people must be removed; and things must be done that would be "grateful and pleasing" to them. He then mentioned the universal belief that James was extravagant and that money granted was "mispent in private guifts and not converted to the good of his Estate." To remedy this the council must teach the people that James now saw the errors of his former generosity; it must impress upon the

[20] See pp. 142–45.

35

king the necessity of staying his hand until his finances improved; and it must continue its efforts to introduce economy in all departments of the state. Lake then turned to arbitrary acts of the crown "which had been offensively taken." To remedy these, the council should review the grievances of the last two parliaments. The learned counsel should be consulted. Grievances removable by the law should be recommended to the judges, those which the council could correct should be redressed by them, and those requiring an act of the king should be placed before him with the recommendations of the board. Impositions had been "the Smart which hath most grieved the people." Lake declined to enter into the question of right but recommended the matter to the lords as something for which a solution was essential. Sir Lionel Cranfield had a plan, Lake said, and this should be carefully debated by the council.

Lake then suggested a number of things to please the commons. Measures to promote fishing would benefit the entire realm, especially the maritime counties, and "would be greedely embraced" by the commons if offered to them. Lake also wished an investigation of commercial conditions for the purpose of increasing exports; and here again Cranfield had proposals that should be heard. This also was a matter which the commons would be "very grateful to work on." In addition the council might consider the statute of employments which "enricheth the naturall subject and curbeth the Stranger," measures for the dyeing and dressing of cloth, and the repeal of obsolete and contradictory laws, a matter mentioned by the king and "often spoken of in Parliament." These preparations, Lake hoped, would bring a new kindliness between king and people.

Caesar repeated that the king's wants must be relieved in parliament and that the grievances of former sessions, as recorded in the parliament rolls, should be investigated and removed. Sir Thomas Parry said the same.

Coke spoke at considerable length. He pointed to the king's mounting debt and to the constant excess of expenditures over income. He advised that the council investigate every possibility of economy in all spending departments (which he thought should be done by a series of committees) and urged that all pensions be stopped until the king was out of debt. Royal grants should be canceled where the crown had been defrauded. But to cut down the debt a parliament was necessary, and that must not be attempted without preparations. Coke approved the preparations mentioned by other councillors and suggested a collection of all James's expenditures since his accession, "whereby to shew that they were necessary and fit," not springing from prodigality but from unavoidable charges. This "being represented in Parliament he thought would work to good purpose." Too much should not be asked of the commons lest they be discouraged; elections should be free; and the learned counsel should not be members of the house, where their presence was resented.

Greville was more conservative. The council should not remedy "everything that was vulgarly complayned of," for all impositions and all monopolies were neither bad nor illegal. It would perhaps be wise to submit some things to the commons rather than to do them in advance. "It was a pleasing and a popular thinge, to aske a multitudes advice" and would increase trust and confidence between king and commons.

Winwood spoke with great force and energy. He took "for a Foundation" that "there was no way to redeem the king out of his necessities really and substantially but by the good will of his People in Parliament." He made three points regarding preparations. Impositions "had made the hardest Interruption in the last two Parliamentes and was like to be most pressed"; and he wished a special committee of the council to consider what could be done to end that grievance. Secondly, he made the bold suggestion "that the Fraudes committed upon the Crowne by those which had bin trusted in great offices might be called in question as a matter which would be very grateful and popular." Thirdly, assurance must be given the commons that money voted would be used for the public good.

Several short speeches followed. Lord Wotton thought that a Scottish parliament which voted supply would make a good impression in England. Lord Knollys wished James to disforest some of his more distant parks and chases. Lord Zouch suggested that the laws against recusants be enforced more rigidly, that elections be left entirely to the people, and that the government make absolutely clear that parliament was called for public ends and not for the advantage of private persons. The bishop of Winchester urged that the people be taught to relieve the king as part of their religious duty. Lord Fenton remarked that a parliament had been held quite recently in Scotland and had made the king a grant.

The earl of Exeter said that "the ease of the peoples grief" must precede "the relief of the king." Offensive grants must be called in, "especially those of surrounded grounds, which he knew to be very grievious." Expenses must be cut down, for that would bring relief "certayn and perpetuall" while a grant of the commons was only temporary. He desired a law "to redress the excess of apparell, now grown so superfluous."

Pembroke regarded a parliament as essential and had good hopes that preparations would bring results. He especially wished that impositions "be maturely considered by their Lordships, not doubting but if that might be accommodated, the rest would be easy enough." Every effort should be made to cut down expenses, "which conceyt of husbandry would be a great encouragement to the people to give."

The Howards gave formal approval to what had been said but showed their dislike of parliament and their hostility to calling it. Lord admiral Nottingham said that he could not disagree with those who had spoken before him. Yet he feared "that the preparations which had been mooved would not suffyce." The last two parliaments had been offered material benefits by the king and would probably ask the same again, being unwilling to give "but on such conditions." Suffolk "would not dissent from so many great Councelors and men of understanding." Yet "he moved a dowt that struck deeply within him," that the removal of impositions *de facto* would not satisfy the commons. They would insist upon the question of right, which, if once moved, would produce such difficulties that he could not foresee the result.

Lord chancellor Ellesmere said that all the points which he had heard had often been made at the board before. "In the matter of Impositions, which he perceaved was the hardest knott to unty, he would not speake of his Majesties right of imposing, nor ever give consent it should be spoken of in Parliament, or else where: as he had never lyked the mooving of the question; it should suffyse him to talk of conveniency or inconveniency of the rates and quantity: and of the time, when fit, and unfitt: and within those bounds he wished others to be contayned: and would conteyne himself. . . . He never lyked of novelties, especially in Parliament, as were the new termes of Contribution and Retribution, which he thought had done much hurt. He wished the ould course of Parliaments to be houlden between the King and his subjects: that is that his Majesty should grant them good laws, and they give him convenient relliefe, as his occasions should require." He wished, however, that the preparations mentioned would be speeded and deeply regretted that they had not already been put into effect. Some of them, he said, would of themselves give the crown relief, some might be done as preparations for a parliament, and some might be presented to the commons when they met.

The debate was concluded by archbishop Abbot, who took "as great pleasure in this days work as in any that ever he had been at in that place." For though these matters had been discussed before, they had never been "handled so seriously and methodically, nor to such an end, as was now aymed at." He believed that a parliament was necessary and approved the preparations mentioned by others. He added nothing of himself but pleaded that secrecy be maintained concerning the debate. The council's discussion was then reported to the king. James disliked deforesting his parks, said it would be very difficult to stop the pensions, and remarked that a parliament had recently been held in Scotland. Otherwise he approved further discussion of the points that had been raised.[21]

As in 1614, this debate was largely a search for concessions that might induce the commons to vote supply. Yet it is obvious that the council here was much closer to reality than before. It is true that the religious problem was scarcely touched; and only the impetuous Winwood dared suggest that peculation and fraud in

[21] Harl. MSS 4289, f. 224v–31; *Spedding,* V, 194–207. A similar debate occurred in November. The council wrote James that in a debate on his finances (which they "resolved could not be relieved without the help of the people"), they had fallen "by way of discourse into mention of a parliament." But many councillors were absent and "yt was unfitt for soe weighty a business to be treated (much less resolved on) the board not being full." They understood that James wished them to debate the matter and asked him to set a date when the councillors with him at court might come to London for a full-dress debate. We may assume that this debate took place. The council to the king, November 27, 1615, St. P. Domestic, 14/83:68. This debate should be compared with Bacon's advice to the king. See pages 132–35, and especially Bacon's letter to James in 1615 (*Spedding,* V, 176–91), in which he approved Cranfield's plan to transform impositions into higher import duties on all foreign commodities. Bacon also liked the idea of assigning the revenue to necessary expenses and using only the surplus for other purposes.

high places be investigated. Yet the financial crisis was squarely faced and impositions were not dodged. The council was ready to make important concessions. It was a debate that might have laid foundations for important reforms and might have made the future much easier. But it was extremely difficult to translate such a discussion into action. The Howards were ready to make difficulties at every turn. Ellesmere displayed a rigid conservatism. James offered nothing but hostile criticism. And as a result the recommendations of the council simply remained in abeyance. Later reforms by Cranfield and other officials cannot be traced to this debate or to the work of the council as a whole. And grievances increased rather than diminished in the years that followed. Parliament, of course, was not summoned at this time; and here again the advice of the council was disregarded. The Spanish party in whom James put his trust regarded parliament as a dangerous enemy and succeeded in persuading the king not to summon it. Private interests and an un-English foreign policy frustrated the sounder advice of the council.

Preparations for the parliament of 1621 were not at first entrusted to the council but to a group of judges headed by Bacon. He was instructed to consult with Hobart and Montagu, the two chief justices, with Coke, with Sir Randall Crew, who had been speaker in 1614, and with any other judges whom he wished, "touching that which mought in true policy, without packing or degenerate arts, prepare to a Parliament." The results might be placed before the council; but both James and Bacon considered that "all things were not at first fit for the whole table." [22] This seems somewhat strange. But at the time that Bacon received his instructions, James had not yet decided whether he would summon parliament or not. He was, in fact, most uncertain; and may well have thought that quiet consultation by the judges would leave him more complete freedom of action than formal deliberations in the council. While the council as a whole urged James to summon parliament, there was a small but powerful group working against it, and James may have thought that discussion of preparations would increase divisions and antagonism. Deliberation by the judges, moreover, would be an answer to those who were urging a parliament and would give the king more time to

[22] Bacon to Buckingham, Bacon to the king, October 2, 1620, *Spedding*, VII, 113–15.

make up his mind. Bacon had been prolific of advice to James upon parliamentary affairs for many years and was in a better position than anyone else in public life to make preparations that would be adequate. The judges whom he consulted were all old parliament men with more knowledge of the commons than that possessed by the majority of councillors. Certainly the parliament of 1614 had shown the need for secrecy and caution. In fact, the plan was a very sensible one. At the same time it was an indication that the council was slipping and that affairs supposedly within its province were now decided elsewhere. For many reasons Bacon would welcome a solution that placed preparations in his own hands.

The judges got to work at once. Bacon reported within a few days that he had consulted Hobart, Montagu, and Crew (Coke being at first omitted) and that they had divided the subject into four parts. Firstly, they had begun a collection of the grievances of parliament in 1614 as well as of those that had appeared more recently. Secondly, they discussed a fitting proclamation to announce the parliament. Thirdly, they considered what persons were fit to be members of the house and how they might be placed. Fourthly, they began to prepare a list of bills affecting the welfare of the state, "not wooing bills to make the King and his graces cheap; but good matter to set the Parliament on work, that an empty stomach do not feed upon humour." These four points may be taken up in turn.

The main work of the judges concerned grievances. In an interview with the king, of which we do not have the exact date, they "went over the grievances of the last parliament," giving James their opinion, "by way of probable conjecture, which of them were like to fall off, and which might perchance stick and be renewed." They also discussed with James more recent grievances which were likely to come up in the commons. These were of two kinds, "Proclamations and Commissions, and many Patents." They soon pushed earlier grievances into the background.

Early in November James publicly appointed Bacon and the other judges as commissioners to survey all monopolies and patents that were grievous to the commonwealth.[23] The commission-

[23] Chamberlain to Carleton, November 4, 1620, *Court and Times, James I*, II, 211. "To make way hereto [the parliament], and to prevent a maine opposition against his

ers soon reported to the king. They carefully pointed out that they were not necessarily expressing their own opinions but were trying "to personate the Lower House, and cast with themselves what was like to be stirred there." Thus the government would not be taken by surprise if parliament met before grievances were redressed. The patents likely to be "most subject to exception" were patents of old debts, of concealments, of monopolies, and of forfeitures and dispensations connected with penal statutes. The commissioners recommended that patents of old debts and concealments be done away with by an act of parliament as soon as the commons met. To remove them in the courts would be too slow, and action by the council would open a flood of courtiers seeking compensation. Better to have "some modest motion" in the house "by some grave and discreet gentlemen of the country, such as have least relation to the court," this to be followed by an act taking these patents away. On the other hand, such patents of monopoly as the king was willing to forego should be examined by the council and there revoked. This should not appear to be done as a preparation for parliament but as action taken in the ordinary course of the council's business. Thus the king "should keep his greatness, and something should be done in Parliament and something out of Parliament." The commissioners submitted a list of patents they wished revoked. There were many others; but to take them all "away now in a blaze would give more scandal that such things were granted, than cause thanks that they be now revoked." Many proclamations and commissions which were regarded as burdensome grew originally out of patents and would disappear with them.[24]

On December 14 the commissioners, with the king's consent, placed their findings before the council. To many things the lords agreed. For some things we provide, wrote Bacon, for some things we arm. But the council opposed a sweeping revocation of monopolies. Bacon argued before the council that if patents were removed the commons "would go better and faster to the main

prerogative, the king hath granted a commission to inquire of all Monopolies that are grevious to the subject, which to save the house that labour, himself will suppress." Burton to Carnsew, November 4, 1620, St. P. Domestic, 14/117:55.

[24] Bacon to Buckingham, October 7, Buckingham to Bacon, October 9, Bacon, Hobart, Montagu, Coke, and Crew to Buckingham, November 29, 1620, *Spedding*, VII, 115–18, 145–48.

errand, that these things should not be staged nor talked of, and so less fuel to the fire." He pointed out that the council had revoked many patents in the past and would therefore only be acting as it had often done before; and that it should watch over the public interest "as if it thought not of a Parliament." But other councillors answered that to revoke patents now would be regarded as mere humoring of the commons, who would suspect that once the parliament was over patents would reappear. The commons should be allowed to select the grievances they wished to present, especially as their actions could not be final; patents were normally revoked upon the complaint of injured parties and not from a clear sky; and offered graces "lose their thanks." To these arguments Bacon yielded with reluctance. He approved of patents in theory but he saw the practical necessity of meeting adverse criticism.[25]

The opposition of the council can only be explained by Buckingham's influence. Certainly Cranfield would have wished to see the monopolies ended. They were certain to cause trouble in the coming session, and there were many councillors who longed with all their hearts for a reconciliation of king and people. But Buckingham, although he got little from the patents himself, had been defending them with his usual violence and impetuosity. He had recently ruined Yelverton for opposing them. Bacon twice appealed to him to give them up, "to put off the envy of these things (which I think in themselves bear no great fruit), and rather take the thanks for ceasing them, than the note for maintaining them." [26] Bacon's letters show clearly that Buckingham could have ended the patents had he wished. But he was not convinced. And James, who regarded the patents as a cheap way of

[25] Naunton wrote Calvert, "To morrow I have warned all the Council to meet, when the Committees for the preparation to the Parliament are to put their advices to the Table." December 13, 1620, St. P. Domestic, 14/118:25. "The king is already preparing and arranging many things to give some satisfaction before the parliament meets, as he prudently wishes to make a show of granting voluntarily what he would be compelled to concede by necessity." November 20, 1620, Cal. St. P. Venetian, 1619–1621, 479. Tillières speaks of "le Parlement, apres lequel Messieurs du Conseil travaillent continuellement pour trouver quelque milieu par laquel le peuple soit contente et peu ainsy oblige a fournir de l'argent et le Roy conserve ses preroatives." October 18, 1620, Paris Trans., 3/54. Sir Edward Coke told the commons, February 19, 1621, "I was against the callinge in of theis Pattents before the Parliament, because then they would have been kept in store for a newe suite." Commons Debates 1621, IV, 79. Bacon to Buckingham, December 16, 1620, Spedding, VII, 151–52.
[26] Bacon to Buckingham, November 29, December 16, 1620, Spedding, VII, 148–52.

rewarding his servants, allowed the inevitable and bitter assaults of the commons to come without any indication on the part of the government that it was ready to meet parliament halfway.

The second part of the work which the judges had originally set themselves concerned a fitting proclamation to announce the parliament. The proclamation was of unusual importance: it must assure the people that there would be no undertaking as in 1614 and it must give a firm and statesmanlike lead in foreign policy, now of the greatest importance. The judges prepared an able document. James was made to say that he would retain the Palatinate at all costs and that advice and money for this end were the causes of summoning the commons. A secondary cause was to remove any abuses that had recently crept into the administration. The people were admonished to elect experienced and substantial members. But while the proclamation was an excellent one, James did not like it. It took too strong a tone in foreign policy and spoke of matters above the people's capacity. He told the judges he would write his own proclamation.[27] When it appeared, it was quite colorless. James thus rejected an important part of the judges' advice.

A third part of the judges' preparation, which concerned the election of proper members wherever possible, is discussed in another connection.[28] Finally, the judges did something to prepare a list of public bills to be submitted to the commons. Bacon spoke of this list in several of his reports, and on November 29 the judges sent it to the king for approval. "I have prepared some [laws]," James told the commons in April, "and left others for you to think on." Exactly what these laws were we do not know. Shortly before parliament met, Noy, Hakewill, and Heneage Finch had been instructed to review the penal statutes and had found many that needed to be repealed.[29] Cranfield's papers contained a vast quantity of material for paternalistic legislation if Bacon had been willing to use it.

The judges made other suggestions. They advised that the general pardon be more liberal than had been the case in recent years.

[27] "I send you the proclamation for the parliament, penned by the king himself, and would not be entreated by the lord chancellor and lord chamberlain to leave out the words, 'wrangling lawyers.'" Chamberlain to Carleton, November 9, 1620, *Court and Times, James I,* II, 214.
[28] See pp. 156–57.
[29] *Commons Debates 1621,* II, 304, 72. *Spedding,* V, 84–86; VI, 71; VII, 181.

They submitted a list of names from which the speaker might be chosen. When a proclamation was issued against licentious speech, Bacon urged in the council that it should not be "oversharp." When Hobart became ill, Bacon asked the king to appoint another member of the commission for preparations. Bacon also gave James advice about his opening speech to parliament, advice which, it seems, James rejected. He also sent James a forecast of what he anticipated might happen in the commons, a paper which unfortunately we do not now possess. "I have broken the main of the Parliament business into questions and parts, which I send," he wrote; "it may be, it is an over-dilligence: but still methinks there is a middle thing between art and chance: I think they call it prudence." Bacon asked the king to read this paper and "refer it to some few of the Council." [30]

Throughout these preparations in 1621 we may see the pervading spirit of Bacon. His suggestions were both wise and practical, but many of them were frustrated by the opposition of Buckingham and the council and by the drifting policy of the king. The part played by the council was comparatively minor; and its chief act was to reject Bacon's advice concerning monopolies. This was a surprising reversal of the council's attitude in 1615, when it had appeared ready to advocate drastic concessions to the commons. Doubtless certain councillors were personally interested in maintaining the monopolies. Yet the principal cause of their opposition must be found in Buckingham's influence. James played a rather sorry part. He rejected the judges' advice to take a firm tone in foreign affairs and put no pressure on the council to back the judges regarding patents of monopoly. He met parliament without a policy and without promise of reform.

Events in the parliament of 1621 forced a change in the government's approach to grievances. James allowed the commons considerable latitude in dealing with domestic policy, and not only did they unearth an amazing amount of injustice and corruption but began an ambitious and far-reaching program of reform in government, trade, and the courts of law. Their work, however, was cut short when far from completion by James's sudden adjournment in June. The commons were extremely angry; and even Weston spoke of "the sudden, and much wondered at, and

[30] *Spedding,* VII, 115–18, 123–29, 145–50, 155, 167.

much lamented adjournment." But the government was seriously alarmed at the extent and gravity of the disclosures made in parliament. And it was felt that if the commons were not to be allowed to complete their work, the government must prove that it could provide its own program of reform. James had been appalled at the findings of the commons. Bacon, who was still in London, strongly urged him to "pursue the reformation which the parliament hath begun" and outlined a declaration to that effect which he wished the king to make in the Star Chamber. Williams, the new lord keeper, constantly advocated conciliation of the commons, so that when king and parliament met again they should, to use Hacket's phrase, "be like a Mixture of Roses and Woodbinds in a sweet Entwinement." [31] But the strongest force toward reform came from Cranfield, who had promised the commons in the last days of their meeting that the government would do all in its power to promote trade. He had many ideas on the subject and was determined to redeem his pledge. After the adjournment in June, the council made a strenuous effort to carry out many reforms inaugurated by the commons and to show the nation that a program of reform could safely be entrusted to the crown.

On June 21 James instructed the council to debate a wide variety of abuses and grievances; and in the weeks that followed the council worked over the details of a sweeping proclamation issued on July 10. The council first debated a list of fifteen patents "which his Majesty in his own judgement did condemn" and a second list of seven more "which his Majesty did not now condemn but did commend to the lords of his Privie Council to consider of and to report." Later the council considered all other patents debated in the commons, whether the commons had condemned them or not, besides a long list of seventy-nine more (all that could be discovered) which had not been mentioned in parliament. Solicitor Heath kept notes of these debates and of the council's decision in each case. The proclamation of July 10 was based upon these decisions. It swept away eighteen patents at a stroke and listed seventeen more which the crown would not defend if legal proceedings were begun against them.[32]

[31] Sir Richard Weston to Lord Digby(?), June 25, 1621, Aston Papers, Add. MSS 36445, f. 148. Bacon to the king, June, 1621, *Spedding*, VII, 289–91. Hacket, *Williams*, I, 81, 85, 104, 109–10.

[32] St. P. Domestic, 14/121:48, 49, 122, 125. *Commons Debates 1621*, VII, 309–564, contains a detailed account of the history of all patents brought up in this parliament. See

The council was also instructed to deal with many other grievances complained of in the commons, so that either "by proclamation or otherwise . . . happily such present course may be taken as may prevent new complaint." Throughout the summer and autumn of 1621 a strenuous effort was made to improve trade and settle disputes arising from commercial competition. Trading privileges in the new draperies and in Welsh cottons were extended; new negotiations were begun with the Dutch in the interest of the East India Company; interlopers complained of by the Eastland Company were restricted. In addition, the council debated the scarcity of money, the value of exchange, the excess of imports over exports, and the rates charged as customs. Representatives of commercial companies and of the outports were called to London, and a committee of the council considered their advice. A committee of merchants was appointed in November to suggest means for balancing trade. In September Cranfield was collecting information on imports from the Netherlands. New restrictions were drawn against the exportation of iron ordnance, of which the commons had bitterly complained. An attempt was also made to carry out certain legal reforms suggested by the commons. And a commission was set up to consider abuses and grievances in the government of Ireland. Many of these points were touched upon in the proclamation of July 10. Thus the government sought to implement the program begun in the commons. The summer of 1621 also saw the release of a number of political prisoners, largely at Williams' solicitation.[33]

This reforming zeal continued, with somewhat abated ardor, through 1622 and 1623. A commission of councillors was appointed, September 28, 1622, to investigate the size of fees taken in all the courts of England and Wales, both temporal and ecclesiastical. A proclamation of July 28, 1622, announced a committee of the council to investigate the decay of the wool trade and prom-

also *ibid.*, III, 416, note 25. Robert Steele, *Tudor and Stuart Proclamations, 1485–1714* (2 vols., Oxford, 1910), I, 155. But the commons in 1621 had taken the stand that a proclamation was insufficient in dealing with a parliamentary grievance.

[33] This paragraph is based upon *Commons Debates 1621*, III, 415–17, notes 23–26. See also Hacket, *Williams*, I, 68–70; *Court and Times, James I*, II, 268–70; *Cal. St. P. Venetian, 1621–1623*, 108; *Gardiner*, IV, 133–37. Williams also objected to a mitigation of Bacon's sentence and to the appointment of Arundel as lord marshal on the ground that parliament would be offended. *Spedding*, VII, 291, 310–11; Williams to Buckingham, September 15, 1621, Harl. MSS 7000, f. 61.

ised a commission for the general furtherance of industry and commerce. This commission was appointed and made important recommendations. But Brooke wrote Conway in March, 1623: "The commission for trade, being of so great weight, proceeds slowly; that for fees seems dead." Meanwhile, October 12, 1622, the council wrote James that it "had appointed a day to take into consideration the remaine of all those things that were spoken of as grievances in the last Parliament." About the same time there was a rumor of a general pardon, though it did not appear. According to Hacket, Cranfield opposed it on financial grounds. But if he did so, he also appears to have withstood pressure from courtiers and other interested parties to renew under different forms the monopolies and patents of 1621. Another commission, appointed early in 1623, named five important councillors to whom anyone might bring grievances that had no legal redress. The commission for Ireland, which had at first seemed largely a means of punishing those selected as commissioners, came to assume more aspects of an attempt at reform.[34] Thus the council sought to prepare for future sessions of the commons by meeting the demand for sweeping changes that had arisen in the cataclysmic parliament of 1621.

Nevertheless, the months preceding the parliament of 1624 saw a minimum of formal preparations. Charles and Buckingham had now returned from Madrid demanding a reversal of English policy and a war with Spain. Their plans included a parliament. They began a campaign to force the king into line with their new policy and brought tremendous pressure to bear upon pro-Spanish ministers. It was of this struggle that councillors were thinking and not of preparations for the coming session. There was, indeed, a rumor in October that a general pardon was to be issued as the "forerunner of a parliament." And on December 20 the council was to have met to determine what advice it should offer the king upon summoning parliament and what should be done to prepare for a session. But at the last moment James, still undecided and knowing that the council would follow the prince

---

[34] *Acts of the Privy Council, 1621–1623*, 325. Steele, *Proclamations*, I, 157–59. *Cal. St. P. Domestic, 1619–1623*, 477. Lord Brooke to Sir Edward Conway, March 6, 1623, *ibid.*, 512. The council to the king, October 12, 1622, St. P. Domestic, 14/133:45. Sir Francis Nethersole to Carleton, September 28, 1622, St. P. Holland, 84/109. Hacket, *Williams*, I, 81, 85, 104.

and Buckingham, forbade the debate.[35] Despite this lack of preparation, Charles and Buckingham had their way with parliament in 1624; ending the Spanish treaties was for the moment far more attractive than any other concession the government could offer. Other preparations were not necessary. But in later parliaments Buckingham's lack of preparations formed an additional handicap in his dealings with the commons.

Indeed, we come here to a sharp break in the matter we have been following. There were scarcely any preparations made by the government before the parliaments of 1625, 1626, or 1628. Charles and Buckingham seem to have assumed that the parliament of 1625 would be as accommodating as that of 1624. The writs were issued in great haste immediately after James's death, and there were none of the preparations that preceded earlier parliaments. Williams warned that delay was advisable to allow courtiers time to secure election. And Conway protested that concessions to Catholics, called for in the marriage treaty with France, were most inexpedient before a parliament.[36] These cautions were ignored with serious results.

In the six months that intervened between the parliament of 1625 and that of 1626 one important concession was made to public opinion. A series of proclamations reimposed the penal laws against the Catholics and inaugurated a brief period of persecution. This had been offered to the commons, though with small effect, in the closing days of the 1625 parliament. The penal laws were now enforced, in spite of the promises to France; and were obviously inspired by the hope of winning approval in the commons.[37] Apart from this, the government did very little.[38] Buckingham clung to the hope that a brilliant success in his foreign

[35] Chamberlain to Carleton, October 25, 1623, *Court and Times, James I*, II, 425; *Cal. St. P. Venetian, 1623–1625*, 157. Conway to Buckingham, December 20, 1623, St. P. Domestic, 14/155:65. J. J. von Rusdorff, *Mémoires et négociations secrètes* (2 vols., Leipzig, 1789), I, 156. The last of these references I owe to *Gardiner*, V, 157.

[36] Hacket, *Williams*, II, 4–5. Conway to Buckingham, June 4, 1625, St. P. Domestic, 16/3:25.

[37] *Gardiner*, V, 417–18; VI, 3, 32–33. "Here be daily proclamations come forth; one strict enough against papists and recusants, if it may be duly executed; but it is thought to look towards the parliament . . . For my part, I look for no good of this parliament, the world being so far out of tune every way." Chamberlain to Carleton, January 19, 1626, *Court and Times, Charles I*, I, 72.

[38] I find but one indication of any attempt to remedy grievances. A state paper, endorsed "Remembrances against the Parliament," suggests laws correcting two minor grievances complained of by the commons. *Cal. St. P. Domestic, 1625–1626*, 242.

policy would win the hearts of the people and force the commons to follow his leadership. But his hopes faded one by one and he was forced to meet the commons with the disastrous expedition against Cadiz fresh in their minds. Grievances of many kinds were allowed to accumulate without any attempt of the government to redress them. The greatest grievance of all was the position of Buckingham himself; and this was a point on which the crown refused to compromise. Nor were more preparations made for the meeting of parliament in 1628.

Indeed, by 1626, Charles was more inclined to employ force than conciliation in dealing with the commons. The Venetian ambassador, after discussing the possibility of concessions by Charles in 1626, wrote, "I fancy that the king has received advice of a diametrically opposite tenor, to insist upon his prerogative" and to seize what the commons refused to grant. "In order to fortify the king's authority they speak of bringing the troops from the fleet to the Tower and its neighborhood. This would be a very violent innovation, very ill-adapted to the humour of the country." Threats preceded the parliament of 1628. Charles attempted to collect money before it was voted, under the threat that unless it was paid no parliament would be called. He asked for some £173,000 as ship money and issued privy seals demanding loans from wealthy men. But opposition was so intense that these measures were dropped. This was most fortunate, "for in all men's minds," as Woodward wrote Windebank, "there will be no parliament if they go forth." "That fearful preludium of Privy Seals and letters are not to be represented on the stage, so that now there is more hope of better harmony in the Lower House." Nevertheless Charles was still toying with the idea of violence. "I hear," wrote the Venetian ambassador, "it has been voted in the Council that unless the Commons grant the money immediately and without further debate, the king will be justified in exercising his prerogative burdening them with taxes and compelling them. For this end it is said that they have raised the thousand Reiters, given the orders for corslets and for the Scottish and Irish regements. I do not know how these sudden and violent remedies can cure a feeble frame." [39]

[39] *Cal. St. P. Venetian, 1625–1626,* 319; *1628–1629,* 10. John Beaulieu to Sir Thomas Puckering, February 20, 1628, *Court and Times, Charles I,* I, 323. Rowland Woodward to Francis Windebank, February 6, 20, 1628, St. P. Domestic, 16/92:55; 16/93:87.

Between the prorogation of parliament in June, 1628, and its meeting in January, 1629, there was some attempt on the part of the government to conciliate public opinion and prepare it for the coming session. The summer of 1628 saw important changes in the government. Buckingham resigned his office of warden of the Cinque Ports, though his successor, the earl of Suffolk, was one of his creatures. Arundel, Bristol, and Abbot were restored to favor, Buckingham became reconciled to Williams, Weston became lord treasurer, Wentworth was taken into the royal service. The policy of these men would be for peace abroad, or at least a great curtailment of the scope of the war, and for a sounder and more conservative administration at home. They would advocate a more conciliatory policy toward the commons. This was evident in the way in which Weston handled the question of tonnage and poundage. The government was greatly embarrassed by the refusal of many merchants to pay the duties. But Weston held that the question must be reserved for the commons and kept the actions of the government within reasonable limits until parliament assembled. Stricter measures were taken against Catholics; and leading churchmen close to the king were asked to renounce publicly any connection with Arminianism. Felton, the assassin of Buckingham, was "punished for simple murder, in order not to exasperate the people." "All things," wrote Dorchester, "by his majesty's personal order in council, as well as in church as commonwealth, are provisionally so disposed, that he may the better hope for a fair and loving meeting with his people." [40]

But if the desperateness of 1628 forced a more conciliatory attitude on the part of the government, the time was past when such things could affect the disposition of the commons. And the results of these concessions were nil. Salvetti wrote in December "that all these anticipations and preparations . . . are already regarded with suspicion." Sir Robert Aiton wrote Carlisle that the government was "about to satisfy some things both in religion and government to sweeten things to the parliament, but most

[40] Weston to Buckingham, August 18, 1628, St. P. Domestic, 16/113:14. Dorchester to Carlisle, September 30, December 19, John Pory to Rev. Joseph Mead, November 28, Beaulieu to Puckering, December 24, 1628, *Court and Times, Charles I*, I, 403–04, 438–39; II, 2–3. *Cal. St. P. Venetian, 1628–1629*, 242, 394–95, 432, 493. Salvetti Correspondence, *Skrine MSS, H. M. C.*, 173. Dorset to Carlisle, November 24, 1628, *Cal. St. P. Domestic, Addenda, 1625–1649*, 303. See also *Gardiner*, VII, 1–7, 28–29.

men doubt that they are not sincerely intended, and so will give little satisfaction." [41] Preparations were hopeless in 1628.

As we survey these preparations of the council between the accession of James and the dissolution of parliament in 1629, it is obvious that they were far from satisfactory. There was always one difficulty or another. Preparations were either too superficial, or were presented to the commons in an unsatisfactory manner, or were ruined by divisions in the council itself. As time went on, the council became more subservient to Buckingham. This subservience had hampered preparations in 1621, and in later parliaments it prevented councillors from making any preparations at all. Many councillors during the early years of Charles's reign desired to conciliate the commons but were unable to secure the adoption of their policy until, in 1628, concessions were hopeless. The council could discuss only those matters which the king ordered it to discuss; and if the king decided that councillors should not participate in a given business, they had no recourse but to obey. This was a fundamental difficulty running through all debates in the council upon preparations for parliament. The council's position in the framework of the constitution precluded it from attempting to solve the more fundamental problems confronting the crown.

But if the advice of the council fell short of what it might have been, it was, on the whole, advice toward a moderate and conciliatory policy. The council's judgment was surprisingly constant that parliaments were essential and must be conciliated, summoned frequently, and not dissolved in anger. The violent courses adopted by the crown and wild notions that the king could rule without meeting his people might find support from a few stray councillors but never from the council as a whole. Salisbury, though he did not relish meetings of the commons, advised James to summon parliament in 1610 and struggled desperately to avoid the rupture which took place between James and the commons in the autumn of that year. He and the council made every effort after parliament had been dissolved to dissuade the king from punishing those members who had spoken most violently. The council's advice to James in 1614 was in favor of a

[41] *Skrine MSS, H.M.C.*, 173. Aiton to Carlisle, December 19, 1628, St. P. Domestic, 16/152:58.

parliament, although it realized fully that difficulties would be very great. Twice in 1615 the council forced the possibility of calling parliament upon the attention of the king. In the long debate in 1615, which we have cited, every councillor except the Howards began his speech by declaring that a parliament was absolutely necessary; and James was plainly told "that there was no likelyhood of a perfect subsistance for him, but by a releefe of his people, which must be by parliament." There was no other way. The Howards might demur, but the council was overwhelmingly against them. Again in 1621 the great majority of councillors advised James to summon parliament; they had, indeed, been urging him in that direction since the beginning of the Thirty Years' War in 1618. Buckingham was against calling parliament, but in spite of his influence the advice of the council was in its favor. The dissolution of the parliament of 1621 and the acts of violence that accompanied it were carried out over the protests of leading councillors. And if certain councillors opposed a parliament in 1624, it was because parliament at that time meant a war with Spain.

Councillors objected to every dissolution from 1625 to 1629 without the slightest effect upon events. They deplored the haste with which the parliament of 1625 was summoned, the rash adjournment to Oxford, and the angry dissolution in August. But the advice of the council was now a matter of small importance. "The king summoned his council to Woodstock," wrote the Venetian ambassador, "to inform them of his determination to dissolve parliament, but to ask their advice about the way of doing it." Again in December the council was merely informed of the decision of the king to summon another meeting of the commons. Coventry wrote on December 26, 1625, that "his Majestie hath this day resolved to holde a parliament at Westminster the 5th of February next."[42] The decision to dissolve in June, 1626, was opposed by all the council except the duke. On June 14 "the lords sitting in council at Whitehall to argue whether it should be dissolved or not, were all with one voice against the dissolution of it." Coventry was said to be in some danger of disgrace for his opposition; and a letter to Buckingham from solicitor Heath, the

[42] *Cal. St. P. Venetian, 1625–1626,* 146–47. See also Hacket, *Williams,* II, 15–16; *Negotium Posterorum,* II, 104. Coventry to Sir Heneage Finch, December 26, 1625, *Finch MSS, H. M. C.,* I, 43.

ablest adviser trusted by the crown on parliamentary affairs, contained a plea for moderation. The house of lords opposed the dissolution. They sent a deputation of four peers, Pembroke, Carlisle, Holland, and Manchester, to point out to the king the disorder and inconveniences which were bound to ensue. But Charles was not to be moved. According to one account these four lords begged him to continue the parliament "but two days longer. He answered, 'Not a Minute.'"[43]

The desperate lack of money in the latter part of 1627 forced Charles to heed the advice of his council; and the council again told him that parliament was the one way to obtain adequate supply. Buckingham, always hopeful of success and ready to take chances, also advised this step. But Charles was most reluctant and had to be persuaded. In December and January, 1627–28, there were almost daily consultations in the council upon all possible means of raising revenue; and at a very late hour on January 30 Charles finally consented to calling a parliament. "This decision," wrote the Venetian ambassador, "was due to compulsion, from the impossibility of self-defense in any other way, and from the promises made by many of the chief personages that nothing should be said about the duke." Toward the end of February the king and council, alarmed at the violence of some of the election contests and at the universal defeat of government candidates, postponed parliament from March to April; but other means of raising money were so universally opposed that "the council again met several times and the original decision for parliament to meet on the 29th of March was confirmed."[44] Sheer necessity forced the king to accept the advice of those of his council who wished parliament to meet.

On several occasions during the parliament of 1628 the council acted as a modifying influence and restrained the king from dissolving the commons.[45] And even after the events of March 2,

[43] *Court and Times, Charles I,* I, 111. *Cal. St. P. Venetian, 1625–1626,* 452–53, 462. Heath to Buckingham, June 13, 1626, *Cal. St. P. Domestic, Addenda, 1625–1649,* 133–34. *Cal. St. P. Domestic, 1625–1626,* 354. *Buccleuch MSS, Montagu Papers, H. M. C.,* III, 304. Salvetti Correspondence, *Skrine MSS, H. M. C.,* 75.

[44] Rev. Joseph Mead to Sir Martin Stuteville, December 15, 1627, February 2, 1628, *Court and Times, Charles I,* I, 305, 316–17. *Ibid.,* I, 323–24. Registers of the Privy Council for January 2, 1628 (cited in *Gardiner,* VI, 225). *Cal. St. P. Venetian, 1626–1628,* 558–59, 584, 588–89, 605–06. John Hope to ———, January 31, 1628, St. P. Domestic, 16/91:93.

[45] Nethersole to the queen of Bohemia, June 7, 1628, St. P. Domestic, 16/106:55. Diary of Walter Yonge, Add. MSS 35331, f. 20v. In June the council urged Charles to adjourn,

1629, there was a group in the council that advocated moderation. "Cabinet councils have been held very frequently," wrote the Venetian ambassador, "both day and night, the king always being present. It was difficult to decide, as the Council was divided. The Lord Keeper [Coventry] with a great party was in favour of gentleness. The treasurer [Weston], with the others, seeing themselves in danger, insisted on force and a rupture, the course followed." [46] The commons had attacked Weston with much bitterness, and he now wished to be rid of them as soon as possible. Thus personal interests again played a great part in the advice of certain councillors. Nevertheless, generally speaking, the council's advice upon calling and dissolving the commons was sound. The council was on the decline; but its advice was far better than that of the individual ministers selected by the early Stuarts. [47]

as the commons wished, rather than prorogue. *Court and Times, Charles I,* I, 370. About prolonging the time of the prorogation from autumn to winter the council's opinion was not asked. Dorchester to Carlisle, September 30, 1628, *ibid.,* I, 403–04.

[46] *Cal. St. P. Venetian, 1628–1629,* 580. *Gardiner,* VII, 77.

[47] See D. H. Willson, "Summoning and Dissolving Parliament, 1603–25: The Council's Advice to James I," *American Historical Review,* 45:279–300 (January, 1940).

3

The Councillors Are Placed in the House

If James and Charles were to deal with parliament on the lines laid down by the Tudors, it was essential for them to select councillors of the proper type and place them in the commons. Broadly speaking, the early Stuarts realized that this was so. There was constant government pressure to secure the election of councillors; and appointments to the council were occasionally made with the purpose of strengthening its position in the house. But here, as elsewhere, James and Charles did not act with constancy or firmness. James was slow to realize the importance of the problem; other considerations were constantly allowed to intervene; grave mistakes were made in selecting the proper men; and as a result the Stuarts were, as a rule, poorly represented by their councillors in parliament. It is, therefore, important to follow the policy and fortunes of James and Charles in placing their councillors in the commons and to see what kind of men these councillors were.

When James ascended the English throne, he did not know that the problem existed. In his first parliament the strength of the council in the commons was allowed to shrink to pitiable weakness. During the first session in 1604 there were but two councillors in the house, Sir John Herbert, the second secretary of state, and Sir John Stanhope, the king's vice-chamberlain, both very mediocre persons.[1] The influence of the council in this session stood practically at zero. As a result the opposition was encouraged to assume a bolder and more aggressive tone; and had not Salisbury been directing parliamentary affairs from the lords, the consequences might have been most disastrous.

The government had planned, indeed, to have a more influential councillor in the commons. At Elizabeth's death Sir John Fortescue held the offices of keeper of the great wardrobe, chancellor of the duchy of Lancaster, and chancellor of the exchequer.

[1] A list of the privy councillors in the house of commons will be found at the end of this chapter (pp. 99–101).

He was removed from the last of these by James, who, according to Goodman, "never favoured him," but he was, nevertheless, the most distinguished councillor in 1604 who was not a peer. He stood for Buckinghamshire but was defeated by Sir Francis Goodwin. The government then attempted to obtain the seat for him in spite of his failure. Cecil wrote to Parry: "Sir Francis Goodwin having labored to be knight of Buckinghamshire, to the exclusion of an Ancient Councillor, Sir John Fortescue, it was advised by the King's learned Council and Judges, whether there were not some means (by the law) to avoid it, whereupon it being found that Sir Francis was out-lawed and so certified by the sheriff, consequently a new writ was sent forth, by virtue whereof Sir John Fortescue was chosen." When the sheriff of Bucks was examined by the house, he confessed he had certified Goodwin as an outlaw at the direction of the attorney-general.[2]

Thus the famous case of Goodwin vs. Fortescue originated in the wish of the government to add another councillor to the small number already in the commons. The house, however, resisted this interference in elections. "If it shalbe Lawfull," said Sir Robert Wingfield, "for any great Offycers about the Kings Majestie to alter the free Choyce of Burgesses, what inconvenyence that will Come unto, I will not speake of but only leave it to your Judgments." The commons, therefore, as Cecil wrote Parry, "somewhat suddenly fearing some opposition (which was indeed intended) allowed of Goodwin and rejected the other." When the lords requested a conference, the commons refused. They laid their case before the king, who suggested a conference with the council and judges, himself to be present; and here a compromise was effected by which neither Goodwin nor Fortescue was to have

[2] *Goodman*, I, 26. Lord Cecil to Sir Thomas Parry, April 14, 1604, St. P. Domestic, 14/7:27. April 2, 1604, *C. J.*, I, 161. The sheriff said, "He being here in London, Mr. Attorney General, the second of March, at his Chamber in the Inner Temple, delivered him Two Cap. utlagat. against Sir Francis Goodwin; and, before he made his Return, he went, and advised with Mr. Attorney about his Return; who penned it; And so it was done by his Direction." Speech of Sir Robert Wingfield, April, 1604, St. P. Domestic, 14/7:2.

James later declared, "That, for his Part, he was indifferent which of them were chosen; Sir John or Sir Francis: That they could suspect no special Affection in him, because this was a Counsellor not brought in by himself." *C. J.*, I, 158. He may have been thinking in terms of the Scotch parliament; or Salisbury may have handled the matter at first without the knowledge of the king. Sir Francis Goodwin was a good candidate from the government's point of view. He urged the freeholders to elect Fortescue in the original election. A letter from the council to the bailiff and burgesses of Buckingham borough, February 21, 1606 (Add. MSS 11402, f. 110), urged the election of Goodwin. He was returned by this corporation.

the seat in question. Thus the house rejected Fortescue although he was a councillor. When at the beginning of the next session James asked the commons to admit Fortescue if he was elected from a new constituency and the commons gave a somewhat reluctant consent, a member remarked that he was "a litle ielous what maie follow if wee receave Burgesses by his Majesties commendacions"; and the house showed its uneasiness by directing the clerk to make no entry of their decision in the *Journals*.[3]

If the situation in 1604 was extraordinary, that in the second session in 1606 was even more so. Stanhope was now in the lords, and for the first month of the session Herbert was left as the sole representative of the council in the commons. He was then joined by Sir John Fortescue, who came in through a by-election for Middlesex. The influence of the council in the house was even less than it had been in 1604; the same is true of the third session of the parliament held in 1606 and 1607. When the commons met in 1610 for the fourth and fifth sessions of this long parliament, Fortescue was dead; but Herbert was supported by two new councillors, Sir Thomas Parry, chancellor of the duchy of Lancaster, and Sir Julius Caesar, chancellor of the exchequer. Yet even so, the end of this parliament found only three councillors in the house, while at the beginning there had been but two and for a short period in 1606 but one. In comparison with the days of Queen Elizabeth the representation of the council in the commons was at an extremely low ebb, in ability as well as in numerical strength.

The explanation is not that councillors were unable to secure election, but that the council consisted too exclusively of peers. At Elizabeth's death there were six members of the council who were commoners: Herbert, Stanhope, Fortescue, Knollys, Cecil (all of whom served in the parliament of 1601), and Sir Edward Wotton, who became a councillor in December, 1602. But in May, 1603, Cecil, Knollys, and Wotton, while retaining their offices, were elevated to the peerage. There were thus but three councillors eligible for election in 1604, Stanhope and Herbert, who were returned, and Fortescue, who was defeated. Stanhope became a baron in 1605; and thus during the session of 1606 the council

---

[3] Speech of Sir Robert Wingfield, April, 1604, St. P. Domestic, 14/7:2. *Bowyer*, 15, 52 note.

contained but two men who were not peers, Fortescue and Herbert, who were both members of the commons. Caesar and Parry were the only other commoners added to the council until after the dissolution of James's first parliament.[4] Thus, with the exception of Fortescue in 1604, the councillors in the commons at this time, few as they were, were identical with those members of the council who were not peers. So began a process which, throughout the reign of James, was to drain the commons of many of the most able supporters of the crown. It was natural enough that James should ennoble those of his servants whom he wished to honor; Elizabeth had been unnecessarily sparing of such honors. It is probable that James at the beginning of his reign, deriving his ideas from Scottish practice, envisaged a royal council as a body composed primarily of nobles. He declared in 1603 that he wished to make room in the council "for such of the ancient Nobilitie whose birth and meritt make them more capable then others," as if nobles only were to be selected. Whatever the cause, the number and personnel of his creations undoubtedly removed from the commons many of those councillors best able to serve him in the lower chamber.[5] In this first parliament, as a result of his creations, the number of councillors eligible for election was extremely small.

James's error was soon pointed out to him. "For the king," wrote Chamberlain in 1612, "is given to understand that he is ill served in parliament by reason of the paucity of councillors and officers of household, that were wont to bear great sway in that House . . . " In urging a parliament in 1613, Bacon advised the king to consider "whether it be fit to strengthen the lower house with any Counsellors of estate . . . " And in 1606 Hoby wrote Edmondes that the subsidy of that year was "propounded by Sir Thomas Ridgeway, and seconded by such like (for I must tell

[4] Caesar became a councillor on July 5, 1607, and Parry on December 24, 1607. Attendance lists of the council during this period include the names of no commoners except Herbert, Parry, and Caesar. Add. MSS 11402, f. 99, 128, 134, 154, 156v, 158. I am leaving out of account the Scots who were councillors, even though they had been naturalized by act of parliament.

[5] Declaration of the king in council, May 10, 1603, St. P. Domestic, 14/1:73. The following councillors were raised to the peerage at times when they might have served in the commons: Sir John Stanhope (1605), Sir Lionel Cranfield and Sir Fulke Greville (1621), Sir Edward Conway (1625), Sir Dudley Carleton (1626), and Sir Richard Weston (1628). Sir Henry Cary was made a Scottish peer in 1621, which raised a question of his eligibility to sit in the commons.

you, that I think the State scorneth to have any privy counsellors of any understanding in that House) . . . " Chamberlain, writing in 1612, reported a plan for a partial solution of the difficulty. James, he said, was "minded to reduce the House to the form it had in the late queen's time" and therefore offered Knollys and Wotton a yearly pension of £2,000 each if they would resign their places, thus making way for councillors who could sit in the commons. "But the Lord Knollys stood upon an earldom and the Lord Wotton had rather have £5,000 in hand: and so the matter rests." [6] Of this plan nothing more was heard.

Salisbury's death in 1612 greatly increased the need for placing able councillors in the house and at the same time opened the way for new appointments to the council. Yet the situation in the parliament of 1614 showed only a slight improvement. When that parliament began, the council contained five men eligible for election. Four of them became members: Sir Ralph Winwood, Sir Thomas Lake, Sir Thomas Parry, and Sir Julius Caesar; the fifth, Sir John Herbert, did not. The government had sought to remedy its earlier error, but its efforts were only a qualified success. None of these councillors were properly fitted for their task, and the strength of the council in the house remained far from satisfactory. This can no longer be attributed to the inexperience of the king. It was rather that he did not select the best men for office, but allowed other considerations besides the qualifications of the candidate to play a part in appointments.

When the commons met again in 1621, a new and distinctly superior group of councillors took their places in the house. The council had grown in size and now contained a larger number of non-noble members. The government was determined that all available councillors should be placed in the commons. The work of preparation, as we have seen, was entrusted to Bacon and certain other judges, who drew up lists of desirable members; and their first list contained "the privy councillors and principal statesmen or courtiers." [7] The efforts of the government resulted in the remarkable fact that every councillor eligible for election found a seat in the commons in 1621. Nine privy councillors were elected to the

[6] Chamberlain to Carleton, June 17, 1612, *Court and Times, James I*, I, 176. Bacon to King James, *Spedding*, IV, 368. Sir Edward Hoby to Sir Thomas Edmondes, March 7, 1606, *Court and Times, James I*, I, 59–60.
[7] *Spedding*, VII, 116.

house; and though their actual strength in daily debate was below that figure, they formed nevertheless the ablest and strongest group of councillors in any of the parliaments of James and Charles. And their influence was greater than in any other parliament of the period.

The government's desire to place councillors in the house is well illustrated by the case of Sir Fulke Greville. Greville had been chancellor of the exchequer since 1614, but he resigned his office in January, 1621, and was raised to the peerage, his patent bearing the date of January 29. Yet he sat in the commons in 1621 until the adjournment in June. Gardiner's explanation is that although it was quite natural for Greville to resign at this time, the government strongly disliked the prospect of meeting parliament after an interval of seven years with a newly appointed chancellor of the exchequer as yet unacquainted with his department; and therefore devised an ingenious method of escape. Woodford, writing on February 2, said that Greville was to become Lord Brooke, "but his pattente is not yet sealed." This may be taken to mean that while the patent was made out and the rank conferred, it did not become valid until Greville passed it under the great seal; and he deferred this final step until the summer. In the meantime he sat in the commons, where he was often referred to as chancellor of the exchequer, although the office had been conferred upon Sir Richard Weston on January 29.[8]

In the parliaments following 1621 it is obvious that the government continued its efforts to place as large a number of councillors as possible in the commons; and with the exception of the parliament of 1628 it was markedly successful. There were six councillors in the parliament of 1624, six in that of 1625, and seven in that of 1626. Caesar was the one eligible councillor not in the commons during these years.[9] The government's efforts appear most clearly in its constant interference in elections in behalf of councillors, a point which will be discussed presently. There is also other evidence. In 1624 Sir Robert Naunton wrote Buckingham

[8] *Notes and Queries,* 4th series, 8:22, 88–89, 217, 234. Weston did not enter the commons until November, 1621.

[9] It is just possible that Caesar was a member of parliament in 1626, which would make eight councillors in that session. His name does not appear in the list of members, but Whitelocke refers twice to speeches by the master of the rolls. March 8, April 27, 1626, Whitelocke, f. 34v, 163. But it is more probable that these speeches were by Henry Rolle, whom the diarists called "Mr. Rowles," which in copying became "Master of the Rolls."

that he understood the king planned to use his services in the coming parliament. Naunton was in disgrace for some indiscreet remarks about the Spanish match and was anxious to retrieve his fortunes. "For the Parliament," he wrote, "I gave your Lordship account [in a former letter] how my Lord Keeper had acquainted me, that it was his Majesty's pleasure to use my service in it, and how his Lordship had written to the university [of Cambridge] to choose me one of their burgesses, which I since understand that they have already done. . . . As for any honour in Parliament, my Lord, I have no other ambition there than merely to follow and observe his Majesties direction. Only my desire and hope is, that his Majesty will not draw me out onto that stage, after all these sufferings, less than formerly I was." [10]

In the parliament of 1628, however, we find a new situation. Seven councillors were eligible for election, but only three were returned. Sir John Coke, May, and Edmondes secured seats; Weston, Savile, Naunton, and Caesar did not. Sir Francis Cottington, elected a member of the commons in 1628, became a councillor in November, making a fourth councillor in the house during the short session of 1629. We have here for the first time a number of eligible councillors who were not members. This was due in part to increased difficulty in obtaining election, since both Savile and Edmondes were defeated, though Edmondes later obtained a place from a small Cornish borough. But Weston was raised to the peerage shortly after the session began and may not have sought election to the commons; [11] while Naunton had once more incurred the displeasure of the court and probably was not wanted in parliament by the government. Thus the desire of the crown to strengthen its position in the lords and its propensity to punish those who differed with its policies also help explain the lack of councillors in the commons at this time.

Although this study does not extend beyond 1629, it is interest-

[10] Naunton to Buckingham, January 14, 1624, St. P. Domestic, 14/158:30. Naunton, who was confined to his own house, wrote that if his enlargement was further delayed, the impression might become current that James had released him because of pressure from the commons.

[11] His elevation was reported, though falsely, as having already taken place before parliament met. John Cayworth to Lord Montagu, February 9, 1628, *Buccleuch MSS, Montagu Papers, H. M. C.,* III, 324. On April 14, the day following his elevation, Weston, together with Coventry, Sir Edward Howard, and Goring, was introduced into the lords, obviously with the intention of strengthening the royal party there. *L. J.,* III, 738. Savile was defeated in Yorkshire; I do not know whether Naunton or Caesar sought election.

ing to note that during the Short Parliament and in the early months of the Long Parliament, circumstances prevailed that duplicate the first years of the reign of James. The council was large in 1640 and 1641, containing some forty members; but it was composed almost entirely of peers, and the number of councillors eligible for election to the commons was small. Ten years before the group of non-noble councillors had been large. Sir Henry Vane and Sir Thomas Jermyn were added to it in 1630 and Sir Francis Windebank in 1632. But after that date the group remained constant until June, 1640, after the dissolution of the Short Parliament, when Sir Thomas Roe became a member. Meanwhile the older men — May, Naunton, Caesar, Edmondes, and finally Coke — were dropping out. Their offices were given to noblemen, or to commoners already in the council, or to persons who were not admitted to the council. As a result the crisis of 1640 found the government unprepared to place an adequate number of councillors in the house. When the Short Parliament began, only three councillors were eligible for election; and when the Long Parliament began, only four.[12]

The strength of the council in the house thus appears to follow a curve, beginning with a weak representation in the first parliament of James, then increasing in the parliaments of the 1620's, and finally declining again in the parliament of 1628 and in those of 1640. It is, of course, true that the councillors in the commons were much stronger in the 1620's than at any other time during the period. But if we disregard numbers and look merely at the effective strength of the councillors during these years, the curve begins to flatten out and it is seen that their position during the 1620's was not as great as would at first appear.

When the short session of 1614 was about half over, the commons discovered that Sir Thomas Parry had interfered corruptly in the election for Stockbridge; and for this he was expelled from the house, thus reducing the number of councillors from four to three. His removal did not greatly diminish the council's strength in this house of commons; but it was a blow at its prestige and a dangerous precedent for the future, and it is strange that James made so little effort in Parry's behalf. After a characteristic but futile request that the house allow him to punish Parry, James

[12] Registers of the Privy Council, *passim*.

told the commons they could deal with Parry as they pleased and added the further disgrace of suspending him both from the council and from the chancellorship of the duchy. An explanation is found, perhaps, in a letter of Chamberlain written before parliament opened. "I hear," he wrote, "that Sir Thomas Parry be in some disfavor and like to be suspended from his place of Chancellor, and to be put to his pension." [13] Parry's kindness to Arabella Stuart may have irritated James. But Parry was now an old man and James may well have regarded the attack of the commons as an opportunity to be rid of him.

But if James merely acquiesced in Parry's disgrace, he himself helped reduce the strength of the council at the opening of parliament in 1621. Sir Robert Naunton had aroused the animosity of Gondomar, who on several occasions complained to the king of his conduct and steadily worked for his removal from office. Partly because of Gondomar's intrigues and partly because of an official indiscretion, Naunton incurred James's anger in January, 1621, just as parliament was about to open. He was suspended though not dismissed from office, and placed in confinement until the following August. [14] He never took his seat in this parliament. The commons were inclined to interfere in his behalf as a matter of privilege; and we might have had the paradox of parliament defending a councillor from the wrath of the crown. But Naunton feared that any such move would only increase his misfortunes. When the house ordered immediate attendance of all members, Sir Samuel Sandys moved that Naunton be exempt from the order, since its application would anger the king and prove "hurtful" to the secretary. Naunton himself had prompted this motion and the house did not insist upon his attendance. [15] It is astonishing that James, to please a foreign ambassador, should thus have

[13] C. J., I, 477–80; Court and Times, James I, I, 309–10, 315; Portland MSS, H. M. C., IX, 132. Chamberlain to Carleton, March 17, 1614, St. P. Domestic, 14/76:49.

[14] Gondomar to Philip III, February 10, 1621, Spanish Trans., 12/21. Gardiner's Transcripts, Add. MSS 31111, no. 232. Cal. St. P. Venetian, 1619–1621, 402, 432, 552. Court and Times, James I, II, 219. F. M. G. Evans, The Principal Secretary of State (Manchester, 1923), 77–78.

[15] Commons Debates 1621, IV, 18. Naunton wrote to Buckingham (Goodman, II, 225–27), "I have entreated some of my friends to oppose that motion, if any should be made, for my calling thither, and am resolved they shall send me to what prison they will, yea, and pull me in pieces too, before I will be fetched out of my house with my own consent, till my sovereign dear master shall enlarge me, who hath confined me thither." See also Naunton to Buckingham, January 14, 1624, St. P. Domestic, 14/158:30.

sacrificed his secretary upon the eve of parliament; but the power of Gondomar at Whitehall wrought strange things.

In all probability another councillor also, Henry Cary, Viscount Falkland, never took his seat in this house of commons. In all the voluminous records for 1621 there is no trace of his presence in the house. His election had been questioned because subsequent to it he had been created a Scottish viscount. A newsletter describes him as "unwilling" to continue among the commons;[16] but whether he was offended, as may well have been the case, or whether he regarded a place in the house as incommensurate with his new dignity, is not made clear. Another councillor, Sir Edward Coke, joined the opposition. Sir Richard Weston was not a member of the commons until the autumn. Thus the strength of the council from January to June must be reduced to five. When parliament met again in November, both Cranfield and Greville had been raised to the peerage; and although Weston now became a member, the number of effective councillors was reduced to four.[17]

In 1624, as in 1621, the strength of the council in the house was less than its numbers might imply. Naunton in all probability never attended; Suckling's part was negligible; and both Conway and Calvert were irregular in their attendance. Conway followed the court, and both he and Calvert were ill during part of the session. Conway wrote Calvert on May 20, "His Majesty finds himself less informed at this Parliament than at others from his Privy Councillors of the House, from whom he challendgeth that duty." Calvert replied that "all things have gone so fairly and well" that there was nothing to report but *"omnia bene,"* which he supposed Conway himself had reported since he was "sometimes there, and saw the disposition of the House." Calvert continued, "And certainly it were much for the King's service, if it pleased you to be there oftener, which I remember I was the last Parliament, when his Majesty was at Newmarket, and I sole Secretary at that time.

[16] Mead to Stuteville, February 17, 1621, *Court and Times, James I,* II, 228.

[17] The government apparently felt its diminished strength in the commons. Calvert wrote Caesar, November 25, 1621: "I have received a letter from my Lord of Buckingham even very now, wherein I am required to tell you that it is his Majesties pleasure you fayle not to be at the lower howse to morrow morning being Munday, and so to contynue every day as long as the howse sitts notwithstanding your Term businesse, which may well give way to his Majesties service in the Parliament, rather then be any hinderance to your attendance there. . . . Where hoping to meete you, I will take my leave." Add. MSS 34324, f. 290.

But this is only a wish of mine own for your company and the good of his Majesty's service. Your own wisdom can best tell you what is fit for you to do and what your business will suffer you. Now Sir for that which concerns myself, I must intreat you to be pleased to excuse me to his Majesty, if I do not attend the House so dilligently as I ought, or as I desire, for that, having been of late let blood, I find myself so exceeding much weakened therewith, as I can scarce go up a pair of stairs, and the other day being in the Parliament House, I was overcome with the heat of the season and the Company, and forced to come away within half an hour after I was sat, for fear of souring. This makes me not yet dare to adventure thither again so soon, till I have recovered a little more strength which I hope I shall do within a few days." [18] Thus in 1624 the effective strength of the council was reduced from six to four, and of these four the two secretaries were frequently absent.

Again in 1625 the strength of councillors must be greatly reduced. Conway was now in the lords, and the other secretary, Sir Albertus Morton, was away at The Hague. As far as I know, he never took his seat in the commons,[19] which meant that neither secretary was present in the house. Caesar failed to obtain election, Suckling was quite colorless, and Naunton's part was small. Weston, May, and Edmondes were the only effective councillors in the commons during a most important parliament and they were somewhat disregarded as they did not fully concur with Buckingham's parliamentary policy. The government's most trusted agent in this parliament was Sir John Coke, as yet neither councillor nor secretary. The same situation prevailed in the parliament of 1626. Naunton and Suckling remained inarticulate; and Edmondes' election at Oxford was voided by the commons. This left but four councillors of importance: Coke, Carleton, May, and Weston. Carleton was in France when parliament opened in February, did not return to England until March, and is not mentioned as speaking in the commons until April. In May he became a baron, after a short and unsuccessful career in the commons. Coke had

---

[18] D. Carleton to Sir Dudley Carleton, April 4, 1624, St. P. Domestic, 14/162:13. Conway to Calvert and Weston, May 20, Calvert to Conway, May 21, 1624, *ibid.*, 14/165:4, 11.

[19] *Gardiner*, V, 370. Conway refers to "the absence of my Brother Secretary, casting the whole business upon my hands only." Conway to Carleton, July 7, 1625, St. P. Holland, 84/128.

a spell of illness in May and did not speak in the commons, as far as the records show, between April 21 and June 9, about a week before the dissolution.[20] Thus Carleton and Coke were absent for considerable periods, leaving to Weston and May the hopeless task of defending Buckingham in a house bent on his impeachment. Even in 1628, when there were only three councillors in the commons, Coke was sent to Portsmouth on naval business in May and remained away for the rest of the session.[21]

Finally it may be noted that the small group of councillors in the commons at the opening of the Long Parliament was annihilated within a period of six months. Secretary Windebank was ordered, December 3, 1640, to appear before the commons to face charges of undue leniency toward Catholics.[22] That night he fled the country and, except for a short visit to England in 1642, remained in Paris until his death. The other secretary, Sir Henry Vane, defended the interests of the crown in the first months of the parliament. But his implication in the charges against Strafford rendered his position at court impossible. The king was convinced of his treachery; there were many complaints of his conduct;[23] and on November 4, 1641, he was dismissed from all his offices at court. At once he joined the opposition and became a member of the committee of both kingdoms, though the royalists maintained he had lost the confidence of both camps. Sir Thomas Roe was the most impressive councillor in the house during these months, but he did not attend with any regularity. In February, 1641, D'Ewes wrote that Roe "had been absent from the Howse about eight weekes," apparently owing to illness. In April he was named by the king as envoy to the Diet of Ratisbon, though ill-health and the king's lack of funds delayed his departure until the following month. He did not return until the outbreak of the civil war.[24] A fourth councillor, Sir Thomas Jermyn, also ceased

[20] On April 29, 1626, Sir William Beecher told the house that Suckling was ill. *C. J.*, I, 852; Whitelocke, f. 168v. April 18, 1626, *C. J.*, I, 845; Whitelocke, f. 137. Conway to Sir John Coke, May 30, 1626, *Cowper MSS, H. M. C.*, I, 269; Whitelocke, f. 148v, 227v.

[21] He last spoke in the house on May 17 and left London two days later. Mass., f. 172; *Cowper MSS, H. M. C.*, I, 343, 350.

[22] D'Ewes (*Long Parl.*), 89–91, 101, 103. "Total ruin is predicted for Windebank." *Cal. St. P. Venetian, 1640–1642*, 98. "It was not in the wit of man to save Windebank." *Cal. Clarendon State Papers* (4 vols., Oxford, 1869–1932), I, 212.

[23] *Cal. St. P. Domestic, 1641–1643*, 149–50, 200–01. *Cal. St. P. Venetian, 1640–1642*, 191–92, 198.

[24] D'Ewes reported his speeches with praise, and in Holland in 1641 Roe "left an impression of great ability." *D'Ewes (Long Parl.)*, 51, 87, 330; *Cal. St. P. Venetian, 1640–1642*,

to attend the commons in May. This was due to his son's participation in the first army plot. On June 11 a member, referring to
Jermyn's absence, moved "that there ys an honourable gentleman
that hathe nott bene heere a great whyle. He desyres a writt may
go forthe if he will not come." It was answered that Jermyn "ys
so troubled for hys son that he ys unwilling to come to the
house." [25] Shortly thereafter Jermyn sold his place as comptroller
to Sir Peter Wyche, who was not a member of the commons.[26]
After May, 1641, the crown had not a single councillor in the
house whom it could trust.[27]

Thus while the crown saw the wisdom of placing councillors
in the commons, it allowed other things to interfere with that
policy. Councillors were made lords, or were dismissed from office, or were alienated in some other way. They were frequently
away from London on royal business; and although this could not
be altogether avoided, it might have been reduced by careful planning. The commons, moreover, upon occasion took matters into
their own hands. Parry was expelled from the house; the elections
of councillors were frequently questioned and on three occasions
declared void. Thus many things combined to reduce the fighting
strength of the councillors in the house.

Difficulties such as these were far more serious than those en-
countered in securing seats in the commons for privy councillors.
Councillors, indeed, had to be satisfied with representing small
close boroughs where the crown could influence elections. Under
the Tudors councillors were welcomed as representatives by the
counties and larger boroughs. But as opposition mounted against
the crown in the Stuart period, they were gradually driven from
constituencies where popular opinion could express itself. They

---

135, 139, 144, 158, 162. Roe was himself a disappointed candidate for the secretaryship.
It is a pity he was not secretary during the Long Parliament. See *Cal. St. P. Domestic,
1641–1643*, 294.

[25] Gawdy Notes of the Long Parliament, June 11, 1641, Add. MSS 14828, f. 71.

[26] *Cal. St. P. Domestic, 1641–1643,* 73, 77.

[27] In January, 1642, when affairs were at the breaking point between king and parliament, Charles admitted to the council two men who had become leaders of the royal party
in the commons. Lucius Cary, Viscount Falkland, became secretary, and Sir John Culpepper
chancellor of the exchequer. Hyde was offered the solicitorship but declined it because he
thought he could do better service as a private member. Charles promised that he would
consult these men on all business concerning the commons; but almost at once he carried
out the attempted arrest of the five members without their knowledge, which left them "so
much displeased and dejected" that only "duty and conscience" prevented them from leaving Charles's service. *Clarendon,* IV, 126, 158.

were not, for the most part, men of great wealth or family connection and could not rely upon their own prestige or influence in any particular locality. Hence they were forced to seek election in boroughs where the influence of the crown could sway the issue or where their official position gave them a preponderating influence. The number of such boroughs, however, was fairly large; and as far as I know, there are only three instances in the early Stuart period in which a councillor who sought election was unable to obtain a place. Yet even in small boroughs things might go wrong and councillors might be defeated. They met with difficulties, although those difficulties were not insuperable.

That councillors were pushed from large open constituencies is well illustrated by the elections in the counties. Councillors had no great difficulty in obtaining election from counties during the first two parliaments of James. Sir John Herbert represented Monmouth in 1604, and although Fortescue was defeated in the famous election in Buckinghamshire, he secured a seat from Middlesex in the second session of the parliament. In 1614 Middlesex returned two councillors, Caesar and Lake, the government having taken the precaution of ordering another candidate to retire from the contest. "Upon Thursday last," wrote Chamberlain, "was a great concourse at Uxbridge for the choosing of Sir Julius Caesar and Sir Thomas Lake Knights for Middlesex. Sir Walter Cope stood not; but Sir Francis Darcie had a man there who getting up upon a table told the assembly that his Master meant to have stoode, but was forbidden by the King, wherefore he desired all his well willers to geve theyre voyces to Mr. Chancellor [Caesar], and for the second place to do as God should put in theyre mindes. For this saucie part he is committed and his master called in question." Sir Thomas Parry was returned by Berkshire, where, Chamberlain implies, he experienced no great difficulty. Thus three of the four councillors in the parliament of 1614 represented counties. Two points, however, must be made. Lake's appointment to the council, which immediately preceded the opening of parliament, was subsequent to his election, and this was also the case with Winwood, who represented Buckingham borough, a small corporation that the council had been able to control in James's first parliament. The councillors were rather fortunate; for this election, the first in which the country had an opportunity of passing judgment upon James's government, went heavily against the crown and "letters and countenance, even in meaner boroughs, proved not so powerful as was ymagined." [28]

In 1621 we find a different story. Of nine councillors in the house only three — Greville, Falkland, and Calvert — represented counties. Sir Fulke Greville was one of the very few councillors in the commons who possessed sufficient local influence to carry elections. The Greville interest in Warwickshire returned Sir Fulke from the county in 1621 and also John Coke, formerly in Greville's service, from Warwick borough. Sir Edward Conway, who was Greville's first cousin, secured his son's return from Warwick borough in 1624, and was urged by Greville, now Lord Brooke, to stand for the county in 1626.[29] The return of Henry Cary, Viscount Falkland, as knight from Hertford was perhaps due partly to similar influences. But we know that he sought the aid of the local nobility, especially the earl of Salisbury, whom he regarded as his chief support and who made a public "declaration of affection" in his behalf. "I thank you for your favor and counsel," he wrote Salisbury, "I have written to my Lord of Hunsdon and others; from some I have received kind answers, from others none at all." [30]

Calvert's election from Yorkshire, on the other hand, emphasized the weakness rather than the strength of councillors. For Calvert obtained a seat only through the influence and energy of his popular running mate, Sir Thomas Wentworth. Wentworth, having been persuaded, as he wrote, by Calvert and other friends to stand with Calvert as knight of the shire, began a vigorous campaign for their joint election by writing his friends and by the dubious expedient of obtaining written promises of support from many freeholders. He was soon satisfied that his own election was secure, but that the county was "not so well affected" to Calvert because he was "his Majesty's Secretary" and "the king's servant." Wentworth hoped to secure first place at the election for Calvert

[28] Chamberlain to Carleton, March 17, 1614, St. P. Domestic, 14/76:49. "I have heard, that when Sir Francis Darcy opposed Sir Thomas Lake in a Matter of like Nature, the Lords of the Council writ to Sir Francis to desist." Sir Thomas Wentworth to Calvert, December 5, 1620, *Strafford's Letters,* I, 10.

[29] Conway to William Chesterman, January 31, 1624, St. P. Domestic, 14/158:71. Brooke to Conway, January 2, 1626, *Cal. St. P. Domestic, Addenda, 1625–1649,* 94–95. Brooke's suggestion in 1626 rather strangely ignored the fact that Conway had recently become a peer.

[30] Cary to the earl of Salisbury, December 7, 11, 1620, Hatfield House MSS.

and obtain the second for himself, but as the day for election approached, he wrote Ingram, "In good faith, I think it very improbable we shall ever get the first place for Mr. Secretary, nay I protest we shall have need of our Strength to obtain him a second Election: So as the likeliest way so far as I am able to judge, to secure both, will be for me to stand for the Prime, and so cast all my second Voices upon him, which notwithstanding we may help by putting him first in the Indenture." Once he had obtained first place, Wentworth thought, the vote for second place "might be so suddenly carried" that the opposition "should have no time to move." He also suggested certain steps to Calvert. Calvert should write Lord Scrope, president of the council in the north, to "shew himself . . . in the Castle-Yard" on Calvert's side during the election. Calvert should also secure a letter from lord chancellor Bacon commanding Sir John Savile, the opposition candidate, to abandon the contest, as the council had commanded Sir Francis Darcy in the Middlesex election of 1614. "Such a letter," Wentworth thought, "would make an end of all." Yorkshire returned both Wentworth and Calvert, and Calvert's name stands first in the return.[31]

Moreover, two councillors were defeated in Middlesex. "Sir Thomas Edmondes and Sir Julius Caesar," wrote Locke, "made all the means they could to have bin knights of the shire for Middlesex, but the Freeholders would have none of them. Their reason was, by cause they could not have accesse to such great persons as privie Counsellors and therefore they chose Sir Francis Darcie and Sir Garret [Sir Gilbert Gerrard] their neighbours, though Sir Francis Darcie did openlie att the election desier all his Tenants and friends to give their voices to Sir Thomas Edmondes."[32] This was a defeat, under the very eyes of the court, in a constituency

---

[31] Wentworth to Sir Thomas Fairfax, Sir George Calvert, Sir Arthur Ingram, Sir Henry Slingsby, Thomas Wentworth; Samuel Casson to Wentworth, December 3 to December 12, 1620, *Strafford's Letters*, I, 10–13.

[32] Locke to Carleton, December 16, 1620, St. P. Domestic, 14/118:30. Sir Charles Montagu wrote to Sir Edward Montagu, who was a member of the commons, "You shall meet there it seems with many of your old acquaintance, for the countries care not for courtiers, nor councillors, for the[y] choose freely, and here in Middlesex they have given two privy councillors the canvise [*sic*], but I think very unwisely and not fairly carried." December 13, 1620, *Buccleuch MSS, Montagu Papers*, H. M. C., I, 256. The Venetian ambassador wrote that although James tried to influence elections "and succeeded in some towns and counties, he could not manage it as a general rule, the relations of the favorite and even his own councillors being rejected." September 21, 1622, *Cal. St. P. Venetian, 1621–1623*, 438.

where councillors had been returned in both of James's earlier parliaments. Both Caesar and Edmondes obtained seats elsewhere, Caesar from Maldon,[33] and Edmondes from Bewdley and Dorchester, choosing to serve for the first.

Middlesex returned the one councillor elected from a county in 1624. This was Sir John Suckling, certainly a person of small significance in the commons, who won by a very narrow margin and suffered the added embarrassment of having his election questioned by the house. Three candidates appeared at the election, Suckling, Sir John Apsley, who was "countannanced by the Duke of Buckingham," and Sir John Franklin. But a fourth candidate, Sir Gilbert Gerrard, though not present, "carried away the first place clere from them all." Sir John Apsley was second, but many of his followers were "from the stable" and "minutemen" brought by the lieutenant of the Tower, Sir Allen Apsley; and these would not be admitted as freeholders, "so that he came short of Sir John Suckling ten or twelve voyces." Thus Suckling won by a very close count and by squeezing out another candidate from the court. When the electors were asked whether Suckling or Gerrard should have first place in the indenture, "the whole cry went for Gerrard." Moreover, the election was questioned by the house. A group of Middlesex freeholders petitioned the commons that Gerrard and Franklin had been rightfully elected but that Suckling had been "unduly returned" in Franklin's place. When the committee for returns came to examine the case, however, it was surprised to learn that the petitioners wished to withdraw their petition. At first the committee, fearing "some underhand combination," considered an inquiry on the grounds that the house could investigate any election it chose; but no corruption appearing, the committee considered Suckling's election good and the house approved.[34] Suckling was also returned from Litchfield city and Kingston-upon-Hull.

[33] Where a court candidate had been placed in 1605. Bailiffs of Maldon to the privy council, October 16, the same to the earls of Northampton and Salisbury, October 26, 1605, Hatfield House MSS. Caesar's fellow member was Sir Henry Mildmay, who was appointed high steward of the borough on the very day on which the return is dated, December 20, 1620.

Since this book went to the printer, a new volume of Hatfield House MSS, covering the year 1605, has been published. The letters I cite from this collection may be identified by their dates.

[34] Chamberlain to Carleton, January 31, 1624, St. P. Domestic, 14/158:72. J. Topham (ed.), J. Glanville, *Reports of Cases Determined by . . . Parliament* (London, 1775), 117–19.

He lost the seat for Middlesex, however, in the parliament of 1625. "Sir John Franklin and Sir Gilbert Gerrard carried it away in Middlesex from Mr. Controller," wrote Chamberlain, "though he were present, which was thought not so wise a part for a privie counsaillor to take the foil in person."[35] A place was found for him at Yarmouth, Isle of Wight, where Conway, recently appointed captain, had some influence in elections. The election at Yarmouth had already taken place; but one of its members, also returned at Hythe, elected to serve for that borough and left a vacancy at Yarmouth.

The one councillor serving for a county in 1625 was Sir Albertus Morton, who was returned by Kent and also by Cambridge University. He was supported in Kent by letters from the earls of Westmorland and Dorset, and Buckingham wrote the mayor of Rochester in his behalf. Morton did not spare expense and won in Kent "three to one," electing to serve for the county rather than for the university; though Chamberlain wrote, "If I had ben as Secretarie Morton I should have estemed as much the choise of the Universitie of Cambridge (where he was elected) as this higher title in shew with the expense of two or three hundred pounds they say at least."[36] Thus in this parliament one councillor was elected from a county but only by a considerable outlay of money and by the support of unusually influential persons; while another was defeated and only squeezed into the house through a by-election in a small borough.

Of seven councillors elected to the parliament of 1626 only one, Sir Robert Naunton, represented a county. Naunton was returned from Suffolk.

In the parliament of 1628 no councillor represented a county. Sir Thomas Edmondes sought election in Essex and Sir John Savile in Yorkshire, but both were defeated. In Essex the government resorted to trickery. An attempt was made to hold the

[35] Chamberlain to Carleton, May 6, 1625, St. P. Domestic, 16/2:27. Printed in rather garbled form in *Court and Times, Charles I*, I, 18–19.

[36] Earl of Westmorland to Sir Edward Deering, April 13, 1625, earl of Dorset to the same, 1625, Stowe MSS 743, f. 60, 64. Earl of Montgomery to the mayor of Rochester, April 20, 1625, *Gentleman's Magazine*, 1798, 1:116–17. A letter from Hippesley to Buckingham in 1626 shows one means by which the duke could influence the county election in Kent. Hippesley wrote, "If you please this night to send to all those of the Navie to be there for Sir Sandes to morrowe I doe thinke he will carrie it, other wise I thinke you must bringe him in [for] the Portes." St. P. Domestic, 16/18:28. Chamberlain to Carleton, May 6, 1625, *ibid.*, 16/2:27.

county election unexpectedly before the main body of electors were aware of what was going on. "Sir Thomas Fanshaw and Sir Thomas Edmonds had privately procurred the writ for Essex, and the Sheriff to come to Stratford," wrote John Cayworth to Lord Montagu, "but the country, having intelligence from London, came in so fast that they durst not trust them and so were dismissed without doing anything." Another type of interference was also attempted. At the direction of the privy council, the justices of the peace in Essex instructed the high constables to ask freeholders to support such candidates as the majority of the justices at the election should recommend, that is to say, "to give their voices on that side which most of the Justices of the Peace doe." [37] The net result of these expedients was to make the election so tumultuous that it was almost a riot and to give the popular candidates an overwhelming victory. Mead wrote of "our famous election in Essex, where Sir Francis Barrington had all the voices of 15,000 men, those who say least, and were there, 10,000 freeholders, with more passages than I have time to tell you." The government had provoked a striking display of resistance which became an example for other sections of the country.[38]

Thus the councillors were driven from the counties and were forced to seek election in cities and boroughs where influence of some kind could be applied. It is not easy to classify these elections, for influence was a capricious factor that often rose and fell in a given community; and there was a tendency as the period pro-

[37] John Cayworth to Lord Montagu, February 7, 1628, *Buccleuch MSS, Montagu Papers, H. M. C.,* III, 324. See also Beaulieu to Puckering, February 20, 1628, *Court and Times, Charles I,* I, 323. Justices of Essex to the high constables, February, 1628, St. P. Domestic, 16/94:87; Edward Nuttall to Edward Nicholas, March 4, 1628, *ibid.,* 16/95:35. See also Mead to Stuteville, March 22, 1628, *Court and Times, Charles I,* I, 333.

[38] Mead to Stuteville, March 15, 1628, *Court and Times, Charles I,* I, 329. "What lord in England would be followed by so many freeholders as some of those [members] are?" *Ibid.,* I, 331. The Venetian ambassador wrote that "after the riot in Essex, the meeting [of parliament] was postponed until the 29th of April" and that many counties were "following the example of Essex." *Cal. St. P. Venetian, 1626–1628,* 605. Trickery in the Essex election was not confined to the government. A number of wealthy men sold small parcels of land just before the election, thus creating new forty-shilling freeholders, on the understanding that the land would be resold to its former owners immediately after the election. The new electors voted against the government. Edward Nuttall to Nicholas, March 4, 1628, St. P. Domestic, 16/95:35.

No councillor represented a county in the Short Parliament or in the first year of the Long Parliament. Sir John Culpepper, who sat for Kent, was made a councillor in January, 1642. During the elections to the Short Parliament Windebank suggested to Sir Richard Harrison that they stand as knights for Berkshire but received a most discouraging reply. *Cal. St. P. Domestic, 1639–1640,* 153.

gressed for electors even in subservient boroughs to rebel against the influence of the court. A number of constituencies may be pointed out, however, where councillors sought election with more or less constant success.

The universities of Oxford and Cambridge, having obtained the right to return members at the beginning of James's reign, sent many councillors to parliament during these years. Oxford returned Sir George Calvert in 1624, Sir Thomas Edmondes in 1625 and again in 1626, Sir Francis Windebank to the Short Parliament, and Sir Thomas Roe to the Long Parliament. Cambridge returned Sir Robert Naunton in 1621, 1624, and 1625, and Sir John Coke in 1626 and 1628. It is perfectly clear that these elections were the result of letters from influential persons. There were many junior electors in the universities, and at Oxford in 1626 we find them for a moment in revolt. But normally the heads of houses and older doctors determined the elections, and were influenced very largely by letters from the king, from their chancellor, who was ordinarily a great official at court, and from other important personages. Naunton owed his election at Cambridge in 1621 to Buckingham's influence and his election in 1624 to a letter from lord keeper Williams, written at the direction of the king. Buckingham became chancellor of Cambridge in 1626; and at the next election, that of 1628 when Sir John Coke was chosen, Robert Mason at Cambridge wrote Buckingham's secretary, Edward Nicholas, that "the University most earnestly desired his Grace would declare himself for the election of our Burgesses." Windebank's son wrote of the election at Oxford for the Short Parliament, "This afternoon the whole university are assembled to elect our burgesses. I intend on Wednesday to acquaint my father with the proceedings. I hear already that the vice-chancellor has given order to the masters of arts to name my father burgess in the first place before Sir John Danvers." And although Windebank lost his seat at Oxford in the elections to the Long Parliament, it was not because of his unpopularity, or even because a group at Oxford opposed his election, but because he was not supported by the usual letters from important people. His nephew, Dr. Thomas Read, wrote that "most of our Doctors and the principal men of the University were well inclined towards him, but I am informed that some higher power was directly or indirectly interested in the election" of another candidate.[39]

A revolt against these practices occurred in 1626. Sir Thomas Edmondes was returned from Oxford; but a group of the junior bachelors and masters who had taken part in the election petitioned the house against its validity. Whitelocke supplies a long account of the hearing before the committee of privileges and returns. At the university convocation called to elect members the vice-chancellor "read publiquely the letters of great men both to the convocation house and to himself directed, and seeing some contradiction when he named Sir Thomas Edmondes, the vice-chancellor said *facilius est invitare magnatus quam reconciliare.*" But many of the junior electors cried *non placet* and demanded a scrutiny of voices. This the vice-chancellor did not allow but asked them to name some other candidate, which, he claimed, they did not do; and he therefore pronounced the election concluded in favor of Edmondes. The petitioners claimed firstly that they had named another candidate, Sir Francis Stewart, and one witness said that "three parts of five were for Sir Francis"; and secondly that they had wished to go to a fresh election "but the Vice-Chancellor said *literae eligunt et eligent.*" It was thus a contest between the junior bachelors and masters on one hand and the vice-chancellor and senior electors and doctors on the other; and Edmondes' election had obviously been railroaded through against the wish of the majority. The commons voided the election, a new writ was issued, and Sir Francis Stewart returned.[40] Edmondes did not obtain another seat in this parliament.

The crown's influence at the universities cannot, of course, be explained by the fact that they had recently acquired the right to return members. Yet newly enfranchised boroughs might easily come under the domination of the crown or of individual councillors. Hertford, for example, which regained its medieval right in 1624, was approached by the council of the duchy of Lancaster and by the council of Prince Charles even before its new privi-

[39] *Goodman*, II, 226; St. P. Domestic, 14/158:30. Robert Mason to Nicholas, March 3, 7, 1628, *ibid.*, 16/95:23, 47. John Windebank to Robert Read, March 9, 1640, *Cal. St. P. Domestic, 1639–1640*, 531; Dr. Thomas Read to Robert Read, October 26, 1640, *Cal. St. P. Domestic, 1640–1641*, 197.
[40] March 16, 1626, Whitelocke, f. 23–20v. See also J. Gutch (ed.), Anthony à Wood, *The History and Antiquities of the University of Oxford* (3 vols., Oxford, 1792–96), I, 356; *C. J.*, I, 837; *Court and Times, Charles I*, I, 84–85.

lege became operative.[41] Another borough, Evesham, which had regained its medieval right, returned Sir Edward Conway in the parliaments of 1621 and 1624. James's charter provided that all burgesses of Evesham should take part in the elections, but the right was at once monopolized by the mayor, aldermen, and incorporated burgesses, who wrote Conway in 1621 promising to return him from the town. Conway also secured the return from Evesham of his son-in-law, Sir Robert Harley, in 1628, though not without some difficulty and only by interviewing some of the important men of the borough who were fortunately in London just before the election.[42] Sir Thomas Jermyn, a councillor who sat in the Short and Long Parliaments, was elected by Bury St. Edmunds as soon as that borough was enfranchised in 1621, and he retained his seat during the entire period from 1621 through the Long Parliament.

Councillors also found seats in boroughs where the duchy of Lancaster had some influence, in Cornwall, in the Cinque Ports, and in the Isle of Wight. The chancellor of the duchy of Lancaster had the traditional privilege of naming one member in boroughs which formed part of the property of the duchy, though that privilege was frequently challenged by the electors. Leicester and Stockbridge were duchy towns. Yet Sir John Fortescue failed to obtain the return of his son-in-law, Sir John Poultney, from Leicester in 1604;[43] and Parry had to resort to violent methods to coerce the electors of Stockbridge in 1614. Nevertheless, Sir Humphrey May, chancellor of the duchy, certainly a man of whom any constituency might be proud, was returned by Lancaster borough in 1621, 1624, 1625, and 1626 and by Leicester borough in 1624, 1625, 1626, and 1628,[44] an excellent example of a councillor's using his official position to secure continuous membership in the commons.

[41] Corporation of Hertford MSS, H. M. C., Fourteenth Report, Part 8, 162.

[42] G. May, Descriptive History of the Town of Evesham (Evesham, 1845), 279–82. Fulke Reed to Conway, February 14, 1628, St. P. Domestic, 16/93:32.

[43] The earl of Huntingdon had also supported Sir John Poultney. In 1610 the earl asked the town to return Henry Rich, to which it acceded. Both the earl and Parry offered candidates to the town in 1614, and two courtiers were returned. The earls appeared to act in harmony with the duchy officers, but occasionally the town turned against them both. Corporation of Leicester MSS, H. M. C., Eighth Report, Part 1, 434–35. James Thompson, The History of Leicester (Leicester, 1849), 326–27, 342, 344. See also Miss Winifred Taffs, "Borough Franchise in the 17th Century," M. A. thesis, University of London.

[44] May's relations with the town of Leicester appeared to be especially cordial. Before his election in 1624, he wrote that he wished his constituents to approach him freely on all

Cornwall returned far more courtiers during the period than any other county. Dues levied on the ore from mines and the tenure by which much property was held gave the duchy of Cornwall great influence in many boroughs. And the crown was fortunate in possessing the loyalty of influential families and other interests. In James's first parliament Calvert, Naunton, Lake, Conway, and Carleton, all future councillors, sat for Cornish constituencies, along with numerous other courtiers. Sir Richard Weston sat for Bossiney in 1624, Callington in 1625, and Bodmin in 1626. In 1614 he had been knight of the shire for Essex, but ten years later he could not hope to represent such a popular constituency. In 1621 Liskeard returned Sir Edward Coke, then a councillor, "by the king's commandment." [45] Sir Francis Cottington sat for Camelford in 1624, Bossiney in 1625, and Saltash in 1628; and Edmondes for Penryn in 1628. Yet boroughs which normally responded to court influence might now rebel. St. Germans, enfranchised by Elizabeth, had long permitted the bishop of Exeter to nominate one of its members; and Sir John Coke had held the seat in 1624 and 1625 through the interest of his brother-in-law, then bishop. But Coke was defeated in 1626 because Sir John Eliot, whose country seat was at St. Germans, had turned against the government and used his influence in favor of other candidates. On January 13 the bishop wrote Coke that he had sent a letter to St. Germans and afterward "a direct messenger . . . requesting the like favour of that Corporation as his predecessors and himself had formerly had." He asked for a blank indenture, but the portreeve of St. Germans replied that a blank could not be procured, although he thought that Coke would be returned. He could promise nothing, however, "it being a business resting in the wills of others . . . and chiefly in Sir John Elliot." The bishop, writing on January 22, still "rested very well assured he [Eliot] could not divert them from due respect to me." [46] But St. Germans returned Eliot and Sir Henry Marten, and Coke was forced to look elsewhere.

matters of business, and the corporation noted his "love and respect" for them. When May was elected both at Leicester and Lancaster in 1625, he asked Leicester to elect Thomas Jermyn in his place; the town replied that they would trust his judgment in the matter, though they would not do the like for any other person. Thompson, *Leicester,* 349–51.

[45] Holkham MSS 727, quoted in article on Coke in *D. N. B.*

[46] Valentine Carey, bishop of Exeter, to Sir John Coke, January 26, 1624, January 13, 22, 1626, *Cowper MSS, H. M. C.,* I, 157, 249, 251.

Coke was returned from Cambridge University; but he had another opportunity from Cornwall. Sir George Chudleigh, of Ashton, Devon, wrote Coke that he had heard his election at St. Germans was uncertain and that "Cambridge was in some competition," and therefore offered him a seat at East Looe. Chudleigh had received a blank indenture from that corporation and had planned to insert his own name or the name of his son, but he offered "to hold it still a blank till I be certain from your honour or some other way that you have elsewhere a place in parliament." [47]

It is rather surprising that no privy councillor was returned from the Cinque Ports during the reign of James and only three during the reign of Charles, one of whom, upon a double return, elected to serve elsewhere. The lord warden [48] normally could nominate one member from each town and occasionally influenced the choice of both members. Certainly many courtiers were returned from the Cinque Ports. But the Ports were not unaffected by the growing dissatisfaction with the government. Nor was Lord Zouch an ardent supporter of the Buckingham regime. He was opposed to the Spanish match and would hardly have used his influence in obtaining seats for councillors of the Spanish faction. In 1621 he promised places to various individuals without consulting the king, and when James sent him a list of men whom he wished returned, Zouch replied that he was already engaged. To this Buckingham answered, "I have acquainted his Majesty with your letter, who would have been glad that any of those men he recommended might have been placed, but seeing your Lordship was otherwise engaged before, he reserveth all to yourself, not doubting that you will be careful to nominate such as will be serviceable to his Majesty and his Kingdom." [49]

Buckingham became lord warden in 1624. But although the Cinque Ports returned a number of courtiers in the following parliament, there were no councillors in the list. In 1626, however, Buckingham attempted to secure seats at the Ports for several councillors. One of them, Sir Dudley Carleton, was in France

[47] Sir George Chudleigh to Sir John Coke, February 1, 23, 1626, *ibid.*, I, 252–53, 257.
[48] Northampton was lord warden from 1604 to 1614, Lord Zouch from 1615 to 1624, and Buckingham from 1624 to 1628.
[49] Buckingham to Zouch, December 14, 1620, St. P. Domestic, 14/118:27. A list of men to whom Zouch had promised places is in *ibid.*, 14/118:26.

during the election; but Sir John Hippesley, lieutenant of Dover Castle, wrote Buckingham, "Sir Dudley Carleton doth expect a place from you as he tolde me at his goine over. I could wish that you would not put him upon Dover, the reason I shall tell you at your cominge." Carleton was returned at Hastings; as a matter of fact Buckingham's letters arrived at Dover so late that his candidate there was defeated.[50] He also planned to place Sir Richard Weston at Hythe, but again the town, acting with considerable haste, held its election before Buckingham's letters arrived. The members of the corporation at Hythe excused themselves by saying that they had received the writ on January 7, had proceeded at once to an election as the writ directed, and afterward on January 11 had received the duke's letters (dated the tenth) recommending Weston, "an honourable and worthy person whome we in due respect to your grace would willingly have accepted of." They were obviously somewhat taken aback at having refused so important a person as Weston, and Hippesley wrote that they were "sorofull men" for what they had done. But they had allowed little time for the warden to send them his wishes.[51] A third councillor, Sir John Suckling, was returned at Sandwich, but was also elected at Norwich and chose to represent that city. In 1628 the Cinque Ports, apparently having repented of their former independence, returned royalists; but there was no councillor in the list.

Councillors occasionally represented boroughs on the Isle of Wight. Sir John Stanhope was returned by Newtown in 1604 and Suckling by Yarmouth in 1625 after his defeat in Middlesex. But Suckling failed at Newport in 1626. William Weld, Conway's secretary, wrote that "my Lord [now captain in the Isle of Wight] hath written to the three corporations of the Isle of Wight and hath recommended Sir John Suckling to Newport, Sir Edward Conway to Yarmouth, and Mr. Mallett to Newtown. My Lord makes no question of their accepting his recommendations for one in each town." Yarmouth and Newtown did as they were asked, but Newport made its election before Conway's letter arrived. "I am sorry," wrote Philip Flemyng, a deputy lieutenant, "that my neighbours of Newport have so little respect to my Lord

[50] Hippesley to Buckingham, January 8, 12, 14, 1626, St. P. Domestic, 16/18:28, 37, 58.
[51] Hippesley to Buckingham, January 14, corporation of Hythe to Buckingham, January 13, 1626, St. P. Domestic, 16/18:60. The same thing happened at Romney. *Ibid.*, 16/18:97.

as to proceed so hastily to an election for the next Parliament without expecting a particular nomination."[52] In 1628 Conway's recommendations to the boroughs in the Isle of Wight were entirely ignored.

Most of the councillors in the commons were elected from the constituencies we have been mentioning; the elections which remain are too scattered to classify. In a number of them, however, the influence of the government may be seen or suspected, and for the most part they confirm the opinion that councillors were driven to cover in boroughs that could easily be controlled.[53]

The government turned occasionally to the earls of Pembroke for aid in placing councillors. The earls had many seats at their disposal, and there is evidence that Buckingham's adherents advised him to come to terms with Pembroke and secure his help in elections.[54] When in 1625 Carleton asked Nethersole to find a seat for him, Nethersole, having consulted Conway, replied, "My Lord Conway, though he be desirous to pleasure you with a Burgessship, yet gave me small hope of one by his means when I spoke with him; but put me off to my Lord Chamberlayne [Pembroke] . . . [whose] answere is that he hath two Privy Counsellors newly put upon him, els he could have setled you at first hand, as he hopeth he shall do yet at the second upon some double returne."[55] Who these councillors were it is impossible to say. As chancellor of Oxford, Pembroke may have aided Edmondes' election there, and his power in Cornwall may have influenced the election of Weston from Callington. This is the merest guesswork. But Vane certainly owed his seat at Wilton in the Short and Long Parliaments to the aid of the fourth earl. Vane wrote Windebank, September 27, 1640, that it was the king's "pleasure you speak with the Lord Chamberlain [Pembroke] concerning" the elections, "his Majesty expecting some help from him."[56]

In conclusion, two points may be emphasized. Although coun-

[52] William Weld to Philip Flemyng, January 16, Philip Flemyng to William Weld (two letters), January, 1626, *Cal. St. P. Domestic, Addenda, 1625–1649*, 96–97, 100–01.
[53] Caesar was returned for Westminster in 1610, Winwood for Buckingham borough in 1614, Caesar for Maldon and both Cranfield and Weston for Arundel in 1621, Edmondes for Chichester, where Arundel was high steward, in 1624, Windebank for Corfe Castle at the time of the Long Parliament.
[54] Hippesley to Buckingham, February 2, 1628, St. P. Domestic, 16/92:12.
[55] Nethersole to Carleton, April 24, 1625, St. P. Domestic, 16/1:83.
[56] Sir Henry Vane to Sir Francis Windebank, September 27, 1640, *Cal. St. P. Domestic, 1640–1641*, 104–05.

cillors were, on the whole, successful in entering the commons, they nevertheless met with frequent defeats. Fortescue was defeated in 1604, Edmondes and Caesar in 1621, Caesar [57] and Suckling in 1625, Sir John Coke and Suckling in 1626, Edmondes and Savile in 1628. Secondly, a new determination appeared among the commons to investigate irregularities in elections, a determination applied with remorseless impartiality to councillors and non-councillors alike. It is seen with surprising clearness and vigor in the case of Goodwin vs. Fortescue, which began a new era in the commons' control over election returns. It continued with increased daring in 1614 when the commons expelled Parry for corrupt electioneering practices. The importance of Parry's expulsion can hardly be exaggerated. In 1621 the elections of both Calvert and Falkland were questioned; in 1624 that of Suckling. In 1626 the commons voided Edmondes' election at Oxford and in 1640 Roe's election from Windsor.[58] This new scrutiny of election returns narrowed the chances of councillors to become members.

Finally, something must be said of the personalities and abilities of these men. The councillors in James's first parliament were an extremely mediocre group, and especially was this true of Sir John Herbert, the second secretary. He contrasted so sharply with Salisbury that he was nicknamed Mr. "Secondarie" Herbert; and this phrase and others, such as "old Secretary Herbert," indicate a certain contempt on the part of his contemporaries. When Salisbury's death in 1612 left vacant the office of principal secretary, no one dreamed of promoting Herbert, except, indeed, himself. Had he been a more forceful personality, he might have played an important part in combination with Salisbury, the principal secretary being in the lords and the second secretary in the commons. But he was unable to do so, and Salisbury, assuming the task of managing both houses from the lords, employed other agents in the commons. Nor was Herbert of more consequence in the circle

[57] Bailiffs of Maldon to Sir Julius Caesar, April 13, 1625, Add. MSS 12496, f. 106. The bailiffs wrote that they had received Caesar's letter asking to be elected and had imparted its contents first to the aldermen and common council and later at the election to the assembled burgesses. "But those of the Commonality which are free Burgesses meeting and being many in number, the greater part of the assembly (without us) prevailing gave their voices" for other candidates.

[58] The Windsor election was questioned by the house because it was thought that sufficient notice had not been given to the electors, a view supported by Roe himself. The election was voided and a new writ issued. December 8, 1640, D'Ewes (Long Parl.), 120–21. Roe had also been returned by Oxford University.

of the court. It might be supposed that in the period following Salisbury's death, when there was no principal secretary, Herbert would have been of some importance. Yet he is scarcely mentioned in the records of these years. The informal bedchamber methods by which the functions of secretary were performed left him with little or no employment. He was still at court in 1614, though he was not a member of parliament in that year. But Chamberlain wrote in April that Winwood, after a struggle, had obtained Herbert's lodgings, which doubtless indicated his complete eclipse as an official of any consequence.[59]

Sir John Stanhope had had considerable experience both in parliament and as a minor officeholder, but his part in the commons in 1604 was negligible. Fortescue was now an old man (he died in December, 1607) and was apparently failing during the last years of his life. "Sir Jhon Fortescue is at this present only said to be deade," wrote Northampton in January, 1608, "for he was deade befor to the State, though as longe as a man can walke in this place he dreames of immortality."[60] Parry may be placed in the same category. In 1612 Chamberlain wrote of Parry as "the old chancellor of the duchy," and in speaking of his disgrace in 1614, he said, "He is grown so dull and stupid, that unless this awake him, he is thought scant sensible of anything that befalls or concerns him."[61] Thus Parry, Fortescue, and Herbert were superannuated Elizabethan officials, still clinging to office but of little value to the state. Sir Julius Caesar was of more importance, though this was due rather to the abject mediocrity of his colleagues than to any distinction of his own. He was an official of merely ordinary capacity and little more than a clerk of the treasury; yet he was a fair debater, had much detailed knowledge of exchequer business, and extraordinary confidence in his own powers. He was the one councillor in this parliament who could make the slightest pretense to effectiveness.

[59] Chamberlain to Carleton, May 28, 1600, June 11, 1612, April 14, 1614, July 19, 1617, Sarah Williams (ed.), *Letters Written by John Chamberlain during the Reign of Queen Elizabeth* (Camden Society), 75; *Court and Times, James I,* I, 172; St. P. Domestic, 14/77:7; 14/92:96. Sir Gerald Herbert to Carleton, September 2, 1617, *ibid.,* 14/93:76. Evans, *The Principal Secretary of State,* 68. "The second secretary hath small things, and must in a manner feed upon hope." Chamberlain to Carleton, February 21, 1609, *Court and Times, James I,* I, 88.

[60] Northampton to Mar, January 1, 1608, *Mar and Kellie MSS, H. M. C.,* I, 59.

[61] Chamberlain to Carleton, July 18, 1612, May 12, 1614, *Court and Times, James I,* I, 187, 310.

Two new councillors appeared in the parliament of 1614, Winwood and Lake. Sir Ralph Winwood, a diplomat who had been serving in Holland, possessed certain attributes that would commend him to the commons. He firmly believed that parliament was the only cure for the ills of the state. He was an ardent Protestant and a good hater of Spain and Catholicism; and won great applause early in the session by a speech "against recusants and idle churchmen." He was honest and straightforward and possessed great courage and resolution. But he was rash, combative, and overconfident. "In his self-conceitedness," wrote Dudley Carleton, "he will only prove his own enemy." [62] "I commend his courage in resisting and contemning danger when he is in it," wrote Chamberlain, "more than his forwardness in running into it." His total lack of parliamentary experience caused him to speak in the house with too much vehemence and to win a reputation for tactlessness and arrogance that was not entirely deserved. "He is noted to be busy and practicke," wrote Chamberlain, "and withal very lofty and peremptory, which qualities though I do not descern in him, yet he hath the ill luck to be so reputed." "He is reputed somewhat harsh," Chamberlain wrote again, "and too plain a speaker for the tender ears of this age. Indeed, he is somewhat too quick and nimble to keep tune with the slowness of this time." And Sir Thomas Wentworth said that Winwood had "a kind of Hollander's Austerity." [63] Plain and forceful speaking, if skillfully employed, might have considerable effect upon the commons, but Winwood merely increased opposition. The majority of the commons in 1614 had no more parliamentary experience than Winwood himself and, angry and suspicious, they answered his rough asperity with even greater violence. Sir Thomas Lake was active in this house of commons. But he was merely a com-

[62] Winwood to Carleton, September 28, 1613, St. P. Domestic, 14/74:60. Chamberlain to Carleton, May 12, 1614, *Court and Times, James I,* I, 310. Same to same, May 19, 1614, St. P. Domestic, 14/77:26. Carleton to Edmondes, March 30, 1609, T. Birch, *Negotiations between the Courts of England, France, and Brussels* (London, 1749), 297.

[63] Chamberlain to Carleton, December 23, 1613, May 26, February 10, 1614, *Court and Times, James I,* I, 282, 314; St. P. Domestic, 14/76:20. Wentworth to Sir Henry Wotton, November 8, 1617, *Strafford's Letters,* I, 5. Salisbury once hinted to Winwood that he was too passionate in certain negotiations with the Dutch. *Winwood,* III, 316. Carleton complained of his "magisterial gravity and supercilious look." Carleton to Edmondes, April 26, 1609, Birch, *Negotiations,* 298. Chamberlain wrote Carleton, June 1, 1614, "Our good friend the while is neither idle nor always well occupied, neither greatly giving nor receiving satisfaction, but held opiniative and peremptory to the proof, which kind of carriage is nothing pleasing, which makes him subject to much censure." Parliament judges him "ill-favouredly." *Court and Times, James I,* I, 320.

petent bureaucrat and had, wrote Gardiner, "no pretensions to be anything more than a diligent and ready official." [64]

Aside from Sir Edward Coke, who joined the opposition, Cranfield was the ablest councillor in the commons in 1621. He was the one outstanding man among the bureaucrats now coming to the fore through industrious and efficient administration. He had made his mark early in life as a successful merchant in the City, and soon attracted attention at court. "The first acquaintance I had with him," said James in 1624, "was by the Lord of Northampton, who often brought him unto me a private man before he was so much as my servant. He then made so many projects for my profit that Buckingham fell in liking with him after the Earl of Northampton's death, and brought him into my service . . . He found him so studious for my profit that he backed him against great personages and mean, without sparing any man; Buckingham laid the ground and bared the envy; he [Cranfield] took the laborious and ministerial part upon him, and so he came up for his preferment." [65] He first entered the king's service in 1605 but held only minor office until he was appointed a master of requests in 1618, master of the court of wards and chief commissionary of the navy in 1619, a privy councillor in 1620, and lord treasurer late in 1621.

Cranfield cannot be regarded as a great parliamentarian. Yet he won the respect of the commons as a shrewd and practical man of business with long experience and exact information in matters of commerce and finance. He was known to have carried through substantial reforms in various departments of the government. "Sir Lyonel can instruct us well," said Phelips in a debate on trade, "so doth [he] ever informe us faithfullie." Clarendon called him a man "of great parts and notable dexterity . . . of great wit and understanding in all the mysteries of trade." [66] He was placed in the chair in important committees on the scarcity of money and the decay of trade; and he spoke continually on all economic questions, strengthening his arguments with facts and figures. Thus

[64] *Gardiner,* II, 147.
[65] *Parl. Hist.,* VI, 193. Goodman (I, 306) wrote: "My Lord of Northampton taking a great good liking of Mr. Cranfield, he brings him to the King and recommends him to him, with whom the King had some conference, and having a great reach and seeing far into a man, finding great abilities in Mr. Cranfield, he thought fit to draw him into some nearness unto himself."
[66] *Commons Debates 1621,* V, 518. *Clarendon,* I, 27.

the commons, involved as they were in economic matters, found in Cranfield a councillor whose sane and practical observations were always to the point and whose opinions could not be ignored. He stood, moreover, for freer trading conditions, opposed monopolies, and supported the commons' demand for administrative and legal reform.

He was a ready and able speaker. His speeches were effective because of their clearness and utility, their incisive analysis and forceful exposition. They had the ungarnished directness and simplicity of the best type of modern public speaking. Yet there was subtlety in them also, for without resorting to vague exhortations to loyalty, in which councillors so often took refuge, Cranfield managed to present James to the commons in a very favorable light, ready to correct evils and remedy abuses if only they were made clear to him and presented with becoming deference.

Yet while Cranfield won the respect of the house, he did not win popularity. His chairmanship of the committee on trade was disappointing. His chief difficulty was his manner, which won him much ill will. He had something of the arrogance often found in self-made men of business, and his manners were frequently rough and uncourteous. His portrait at Knole is that of a City man highly pleased with his own success; and one may read in his face a certain irrepressible effrontery. He had supreme confidence in his own opinions and expressed them with more forcefulness than tact, which gave offense to many and involved him in numerous quarrels. These were not confined to the house of commons. His quarrel with Buckingham was to his credit; but he also quarreled with Bacon, with Digby, and with Williams, all of them moderate men. And the attacks upon him by his fellow councillors in 1624, although they originated at court, have a distinct ring of sincerity. As a member of the commons, he used sharp language in debate and assumed a hectoring tone which the house was quick to resent. His language in attacking Bacon in 1621 was violent and unguarded. Later in the session he spoke very sharply to Sir Samuel and Sir Edwin Sandys and blurted out that after the parliament certain members would be questioned for their speeches in the house.[67] On May 31 his friend Ingram wrote him begging

[67] Locke to Carleton, March 3, 1621, St. P. Domestic, 14/120:6. *P. and D.,* II, 121–22, 142–43, 151–53. Gardiner remarks that while Cranfield was subservient to Buckingham, he found compensation by snarling at everybody else.

that if he spoke in the commons he would use due moderation and restraint.[68] It is not surprising that, able as Cranfield was, he became increasingly unpopular; and injured his chances of success by the roughness and tactlessness of his manner.

Sir George Calvert had first entered public life as Salisbury's secretary and had received his training in that capacity, "being then esteemed a forward and knowing person in matters relating to the state." After Salisbury's death he held several minor offices, won the favor of Buckingham, and became principal secretary in 1619 largely through Buckingham's patronage. He proved himself a highly efficient secretary and a capable man of business, more skillful than his colleague Naunton; and since he favored the Spanish match, most of the correspondence with that country passed through his hands. Tillières, the French ambassador, described him in 1621 as "an honourable, sensible, well-intentioned man, courteous to strangers, full of respect to ambassadors, zealously intent for the welfare of England, but by reason of these good qualities entirely without consideration or influence." [69] Calvert did not aspire to be more than a successful and trusted bureaucrat; he waited for instructions and addressed Buckingham with humility though not with undue flattery. But though he was by no means a great man or a distinguished parliamentarian, he played a difficult part with skill and some success. By his constant attendance, his courteous and conciliatory manner, his reasonable presentation of the crown's point of view, and his skill as a debater, he rendered better service in the lower house than any secretary of the period.

His politeness and moderation were a distinct asset in parliament, where he had constantly to defend unpopular policies and deliver messages that were certain to irritate. When on February 5 he and Alford rose to speak at the same instant and Alford began with some vehemence, Calvert allowed him to continue and

[68] "Let me entreat your honour to be at the House today and that you will likewise be pleased to be careful that if you speak, it may be with such moderation as it may give no cause of exception. I know the strength of your wisdom to be such as that you are much better able to direct yourself in your own ways than to be advised by me. But, hearing what I have, I could not do less out of the true respect I bear you than to write these few lines to you, craving your pardon if I shew too much boldness therein. And if you please to take a bad dinner I shall take it as a kind favour." *Commons Debates 1621*, III, 358 note.

[69] P. Bliss (ed.), Anthony à Wood, *Athenae Oxonienses* (5 vols., London, 1813–20), II, 522. F. L. G. von Raumer, *History of the Sixteenth and Seventeenth Centuries* (2 vols., London, 1835), II, 263.

said he was glad to give place to him. On November 23 Calvert protested against some words by Alford criticizing the king; but later he let the matter drop with the remark that since the house did not think fit to question Alford for his words, it was of small moment whether he himself was satisfied or not. When the house refused to follow the wishes of the king by preparing legislation for the royal approval in June, Calvert mildly protested that "it would not stand with good Manners in us, neither with our Duties to the Places we serve for." The irritating words of the king's letter of December 14 were, said Calvert, "only the Slip of a Pen in the End of a long Answer." [70] At the same time he defended the actions and honor of the king with force and dignity and, what was more difficult, the honor of the king of Spain and English relations with that country. He presented the policies of the crown in a plausible and reasonable light, minimized attacks upon parliamentary privilege, counselled moderation, and sought methods of procedure that would not offend the court. His speeches were always lucid and sometimes rather impressive. After Cranfield was raised to the peerage, Calvert was the most important councillor in the house.

But he was distrusted and unpopular in the commons. This was due to his leanings toward Catholicism, which he made little effort to conceal, and to his sympathy with Spain and the Spanish match. The commons assumed that such a man could not be honest. His defense of Spain produced angry scenes in the house; and on one occasion, when he explained an action of the government, a diarist remarked, "the House would scarce believe Mr. Secretary, but thinketh he equivocateth." [71] To the commons he was "an Hispaniolized Papist" and the king's "Popish Secretary." But this was quite unjust to Calvert. As an intermediary between king and commons he appears honest and straightforward. His sympathy with Spain never led him to betray the interests of his country; and his policy should be compared with that of Bristol (who was his political ally) rather than with that of James, for Calvert was ready for a stronger stand in the Palatinate. Nevertheless

[70] C. J., I, 508; Commons Debates 1621, II, 18 note; IV, 12. P. and D., II, 198, 305, 139, 338.
[71] Goodman, I, 376. Cal. St. P. Venetian, 1619–1621, 577; Commons Debates 1621, II, 39 and note; VII, 628; Chamberlain to Carleton, February 10, May 2, 1621, Court and Times, James I, II, 222; St. P. Domestic, 14/121:5; P. and D., II, 200.

the failure of the Spanish match was a bitter blow to him. Even before the Spanish negotiations ended, he found himself superseded at court by Conway's rising fortunes; and important affairs began to pass through Conway's hands. "Secretary Calvert droops," wrote Chamberlain, "and keeps out of the way"; and he was described as never "looking merrily since the prince his coming out of Spain." In 1624 he talked of resigning his office and did so in the following January. Buckingham had found a new secretary more to his liking, and Calvert found it impossible to alter the fundamentals of his policy at the bidding of the favorite. He therefore dropped out of public life and devoted himself to "that ancient, primitive, and heroic work of planting the world." [72]

One is not accustomed to think of Sir Edward Coke as a councillor placed in the commons to aid in controlling that body. But Coke's career in the Stuart period had many ups and downs; and when parliament opened in 1621, James undoubtedly regarded him as a person who might be useful. It was Bacon's opinion in 1613 that if Coke became chief justice of the king's bench, he would "think himself near a privy counsellor's place, and thereupon turn obsequious." And in 1621 it was still Bacon's opinion of Coke that "a word from the King mates him." [73] Since his disgrace in 1616 Coke had gradually come back into public life, and in 1620 he apparently had some hope of becoming lord chancellor. James's attitude is clear from the fact that Coke was included in the commission of judges to make preparations for the session and was also provided with a seat in the commons.

But Coke, of course, threw himself, with all the authority of his learning, experience, and personality, into the support of the popular cause. He became one of the most important of the popular leaders. He was placed in the chair for the committee of grievances, attacked monopolies vigorously, suggested remedies, and introduced laws against specific abuses. He boldly named the referees when other members hesitated to do so; he took a leading

[72] See *Gardiner*, IV, 411 note. Goodman says that Calvert "did protest to a friend of his own that he never got by the Spaniards so much as a pair of pockets." *Goodman*, I, 377. Arthur Wilson, *The History of Great Britain* (London, 1653), 97, 171. Chamberlain to Carleton, August 7, 1624, *Court and Times, James I*, II, 470; John Maclean (ed.), *Letters from George Lord Carew to Sir Thomas Roe* (Camden Society), 372. See also *Cal. St. P. Venetian, 1623–1625*, 127. D. Carleton to Sir Dudley Carleton, April 4, 6, 1624, St. P. Domestic, 14/162:13, 25. *D. N. B.* under Calvert.

[73] *Spedding*, IV, 381; VII, 192.

part in the attack upon legal abuses. In these matters he was doing no more than Cranfield; but his tone was very different and he went much further. Grievances must precede supply. "Let the greivances be first prepared," he said in February, "and we shalbe more ready to give when we are better able to geve."[74] He strenuously defended the privileges of the house, he shared to the full the commons' hatred for Spain, and he helped prepare both the petition concerning the marriage of the prince and the Protestation of Liberties at the end of the parliament.

For all this he won the unstinted praise of the commons, who taxed their powers of eloquence to provide him with compliments. "This was the first Parliament," said Alford, "that ever he saw Counsellors of State have such Care of the State."[75] But Coke's actions were naturally viewed very differently at court. His precedents were "not liked nor allowed, as falling out in weak reigns and turbulent times." There was a rumor in June that he was to be sequestered from the council. When in the autumn the commons took up his case against Lepton and Goldsmith, the king ordered the house not to meddle in "Coke's foolish business." In December James asked the council how Coke might be excluded from the general pardon. After the final sitting he was brought before the council and "was told he had incurred the King's displeasure for having forgotten the duty of a servant, the duty of a Councillor, and as might be thought the duty of a subject." He was then deprived of his place in the council, his papers were examined, and he was kept close prisoner in the Tower for nine months. Even after his release his movements were strictly curtailed. These things were not done without the protests of many councillors.[76] But James was determined upon severity.

Sir Richard Weston, the chancellor of the exchequer, was a courtier of some administrative and diplomatic ability. "His edu-

[74] February 5, 1621, *Commons Debates 1621*, IV, 16.

[75] *P. and D.*, I, 66. For praise of Coke, see J. O. Halliwell (ed.), *The Autobiography and Correspondence of Sir Simonds D'Ewes* (2 vols., London, 1845), I, 213; Chamberlain to Carleton, February 10, March 10, 1621, *Court and Times, James I*, II, 222; St. P. Domestic, 14/120:13. See also *C. J.*, I, 546; *Cal. St. P. Venetian, 1621–1623*, 199; St. P. Domestic, 14/119:103; Sir Dudley Digges to Carleton, March 11, 1621, St. P. Holland, 84/100. For a word of criticism, see Chamberlain to Carleton, March 28, 1621, St. P. Domestic, 14/120:52.

[76] Chamberlain to Carleton, January 4, 1622, St. P. Domestic, 14/127:8. Meddus to Mead, June 22, 1621, Locke to Carleton, January 12, 1622, *Court and Times, James I*, II, 259, 283. *P. and D.*, II, 326. The council to the king, December 17, 1621, *Cal. St. P. Domestic, 1619–1623*, 322. *Commons Debates 1621*, VII, 626–27.

cation," wrote Clarendon, "had been very good among books and men"; and he proved both industrious and efficient in public life. But he displayed traits and supported policies which eventually won him such universal unpopularity that toward the end of his life he lived in constant fear of assassination. Like Calvert, he had strong Catholic sympathies and favored political alliance with Spain; and these things alone were sufficient to damn him in the eyes of the commons. In 1625 and again in 1626 the commons considered placing his name among those presented for recusancy, for although he and his sons attended the established church, his wife and daughters did not. He was much more of a political sycophant than Calvert. He devoted himself completely to winning the good will of Buckingham, whom he treated with the most cringing subservience, and altered his political opinions with the greatest facility to keep them in line with those of his patron. He had at first opposed the break with Spain and voted against summoning parliament in 1624; but finding that Buckingham was determined upon war, he acquiesced at once and won a momentary popularity in the commons by his disclosures of Spanish duplicity. While he had given himself body and soul to Buckingham, he managed with considerable skill to retain the good opinion of other important persons at court. "To please some very much and to displease none," wrote Clarendon, was an art in which he excelled. Williams had strongly opposed his appointment as chancellor of the exchequer in 1621 because he feared that Weston's "daring and boldness" would be placed too completely at Cranfield's disposal; yet Williams confessed in 1624 that Weston had remained entirely faithful to Buckingham at all times. Weston was the sort of man who is spoiled by prosperity. "He quickly lost the character of a bold, stout, magnanimous man, which he had long been reputed to be in worse times," wrote Clarendon, "and in his most prosperous season he fell under the reproach of being a man of big looks and of a mean and abject spirit." His former subservience changed to insolence, and he offended many, although he greatly feared the vengeance of those whom he had made his enemies.[77] Such a man could not hope for

[77] *Clarendon*, I, 59. February 27, March 2, 1626, Whitelocke, f. 15, 50–51. May to Buckingham, October 7, 1627, St. P. Domestic, 16/80:60. D. Carleton to Sir Dudley Carleton, March 5, 1624, *ibid.*, 14/160:33; March 11, 1624, Holles, f. 95v. Williams to Buckingham, May 24, 1624, *Cabala*, 94.

success in the commons. His unpopularity steadily increased, and by 1629 he was the object of such detestation, as the disciple upon whom Buckingham's mantle had fallen, that he would certainly have been impeached if parliament had not been dissolved. Although he served in every parliament from 1604 to 1626 (and became a councillor in 1621), he did the cause of the crown little good in the commons.

Sir Thomas Edmondes, the treasurer of the household, was a diplomat of considerable spirit and ability. He had been employed in Paris and Brussels by Cecil, who called him "very trusty and sufficient"; and his resolute carriage and knowledge of affairs made him respected and even feared by foreign governments. In 1621 he followed Cranfield in attacking abuses and advocating reform, and wrote that grievances had piled up to such an extent that the kingdom would have been ruined had not the king summoned parliament.[78] His dispatches from abroad and his speeches in the commons, where he served from 1621 to 1628, are always clear and to the point; and it is strange that he did not make more of a mark in the house. Perhaps this was due to his error in constantly stressing the good intentions and honesty of James and Charles, an argument that was beginning to pall. But more probably it was simply because the position of councillors in the house had now grown so extremely difficult that only a man of most exceptional ability and parliamentary skill could hope for success.

The other councillors in the parliament of 1621 may be passed by with a word. Sir Fulke Greville, the elderly chancellor of the exchequer,[79] spoke on numerous occasions and did good service without making any great impression; the same may be said of Caesar, now master of the rolls. Naunton never took his seat in the commons nor, in all probability, did Falkland.

Of the six councillors in the parliament of 1624 three have already been mentioned, and the remaining three require only brief description. Sir Robert Naunton was a scholarly person who had been public orator at Cambridge and had had some experience in diplomacy in the reign of Elizabeth. He had become a master of requests in 1616, later surveyor of the court of wards, and finally

[78] See *D. N. B.* under Edmondes. Edmondes to Carleton, June 12, 1621, St. P. Domestic, 14/121:96.

[79] Greville had been made chancellor "in spite of his age." Chamberlain to Isaac Wake, October 12, 1614, *ibid.,* 14/78:29.

secretary upon Winwood's death in 1617. He displayed no great ability as either lawyer or official. Whitelocke called him "a scholar and a mere stranger to the law"; and Wood wrote that Calvert's appointment as secretary was in part to "help Sir Robert Naunton, . . . who had not then that faculty of managing and expediting matters of state as Calvert had." It was said that James did not appoint a more eminent man than Calvert "for fear of reflecting on Secretary Naunton." Naunton was, in fact, a quiet, unpretentious person of no outstanding ability, acceptable as an official largely because he followed instructions and did nothing without warrant.[80] He was, however, a strong Protestant, a constant enemy of Spain, and an advocate of interference in defense of the Palatinate. He had taken the lead in urging James to summon parliament in 1621, and his Protestant and anti-Spanish zeal might have had some effect in the commons.[81] But he fell into difficulties at court and lost both his influence in the council and his interest in politics, so that although he spoke occasionally for the government in 1624 and in later parliaments, he did not have the authority of a councillor closely in touch with the secrets of the state. His speeches were cold, formal, and academic and did not possess "that moving eloquenc which does affect a parliament."[82] He was thus a very minor figure in the commons.

Sir Edward Conway, who became secretary in 1623, was a military man, on the whole honest and well intentioned, but entirely devoid of capacity for business and utterly dependent on Buckingham. Buckingham had decided to have a secretary with whom he could discuss military affairs, and Conway became a favorite who followed the court, transmitted Buckingham's instructions to lesser officials, and left the more difficult work of the secretary's office to Calvert, who remained in London. "This Conway constantly follows his Majesty and grows in favor daily," wrote the Venetian ambassador, "but the Spaniards hate him extremely, refuse to recognize him, and only negotiate with the

[80] John Bruce (ed.), *Liber Famelicus of Sir James Whitelocke* (Camden Society), 54, 62. Anthony à Wood, *Athenae Oxonienses*, II, 523. Sir Edward Harwood to Carleton, February 16, 1619, St. P. Domestic, 14/105:112. Bacon wrote that "Secretary Naunton forgets nothing." *Spedding*, VI, 320.

[81] *Cal. St. P. Venetian, 1621–1623*, 64. In October, 1622, when another parliament was being contemplated, the Venetian ambassador wrote, "Certainly to give parliament a good start it would be necessary to reinstate and rehabilitate Naunton." *Ibid.*, 476.

[82] *Negotium Posterorum*, II, 80.

other secretary Calvert." [83] At the time of Conway's appointment James "recommended him to the Lords for his birth, for his soldiery, for his languages, for his sufficiency, and for his honesty," which was giving him the benefit of many a doubt. But other courtiers believed that his success was due to "his courtship and courtesy, in seeking to fasten the title of excellency on the lord marquis." In other words, Conway owed his appointment to his abject fawning upon the favorite, and he continued, after he became secretary, to call Buckingham his noble patron, which aroused the disgust of the commons. Moreover, he had no aptitude for business. Clarendon wrote that in 1628 Conway "for his age and incapacity was at last removed from the Secretary's office which he had exercised for many years with very notable insufficiency." Clarendon added that James was wont to remark pleasantly that Stenny had given him a secretary who could neither read nor write.[84] Conway had few ideas of his own and was merely a mouthpiece for Buckingham's policies and opinions. As a member of the commons, he had no asset beyond a certain soldierly bluntness which was not ineffective in certain types of debate. He told the commons plainly in the early debates on supply that their fine phrases promising support in principle were quite worthless unless they added a large and substantial grant. Conway, however, never proved his ability to do more than speak plainly. He became a peer before the commons met again in 1625.

Sir John Suckling, the comptroller of the household, was so completely colorless that he may be dismissed with the remark that he spoke occasionally in the interests of the crown.

The parliament of 1625 contained two councillors whose names have not been mentioned. One of them, Sir Albertus Morton, was away on a diplomatic mission during the parliament and never took his seat in the commons. The other was Sir Humphrey May. He was a far abler man than those we have been describing, a more skillful debater in the commons, a man

---

[83] Buckingham "doth advise much and often with him about the ways of redressing the affairs and vindicating the King our Masters honor." Nethersole to Carleton, September 28, 1622, St. P. Holland, 84/109. *Cal. St. P. Venetian, 1623–1625,* 106. D. Carleton wrote to Sir Dudley Carleton that Conway "doth all the business and growes much in credit." April 4, 1624, St. P. Domestic, 14/162:13.

[84] Chamberlain to Carleton, January 25, 1623, *Court and Times, James I,* II, 358. *Clarendon,* I, 80.

of keener insight into the problems of the day, of more independent judgment and greater serenity of view, of a broader and more tolerant outlook upon the world.[85] He was as able a servant as Charles possessed in the early years of his reign. But ability and intelligence were not the keys to success at court, and May was condemned by his very qualities to minor office. He had been chancellor of the duchy of Lancaster for many years before he was admitted to the council in 1625. At least twice, in 1617 and in 1625, he had hoped for the secretaryship, but he stood none too high in the favor of Buckingham, whose policies he distrusted and sought to dissuade.[86] But if he failed to secure high office, he at least retained some independence among a host of sycophants.

May had been a member of every house of commons since the accession of James and had done excellent service for the crown. He spoke with ease and authority and could hold his own with Eliot and the best of the opposition leaders. He had a way with him in the commons. "The witt of this gentleman alwaies drew the attention of the house, though his motions seldome relisht it," wrote Eliot, who was not given to praise of the ministers of the crown. Again Eliot wrote that May spoke in the house with "much art" and left an impression upon his hearers, who perforce "measured his words by his intelligenc."[87] May refused to worship precedent in the way in which most of the commons worshiped it, and on many occasions threw the dry light of reason and intelligent moderation upon the excited passions of the house. That he succeeded no better in the commons is a reflection upon the cause he had to defend and upon the unreasonableness of the opposition.

The parliament of 1626 contained two new councillors, Sir John Coke and Sir Dudley Carleton. Coke was an honest, faithful, and industrious bureaucrat, without the slightest spark of imagination or originality, wholly intent upon obeying instructions and quite beyond his depth except within the small sphere

---

[85] See his marvelous letter to Buckingham upon the Spanish match, which he hoped would "allay the cruel hatreds, detestations, and persecutions that are on all sides amongst Christians." Harl. MSS 1581, f. 358.

[86] Chamberlain to Carleton, October 31, 1617, March 23, 1625, *Court and Times, James I*, II, 46, 508. May to Buckingham, October 7, 1627, St. P. Domestic, 16/80:60; Hacket, *Williams*, I, 81.

[87] *Negotium Posterorum*, II, 26–29, 84–85.

of his own official duties, which concerned the navy and which he knew well. "He was a man of a very narrow education," wrote Clarendon, "and of a narrower nature." He had been long at the University of Cambridge and held only minor office until he was past fifty. Eliot wrote that his "conversation being with bookes, and that to teach not studie them, men and business were subiectes which he knew not, and his expressions were more proper for a schoole, then for a State and councell." This was rather hard on Coke, for he performed his duties in the navy with much practical efficiency and acquired great experience in naval administration. His relations with his colleagues were unusually cordial, justifying Brooke's prophecy to Conway that Coke would prove "a passing safe and easy yoke fellow." Buckingham spoke of his "care and abilities" in business and found him "both honest and wise." His relations with May, however, were not so satisfactory. "His cardinal perfection was industry," said Clarendon; "his long experience had informed him well of the state and affairs of England; but of foreign transactions, or the common interests of Christian princes, he was entirely ignorant and undescerning." The Venetian ambassador, having sought some information from him in 1627, wrote that Coke "gave him no account of anything whatever, and indeed it is not his business to attend to foreign affairs, all of which remain in the hands of Secretary Conway, who is a hundred miles away with the king." Miss Evans has shown, however, that Coke was not entirely excluded from the conduct of foreign affairs.

But he was essentially mediocre. Clarendon remarked that he "was a man rather unadorned with parts of vigor and quickness, and unendowed with any notable virtues, than notorious for any weakness or defect of understanding, . . . or transported with any vicious inclination, appetite to money only excepted." And Eliot sneered at his "great abilities" with bitter sarcasm. In the commons, with whom Coke had constantly to deal from 1625 to 1628, he was an actual liability. His rapturous praise of Buckingham at the most inopportune moments grated on the nerves of members. Coke was, in fact, constantly blundering in the commons. Once a line of conduct was marked out for him by the court, he followed it to the letter, with plodding earnestness and an inept, irritating zeal, and "labor'd," said Eliot, "as a woman does with child, in desire to bring it foorth." [88] He made no allowance for the temper of the house and could not shift his ground or alter his tactics on the spur of the moment, as a skillful debater must do. He prepared his speeches with such care that they lacked spontaneity. He made damaging admissions which on several occasions increased the difficulties of the government. He was, in short, a clumsy parliamentarian, too slow and heavy for the give and take of debate. His laborious industry and devotion to duty were no great assets in the commons, and that was all he had. Even so, the intense unpopularity, almost hatred, with which he was regarded comes as something of a surprise. Many of the things he did in the commons which proved so irritating to members were the result of Buckingham's faulty instructions. Coke was the sort of member who would doubtless empty the benches in a modern house; but not one who would arouse intense dislike. It was the cause Coke served that turned him, in the minds of the commons, from a blundering but devoted official to a dangerous enemy of liberty and the public good.

Clarendon draws a sharp contrast between Coke and Sir Dudley Carleton. Carleton, he wrote, "understood all that related to foreign employment, and the condition of other princes and nations, very well; but was utterly unacquainted with the government, laws, and customs of his own country, and the nature of the people." As a student at Christ Church Carleton was regarded as "a young man of parts and towardly expectation," and he developed into the most gifted and successful diplomat of the early Stuart period, "the ablest man the king has abroad." He did not, however, take a large or exalted view of foreign or domestic policy, and was anxious to make his way in the world. "He is a prudent man," wrote the Venetian ambassador, "who knows the abuses and disorders and that to follow is a necessity for those who wish to hold any reputable post." He was unsuccessful in the commons because he knew so little about conditions in England and even less about the prejudices and susceptibilities of the house. "Sir Dudley Carleton is a stranger in Israel," said Digges,

[88] *Clarendon,* I, 80–81. *Negotium Posterorum,* I, 113–14; II, 18. Brooke to Conway, September 22, 1625, *Cal. St. P. Domestic, Addenda, 1625–1649,* 52. Conway to Coke, May 30, 1626, Buckingham to Coke, June 14, Thomas Alured to Coke, June 21, 1628, *Cowper MSS, H. M. C.,* I, 269, 349–53. *Cal. St. P. Venetian, 1626–1628,* 312. Evans, *The Principal Secretary of State,* 87.

"he knows not our reasons here." [89] He caused an uproar in the house by warning the commons that Continental sovereigns, finding their parliaments unruly, were fast doing away with them and were turning to "new counsels." Thus, because of lack of knowledge and experience in parliament, and because he spoke as a diplomat and not as a statesman, he was able to do little good in the commons.

Looking at these men as a group and judging them primarily as parliamentarians, we cannot call them impressive. They fall roughly into three classes. There was, in the first place, a group of really able men who might in other times have proved leaders of the commons. In this group may be placed Sir Edward Coke, who threw in his lot with the opposition, Sir Lionel Cranfield, made a peer too soon and then sacrificed by Charles and Buckingham, and Sir Humphrey May, who had the makings of a great parliamentarian. Secondly, there was a considerably larger group, of far more mediocre abilities, who nevertheless took or were forced to take, often because of the offices which they held, some share in the work of the commons and who had some influence there. Such men were Caesar, Winwood, Calvert, Weston, Edmondes, Conway, Carleton, and Sir John Coke. They were not impressive, but they played a part. And finally, there was a large number of nonentities, who, either because of lack of ability or irregularity of attendance or for some other reason, played so colorless and minor a role that they might as well not have been members.

There is something the matter with almost all of them. They are either too old, or too inefficient, or too cringing to the great, or too arrogant to their inferiors, or too engrossed in their administrative duties, or too ignorant of English affairs, or too inexperienced in the house of commons. Considering the importance of the commons during this period and the efforts of James and Charles to select councillors who would serve them well in the house, one is forced to the conclusion that the Stuarts were unable to judge the merits of the men to whom they gave responsibility.

[89] *Clarendon*, I, 81. *Cal. St. P. Venetian, 1628–1629*, 37. April 20, 1626, Whitelocke, f. 141. He had been a member of James's first parliament, in which he warmly supported the crown, but was abroad for most of the remainder of the reign. John More to Winwood, October 29, 1611, *Buccleuch MSS, Montagu Papers, H. M. C.,* I, 102.

1604–1611	*Office*	*Constituency*
FIRST SESSION		
Sir John Herbert	Secretary of state	Monmouth County
Sir John Stanhope	Vice-chamberlain	Newtown, Isle of Wight
SECOND SESSION		
Sir John Herbert		
Sir John Fortescue	Chancellor of the duchy of Lancaster	Middlesex County
THIRD SESSION		
Sir John Herbert		
Sir John Fortescue		
FOURTH AND FIFTH SESSIONS		
Sir John Herbert		
Sir Thomas Parry	Chancellor of the duchy of Lancaster	St. Albans
Sir Julius Caesar	Chancellor of the exchequer	City of Westminster
1614		
Sir Ralph Winwood	Secretary of state	Buckingham Borough
Sir Thomas Lake	No office	Middlesex County
Sir Julius Caesar	Chancellor of the exchequer	Middlesex County
Sir Thomas Parry	Chancellor of the duchy of Lancaster	Berkshire County
1621		
Sir George Calvert	Secretary of state	York County
Sir Robert Naunton	Secretary of state	Cambridge University
Sir Lionel Cranfield	Master of the wards	Arundel Borough
Sir Richard Weston	Chancellor of the exchequer	Arundel Borough
Sir Edward Coke	No office	Liskeard Borough
Sir Thomas Edmondes	Treasurer of the household	Bewdley and Dorchester boroughs, electing to serve for the first
Sir Julius Caesar	Master of the rolls	Maldon Borough
Sir Fulke Greville	Chancellor of the exchequer	Warwick County
Henry Cary, Viscount Falkland	Comptroller of the household	Hertford County
1624		
Sir George Calvert	Secretary of state	Oxford University
Sir Edward Conway	Secretary of state	Evesham Borough

99

1624 (cont.)	*Office*	*Constituency*
Sir Richard Weston	Chancellor of the exchequer	Bossiney Borough
Sir Thomas Edmondes	Treasurer of the household	Chichester City
Sir John Suckling	Comptroller of the household	Middlesex County, Kingston-upon-Hull, and Litchfield City, electing to serve for the first
Sir Robert Naunton	Master of the wards	Cambridge University
1625		
Sir Richard Weston	Chancellor of the exchequer	Callington Borough
Sir Thomas Edmondes	Treasurer of the household	Oxford University
Sir Albertus Morton	Secretary of state	Kent County and Cambridge University, electing to serve for the first
Sir Humphrey May	Chancellor of the duchy of Lancaster	Lancaster and Leicester boroughs, electing to serve for the first
Sir John Suckling	Comptroller of the household	Yarmouth, Isle of Wight
Sir Robert Naunton	Master of the wards	Cambridge University
1626		
Sir John Coke	Secretary of state	Cambridge University
Sir Richard Weston	Chancellor of the exchequer	Bodmin Borough
Sir Thomas Edmondes	Treasurer of the household	Oxford University (election voided by house)
Sir Humphrey May	Chancellor of the duchy of Lancaster	Leicester and Lancaster boroughs, electing to serve for the first
Sir Robert Naunton	Master of the wards	Suffolk County
Sir John Suckling	Comptroller of the household	Norwich City and Sandwich Borough, electing to serve for the first
Sir Dudley Carleton	Vice-chamberlain	Hastings Borough

1628	*Office*	*Constituency*
Sir John Coke	Secretary of state	Cambridge University
Sir Humphrey May	Chancellor of the duchy of Lancaster	Leicester Borough
Sir Thomas Edmondes	Treasurer of the household	Penryn Borough
Sir Francis Cottington	No office	Saltash Borough
1640 (Short Parl.)		
Sir Francis Windebank	Secretary of state	Oxford University
Sir Thomas Jermyn	Comptroller of the household	Bury St. Edmunds Borough
Sir Henry Vane	Treasurer of the household and second secretary of state	Wilton Borough
1640 (Long Parl.)		
Sir Francis Windebank	Secretary of state	Corfe Castle Borough
Sir Thomas Jermyn	Comptroller of the household	Bury St. Edmunds Borough
Sir Henry Vane	Treasurer of the household and second secretary of state	Wilton Borough
Sir Thomas Roe	No office	Oxford University and Windsor, electing to serve for the first (Windsor election voided by house)
In January, 1642, two men in the house became councillors:		
Lucius Cary, Viscount Falkland	Secretary of state	Newport, Isle of Wight
Sir John Culpepper	Chancellor of the exchequer	Kent County

4

The Earl of Salisbury as Parliamentary Manager for the Crown[1]

The councillors in the commons were merely part, though a highly important part, of a larger framework. They were not the most influential ministers of the crown; and for the most part they advocated policies and pursued parliamentary tactics that had been determined upon elsewhere. We must look behind them, therefore, to their superiors at court, where parliamentary policy was largely formulated and whence the councillors in the house received their instructions. Nor were councillors the only officials in the commons. Many other members were connected in one way or another with the government; their work in the commons could supplement that of councillors; and certainly councillors had small hope of success without their support. Thus we must also look at other officials in the house and at their relations with the government.

In both of these respects the first parliament of James was unique. The crown possessed in Salisbury an able parliamentary manager, ready to assume responsibility for events in the commons. He gathered into his own hands the many threads of the crown's parliamentary business and directed the details of parliamentary policy and manipulation with greater care and thoroughness than any later minister of James or Charles. He also sought to strengthen and solidify the group of officials and courtiers in the commons and gave that group more party organization and abler leadership than it possessed at any other time before the Long Parliament.

Of the Elizabethan parliamentary system Salisbury was the very incarnation. He had first entered the commons as a young man in 1586, but already as the representative of the government and the son whom his father, Lord Burghley, was training for high

---

[1] A portion of this chapter is reprinted from an article, "The Earl of Salisbury and the 'Court' Party in Parliament, 1604–1610," *American Historical Review*, 36:274–94 (January, 1931).

executive office. During his first sessions as a member of the house he took little or no part in its deliberations.[2] But in the parliament of 1592–93 he became more prominent as a member of that group of councillors who from the floor of the house did so much to control its actions. In this parliament Cecil was no more important than other councillors. But his authority was increased in 1596, when he became principal secretary; and in the last two parliaments of Elizabeth, those of 1597 and 1601, he stood out as the foremost spokesman of the crown in the house of commons. He was, in effect, the crown's parliamentary manager. In this role he was continued by James, and it was therefore on his shoulders that there fell the task of continuing into the altered atmosphere of a new dynasty the Elizabethan system of parliamentary control.

But for all his wisdom and judgment, his "infinite wit and policy," Salisbury was not a man to change with changing times. His genius was Elizabethan, and the ideals and traditions of Tudor government were part of his very being. The house must be controlled so that the state could be run efficiently with as little interference as possible from the misguided meddling of the commons. Parliament was an unfortunate interruption to good government, unhappily necessitated by the financial need of the crown. He saw no reason for modifying in any way the Elizabethan system of church and state. He felt no necessity for allowing parliament more power in government or more freedom in conducting business within its own walls. He considered it the duty of the commons to vote money merely because the crown asked for it. In 1603, then, he began his task with his mind made up and his eyes fixed upon the past.

One phase of Salisbury's management has already been discussed: his care in preparing legislation to be placed before the commons and his efforts to placate public opinion by redressing grievances before a session opened.[3] That parliament might be called and dismissed at propitious times, he assumed responsibility for prorogations and adjournments. He consulted with the king, with his more important colleagues, and laid his plans before the council, seeking its advice. But his was the directing

[2] D'Ewes mentions his name but once in the parliament of 1586 and once in that of 1588–89. *D'Ewes (Elizabeth)*, 404, 454.
[3] See pp. 25–29.

brain. Thus in the summer of 1605 he wished to postpone the meeting of parliament for several months so that the people might gradually cease to fear certain royal commissions for raising money. Having consulted with Ellesmere, the chancellor, and with Dorset, the treasurer, he approached the king and obtained his consent.[4] Salisbury did not relish meetings of the commons;[5] but knowing that they were necessary, he sought to time them properly.

Interference in elections had clearly proved to be of importance to the crown in Tudor parliaments and had been used effectively by Salisbury in the last two parliaments of Elizabeth. Unfortunately there is little evidence of any kind concerning the election of 1604, which must probably be taken to mean that there was less interference at this time than in earlier or later parliaments. James certainly made no move toward influencing elections, issuing instead a proclamation declaring that elections should be free. But why Salisbury left the elections to chance, as Bacon later accused him of doing,[6] is extremely difficult to explain. Perhaps already affairs were crowding upon him and he was too occupied with other business. Or perhaps, with his customary assurance concerning parliament, he was confident that with a new and still popular king upon the throne parliament could be easily controlled. As a matter of fact, the number of officials and courtiers who secured election in 1604 was greater than is commonly supposed. Yet it seems clear that elections, broadly speaking, were neglected.[7]

[4] Ellesmere to Salisbury, July 30, August 1, 1605 (two letters), Hatfield House MSS; Salisbury to the council, 1605, *Cal. Hatfield House MSS*, XVI, 425 (where the letter is dated 1604). See also Salisbury to Nicholas Faunt, December 4, 1605, Hatfield House MSS; Lake to Salisbury, November 23, 1610, St. P. Domestic, 14/58:31.

[5] See Salisbury to Sir Charles Cornwallis, September 12, 1605, *Winwood*, II, 132. Salisbury preferred to prorogue and not to dissolve parliament. Tate wrote in Elizabeth's reign that "to have a Parliament lest offensive" it was best "to hold it upon Prorogation, without dissolution." An election was costly in new fees and wasted time in formalities at the first of the session. Moreover "new men . . . are commonlie most Adventerous, and canne be gladdest of Longe Parleamentes to learne and sea fashiones where the olde contineurers have amonge other thinges learned more advisedness." Harl. MSS 253, f. 32. Salisbury urged James to summon parliament in 1610. Add. MSS 22591, f. 191v–213.

[6] Bacon to King James, *Spedding*, IV, 368.

[7] Evidence of interference by the government is surprisingly meager. The council interfered in the election of Fortescue and in that of Sir Edward Denny. See Mary Elizabeth Bohannon, "The Essex Election of 1604," *English Historical Review*, 48:395–413. Sir Edward Coke secured the election of Sir John Hobart at Corfe Castle. H. A. Merewether and A. J. Stephens, *The History of the Boroughs and Municipal Corporations of the United Kingdom* (3 vols., London, 1835), II, 1350–51. Salisbury wrote the earl of Shrewsbury,

The king and Salisbury soon recognized their error as the temper of the commons became more apparent. "The King," wrote the Venetian ambassador in 1605, "desires to order fresh elections in the case of certain turbulent spirits, who are little to his taste. He is well aware how much his neglect of the elections cost him last year."[8] Members once elected could not be turned out. But Salisbury attempted to remedy his initial error by a systematic interference in by-elections throughout the remainder of the parliament. In a house undissolved for seven years numerous vacancies were bound to occur; and the mortality among members of this parliament chanced to be unusually high.[9] A number of members, moreover, were appointed to governmental positions which debarred them from the commons. As a result there were some ninety-five by-elections during the parliament.[10] Salisbury made every effort to place court candidates in these vacancies and was, on the whole, quite successful, occasionally receiving a refusal from a town corporation or local magnate,[11] but much more frequently meeting with submissive acquiescence. The country as a whole was not yet aroused against the Stuart dynasty. At least a third of these by-elections resulted in the return of an official or an individual closely connected with the government; and in the majority of these by-elections won by the crown its interference may be proved.[12]

December 23, 1603, that "you forget me not for a burgess-ship." Edmund Lodge, *Illustrations of British History* (3 vols., London, 1838), III, 83. Arthur Hall wrote the king that there had been packing in 1604 and declared, "I believe you will finde not fewe of them crepte in, by means of some, in great credit, and nere about your Majesty." But though he promised a long list of men corruptly returned, he could name but ten, of whom several should have been debarred merely because of technicalities, such as their being sheriffs. H. G. Wright, *Life and Works of Arthur Hall of Grantham* (Manchester, 1919), 206–07; St. P. Domestic, 14/7:82.

[8] *Cal. St. P. Venetian, 1603–1607*, 268.

[9] "It is observed that many Parliament Men of Mark are dead since the last Sessions." Chamberlain to Winwood, October 12, 1605, *Winwood*, II, 141.

[10] H. Hulme, "Corrections and Additions to the Official 'Return' of Members of Parliament, 1603–04," *Bulletin of the Institute of Historical Research,* 5:96–105.

[11] For failures to place candidates see: Ralph Sneyde to Salisbury, August 9, 1605; Robert (Bennet), bishop of Hereford, to the same, August 9, 1605; mayor and burgesses of Kingston-upon-Hull to same, March 12, 1607, Hatfield House MSS. Corporation of Ludlow to the same, December 1, 1609, St. P. Domestic, 14/50:5.

[12] For by-elections in which Salisbury interfered successfully see: Sir George Carew to Salisbury, July 27, 1605; bailiffs of Maldon to the privy council, October 16, 1605; bailiffs of Maldon to Northampton and Salisbury, October 26, 1605; Salisbury to the mayor, etc., of Beer Alston, October 30, 1605; Thomas Provis to Salisbury, October 21, 1605; mayor and burgesses of Portsmouth to Salisbury, January 12, 1607, Hatfield House MSS. Bailiffs of Eye to Salisbury, October 16, 1609; John Hender to Salisbury, October 21, 1609; bailiffs,

Partly as a result of these tactics the number of officials in this parliament was unusually large. The heart of the royal faction was normally the privy councillors, but the council was exceptionally weak in this house of commons. A more important group consisted of the legal advisers of the crown, the king's learned counsel, of whom Bacon was the chief figure, striving to make his activities in the commons a stepping stone to advancement. During the first sessions of the parliament he was of the king's counsel extraordinary, a new and somewhat anomalous office which he had persuaded James to create for him; and in 1607 he became solicitor. Sir Henry Hobart was attorney of the court of wards and was appointed attorney-general in 1606 without losing his seat in the commons. Sir Thomas Fleming was solicitor in 1604 but became chief baron of the exchequer in October of that year. He was followed as solicitor by Sir John Doderidge, who held the post until it was conferred upon Bacon in 1607. All three of these men were members of the commons in 1604, and Doderidge and Bacon served throughout the parliament. Sir Henry Montagu, recorder of London, was appointed king's counsel in 1607; and Sir Robert Hitcham, attorney to Queen Anne, was also a member of the house. These men were of great importance to the government in dealing with the commons.

The serjeants, except for the king's serjeants,[13] were not officers of the crown; but they were lawyers upon whom the crown had bestowed special honor and privilege and from them the bench was recruited. The serjeants were on their way to be judges. I know of no serjeant who did not support the crown in the commons. Bacon wrote in 1613 that "Crew and Hide stand to be serjeants" and would therefore cease their opposition if another parliament was summoned; and in 1623 Williams advised a call of serjeants as a means of securing support in the next parliament.[14] The parliament of 1604–11 contained twelve serjeants,

etc., of Boroughbridge to Salisbury, November 5, 1609; mayor, etc., of Headon to Salisbury, November 13, 1609, March 3, 1610; William Gee to Salisbury, March 4, 1610; mayor and bailiffs of Weymouth to Sir Julius Caesar, June 13, 16, 1610, St. P. Domestic, 14/48:109, 116; 14/49:10, 25; 14/53:2, 3; 14/55:20, 23. The privy council to the corporation of Buckingham borough, February 21, 1606, Add. MSS 11402, f. 110. Northampton to the mayor and jurats of Rye, September, 1607, Rye MSS, H. M. C., Thirteenth Report, Part 4, 135. In other by-elections involving officials we may fairly suspect interference but have no proof.

[13] Sir John Doderidge became king's serjeant in 1607 and Sir Henry Montagu in 1611.

[14] Spedding, IV, 365, 370. Hacket, Williams, I, 110.

though it is true that some of them were not in the commons for very long. Four have been mentioned among the learned counsel. The others were Robert Barker, Edward Bromley, Sir James Ley, Sir Edward Phelips, who was speaker, John Shirley, George Snigg, Lawrence Tanfield, and Sir Humphrey Winch.[15] Of eleven serjeants called in 1603 seven were elected to the commons in the following year.

Legal officers in the commons also included: Sir George Carew, a master in chancery; Sir Thomas Hesketh, whom Hobart succeeded as attorney of the court of wards; Sir Roger Wilbraham, who had been solicitor in Ireland, was now a master of requests, and became surveyor of the king's liveries and of the court of wards in 1607; Sir Daniel Dunn, who had been dean of arches and master of requests and was now a master in chancery; and Sir Thomas Crompton, who was connected with the ecclesiastical courts. Anthony Dyott, Heneage Finch, and Thomas Trevor were lawyers ready to serve the crown.

But the rank and file of the king's servants in the commons were men who held minor office or were the direct dependents or private servants of important councillors. Minor officeholders included: Robert Bowyer, the keeper of the records in the Tower; Sir William Bowyer, a teller of the exchequer; Sir George Carew, the queen's vice-chamberlain; Sir Walter Cope, a chamberlain of the exchequer; John Corbett, one of the clerks of the privy council; Sir William Fleetwood, receiver-general of the court of wards; Thomas Fanshawe, auditor for the northern part of the duchy of Lancaster, surveyor-general and clerk of the crown; John Ferne, secretary to the council in the north; John Hare, clerk of the court of wards; Sir George Harvey and Sir William Waad, successively lieutenants of the Tower; Sir Robert Johnson, an officer of the ordnance; Sir William Killigrew, chamberlain of the exchequer; Sir Robert Mansell, treasurer of the navy; Griffith Payne, a purveyor; Thomas Lake, clerk of the signet, secretary of the Latin tongue, and keeper of the records at Whitehall; Humphrey May,

[15] Of these men Bromley became a baron of the exchequer in 1610; Ley, chief justice of the king's bench in Ireland in 1604 (he was re-elected to the commons in 1609, when he was again in England as attorney of the court of wards); Snigg, a baron of the exchequer in 1604; Tanfield, a judge of the king's bench in 1606 and chief baron of the exchequer in 1607; Winch, chief baron of the exchequer in Ireland in 1606 and later a judge of the common pleas in England. Thus some of these men were not members of the commons for very long.

groom of the privy chamber and holder of grants in reversion of several minor offices; Richard Percival, remembrancer of the court of wards; George Rivers, of the alienation office; Sir Thomas Ridgeway, vice-treasurer, and Sir Oliver St. John, master of the ordnance, in Ireland. Officials of local importance included Sir Thomas Waller, lieutenant of Dover Castle; George Fane, who had acted as temporary lieutenant; Sir William Selby, gentleman-porter of Berwick; and the stewards of various castles and boroughs, such as Sir Richard Assheton, Talbot Bowes, and Sir Robert Wingfield.

Members with diplomatic hopes or experience included Sir Charles Cornwallis, a dependent of the Howards, Sir John Digby, later the earl of Bristol,[16] Sir Thomas Edmondes, Sir Henry Neville, and Sir Christopher Perkins. Salisbury's dependents in the commons included his secretary, George Calvert, who was clerk of the crown for parts of Ireland and a clerk of the English privy council, Sir Vincent Skinner, a former secretary of Burghley, Sir Michael Hicks, Sir Thomas Holcroft, and Thomas Wilson, men employed by him on both private and public business. Dudley Carleton, secretary to Sir Thomas Parry and later to the unfortunate earl of Northumberland, and John Griffith,[17] Northampton's secretary, were also in the commons. A number of men, some of importance later, were still hangers-on at court, looking to Salisbury for employment: Edward Conway, Richard Weston, and Robert Naunton, all later privy councillors, Sir George St. Paul, Sir Thomas Jermyn, John Holles, and Sir Edward Stafford, still seeking office after many years at the court of Elizabeth.

Another large group was composed of courtiers, men who held some honorary post about the king, or were living on the royal bounty without holding any office at all, or were hanging about the court in the hope of securing a place. This list included such men as Sir Roger Aston, a servant of his majesty's bedchamber, Sir Richard Lewison, a gentleman of the privy chamber, Sir Lewis Lewkenor, master of ceremonies, and Sir Thomas Vavasour, marshal of the court; patentees such as Sir Jerome Bowes, Sir Edward Hoby (who was also a gentleman of the privy cham-

---

[16] G. R. Park, *The Parliamentary Representation of Yorkshire* (Hull, 1886), 255, does not identify this member with the great diplomat; but W. W. Bean, *The Parliamentary Representation of the Six Northern Counties of England* (Hull, 1890), xvii, does so.

[17] *Goodman*, I, 53.

ber), his brother, Sir Thomas Posthumous Hoby, and Sir Arthur Ingram, who was already important in the customs and full of plans to enrich the kingdom and himself. Other courtiers in this house of commons included Sir Henry Rich, later Lord Kensington and earl of Holland; Sir Philip Herbert, whom James made earl of Montgomery in 1605; his cousin, Sir Edward Herbert, knight of the Bath; Sir Robert Killigrew; Sir George More, a fine type of courtier-officeholder; Francis Clifford, who became the fourth earl of Cumberland in 1605; Sir Robert Cotton; Sir Edward Denny, later the earl of Norwich; Sir John Egerton; Sir William Strode; Sir William Maynard; Sir Richard Warburton; and such inconsequential persons as Tobie Matthew and Edward Wymarke.[18] The list could also include the relations of great officials, such as Sir William Cecil, Salisbury's son, and Sir Edward Cecil, his cousin, later Viscount Wimbledon; Theophilus, later Lord Howard de Walden, and Sir Thomas Howard, sons of the earl of Suffolk; and Robert Sackville, Dorset's eldest son.

I do not pretend that this list is at all complete or that these men were all equally zealous in the royal cause; nor have I attempted to analyze the royalist elements among the gentry, a difficult if not an impossible task. I merely wish to show that the officials and courtiers in the commons were sufficiently numerous to become, with proper leadership, a political force in the house and the nucleus of a royal party.

Of the king's supporters in the house Salisbury was the party chief. He not only directed the general policies to be pursued by his followers in the commons but supervised with characteristic minuteness their daily acts and maneuvers. Before the session of 1606 he sought to coordinate the work of various officials in the commons. He wrote to the councillors, outlining the measures that the government proposed to introduce. Some of the commons, he said, would delay their consent to these measures until they saw some hope of retribution; while others would be absolutely opposed and would come prepared with as many arguments as wit or will could furnish them. He therefore saw "great necessity that such consultations might precede the general assembly as might prepare some good way to the mutual satisfaction both of

[18] We know that Sir Francis Goodwin, Thomas Provis, and Sir John Kaye owed their election to the efforts of Salisbury or the council. Sir Edward Coke secured the election of Valentine Knightly at Dunwich. *Dunwich MSS, H. M. C., Various Collections*, VII, 88.

the King and his subjects, without which whatsoever shall be resolved may be accounted a lame work." Indeed, Salisbury had advised and secured a short prorogation for the express purpose of holding these consultations. He foresaw, he wrote, that unless more time was allowed, "his Majesty's Privy Council, judges, his learned counsel, and officers of several qualities," who were like to bear the principal burden in parliament, would be so occupied when parliament opened with their courts of justice, offices in court, and many other distractions that they would hardly "be able to hold ordinary sessions, and to meet for these things which they already knew, besides those other matters which would arise *ex re nata.*" Without the prorogation officials "could not possibly assemble together to do that which they ought to arm themselves against prepared and studied arguments, and to preoccupate those jealousies which most men are like to apprehend." Especially in the question of the union with Scotland, Salisbury confessed, there were "many things so far out of my exact remembrance, as a weak man, that hap had nothing else to do but study the same, might quickly put me such a book case in a public meeting as I should be loath to reply without a further respite; which, if it fall out to be others' state as well as mine, time will be spent in argument which would be saved if some of those who cannot pass the talking cap might lay their heads together, and second one another constantly without distraction." [19] Thus Salisbury called upon the officials to plan and integrate their efforts.

Once the session opened, Salisbury kept in the closest touch with every turn of events and every shade of opinion in the commons. He was now a member of the lords, but he received constant reports of the doings of the commons from his followers there. His confidential agent, Thomas Wilson, sent him many reports written after the house had adjourned, recounting events and speeches in considerable detail. Wilson also supplied him with the principal arguments put forward in the commons so that Salisbury could answer his adversaries sentence for sentence

[19] Salisbury to the council, autumn of 1605, *Cal. Hatfield House MSS,* XVI, 425–26. In October, 1605, James wrote Salisbury and the council to devise some means to prevent the commons from debating the prerogative government in Wales and the adjacent English counties. "It will be both a great dishonour and inconvenience unto me, that the parliament should bandy that matter amongst themselves." James to Salisbury, October 7, 1605, *ibid.,* XVI, 325.

and point for point. "The grounds of the arguments *pro* and *contra* I will provide in a breefe against the conference," Wilson wrote in December of 1606. And when his own memory failed him, he consulted his friends, "to draw [them] to some particular recytall of some points" for Salisbury's benefit.[20]

Reports by Sir Edward Phelips, the speaker, a devoted servant of the crown and a man of unusual ability,[21] were of much greater importance; for they told of the temper of the house and contained advice (which was often followed) about what could and what could not be done in dealing with the commons. Phelips was a keen observer and constantly consulted with other members. When in February, 1606, Hare made an indiscreet attack upon purveyors, Phelips "sent to have conference with as manie as the shortnesse of the tyme would permitt"; and as a result he could assure Salisbury that the majority of members, though they opposed purveyance, regarded Hare's speech as unfortunate and utterly condemned his insolence. In June, 1607, Phelips advised Salisbury to permit the commons to read a petition on religion, although James had forbidden them to do so. "I fear me I shall not be able to keep the same from reading," Phelips wrote, "but then I strongly assure myself the same will be suppressed, wherein I humbly beseech your Lordship's direction; for I find the best affected to the King's service strongly bent for the reading thereof." In the same letter Phelips wrote that he had instructions from James to command the commons to drop certain complaints presented by the merchants trading with Spain. Phelips said he did not think the commons would act but they would wish to talk; and he therefore advised that "they might spend their breath in speech, so that they proceed no further." Again Phelips reported that he had "dealt and conferred with many" concerning a point in the act of union and found that if certain modifications were made, "the same would readily be assented unto"; otherwise he "conceived some doubt of the success thereof."[22] Reports such as these, together with others from Bacon

[20] Wilson to Salisbury, December 4, 1606, March 15, 1607, St. P. Domestic, 14/24:13; 14/26:87.

[21] Sir Julius Caesar praised him in 1609 as the best speaker since 1581. *Montacute House MSS, H. M. C., First Report*, 57.

[22] Phelips to Salisbury, February 14, 1606, June 16, 1607, printed in *Bowyer*, 38–39 note, 330–31 note, 339–40 note, 353 note. In December, 1610, James, who was in the country, wrote Salisbury to investigate the authors of certain speeches in parliament against the Scots. Lake, who was with the king, told him that if he "pressed Councillors to discover

and Sir Walter Cope, gave Salisbury an insight into the opinions of the house and enabled him to direct his party with a knowledge of what he was about.

With the situation clearly before him, Salisbury issued instructions to his subordinates, appointing to each the part he was to play in the house. Here again the speaker was of the greatest importance. His letters to Salisbury show clearly how detailed and constant were the instructions he received [23] and how closely they were followed. He quietly directed members to make appropriate motions at appropriate times. In April, 1607, he persuaded Sir Francis Barrington to make an important motion concerning the union, "from whose mouth," he wrote Salisbury, "I held the same not distasteful." He pressed forward certain measures and delayed others; he even introduced legislation as other leaders became fewer. He had a great share in securing an additional subsidy in 1606, when he first delivered an energetic message from the king (which Salisbury had written), begging the house to come to a decision, and then forced a division against the wishes of many members. In this division he cleverly worded the question in such a way that members hesitated to vote in the negative. In 1610 he appeared before the chamber with a message which he declared had come from the king but which was later shown to have come from Salisbury. [24]

He skillfully obstructed the actions of the commons when they ran counter to the wishes of the court. In February, 1606, the commons were debating a bill against purveyance. The government disliked the bill and was urging instead that the commons compound with the crown for relief. When the house was thrown off balance by Hare's violent speech against purveyance, Phelips "endevoured to prevente anie sodayne question to be

those by whom they received intelligence, they should be able to do him no more service in that kind." Lake added that Salisbury doubtless had "many secret informations and many observations of the disposition of the House" of which he did not write. Lake to Salisbury, December 3, 1610, Hatfield House MSS.

[23] Many of his letters to Salisbury are printed in the notes to *Bowyer*. When an important point concerning the union was about to come up in April, 1607, he wrote that "if there be aught that your Lordship shall think fit for his Majesty's service by me to be observed, I beseech your direction therein." In March, 1606, he "humblie desires, as the presente occasion shall require, leave in matter of circumstance to use my poor discretion, not varying from the matter whereunto I shalbe prescribed but therein and in all thinges else I subiect myself unto Direction." *Bowyer*, 255 note, 82 note.

[24] *Bowyer*, 255 and note, 289. In 1604 Phelips "hastened a Conference which was much pressed by the Lords." St. P. Domestic, 14/7:74. See pp. 272–73, 296–97 below.

stirred in the howse untill it were better mollifyed." A few days later the commons wished to protest to the lords, who had reprimanded Hare; "which then I prevented," Phelips wrote Salisbury, "under Cullor to move them to a Committee, to advise of the manner thereof." On February 24 the commons wished to pass their bill against purveyors, but Phelips reminded them it was a matter still in conference with the lords and "drewe them to a Committee to advise what was fitt in theire next conference to your Lordships to be propounded, and till then the Bill to staie. Which the Committee this day reporting what they had concluded of, the howse in the end were enflamed to call for theire proceeding in the Bill, and much pressed me also to make a question whether they would compounde or noe. To satisfie theire ymportunitie, which I could not avoyd, I made the question whether they would proceed with the Bill, but tooke occasion to forbeare the second question concerning the Composition, for that I fownd as the state of the howse then stood, it would be reiected. They then would have pressed me to have made a question uppon the engrossing of the Bill, which by some meanes I delayed to do, not withoute the distaste of some as I understand." [25]

Again on June 16, 1607, Phelips wrote that the house "suddenly and unlooked for" demanded that a petition on religion be read, "which I endeavoured to suppress by declaring his Majesty's pleasure that no further proceeding therein should be had; . . . where I was driven to oppose at several times 10 or 12 speakers, being not backed by the speech of anyone; and in the end not without the distaste of many who misliked that myself should so often oppose their proposition, drew them that a committee" should first seek precedents. [26]

In 1607 the speaker prevented action in the house by exaggerating a slight illness and absenting himself for ten days. James had appealed to the judges on a point in the bill of union, and the commons were considering in reply a declaration that the judges' decision was invalid. This James was most anxious to prevent. Salisbury wrote the king on March 15 that "Mr. Speaker had his direction to remember his Provisionall order in case it

[25] Phelips to Salisbury, February 14, 25, 1606, printed in *Bowyer,* 39 note, 51 note, 54 note.
[26] Phelips to Salisbury, June 16, 1607, *ibid.,* 330–31 note.

should be offered." Salisbury then discovered that the speaker was not well. Phelips wrote that "he could not be in ease to come to the howse, and yet would straine himselfe, if [his absence] . . . would hinder the King's service." Salisbury, with marked solicitation for the speaker's health, told him to stay away for two or three days. Three days later, March 18, Salisbury wrote the king that he "thought it the safer way to prevent all causes" and although "it is most trwe, that the speaker is not so ill as to be in any danger, . . . nevertheless . . . either his sicknes shall sufficiently or artificiently keepe him with in or if he doe come abroad, there shall be a provisionall stay" of any action by the commons. On Friday, March 20, Salisbury wrote that the speaker would be kept away at least until the following Monday and "against that he shall have his provisional directions." Meanwhile the commons were receiving, with great discontent, daily bulletins "that Mr. Speaker's Weakness continued"; but they were helpless without their presiding officer. The speaker did not return until Tuesday, March 24, when, upon another excuse, the house was adjourned till Thursday.[27] Thus business was held up for a week and a half. Phelips was as useful an agent as the government possessed in the commons.

Salisbury also made great use of Sir Francis Bacon in parliament, though consistently opposing his advancement outside the house. Bacon could defend government policy along broad and statesmanlike lines, his speeches were marvels of persuasiveness and eloquence, and he was especially skillful in putting a good face upon an awkward subject. His felicity of phrase was long remembered, and he was spoken of in 1626 as "the best Oratore that ever sat within these walls."[28] He held a unique position in the commons. Though counted as a "royalist," he did not exaggerate when he wrote the king in 1612 that he had never for one hour been out of credit with the lower house. His position there rested upon sheer ability and intellectual eminence. He was chosen to represent the lower house before the king and before the lords at conferences; he made reports to the house, he served on numerous committees, and spoke continually on all subjects.

[27] Salisbury to Lake, March 15, 18, 20, 1607, *ibid.*, 240–41 note. *C. J.,* I, 353.
[28] Speech of Sir Dudley Carleton, May 12, 1626, Add. MSS 22474, f. 144v. See also Rich, same date, f. 87v. In the parliament of 1614 Bacon was called "the Heir apparent of Eloquence." *C. J.,* I, 479.

Salisbury made use of him to draw up bills, to introduce legislation, and to push it through the commons. "I send your lordship a preamble for the Subsidy drawn, which was my morning's labour today," Bacon wrote in March, 1606. "This mould or frame if you like it not, I will be ready to cast it again *de novo,* if I may receive your hon. directions." About the same date Bacon wrote that on a certain day he planned to report the subsidy to the house. "But if," he added, "in regard of the King's servants' attendance [at court], your Lordship conceive doubt the house will not be well filled that day, I humbly pray your lordship I may receive your direction for the forebearing to enter into the matter that day. I doubt not success, if those attend that should." Bacon wrote James in 1606 that in all the important business of the last session "I was ever careful (and not without good success) sometimes to put forward that which was good, sometimes to keep back that which was not so good; so your Majesty was pleased to accept kindly of my services. . . . I was dilligent and reasonable happy to execute those directions, which I received either immediately from your own royal mouth, or from my Lord of Salisbury." [29]

Other subordinates received Salisbury's instructions concerning the house. The attorney, Sir Henry Hobart, and the recorder of London, Sir Henry Montagu, were each assigned a special part in supporting the subsidy in March of 1606. "I was at the Parliament yesterday," Hobart wrote Salisbury on March 13, "and on Tuesday before the Recorder, and pressed the proceeding. . . . They put it off till to-morrow Morning: and I have instructed Mr. Recorder as well with my part, which is not great, as he is instructed in his own. But rather then the least offense should be taken, I will be there to-morrow morning and despatch my part. . . . It is hard if the backwardness of the House should be turned upon my blame, that was most desirous to discharge it. Direct what you please and I will follow it presently." [30] Earlier in 1604 Sir John Stanhope wrote Salisbury concerning a bill which the crown desired the house to pass: "I am not forgetful of your speech with me touching your honourable friend's bill. I have

[29] Bacon to King James, May 31, 1612, Bacon to Salisbury, March 22, 27, 1606, Bacon to James, summer of 1606, *Spedding,* IV, 280; III, 275, 277, 294.

[30] Hobart to Salisbury, March 13, 1606, Hatfield House MSS. Bacon regarded Hobart as a very feeble parliamentarian. *Spedding,* IV, 381.

dealt with divers both yesterday and this day, giving them such reasons as I thought might best prepare their voices and strengthen them to persuade others. If you have thought of any particular motives to further the passage thereof, if you please to impart some of them, I doubt not but you shall see good use made of them. . . . My nephew Hollyer [John Holles] and my brother Rydgway will use their best endeavours, and Rydgway, who is strong with his Devonshire crew, assures me of a good party. If it be not afoot afore Tuesday or Wednesday I hope to be at the House." [31] Thus Salisbury instructed his lieutenants and sought to instill some organization into the royal group.

Yet Salisbury was forced to contend with many difficulties. Despite the unifying force of his leadership, the strength of the court group in this and even more in later parliaments was undermined by the disaffection of its own members. Bacon wrote that in James's first parliament the courtiers and king's servants, instead of being sure and zealous in the royal cause, as was their custom in the past, had turned fearful or popular. The earl of Shrewsbury in a letter to Edmondes in 1606 spoke of the house of commons, "where yourself was wont to be placed amongst the mutineers." In the same year Sir Henry Neville, who was at times considered for secretary, wrote to Winwood, "This Parliament hath done me no good, where not only Speeches and Actions, but Countenances, and Conversation with Men disliked, hath been observed. But in these Points I cannot betray my own Mind, speed as it will." "As a Parliament man," wrote Sir Robert Johnson, an officer of the ordnance, "I was not the second that excepted against the use of that Commission [for digging saltpeter]." An extreme case is that of John Hare who, though "holdinge a good and gaynfull place under his majestie" as clerk of the court of wards, attacked purveyance so violently in 1606 that he angered not only the king but also the majority of the commons. And it is evident from the diary of Robert Bowyer that though he felt himself "tied by special duty" to defend the proposals of the government, in sympathy he was strongly drawn toward the popular cause. [32]

[31] Stanhope to Cecil, 1604 (before August 20), *Cal. Hatfield House MSS*, XVI, 264. In the same session Sir Francis Hastings was asked by the king to sound various members upon the possibility of voting supply. *Ibid.,* XVI, 132.
[32] Bacon to King James, *Spedding,* IV, 367. Shrewsbury to Edmondes, February 12, 1606, *Court and Times, James I,* I, 52. Neville to Winwood, June 4, 1606, *Winwood,* II,

It is not difficult to explain the restlessness of the courtiers. They were not unmoved by the general causes of discontent, and the opposition of the commons was highly contagious. They had their special grievances. They were jealous of the Scots, who received so many marks of royal favor, and of Salisbury, who monopolized so many offices. They were becoming dissatisfied with the king and the nature of his appointments. Sir John Stanhope, the vice-chamberlain, for example, who was a privy councillor and a member of the commons, seldom came to court after James told him to his face that "he could not be quiet" till he had conferred his office upon a certain Scot. "Many such like Wrestlings there are with the old Servants, tho' most of them carry a certaine Shew of Contentment, and Conformity to the King's Pleasure." Young men of good family, such as John Holles, who might reasonably hope for employment, felt themselves neglected. At times, perhaps, would-be officials feigned opposition to attract attention at court and thus obtain promotion more quickly, but without doubt there was deep and bitter resentment among courtiers and officials at the way in which affairs were handled and patronage distributed by those in high places.[33]

To counteract this disruptive tendency and to win new support wherever possible Salisbury made use of the influence and pressure which the government could bring to bear upon individual members. Between 1604 and 1610 there was a great increase in lobbying, in seeking privately to persuade men to vote for certain measures, in bringing pressure to bear through friends or officials in interviews outside the house. The Venetian ambassador reported that the government prorogued parliament in 1604 "in order to have time to deal with the Nonconformist members, and to secure that they would do nothing in favour of their sect"; and again that James prorogued the commons in the

216. Sir Robert Johnson to Salisbury, October 31, 1606, Hatfield House MSS. Lord chancellor Ellesmere, "Speciall observations touching all the sessions of the last Parliament," Ellesmere MSS 2599, Huntington Library, San Marino, California. *Bowyer*, 38–40, xii–xiii.

Neville "ranged himself with those Patriots that were accounted of a contrary faction to the Courtiers." More to Winwood, October 29, 1611, *Buccleuch MSS, Montagu Papers, H. M. C.,* I, 102.

[33] The Venetian ambassador wrote that James on his accession added certain Scots to the council, "to the no small chagrin of the English ministers, not only because the supreme offices are bestowed upon Scots, but because every day posts are taken from the English and given to the Scotch." *Cal. St. P. Venetian, 1603–1607,* 33. Samuel Calvert to Winwood, April 6, 1605, *Winwood,* II, 57, a letter that illustrates the discontent of numerous officials. Alexander Thomson, "John Holles," *Journal of Modern History,* 8:145–72.

spring of 1610 because "he hoped to remove in the meantime some who were hostile to him or to win them over." Near the end of the autumn session in 1610, when the situation between king and commons was very near the breaking point, another short prorogation was contemplated during which "his Majestie's Party will deal every one with his Friend and Acquaintance of the House, to work them to some better Reason." In 1604 Stanhope wrote Salisbury, "I have dealt with divers both yesterday and this day, giving them such reasons as I thought might best prepare their voices and strengthen them to persuade others." Before the session of 1610 the king wrote Salisbury to take all possible measures that the commons "might sit down as well prepared for good and purged of evil as might be," and when a vote on the subsidy was approaching in November, he was to "prepare men as well as he could." The speaker, we know, had private interviews with members of the commons, nominally to seek their opinions, actually in many cases to impress his wishes upon them. When he wished to stop a certain bill in 1604, he asked "that such as were not satisfied, should first repair unto him, before the Bill were put to Question." Bacon disliked this development and advised the king in 1613 to avoid "brigues and canvasses" in his next parliament; but he also told James that means must be found by which the popular party could be dissolved or weakened or won and that members must be made to understand that it was not safe to combine against the king in parliament.[34]

Salisbury was lobbying when in 1610 he "had a private meeting . . . with a select number of the Lower House, in Hyde Park, which were Sir Henry Neville, Sir Maurice Berkeley, Sir Edwyn Sandys, Sir Hor. Crofts, Sir John Scot, Sir Francis Goodwin, and Mr. Alford" to "justify his courses." In November of the same year the king privately "called thirty of the Parliament House before him at Whitehall . . . to ask of them some Ques-

[34] *Cal. St. P. Venetian, 1603–1607,* 202; *1607–1610,* 516. More to Winwood, December 1, 1610, *Winwood,* III, 235–36. Stanhope to Cecil, 1604 (before August 20), *Cal. Hatfield House MSS,* XVI, 264. James to Salisbury, 1610, Hatfield House MSS. Lake to Salisbury, November 23, 1610, St. P. Domestic, 14/58:31. *C. J.,* I, 226. Bacon to James, *Spedding,* IV, 366–68, 372.

Tate had written in the reign of Elizabeth, "It is good now and then, secretlie to call to you some meane men of the House and use their advises, and to make bound unto you as many as you cane that be of any valewe or Credit by trulie reportinge them and defendinge theire honest reputacion with her Majestie." Harl. MSS 253, f. 35–36.

tions." These questions concerned supply and were an obvious attempt to browbeat members into abandoning their opposition. These episodes did not pass unnoticed in the commons. Although the conference with Salisbury had dealt only with impositions, "which was the chief subject of their discourse and the cause of their meeting," the members who took part "were all suspected as plotters of some new design." The meeting with the king caused a much greater uproar; and was followed by an order expressly forbidding its recurrence.[35] Lobbying did not meet with great success. Occasionally a member was enticed from opposition by material rewards. Henry Yelverton, nicknamed "the old Tribune of the house," had incurred the special wrath of the king; but he "made his Peace" before the session of 1610, defended impositions in that session, and became solicitor in 1613.[36] Generally speaking, however, Bacon was probably correct in saying that lobbying merely increased opposition.

In dealing with officials and others who opposed the government Salisbury went no further than warnings and persuasion. In later parliaments more strenuous methods were adopted; but Salisbury knew the value of moderation and relied upon quiet insinuations that opposition meant loss of favor at court and an end to hopes of advancement. After the dissolution in 1610 James was eager to punish certain members, but Salisbury and the council persuaded him not to do so. Nevertheless, both Salisbury and Northampton urged James to show his displeasure to those who opposed him in the commons. "Ye would often tell me," he wrote Salisbury, "that if the Lower House men that most offended looked not to be as welcome to me the next day as the honestest man would be, they durst not presume to do as they did, praising that virtue in the late Queen that she would be loath ever to be reconciled in her countenance to them who had willingly offended her." James followed this counsel. He wrote Sal-

[35] Carleton to Edmondes, July 13, 1610, *Court and Times, James I,* I, 123. More to Winwood, December 1, 1610, *Winwood,* III, 235. The order of the commons read: "That no member of this House do hereafter presume or take upon him as a private man or otherwise to deliver his opinion or the reason of his opinion by way of conference or otherwise touching any matter depending in consultation in this House either to the King's Majesty or any of the Lords [of the council], without the assent, direction, or special order of the House in that behalf." November 22, 1610, Cott. MSS Titus F IV, f. 131. See also *Rutland MSS, H. M. C.,* I, 424–25; *Parl. Debates in 1610,* 137 note.

[36] *Bowyer,* 123 note, 134 note, 281–82; Chamberlain to Winwood, February 13, 1610, *Winwood,* III, 117; *Archaeologia,* XV, 27–52; article in *D. N. B.* on Yelverton; *Spedding,* IV, 365, 370.

isbury in 1610, "I desire to have a roll sent me . . . of all my servants' names that sat against me for the poor fifteenth, for I cannot know them by that scent." Bacon wrote in 1613 that the king in dealing with members who had opposed him "carried himself in that princely temper towards them, as not to persecute or disgrace them, nor yet to use or advance them." [37] There are letters to Salisbury and the king from men who had acted with the opposition, begging that their conduct be forgotten or explaining that in spite of appearances it had been intended to serve the purposes of the government. When Neville intimated to Suffolk in 1614 that he hoped his efforts as an undertaker might bring him the secretaryship, Suffolk replied that "he and the rest should amend the faults they made the last parliament before the king would set marks of favor upon them." [38]

While the royal group was torn by dissension, the popular party was growing in strength, until in 1610 it presented a united and powerful majority, which became the despair of Salisbury and the king. It possessed leaders and debaters who could hold their own with any comer, not only in the house, but in the conference chamber as well. Of these Sir Edwin Sandys was easily the chief. His wisdom and moderation, his powers of debate and wide experience of affairs marked him as the most outstanding of all who opposed the king. He led the house in attacking purveyance in 1606, the union with Scotland in 1607, and impositions in 1610. Other able leaders were not lacking: Wing-

[37] James to Salisbury, December 3, 1607, 1610, Hatfield House MSS. *Spedding,* IV, 370.

[38] Sir Maurice Berkeley to the council, 1606; Sir R. Drury to Salisbury, 1606; Sir Francis Hastings to Salisbury, December 30, 1606; Sir Christopher Pigott to the king, February, 1607; Sir Thomas Heneage to the king, 1605, Hatfield House MSS. Sir R. Drury explained that it was his vote which carried the subsidy in 1606, when the government won by a single vote. Sir Thomas Heneage complained that he was most unjustly accused of offending in the commons. He wrote: "Neither heretofore my best speech with my most willing burden for you could be thought worthy thanks, nor now my silence can stand without blame. Much more happy be they that by popular speeches can purchase credit in the world, and by partial reports procure favor from your Honour. . . . I mean [not] to speak suddenly in such cases as by some experience, I can tell, you may be better served in with silence. As for your Majesty's sharpest speeches, I acknowledge with all humbleness it becomes me to bear them; though it be reputed to others a matter of praise, that was reckoned to me in way of reproach."

A letter, probably from Sir Herbert Croft, explains that the author had displeased the king in the parliament of 1604–10 by urging "perhaps over vehemently" that the council of Wales should cease to have jurisdiction over neighboring English shires. But he had then begged James's forgiveness and in the parliament of 1614 "so much strove to effect his Majesty's purposes . . . as that he was cried downe for a time server and a turne coate." Harl. MSS 1581, f. 356–57. Suffolk to Somerset, end of March, 1614, Cott. MSS Titus F IV, f. 340.

field, Owen, Yelverton, Bond, Hyde, Brooke. Some, such as Wentworth and Fuller, though powerful speakers, were too hot-headed to carry great weight. Nor was the popular party without some organization. In the early sessions this is not apparent, and opposition seems unpremeditated and individual, leadership spontaneous and unplanned. But the sessions of 1610 saw a change. Here for the first time the opposition had a full opportunity to lay its case before the king, and here for the first time we see some party organization. Lord Ellesmere, shortly after 1610, wrote a paper denouncing the commons for their many encroachments upon the prerogative. After recounting their sins, he continued: "But some not contented with that which was so treated of in publicke, dyd single theym from the others, and kepte secrette and privye Conventicles and Conferences, wherein they devised and sett down speciall plottes, for the Carryinge of business in the house, accordinge to theyr owne humour and dryfte, and that in the waightiest and moost Important Causes, as namely touching the great and Royal Contracte which was then intended and in handelinge. And for the stayinge of grantinge any subsidyes and fyfteenes. To which purpose yt was devised that Syxe of them who had great countenance and dyd beare great swaye in the house, shoulde be prepared to speake at large agaynst the grantinge of any subsidy at all, and shoulde sett forth all the arguments and reasons that might be obiected or pretended agaynst yt: And that after those theyr speeches the residue shoulde be silent, and not to speake any thinge therein at all, untille the bylle shoulde be put to the question, and then to overthrowe yt wyth a generall, No." Bacon wrote that the opposition in 1610 arose not only *ex puris naturalibus* but also "out of party"; he spoke of the way in which members "combined and made parties in Parliament." And he also wrote of the various elements "which made the popular party last Parliament." [39] It is thus quite clear that organization was appearing in both camps.

The parliaments of Elizabeth and the early Stuarts saw for the first time the faint foreshadowings of later political parties;

[39] Ellesmere MSS 2599, Huntington Library. *Spedding*, IV, 367, 368, 370. The French ambassador wrote in 1607 that certain things in the house "semblent s'attribuer a ceux qui parlent le moins, faisant parler les autes." January 2, 1607, Paris Trans., 3/41. Two letters in the Hatfield MSS show members of the opposition planning joint action in the house: Sir Herbert Croft to Sir Maurice Berkeley; Sir Robert Wingfield to Sir Maurice Berkeley

and it is worth while to inquire at this point how far the conception of political parties was advanced by the first parliament of James. It was certainly making progress. Salisbury's organization of the court group was more in line with party development than anything to be found under the Tudors. He was, in fact, laying foundations that might have led to rapid party organization. But his death was followed by a period without competent leadership, and leadership was absolutely essential. Party organization among the opposition was also clearer than before. In the parliaments to come its growth was more steady and continuous than that of the court and more in line with the new procedures that were transforming methods of doing business in the commons. Salisbury's organization was the better of the two, but the tables were turned in later sessions.

But in referring to early Stuart times the word "party" is misleading. These were not parties in the modern sense, but ill-defined groups, with little organization at best, bound together largely by common approval or disapproval of certain policies, and only gradually taking shape along the main dividing line of offering support or opposition to the majority of royal measures. Members voted with the king on one issue and against him on another, and often a measure found strange bedfellows among its supporters. There was also, as we have seen, much discontent and disaffection among the courtiers, a disaffection which, in my opinion, was a fundamental cause of the difficulties of the early Stuarts in dealing with their parliaments. It is thus absurd to apply the jargon of modern political organization to these embryonic beginnings.

The terms "court" and "country" were coming to be used. Bacon spoke of "courtiers" in this first Stuart parliament and wrote the king that of a certain matter "both court and country took knowledge." He added that Salisbury "had a kind of party in both houses"; and another member spoke of "his Majesty's party" in the session of 1610. But members of this group were seldom referred to definitely as the "court." More frequently they

and Sir Herbert Croft, 1606. Croft wrote Berkeley warning him that he would be absent on a certain day, "lest you might by occasion in expecting me let slip any opportunity of setting forward so important a cause." He was confident "that those others that purpose to assist you will give you sufficient strength" and promised that "when I may be there I will not fail to put my shoulder to the burden." The occasion of this letter may well have been a move against the jurisdiction of the council of Wales.

were called the king's "counsellours and servants," or "his servants and well-wishers," or merely "the King's servants." At times they were referred to even more vaguely. In 1604 James spoke of his followers in the house as "the Parliament men." Robert Bowyer, the diarist of 1606–07, divided the house into those who "studied to please" and those who spoke and voted "out of conscience." [40] In the same way the members of the country group were called "the popular party," "the populars," "the tribunes of the people," or "the patriots." Party names as well as party lines were shifting and indistinct, and the word "party" meant a group or clique or faction. It might be most temporary in nature. Ridgeway assured Stanhope in 1604 "of a good party" to pass a single measure. [41]

Salisbury had other difficulties besides those we have been mentioning. As a peer he found himself cut off from addressing the commons in their own house. He was thus forced, if he wished to speak to at least some portion of the lower chamber, to summon them to meet the lords in conference. In these conferences Salisbury, nominally as a member of the committee from the lords, but in reality as the chief minister of the crown, to whom was entrusted the management of parliament, laid the needs and desires of the king before the commons. He thus continued his Elizabethan role, though under some disadvantage, and argued and debated in the conference chamber very much as if he were still a member of the lower house.

In thus addressing the commons Salisbury spoke with the skill of an old parliament man and with the ease of a graceful and

[40] Bacon to Salisbury, March 22, 1606, Bacon to James, summer of 1607, Bacon's notes, 1613, *Spedding*, III, 275, 294; IV, 367. James to the privy council, December 7, 1610, Hatfield House MSS. Lake to Salisbury, November 23, 1610, St. P. Domestic, 14/58:31. *C.J.*, I, 197. James to Cecil, October 7, 1604, *Cal. Hatfield House MSS*, XVI, 326. *Bowyer*, 84.

An "anonymous libel" against Salisbury in 1610 divided the house into three groups: "honest wise men," "crafty knaves," and "ignorant fools." The first group was made up of those who opposed Salisbury; the second group consisted of "all his friends and followers"; while the third group was composed of those whom the knaves misled "by their witty and cunning speeches." ——— to Lord Haddington, November 4, 1610, Hatfield House MSS.

[41] *Spedding*, IV, 367; St. P. Domestic, 14/21:17; 14/62:44; *Bowyer*, 46, 123 note; *Buccleuch MSS, Montagu Papers, H. M. C.*, I, 102. Stanhope to Cecil (before August 20, 1604), *Cal. Hatfield House MSS*, XVI, 264.

The terms "court" and "country" were in more general use by 1625, though other names appear — "the Duke's privados," "the Duke's friends," "king's servants," and "royalists." *Negotium Posterorum*, I, 75, 78, 103, 110, 118–19; II, 23, 26, 48, 82, 84, 94, 104, 106. *Commons Debates in 1625*, 16, 33, 156. *Cal. St. P. Venetian, 1625–1626*, 63.

natural eloquence. He was a brilliant extemporaneous speaker, "admirable to all men in eloquence upon the sodaine." Dudley Carleton wrote of a conference in 1610, to which Salisbury "came upon some disadvantage, because our men [the commons] were prepared, but did so well acquit him self *ex re natâ,* and so clearly upon all the particularities of the contract, that he gave very extraordinary contentment." Even when demanding supply, "the Grounds and Strength of his Arguments" were "energeticall" and his speech "persuasive." [42] And to eloquence he added a moderation and a spirit of conciliation very rare in James's councillors. Thus Salisbury made the most of his opportunities.

In conferences Salisbury, or other councillor-peers acting under his direction, invariably took the initiative. Frequently it was Salisbury himself who made the motion in the lords suggesting that a conference be held. When the conference took place and the commons' committee appeared, uncovered and standing, before the seated lords, it was Salisbury who explained the policies of the government or pointed out the difficulties in measures suggested by the lower house. Perhaps he would urge the ever-present subject of the king's financial needs. Or perhaps he was forced to check the commons in their desire to legislate against purveyance and to say bluntly that "the King's Necessity could not admit, that this Bill should pass." Perhaps the commons came armed with arguments against union with Scotland, and Salisbury, finding they were getting the best of the debate, brought the conference to an end. Or perhaps for once the two houses were agreed in framing stricter laws against the Catholics. In all cases Salisbury took the lead, as a prime minister might do today in defending government policy before an opposition party. He was, of course, supported by other councillors from the lords' committee. In a conference in 1606, for example, he was followed by the lord admiral, the lord treasurer, the earl of Northampton, and Lord Knollys.[43] Such an array reminds one of the commons in the days of Elizabeth. And, indeed, the government wished to duplicate that earlier time in bringing the force of a good part of the council to bear upon the members of the house of com-

---

[42] *Camden Miscellany,* X, 106. Carleton to Edmondes, July 17, 1610, *Court and Times, James I,* I, 129. Beaulieu to Trumbull, February 23, 1610, *Winwood,* III, 123.
[43] *L. J.,* II, 266, 550 and *passim.* March 4, 1606, *C. J.,* I, 277. March 14, 1607, *Bowyer,* 239–40. February 20, 1606, *C. J.,* I, 271.

mons. Dominated by Salisbury and the council, conferences ceased to be meetings of committees of both houses to adjust disagreements or to arrange for joint action and became meetings of the commons with the chief ministers of the crown, where the needs of the king were pressed forward with all the weight and influence which the lords, the council, and the crown itself could jointly summon.

In the sessions of 1610 Salisbury relied upon conferences more completely than ever. Realizing the grave necessity of a parliamentary grant, and maintaining a splendid confidence in his own powers of persuading the commons, Salisbury took the whole burden of negotiation upon his own shoulders and conducted the entire campaign from the lords. The sessions became one long series of conferences. Between conferences the commons debated the propositions of the crown, and Salisbury, after reporting the latest conference to the lords, hastened to the king to plan in secret what the next move should be. This, in turn, was related by Salisbury to the lords and was followed by further conferences with the commons. As a house the lords counted but little. Step by step Salisbury led on the negotiations till he had "brought all the great hounds to a perfect tune," and the Great Contract was agreed upon in the spring. When in the fall he saw his scheme come to nothing and all his labor wasted, he continued to urge, in fresh conferences, that the commons grant supply in the ordinary way.

But Salisbury's attempt to control the commons through conferences was a failure. The story of that failure is told in another connection, since it is a matter of the growth of rules of procedure.[44] But it may be said, in a word, that the commons, fearing and disliking conferences, so restricted the authority of their committees sent to confer that all decisions had to be referred back to the commons for debate and determination. Against this development Salisbury protested in vain.

Salisbury, moreover, was at another disadvantage. He was responsible for parliamentary affairs. Yet he was constantly embarrassed and handicapped by the interference and meddling of the king. James demanded long reports from Salisbury and sent

[44] See pp. 225–36.

him constant instructions as to what should be done in the house. In 1604 Salisbury was ordered to see that a certain bill was taken up in committee. In 1606 he was given instructions concerning the form which the subsidy grant should take. In more than one of his speeches in 1610, for which Bacon judged him so harshly, Salisbury appeared before parliament having just returned from the king with instructions and commands. Thus Salisbury was not master of the policies which he advocated in parliament, nor could he control the way in which these policies were presented to the commons. Even in the Great Contract, which was a project peculiarly his own, he was not free from the interference of the king, against which the council as a whole protested in 1608.[45]

During the crisis that arose in the autumn session of 1610, James's normal irritation with the commons turned to bitter hostility and his interference reached a stage that rendered Salisbury's task impossible. Advice was thrown to the winds and events moved swiftly toward an angry dissolution. James had been growing more and more incensed with the commons since the session began in October. He wrote Salisbury that he had now had patience with parliament for some seven years and had received more insults and ignominies than it became a prince to endure. He had followed Salisbury's advice in having patience, but he could not have "assenine patience." "No house save the house of Hell" would treat him as the commons were doing. About the middle of November he left London for Royston, where he remained during the rest of the session, thus greatly increasing Salisbury's difficulties; and refused all entreaties to return to London for consultation on parliamentary affairs. Nothing remained to be decided, he said, save the form the dissolution should take. "Your greatest error hath been," he wrote Salisbury, "that ye ever expected to draw honey out of gall, being a little blinded with the self-love of your own counsel in holding together of this Parliament, whereof all men were despaired as I have oft told you, but yourself alone." James also found fault with the moderate tone taken by his councillors in the house, a

[45] Lake to Salisbury, May 4, 1606, Hatfield House MSS. Sir George Home to Cecil, May 2, 1604, *Cal. Hatfield House MSS,* XVI, 84. Lord Dirleton to Salisbury, February 10, 1606, St. P. Domestic, 14/18:77. Lake to Salisbury, October 21, 1608, *ibid.,* 14/37:23.

moderation that Salisbury had imposed. With the sovereign in this frame of mind Salisbury could do nothing.[46]

Nevertheless, Salisbury struggled desperately, on the one hand to moderate the attitude of the king, and on the other to obtain concessions from the commons sufficient to prevent a rupture. In a meeting of the council about the middle of November he advised against a dissolution, and for the moment he had his way. When the possibility arose that the commons might agree to one portion of the Contract, he rushed details to James at Royston. He managed to avoid a suggestion of the king to force a vote on supply in the commons whether it had any hope of passage or not. He protested, and here he was successful, against James's wish to punish certain members for their speeches. He adjourned parliament for five days (November 24 to 29) to silence angry speeches and advised a further adjournment from November 29 to allow passions to subside and permit time for reflection on both sides. But James ordered a prorogation, which ended the hope of compromise and looked toward the dissolution that took place in January, 1611.[47]

There was a sinister element in James's decision. He had been particularly irritated by speeches in the commons against the Scots. Sir Thomas Lake, who was with him at Royston, discovered, as he wrote Salisbury, "that all this heat expressed in my last two letters is moved by Sir Robert Carr; that your Lordship has been very maliciously dealt with by some of the Lower House, he being the instrument; that the intent of pressing your Lordship and my Lords to discover these names [of members who had spoken against the Scots] and matter is urged by him out of a purpose to cast some distaste between your Lordships and the King." [48] Thus James allowed himself to be swayed not only by

[46] Lake to Salisbury, November 24, 25, 26, 27, 28, 1610, St. P. Domestic, 14/58:32, 35, 36, 38, 40, 41. James to Salisbury, December 6, James to the council, December 7, 1610, Hatfield House MSS. Lake to Salisbury, Northampton, Suffolk, and Worcester, November 21, 1610, St. P. Domestic, 14/58:26. This paragraph and the two that follow summarize material in an article of mine, "Summoning and Dissolving Parliament, 1603–25: The Council's Advice to James I," *American Historical Review*, 45:281–84 (January, 1940).

[47] Lake to Salisbury, Northampton, Suffolk, and Worcester, November 21, 23, Lake to Salisbury, November 23, 24, 25, 26, 27, 28, December 2, 6, 1610, St. P. Domestic, 14/58:26, 30, 31, 32, 35, 38, 40, 41, 54, 62. Salisbury to King James, December 3, Lake to Salisbury, December 3, 4, King James to the council, December 7, 1610, Hatfield House MSS. Earl of Pembroke to Edmondes, January 17, 1611, Stowe MSS 171, f. 358.

[48] Lake to Salisbury, December 4, James to Salisbury, December 6, 1610, Hatfield House MSS. Bacon believed that opposition in this session was due in part to intrigues among the

his irritation with the commons but by the secret persuasions of a Scottish favorite who saw his own interests endangered. Carr appears to have had his own agents in the commons and may even have urged them to bring up delicate points in the hope of exasperating the king.

It was not in the nature of things that Salisbury should either demand or obtain from James that freedom of action which might perhaps have brought better results in the commons. His influence over the king was great, much greater than that of any other member of the council, and certain of his contemporaries believed that it was complete. His power was so great, wrote the Venetian ambassador in 1607, "that he may truly be called the King." And the Spanish council believed that "the King of England is wholly governed by Salisburie." [49] But such was not the case. Salisbury was never more than the first servant of his royal master. And James, though easily influenced, was not to be controlled. His very weakness of character rendered this impossible, for he was easily offended and easily turned aside by advice that appealed to his emotions. Salisbury was keenly aware that his pre-eminent position depended entirely upon the continued favor of the king, and he therefore played upon James's vanity, encouraged him to trust to his little beagle for money,[50] frowned upon possible rivals, and, when necessary, bent to the royal will against his better judgment. In 1612 Sir Walter Cope reminded the king that Salisbury had learned two lessons under him, "as well to obey as to command; and to conclude with Seneca, *Sapiens non se mutat, sed aptat*." [51]

The failure of Salisbury to control the house [52] was more than

commons by important persons. *Spedding*, IV, 366, 368, 371; V, 179. Bacon was thinking of Salisbury when he wrote: "I cannot excuse him that is gone of an artificial animating of the Negative." But this seems impossible. Carr was a far more likely person for such intrigues.

[49] *Cal. St. P. Venetian, 1603–1607*, 515. Sir Charles Cornwallis to Salisbury, November or December, 1606, *Winwood*, II, 275.

[50] James complained to Salisbury in 1610 "that in his letters he had given him hope" of better results than were attained. Lake to Salisbury, April 30, 1610, Hatfield House MSS. More wrote Winwood that the difficulties of the sessions of 1610 were greatly affecting Salisbury's spirits "because (as some suppose) his Lordship may have given the King hope of some real Assistance to be granted, without any great materiall Retribution from his Majesty's part." December 1, 1610, *Winwood*, III, 235.

[51] Sir Walter Cope, *An Apology for the Late Lord Treasurer Sir Robert Cecill, Earl of Salisbury*, in *Collectanea Curiosa* (2 vols., Oxford, 1781), I, 130.

[52] Salisbury wrote the king, "I have seen this Parliament at an end, whereof the many vexations have so overtaken one another, as I know not to what to resemble them so well as to the plagues of Job." Salisbury to Lake, December 9, 1610, Hatfield House MSS.

the failure of a single minister. It was the failure of a system. He had applied Tudor methods of dealing with the commons and had pushed those methods about as far as they could be pushed. He had sought to find new ways of dealing with an increased opposition. But his attempts at lobbying and his use of conferences proved ineffectual, and the king himself hindered rather than helped. The Elizabethan system, without Elizabeth, had broken down and was not to be restored. In attempting to maintain it Salisbury was drawing water in a sieve. He presents the tragic picture of a statesman striving to continue outworn practices and fighting to maintain a political system which the majority of his fellow countrymen would no longer tolerate.

5

The Parliaments of 1614 and 1621

Salisbury had made mistakes in dealing with the commons, but his death left a void that could not easily be filled. Changes and adjustments were inevitable. Yet surely it was James's primary duty to find a successor who could handle with skill and ability the parliamentary business of the crown. James, however, allowed matters to drift and mismanaged appointments so badly that disaster was all but inevitable in the parliament of 1614. That parliament was a period of confusion, intrigue, and conflicting counsels at court, which gave ample scope to treacherous and subversive elements and quickly ended the organization and leadership that Salisbury had given to the court party in the commons.

There was a revulsion of feeling both at court and in parliament against the methods Salisbury had employed. At court this came from men who disliked and envied him and wished to be his successors in power. They could easily point out that his methods had not brought the desired results; and they suggested various alternatives. Thus different lines of policy were open to the crown. James found it difficult to make up his mind and floundered amid conflicting advice. In the commons, unfortunately, resentment at Salisbury's methods was violently increased by the furor over undertaking. The further one investigates this episode the more disastrous it appears. It rendered all forms of governmental interference doubly suspect and made the creation of a royal faction, along the lines laid down by Salisbury, utterly impossible.

Certain alterations were inevitable in the government's approach to the problem of parliamentary management, for many of Salisbury's tactics were peculiarly his own and were the result of his unique position in the state. There was certainly no other peer in 1612 who could hope to conduct the crown's parliamentary business from the lords as Salisbury had done. The commons, moreover, had objected to this device, and James was strongly urged to deal with them through someone of their own number.[1] There was obvious need for an influential councillor in the commons who could speak there with authority and play the part that Salisbury had played in the last parliaments of Elizabeth. This meant in practice that the man selected must be the new secretary of state, for that was the one office, as Salisbury had developed it, which combined great importance in administration with responsibility for the crown's parliamentary interests. "The last parliament in comparison with others in the late Queen's reign," Carleton wrote early in 1614, "sheweth how necessary it is for his Majesty's service to have persons of place and authority in the lower house and chiefly a secretary."[2] Candidates for the secretaryship were therefore considered partly with an eye to their quality as parliamentarians.

James made a great blunder, however, in leaving the office vacant for too long a time, about two years. He apparently wished, now that the pilot had been removed by death, to take the helm himself and to become his own secretary, relying on Somerset for advice and on Lake for clerical assistance. But he could not force himself to go through with the necessary drudgery, and after an early show of energy he neglected the business placed before him. The council was soon begging that a new secretary be named.[3] James's delay in making the appointment intensified and embittered the usual competition for a place of importance. There were many candidates: Sir Francis Bacon, Sir Charles Cornwallis, Sir Thomas Edmondes, Sir Ralph Winwood, Sir Henry Neville, Sir Henry Wotton, Sir John Holles, Sir William Waad, and Sir John Herbert. Competition became fast and furious. Factions and animosities were increased. And as a result the new secretary, whoever he might be, would certainly be surrounded after his appointment by such jealousy and envy that

[1] *Spedding*, IV, 368. Neville advised the king "to make his propositions unto the commons by himself, or by his ministers and servants that are of their own body, and not by mediation of the Lords, for the commons will be rather willing to make oblation of their affections themselves unto his Majesty, than that any other should do it, and intercept both the merit and the thanks for them." He also told James that in summoning members of the commons to have audience with him he should not name the individuals but should leave that to the house. St. P. Domestic, 14/74:44.

[2] Carleton to Winwood(?), April 2, 1614, St. P. Venice Correspondence, 99/15.

[3] Chamberlain to Carleton, January 28, 1612, *Court and Times, James I,* I, 157. Chamberlain to Winwood, January 9, 1613, *Winwood,* III, 421.

his chances of organizing the king's supporters in the commons would be seriously impaired.[4]

The most interesting of these candidates, the one of infinitely greatest powers and potentialities, was Bacon. He represented most strongly the reaction against Salisbury's methods, and he illustrates the choice of policy lying before the king. His legal advancement now seemed assured, but in a letter to James in 1612 after Salisbury's death he had offered himself as a candidate for the office of secretary. "If your Majesty find any aptness in me . . . whereby you may think it fit for your service to remove me to business of state, . . . I will be ready as a chessman to be wherever your Majesty's royal hand shall set me." As the representative of the king in parliament, Bacon would have been the ideal secretary. We have seen his importance in James's first parliament, in which he rendered valuable service to the crown while retaining the esteem of his fellow members. "No man can say," he wrote James, "but I was a perfect and peremptory royalist, yet every man makes me believe that I was never one hour out of credit with the lower house."[5] Much better than anyone else in politics in 1614 he could have pushed the interests of the crown without arousing the hostility of the commons.

Had he been made secretary and admitted to a fuller share of the royal confidence, he might possibly have done much more than this. His political philosophy was essentially Tudor in character, augmented by the sweep of his own rich imagination, and combined a high conception of the king's position and powers with quiet but constant guidance of parliamentary affairs. He might have instructed James to deal with his parliaments in a more statesmanlike as well as a more truly regal fashion. Bacon envisaged the king as the potent head of the state, his powers buttressed by high prerogative, with whom the commons would loyally and gratefully cooperate in building a better society. Grievances should be dealt with justly as they arose, and settled on their merits; but this should be done without calling the prerogative into question or disturbing the partnership of crown and commons, in which the king pointed the way to be followed by a sympathetic and responsive people.

[4] On the contest for the secretaryship, see also Evans, *The Principal Secretary of State*, 65-71 and *Gardiner*, II, 145-48.
[5] Bacon to the king (two letters), 1612, *Spedding*, IV, 280, 282.

With these things in mind, Bacon regarded Salisbury's attempt of 1610 to strike a bargain with the opposition and to create a royal faction in the commons as a colossal and fatal blunder. The Great Contract had introduced the sordid spirit of trade into the relations of crown and commons and had exposed the extreme penury of the king, which became the subject of endless debate and showed the opposition its strength. James must, above all, deal with parliament not as a merchant but as a king, "in a more familiar, but yet a more princely manner." He must not put his favors and graces up for sale. In certain cases, such as the court of wards, events had shown that in 1610 James had set his price too high, which had brought the whole bargain into disrepute. It was infinitely more important for the king to cultivate good relations with the commons than to strive for temporary results; infinitely better to sacrifice immediate subsidies and proceed gradually to a better understanding with the commons. "Until your Majesty have tuned your instrument you will have no harmony. I, for my part, think it a thing inestimable to your Majesty's safety and service, that you once part with your Parliament with love and reverence." Parliament should not be told that it was called for money even though that were the case; some other reason, such as the improvement of trade or the planting of Ireland, should be placed in the foreground, so that members would have something to talk about besides the poverty of the king. Let them imagine that the crown was not wholly dependent upon them to restore its fortunes; and intimate that the king needed money merely because other means could not be harvested in a day. Thus parliament could be dealt with "upon terms of majesty and not of necessity." [6] Nor should the king attempt to form a party or canvass members in seeking support for particular measures. Let "there be no brigues nor canvasses, whereof I hear too much; for certainly howsoever men may seek to value their service in that

[6] After the failure of the 1614 parliament Bacon repeated this advice in even stronger terms. He wrote James in 1615 that when parliament met again the government should not mention money at all. The subject was sure to arise in the natural course of debate. But if it did not do so, the government should remain silent. The king must give the impression that he could subsist on his own resources. He must have money on hand during the session, even though he sold land or created barons to obtain it. No sprigs of the prerogative should be offered to the commons. No leniency in legal matters should be shown immediately before the parliament, "as if he should keep a kind of diet against a Parliament. . . . For these things do but savour of weakness, and whatsoever showeth fear or need of a Parliament hurteth." *Spedding*, V, 183–91.

kind, it will but increase animosities and oppositions." Bacon looked on parliament as a whole, as Elizabeth had done, and could see no hope in a small group of men pledged to support the king. Nothing illustrates better than this the embryonic state in which political parties still remained.

But if the king was not to form a party in the commons, he should prevent the formation of one against him and should seek to win the approval of the entire chamber. Tudor management, modified to suit the times, should continue. Bacon believed that the party of opposition of 1610 was now broken up. That opposition "as much as was not *ex puris naturalibus* but out of party, I conceive to be now much weaker than it was, and that party almost dissolved. Yelverton is won; Sandes is fallen off; Crew and Hyde stand to be serjeants; Brocke is dead; Nevell hath hopes; Barkeley I think will be respective; Martin hath money in his purse; Dudley Digges and Holys are yours. Besides, they cannot but find more and more the vanity of that popular course," especially as James had refused to advance them. Some course should be taken in the next parliament "for the winning or bridling of the Lawyers . . . that they may furder the King's causes, or at least fear to oppose them." Other groups, citizens and burgesses, justices of the peace and country gentlemen, should be persuaded to support the business of the crown. Councillors, speaker, bureaucrats, "courtiers and K's servants" should be sure and zealous for the king, and not, as in the last parliament, fearful or popular. The king should consider "what course may be taken with that combined body, being extracted of all the former sorts, which made the popular party the last Parliament, for the severing of them, intimidating of them, or holding them in hopes, or the like, whereby they may be dissolved, or weakened, or won." Members of "gravity, discretion, temper, and ability to persuade" should be quietly brought into the house and those who were violent and turbulent should be excluded, but this must be done "*bonis artibus,* without labouring or packing." For this purpose the boroughs controlled by the duchies of Cornwall and Lancaster, the Cinque Ports, "and other boroughs at the devotion of divers of the K's counsellors" should be used. Let parliament know that the king had a watchful eye over its proceedings "to make men perceive that it is not safe [to] combine and make parties in Parliament." And all this was to be done without show or scandal.

Further precautions could also be taken. James should "ingage and assure the Judges *in omnem eventum,* for any points of law or right that may be foreseen as likely to come in question in Parliament." Something should be done to bury the issue of impositions. Discussion of grievances should be held back if possible until the commons were at work on other measures brought forward by the crown; and for this purpose plausible and acceptable laws should be prepared and offered to the house. The government should consider whether it was wise to conduct business through conferences with the lords as Salisbury had done. And parliament should be given to understand that its sittings were not to be long.[7]

Such was Bacon's parliamentary philosophy as seen in his private notes and letters to the king. It contained worldly wisdom. It combined princely reticence and moderation with unprovocative manipulation. It suggested a long-time view and offered a dignified avenue of retreat in case of temporary failure. It was Tudor policy at its best molded to meet an increasing opposition. It relied, no doubt, too much upon manipulation, which, as events proved, could not go unnoticed. It did not give members credit for very good memories, and assumed that their opposition was more superficial than was the case. But its chief defect was that James could not play the part assigned to him. He was not cast in the Tudor mold.

We have no evidence that James replied to Bacon's suggestion that he become secretary; it seems to have been scarcely considered. Perhaps Salisbury's distrust of Bacon was still present in James's mind. Diplomacy and administration, rather than the law, for which James had no great liking, were the usual stepping stones to the secretaryship; and when Bacon was made a councillor in 1616, many of the lords disliked seeing the attorney rise from the position of legal assistant to that of full membership at the board.[8] Northampton, whose influence had now greatly increased, was no friend of Bacon. At any rate, the appointment was not made; and one of the most interesting possibilities of the reign remains a subject of mere speculation.

[7] *Spedding,* IV, 313, 365–78.
[8] Chamberlain to Carleton, June 8, 1616, *Court and Times, James I,* I, 411.

Another competitor is also of interest. Sir Henry Neville was distinctly a popular candidate. Though closely connected with the court, he had, as we have seen, supported the popular cause in James's first parliament. In a private meeting in 1610 between James and some thirty members of the house Neville had clearly and emphatically stated the popular point of view. He had lived on terms of intimacy with the leaders of the opposition and knew "their inwardest thought." This sympathy and close acquaintance with the opposition would certainly have won him a following in the house, and he was as good a parliamentarian as the majority of councillors. Parliament men were delighted to find that he was being considered and flocked about him in London. Even before Salisbury's death there had been a rumor that Neville, backed by Rochester and Sir Thomas Overbury, might be made secretary for the purpose of leading the commons. "The plot was," wrote More, "that Sir H. Nevill should undertake to deal with the Lower House, and then (so as my Lord Treasurer [Salisbury] would not intermeddle) there was no doubt but that better effects would come of the next session . . . than did of the former." [9] Had James wished a secretary with whom the commons would sympathize, he could have done no better than Neville.

Neville, who also represented a reaction against Salisbury's tactics, might have taught James some practical ways of lessening friction with the commons. But his real policy was one of concession. His famous scheme, out of which grew the storm about undertaking, was based upon the presupposition of concessions by the crown. These concessions had been rather trivial in nature. And one wonders what he would have done when forced to meet more fundamental issues. It seems probable that he would have counselled James to yield upon one point after another, and this could not have gone on for very long. Neville as secretary would have been supported by Pembroke and Southampton; but Northampton violently opposed him, Bacon was highly suspicious, and Suffolk and Somerset were merely ready to use him. If one may prophesy, he would have continued to be popular with the commons but would soon have met the most serious opposition at

[9] More to Winwood, December 1, 1610, *Winwood*, III, 235. St. P. Domestic, 14/74:44. More to Winwood, October 29, 1611, *Buccleuch MSS, Montagu Papers, H. M. C.*, I, 101.

court; and in all likelihood he could not have retained his place for very long.

Neville was thus too popular a candidate for the king's taste; and his appointment, though highly pleasing to the nation, would have been something like surrender for James himself. Neville's chances, therefore, were slim. In 1612 he had been a leading candidate. He was backed throughout by Southampton and Sheffield, who represented the popular party and the group of courtiers formerly friends of Essex. These men hoped to advance themselves by advancing Neville.[10] He was also backed at first by Somerset and Sir Thomas Overbury, who for a time were the allies of the Essex group and the opponents of the Howards. The Howard candidate was Sir Thomas Lake. But in 1612 Neville's friends apparently pushed him too hard. "It is said too much soliciting hath hindered him; and the flocking of parliament-men about him, and their meetings and consultations with the Earl of Southampton and the Lord Sheffield at Lord Rochester's chamber, hath done him no good. For the king says he will not have a secretary imposed on him by parliament."[11] The disgrace of Overbury and Somerset's alliance with the Howards deprived Neville of his most powerful supporters, and he was considered quite out of the running by the middle of 1613.[12]

The choice fell eventually upon Sir Ralph Winwood. His appointment was a compromise between contending factions and opinions. He had won the support of Somerset, for which it was suspected he had paid hard cash. Somerset, after dropping Neville, had for a time supported Lake, and now in 1614 supported

[10] "Yet there are exceptions taken to him [Neville] that he cannot be content to come in himself, but he must bring in his man Sir R[alph] W[inwood], and his champion the Earl of Southampton, and whosoever he thinks good." Chamberlain to Carleton, November 4, 1612, *Court and Times, James I*, I, 200.

[11] Earl of Dorset to Edmondes, June 22, Chamberlain to Carleton, June 17, 1612, *Court and Times, James I*, I, 179, 175–76.

[12] "I would . . . Sir H[enry] N[eville] had . . . not hung so long by a twine thread till all is fallen to the ground, where though he be no lower then he was before, yet it is with some loss and imputation that he could not discern in time, but suffer himself to be sucked and drawn dry and then left as it were empty." Chamberlain to Carleton, October 27, 1613, St. P. Domestic, 14/74:89. "The great places of the court are not yet disposed of. The manifest faction which is between the family of the Howards on one side, and the Earl of Southampton and Viscount Rochester on the other, is supposed to be the cause thereof. . . . I suppose Sir Henry Neville's hopes quite dashed; for merely depending upon my Lord Rochester, he wants not opposition; and then, besides, Overbury being fallen into disgrace, he is thereby deprived of his best instrument." Rev. Thomas Lorkin to Sir Thomas Puckering, June 24, 1613, *Court and Times, James I*, I, 248. See also Chamberlain to Carleton, October 14, 1613, *ibid.*, I, 277.

Winwood, by which we may gauge the depth of his statesman-ship. Lake was made a councillor on the same day as Winwood, a move to appease the Howards.[13] The appointment of Winwood was also a concession to public opinion. Winwood, as we know, hated Spain and Catholicism. Yet, unlike Neville, he had no connection with the opposition in parliament[14] and had never been a member of the commons before, a fact which handicapped him in the house but undoubtedly aided him in securing his appointment. Indeed, he was selected as much for what he was not as for what he was.

The choice was not a happy one. Winwood's personality was against him in the commons. But quite apart from his personal attributes, there were other factors which practically ensured his failure as parliamentary manager for the crown.

Winwood, in the first place, was badly handicapped by the time of his appointment, which was made exactly seven days before the session opened. An appointment so poorly timed might well cause suspicion and "interpretation" among the commons, as "being done in the very entrance into the Parliament . . . expressly for that purpose."[15] But, what was far more serious, it made any adequate preparations by Winwood clearly impossible and plunged him into the routine of the secretary's place at the moment when its duties were heaviest and one of its most difficult tasks was about to be performed. "He is come to the place at a busy time considering the parliament," wrote Chamberlain, "where he is to have a great part to act, and hath his head so full, that he is sometimes forced to be a songe-cruez."[16] It is small

[13] Chamberlain to Carleton, December 23, 1613, March 3, 1614, *Court and Times, James I,* I, 281–82, 301. *Goodman,* I, 186, 257. Sarmiento to the duke of Lerma, December 26, 1615, Spanish Trans., 12/36. Lorkin to Puckering, June 24, 1613, *Court and Times, James I,* I, 248. Chamberlain to Carleton, March 31, 1614, St. P. Domestic, 14/76:52.

[14] Winwood was "held free from faction, and to have no near dependants on either side." Chamberlain to Carleton, October 27, 1613, St. P. Domestic, 14/74:89. See also More to Winwood, January 1, 1612, *Winwood,* III, 319.

[15] The appointment should be made early, for "if it be held in suspence until the end [of the parliament], no man that hath ben voyced to that place can give a voice or speak without prejudice." On the other hand, if the appointment were held back, all men would be "kept in hope whereby to distaste none, but set every man on work to win the goal." Two dispatches of Carleton, April 2, 1614, St. P. Venice Correspondence, 99/15.

[16] Chamberlain to Carleton, April 14, 1614, St. P. Domestic, 14/77:7. "He [Winwood] hath now his head and handes full of busines what with the parlement where he is all the morning and at committees in the afternoone, and with other affaires pertaining to his place, wherin he is yet scant warme and not thoroughly setled." Chamberlain to Carleton, May 19, 1614, *ibid.,* 14/77:26.

wonder that he was at times a bit bewildered by the mass of business he was suddenly called upon to perform. And here his complete lack of parliamentary experience was an additional handicap. His first speech was criticized as "being in a kind of academical tune." "But he is to be excused," said Chamberlain, "having such a disadvantage that the first that ever he heard speake in that place was himself." Surely, if the new secretary was to deal with the commons for the first time in his life, he might have been allowed a short time to become seated in his place before parliament met. In this important respect James allowed the parliament to begin without any adequate preparation.

Winwood was at once surrounded by a vast amount of jealousy at court. "He must need walk warily," wrote Chamberlain, "having all men's eyes upon him, all ears open, and being set, as it were, a butt for all detracting tonges to shoot at. And indeed he is followed with the same malignity that opposed him at first; so that unless he carry it constantly and temperately and be constantly supported by his founders, he is in a hard case." Again Chamberlain wrote that "every little action or gesture" of Winwood's was "observed to the full and commonly construed to the worst." Winwood was bitterly opposed by the Howards. Lake, Herbert, Caesar, and other disappointed aspirants to the secretaryship placed every obstacle in his way. There was an effort to keep him busy in the council and in parliament, and thus away from court, so that his opportunities of personal contact with the king would be as few as possible. He had to fight for his lodgings at Whitehall. He had never been popular with other officials. And to this unpopularity was now added the jealousy of men who had striven furiously for an office only to see it given to a rival.[17] But it was these very men who were his colleagues in the commons, and their cooperation was essential for success in the house.

Winwood also found himself attacked at court and elsewhere

[17] Chamberlain to Carleton, April 7, 14, 1614, July 2, 1612, *Court and Times, James I*, I, 308, 181; St. P. Domestic, 14/77:7. Evans, *The Principal Secretary of State*, 69. "He hath yet no lodging in court but [is] put off from day to day. Sir John Herbert and he have had some little bustling for place, and Sir Julius Caesar, but he hath carried it from them both; Sir Thomas Edmondes bears it better than I looked for, only he is content to hear and believe the worst." *Court and Times, James I*, I, 308.

The discontent among officials because of appointments made at court continued during this parliament. A good example is the anger of various officials when Sir Arthur Ingram was made chamberlain of the king's household; some courtiers said they would rather be hanged than have "such a scandalous fellow set over them." *Ibid.*, I, 299.

by the upper clergy as the result of a speech he had made in the commons against recusants and idle churchmen. The clergy charged that his former associates were little better than Brownists and pictured him to James as a man who wished to make himself head of the puritan faction.[18]

The animosities and treachery at court went deeper than obstructing the work of an unpopular official. Northampton and the other Howards, with whom Somerset was now allied, regarded this parliament with the deepest aversion and "sought by all means to embroil it and bring it to nothing." They had done all in their power to prevent its summons. Sarmiento wrote that when the council in 1613 was debating the possibility of a parliament, Northampton told the king "that he should in no case call together and join his enemies, for such were those of the parliament, that would do nothing which he desired, as he had seen by experience." In a conversation with Sir Henry Neville in 1612 James had explained "the Reasons why divers dissuaded a Parliament," which, Neville later told the commons, had made him "tremble to think that any should thus breed a Dislike" between king and people.[19] But the Howards had been voted down in the council and the parliament had been called.

Northampton then set himself to wreck its work and bring about its dissolution. There are constant references in 1614 to attempts in high places at disrupting the work of the commons and setting them at variance among themselves.[20] The storm about undertakers gave Northampton an excellent opportunity. The commons' dislike of undertaking "was taken hold of and exasperated" by those who wished "to cover and convey their own secret averseness towards the King's business . . . My Lord Privy Seal [Northampton], who had discounselled the Parliament and hated the persons almost of the Undertakers, what for the glory of his

[18] Chamberlain to Carleton, May 12, 19, 1614, *Court and Times, James I*, I, 310; St. P. Domestic, 14/77:26.

[19] Chamberlain to Carleton, June 30, 1614, *Court and Times, James I*, I, 326. Account of the English court by the Spanish ambassador, 1613, contained in a letter of Sir John Digby to the king, September 22, 1613, St. P. Spanish, 94/20. May 14, 1614, *C. J.*, I, 485.

[20] "Whether it be chance or cunning, there be many bones cast among them [the commons] to set them at variance among themselves." Chamberlain to Carleton, June 1, 1614, *Court and Times, James I*, I, 320. Sir Herbert Croft wrote that the parliament would have been a success "if the Divell had not cast bones among us." Harl. MSS 1581, f. 356v. Sir Samuel Sandys said he had been in the commons for thirty years yet he found "more Bones cast in this Parliament to divert the good Proceedings of the House, than in all the Parliaments he hath known." *C. J.*, I, 500.

opinion and what for the blasting of their services, declared himself in that manner as he set up a kind of flag unto all those that opposed the Undertakers and would frustrate the success of the Parliament." [21]

These efforts culminated in his successful intrigue at the end of the parliament to increase its turbulence and thus anger the king and bring about a dissolution. Two of his agents, Dr. Lionel Sharp, a clergyman, and Sir Charles Cornwallis, formerly ambassador in Spain and a man long connected with the Howard faction, began intriguing among the commons. One member, John Hoskyns, was persuaded to say in the house that a new Sicilian Vespers might take place against the Scots. He apparently did not realize the full significance of the phrase but later confessed that he had obtained it from Sharp, "who had infused these things into him and had sollicited him to impress them in the Parliament." He was promised that in case of trouble he would have the protection of Northampton and also, apparently, of Somerset. His speech was reported to James as a threat of assassination; and after consultations with Northampton and Sarmiento, who offered empty assurances of Spanish friendship, James determined "to break with the Puritans" and dissolve the parliament. A last minute attempt by Ellesmere and Winwood to prevent a rupture was fruitless. They sought, on the one hand, to persuade the king to prorogue rather than dissolve, and on the other, to persuade the commons to vote supply in return for the prorogation. But the commons refused.[22] Thus Northampton's intrigue was only too

[21] *Spedding*, V, 180, 182, 188–89. Bacon warned the king in 1615 that he would not succeed in parliament until he had composed the differences in his own household, "that his Majesty be pleased according to his great wisdom and absolute power to extinguish, or at least compose for a time, the divisions in his own house, which otherwise, as it did the last time, will be sure to have such influence and infusion into the House or perhaps the Houses of Parliament, as we shall only grow and profit in inconveniences. For as long as any popish dissembler, turbulent spirit, ambitious or vainglorious valuer of himself, peevish puritan, seditious bankrout, weak popular or patriot, shall make account that in opposing the King's causes he shall have a retreat and harbour overt or secret in the favour of some great person, let his Majesty look for nothing but tempest. Therefore it must be so handled that factions be so mortified, or at least laid asleep, that all do counsel a Parliament and come cheerfully to it, and join sincerely in helping forwards the King's business, and be all alike sensible of any opposition or frustration thereof, and in a word that the people may as it were read in their faces consent and assurance. As for any undertaking, or opinion of undertaking, it is by all means to be laid aside, [though] it were to be wished that the gentlemen that were noted therefore were not altogether vilipended or discouraged or exasperated; and the like and equal course to be held towards those that were their opposites."

[22] *Gardiner*, II, 247–48, 250–52. Sir Henry Wotton, *Reliquiae Wottonianae* (London, 1685), 434–35. *Court and Times, James I*, I, 321, 324–26. St. P. Domestic, 14/77:42, 43;

successful. The fault in the last resort must be laid at James's door; for he had placed Northampton in power and listened to his advice.

To treachery at court must be added the unusually violent temper of the commons, which precluded either successful leadership by the court or the formation of a royal faction. Old grievances were now augmented by suspicion of the undertakers. Neville's scheme had been innocent enough, but rumor had distorted it into a heinous plot to interfere with elections on a huge scale and thus obtain a house ready to betray the interests of the country at the pleasure of the crown. The wildest reports were current while the elections were in progress. The sober truth was irritating enough. The undertakers had dared to prophesy what the next house of commons would do. This "stirred up a kind of indignation even in those that were very well and honestly affected, that a house of Parliament should become the shadows and followers of a few." Men saw in it such "an Iniurie to themselves, and the Parliament house, as that they began to bandy, and to make a faction which was like to break forth to open discontent at their sitting."[23] James may well have added to the general alarm. Hearing from certain courtiers who had sought election unsuccessfully that "all the shires were disposed to take care that none of his Majesty's servants were chosen" and that the commons were "not willing to have his servants in their company," James wrote in a panic to his principal councillors begging that they use their influence wherever possible to place "men of good disposition" in the house. "Letters fly from great personages extraordinarily," wrote Chamberlain a little later, "wherein, methinks, they do the king no great service, seeing the world is apt to conceive it is a kind of packing." "There was great suing, standing, and striving about elections and places," wrote Bacon, "which joined with the general noise of this undertaking" and made the wisest and ablest persons of the king-

Cowper MSS, H.M.C., I, 87; L. B. Osborn, *The Life, Letters, and Writings of John Hoskyns* (New Haven, 1937), 37–47, 75. Winwood to Carleton, June 16, 1614, St. P. Venice Correspondence, 99/16. S. R. Gardiner (ed.), F. Francisco de Jesus, *The Spanish Marriage Treaty* (Camden Society), 285–93. *Commons Debates 1621,* VII, 652–56; *Portland MSS, H. M. C.,* IX, 137.

This paragraph summarizes material from an article, "Summoning and Dissolving Parliament, 1603–25: The Council's Advice to James I," *American Historical Review,* 45:288–90 (January, 1940).

[23] *Spedding,* V, 180. Cott. MSS Titus F IV, f. 351–52v.

e house, they attempted to regain reputation "by being forward
ıd running violent courses in causes of popularity," in the hope
of checking the house later when their influence had increased,
"wherein they found themselves only able to row with the stream,
but had no arms or powers to row against it." At the same time
they created a habit of boldness and liberty in opposing the causes
of the king.[28]

Another difficulty also became apparent in this parliament.
While Salisbury had been managing the parliamentary affairs of
the crown, James could give him general instructions and leave
him to work out the details. But this was not possible with Winwood. A bureaucrat, and a comparatively insignificant one, had
taken the place of a statesman. Much more responsibility was thus
thrown upon the king. He was now brought more constantly in
touch with the daily business of the house and was forced to be
his own parliamentary manager to a far greater extent. Salisbury
had been something of a buffer between James and the commons.
But now the king was required to apply himself to a daily routine,
which he detested, and to employ tact and forbearance, in which
he was notably deficient.

The effect was apparent at once. James's opening speech was a
curious blend of Bacon's advice, of Neville's, and of his own tendency to compromise and halfway measures. He insisted, following
Bacon, that he would deal with this parliament as a king and not
as a merchant and that this was to be a session of love and not of
bargains. Yet he followed Neville's advice by offering certain concessions to the commons, and these bills of grace were at once
placed before the house in fuller form by the learned counsel.
Bacon regarded this as a repetition of Salisbury's error in 1610.
James disclaimed all idea of a contract, yet his offers were "a kind
of valued gift, which made men take weights and measures into
their hands"; they were wooing bills and their obvious purpose
was to make the demand for money more palatable. James sought
to imply, again following Bacon, that the parliament was not
called for money and that grievances should precede supply. But
before his speech was over, he "laid out his wants, and descended
as it were to entreating to be relieved." [29] Thus James fell between

[28] *Spedding*, V, 181–82.
[29] *C. J.*, I, 458–59. *Spedding*, V, 24–30. Chamberlain to Carleton, April 14, 1614, St. P.
Domestic, 14/77:7.

two stools and created those impressions which Bacon was m.
anxious to avoid.

James's speech was followed at once by a demand for supply in
the commons which caused "infinite animosity and distaste." Nor
was it done with great skill. James was obviously overeager. Bacon
suggests that money was asked immediately "that the weakness
of the Undertakers, whose strength was more in noise than in
strength, mought not be perceived before the King's turn was
served." If James was impatient, Winwood was too peremptory.
He and other courtiers were very vehement and demanded that
a vote be taken at once. But these tactics failed and the house resolved to debate grievances before supply, a course which at once
brought up the dangerous topic of impositions. Thus James was not
consistent, and Winwood added to the blunders of the government. This stumbling at the threshold, wrote Bacon, was never
after recovered.[30]

With such deplorable leadership and with the commons in an
angry mood, it is only natural that there would be little organization or cooperation among the members of the court group. They
worked together only in a casual sort of way, and there was no
directing brain in charge of affairs. The speaker obviously had his
instructions;[31] but we find the courtiers divided in the debates on
Parry's case, and even in such a vital matter as supply there were
differences of opinion among them. In a debate on April 12 Winwood asked for an immediate vote on supply; Caesar wished a
large committee, on the Elizabethan model, with power to deal
both with subsidies and with the bills of grace; Bacon moved for
a committee of the whole; Montagu returned to Winwood's proposal for an immediate vote in the house.[32] Such a difference of
opinion, if only on a point of procedure, shows clearly that the
court group was utterly lacking in organization and party cohesion.

[30] *Spedding*, V, 182. The undertakers, Bacon thought, had already done great harm by
proclaiming before the parliament that the house was called to relieve the king from debt,
thus making money the business of the parliament. *Ibid.*, V, 179. Lorkin to Puckering,
May 28, 1614, *Court and Times, James I*, I, 315–16. Chamberlain to Carleton, April 14,
1614, St. P. Domestic, 14/77:7.
[31] We find him adjourning the house in the middle of a report on impositions, attempting to postpone decisions likely to go against the crown, showing the book of orders to the
king, attempting to force a vote on supply, and absenting himself from the house at a critical
moment. *Commons Debates 1621*, VII, 633, 656. *C. J.*, I, 456, 499. *Portland MSS, H. M. C.*,
IX, 134. *Court and Times, James I*, I, 321.
[32] *C. J.*, I, 478–79, 461–63.

The parliament of 1621, though its history is vastly more extensive and complicated than that of 1614, nevertheless follows somewhat similar lines in the matters we have been discussing. The councillors in the house were more numerous and more able. But there was no one minister at court or in parliament to guide or integrate their efforts. Signs of organization among the courtiers were even fainter than they had been in 1614. Meanwhile, disruptive tendencies continued both at court and in the commons, and the organization of the opposition was making steady progress.

Much depended upon Buckingham. He was now deep in the secrets of the state and formed the channel through which the world at large approached the sovereign. But his attitude toward the parliament of 1621 was that of an irresponsible young courtier who was enjoying the good things of the world and was extremely anxious not to lose them. He had no parliamentary experience and no parliamentary policy beyond the protection of his own interests. For a moment in 1619 he had joined those councillors who wished a war for the protection of the Palatinate and who urged James to summon parliament, without which he could not hope to speak effectively in German affairs. But Buckingham soon realized that a parliament would involve him in some personal danger. "The Puritans have rendered Buckingham Spanish," wrote Tillières, "for seeing that they mean to attack him, he knows no way of securing protection against them except by the Spanish match." When Gondomar returned to England in March of 1620, he had no difficulty in persuading the favorite to use his influence against calling parliament.[33]

But those councillors who hoped that king and commons might find reconciliation in a foreign policy of which they both approved told James that a parliament was essential.[34] Naunton

[33] Buckingham confessed to the commons that "he did never before know what a parliament was." *P. and D.*, I, 150. Tillières to Puisieux, February 13, 1621, Paris Trans., 3/54. Buckingham would carry certain councillors with him: Carlisle, one of his intimates, Arundel, at this time his active supporter, Calvert, and Weston. Gondomar wrote on December 22, 1621, that he had just spent three hours with Charles urging him to support Spain in talking with his father and to break with all other influences. Gondomar to the Archduchess Isabella, Simancas MSS, Gardiner's Transcripts, Add. MSS 31112, no. 291.

[34] Sir Benjamin Rudyard to Nethersole, October 2, 1620, St. P. German, 81/19:17.

This paragraph and two that follow summarize material from "Summoning and Dissolving Parliament, 1603–25: The Council's Advice to James I," *American Historical Review*, 45:292–97 (January, 1940).

was especially vehement; and James later remarked, "I may well thank Naunton, as were it not for him I should not have summoned parliament." Naunton was supported not only by ministers who were violently anti-Spanish but by many more moderate men, including Bacon, Cranfield, Mandeville, Hamilton, Coke, and Edmondes. Their hand was strengthened by the Spanish invasion of the Palatinate and they sought to persuade the king that the commons if summoned would prove tractable and well behaved. Bacon's letters to James in the autumn of 1620 clearly aim to convey this impression. Tillières' dispatches during the same period mention "a promise which the Puritans have made to the king that they would not touch his prerogative" but confine themselves to the defense of Protestantism at home and abroad. The moderation and restraint of debate in the commons during the first weeks of the parliament bear out Tillières' assertion. James finally yielded, though up to the very moment that parliament met there was danger that it would not be called at all. The Venetian ambassador reported that the Spanish ministers sought "to destroy if possible the decision to summon parliament, or at least to postpone the carrying of it into effect. Its destruction may be hoped for from the smallest delay." [35]

Thus the parliament was called in spite of Buckingham's opposition. When it met, his worst fears were realized. His position was an insult to the older nobility, and nascent opposition began in the lords. He was closely enough connected with various patents and monopolies to ensure the hostility of the commons. He had a certain following among the lords but absolutely none in the lower house. When Williams suggested to him means to keep his name out of the debates in the commons, it was not to be done through Buckingham's friends but through Williams "and your other Servants, that have some Credit with the most Active Members." There were, of course, individuals in the commons ready enough to serve the favorite. Sir George Goring reported what was taking place in the house, in part for Buckingham's benefit, in part for the information of the king. Goring wrote on

[35] *Cal. St. P. Venetian, 1621–1623,* 64. Tillières to Puisieux, October 14, 18, November 20, 1620, Paris Trans., 3/54. *Spedding,* VII, 113–67. For attempts to stop the parliament, see *Cal. St. P. Venetian, 1619–1621,* 93, 152, 471, 484–85; Nicholas Burton to William Carnsew, November 4, 1620, St. P. Domestic, 14/117:55; *Court and Times, James I,* II, 239; Tillières to Puisieux, January 29, 1621, Paris Trans., 3/54.

November 29 that he had made a certain motion "according to your Lordship's last directions" and was confident that "his Majestyes ende was not knowen to any."[36] But Buckingham had no influence in the commons. When he found that parliament was not to his liking, his remedy was to obtain a dissolution as soon as possible.

During April and May, we know, Buckingham was urging the king to dissolve; and Gondomar seriously hoped that the adjournment in June might have been a dissolution. James resisted these efforts until the following December, but then, as in 1614, his anger drove him into the hands of the Spanish party. When a crisis arose as a result of the commons' petition that Charles should marry a Protestant, James was foolishly loitering in the country. Buckingham was with him and urged him not to return to London. Shortly before the dissolution took place Gondomar wrote that James, though still undecided, "was being valiantly urged on by the Marquis of Buckingham and other good friends." In the council meeting that voted the dissolution Buckingham silenced Pembroke's objections; and Gondomar wrote in reporting the dissolution to Spain that "the Marquis of Buckingham has had a great part in this and deserves to be thanked." Gondomar's famous letter to James complaining of the commons produced the final crisis. But between the last sitting of the commons (December 19) and the proclamation of dissolution (January 6) Gondomar urged James to punish certain members at once, "that the king should be the more obliged to dissolve." When the council asked delay before the dissolution was proclaimed, Gondomar urged the king to publish it at once.[37] These intrigues were successful; members were punished and the dissolution was carried through.

Against these proceedings other councillors protested in vain. Williams, May, and Cranfield all counseled moderation and advised against the dissolution. "My Lord of Pembroke and Mar-

[36] Hacket, *Williams,* I, 50. Sir George Goring to Buckingham, March 15, November 27, 29, December 3, 1621, *Commons Debates 1621,* VII, 578–80, 620–21; Harl. MSS 1580, f. 428, 430.

[37] *Gardiner,* IV, 85–87, 231, 248–49, 265–66. For Buckingham's early efforts to secure a dissolution, see Tillières to Puisieux, April 3, May 2, May 29, 1621, Paris Trans., 3/55. Gondomar to the Archduchess Isabella, December 22, 1621, Simancas MSS, Gardiner's Transcripts, Add. MSS 31112, no. 291. Gondomar to Philip IV, January 21, 1622, Spanish Trans., 12/26. Tillières to Puisieux, December 20, 1621, January 6, 24, 1622, Paris Trans., 3/55; 3/56.

quis Hamilton spoke vehemently at the council table against the dissolving of the parliament, affirming that the day would come when this error would be imputed to the council, and not the king; and therefore they protested against it." But protests were useless. In the council meeting that voted the dissolution James "gave an account of his determination, with his reasons for doing so, at which those who were badly disposed were frozen to death; they ended by confirming it, with evidence of great inward grief; no one dared to contradict it but the Earl of Pembroke, high chamberlain, a great Puritan. He said there was no need of voting or disputing, for the king had declared his will. The Marquis of Buckingham replied, that if he wished to contradict the king's will he should do so, for he in his case would do the same, although his Majesty were present. This made the Earl hold his tongue, and he and the others approved it." [38] It is against this background of intrigue and dissension at court that we must watch events in the commons.

There was no leader in the lower house who could direct the courtiers or give them some party organization. Secretary Calvert was the ordinary channel through which the government communicated with the commons. He carried out instructions with skill and exactness, but he did little more. At certain times he was given a considerable amount of discretionary power. But he shunned responsibility, kept close to his instructions, and when he did not have them, assumed a purely negative attitude of defense. When on one occasion he acted in the house on his own responsibility, he apologized for the liberty he had taken, "being as I conceived thereunto sufficiently warrented, by the former direccions I had received from his Majestie, both by verball Message and writing, without which I would not have presumed to do it." [39] He apparently had no conception of a royal party in the commons and certainly made no move toward creating one. Cranfield took a far more independent line, but his methods tended rather to disrupt than to build a party organization. His disgust at corruption in government circles and his desire to

[38] Hacket, *Williams*, I, 81; April 16, 1624, Gurney, f. 228; Mead to Stuteville, January 10, 22, 1622, *Court and Times, James I*, II, 281, 287; *Cal. St. P. Venetian, 1621–1623*, 199, 215; Chamberlain to Carleton, January 4, 1622, St. P. Domestic, 14/127:8. Tillières to Puisieux, January 24, 1622, Paris Trans., 3/56; Gondomar to Philip IV, January 21, 1622, Spanish Trans., 12/26; Caesar's notes in Add. MSS 34324, f. 147.
[39] Calvert to Buckingham, December 17, 1621, *Commons Debates 1621*, VII, 626.

shield the king led him to throw his fellow officials to the mercies of the commons and to attack Bacon with great violence. For a councillor to attack other officers of the crown was utterly destructive of any party loyalty or cohesion. The exposure of widespread corruption had already created an atmosphere in which officials ran for cover.[40] And Cranfield added to the general alarm.

Bacon had been the guiding spirit in the work of preparation for the parliament. He had long been urging the king to summon the commons and still believed that his former influence among them could be maintained. In recommending himself for the chancery he wrote that he had always been gracious in the lower house and would "be able to do some effect in rectifying that body of parliament-men, which is *cardo rerum*." During the first weeks of the session the government met the reforming zeal of the commons by a policy of obstruction; and since the commons employed conferences to place their findings before the lords, Bacon, as the presiding officer in the upper chamber, could be very useful.[41] He might even yet have become the chief parliamentary manager for the crown. It is a pity he could not have cooperated with Cranfield in guiding and controlling the commons; in place of collaboration we find bitter rivalry and stinging innuendoes. Bacon's impeachment quickly removed him from public life.

In the autumn, with the king and Buckingham away at Royston, some of the councillors in London met after the house had

[40] Note how quickly Bacon was denounced "by his own creatures."

[41] *Spedding*, V, 243. James wrote Bacon, February 28, to delay if possible a conference about Sir Giles Mompesson for which the commons were to ask the following day. Bacon consulted with Prince Charles and lord treasurer Mandeville, and they agreed that the lords should request delay on the ground of unpreparedness. But this was not necessary. Bacon, finding little business in the lords, was able to adjourn them for the day, before the request for conference came up from the commons. No sooner had he adjourned the lords than the request for conference arrived, and he "perceived a great willingness in many of the Lords to have recalled it." Bacon had also prompted Abbot to move that the lords should not meet on the following day, as the bishops wished to be present in convocation. The conference was thus postponed from March 1 to 3, and in the meantime Mompesson escaped to the Continent. *Spedding*, VII, 190. There is other evidence of obstruction. The speaker adjourned the house in the middle of the morning of March 8, and thus interrupted a report by the managers for a conference on the referees. Thus the managers were unable to tell the house what they planned to do in the conference. "There was means found by some so to employ . . . in other matters" the members of the commons who conducted these conferences "that they should have little time to look to the business to which they were appointed." A later conference was interrupted by the lords on the ground that it was time for dinner. Such systematic obstruction had a guiding hand behind it, and in all probability it was Bacon's. *Commons Debates 1621*, IV, 137. Mead to Stuteville, March 17, 1621, *Court and Times, James I*, II, 238.

risen for the day to determine what their next move should be and what advice they should offer the king. Calvert, Cranfield, Arundel, and May took part in these consultations and doubtless Weston did also, but it is clear that some councillors were excluded.[42] Here, then, is a select group of councillors planning joint action in parliament. Meetings such as these, however, were most unusual; they took place only because of the emergency created by the absence of the king and the alarming crisis in the commons.

It may be noted in passing that Prince Charles had some share in these consultations. "This Evening after the Howse was up," Calvert wrote Buckingham on December 7, "divers of My Lords of the Councell together with my selfe attended the Prince, and acquainted him with the whole proceedings of this day." Two letters from Charles to Buckingham report certain of these meetings. Charles for the most part wrote what the councillors suggested. But he added advice of his own, advice which tended to more vigorous action than that suggested by the council. On November 3 he reported that the house had been somewhat unruly, and, though the council advised patience, he asked for a warrant, to be used at discretion, for punishing members who got out of hand. Charles thus inclined to the high views of the prerogative held by his father. But his influence was slight at this time, and one suspects that councillors consulted him merely to give additional weight to their own decisions.[43]

While the courtiers suffered from lack of leadership, they watched two councillors desert the royal cause and become leaders of the opposition. Sir Edward Coke was by far the more important of the two; and one need not labor the seriousness of his defection. He assumed such a leading role in opposition that

[42] Calvert wrote Buckingham on December 17 that Arundel, who "being well informed of all our proceedings can give his Majestie the best satisfaccion," would be with the king that night. *Commons Debates 1621*, VII, 628. Prince Charles wrote after one of these conferences that he "had spoken with so many of the council as the king trusts most."

[43] Calvert to Buckingham, December 7, 1621, *Commons Debates 1621*, VII, 624. Charles to Buckingham, November 3, 28, 1621, *Goodman*, II, 209–10; Harl. MSS 6987, f. 205. The Venetian ambassador wrote that the commons were "disaffected by hearing that the prince daily utters opinions contrary to the authority of the parliament, and at seeing him, praiseworthy as it is, follow all the movements of his father like his shadow and take his cue and advice from those ministers who are most hated." *Cal. St. P. Venetian, 1621–1623*, 185. Calvert wrote Buckingham, December 17, that he had not used his warrant to announce a dissolution, "which I did forbeare upon advise and dirreccion from the Prince this Morning, whatsoever should happen, untill his Majestie were advertised of the successe of this day, either by Letter or by some of his Councell." *Commons Debates 1621*, VII, 627.

James called him Captain Coke, the leader of the faction in parliament. He not only opposed the policy of the government but clashed fiercely with his colleagues of the council. On various occasions he had heated words with Calvert, Cranfield, and Edmondes.[44] And his exultant participation in the hunt for Bacon's scalp did the royal cause great harm. The man who might have been the crown's strongest advocate became its most successful opponent.

The earl of Southampton also became prominent in opposition. "From the first beginning of the Parliament," wrote Cranfield, Southampton "estranged himself very much from the Court and Council Board as either unwilling to know or careless to further and assist" the wishes of the king, "as though the Parliament time absolved servants and Councillors from all the duties and other relations and gratitude they owe their sovereign. In lieu of his fellow councillors [Southampton] consorted himself during the time of the Parliament with those young lords in the Upper and those knights and burgesses in the Lower House which were most stirring and active to cross the general proceedings and to asperse and infame the present government." Southampton criticized the administration with the greatest bitterness and was "active in ripping up supposed enormities in the state of the King's servants (which was his usual theme at home and abroad)." He was an open opponent of Buckingham. He was accused of saying that "he liked not to come to the Council Board, because there were so many Boys and base Fellows" there and that "there would never be a good Reformation, while one did so wholly govern the King." In the house of lords he clashed so violently with Buckingham that on one occasion swords were all but drawn; he told one of the bishops that his motions were unseasonable; he "crossed" the motions of the prince; and he was more interested in parliamentary liberties "than became any Privy Councillor to be." In fact, he led the opposition in the lords as prominently as Coke was leading it in the commons.

Southampton was in close touch with the leaders of the opposition in the lower house, where, it was said, the most caustic attacks upon the government came from some very near him. In

[44] Mead to Stuteville, February 2, 1622, *Court and Times, James I*, II, 289. Chamberlain to Carleton, February 10, 1621, *ibid.*, II, 221–22; *P. and D.*, II, 63; *Commons Debates 1621*, II, 362; Chamberlain to Carleton, May 2, 1621, St. P. Domestic, 14/121:5.

his examination before the council he was asked whether "some of the Lower House did not usually come up into the Committee Chamber of the Upper House, upon Design and Plot to receive a Direction from him what to do in their House." He was also asked whether he "had not Practice with some of the Lower House to cross the King" in a variety of ways, "whether there were not Meetings and Consultations to that Intent," and whether leaders of the opposition were not constant guests under his roof. We have evidence of meetings at Southampton's house in Holborn and also at Dorset House in Fleet Street. It was of Southampton and his friends that Sir Anthony Ashley wrote Buckingham in May: "Your Adversaries continue their meetings and conferences here in Holborn, how to give his Majestie some foul distaste of you" and have taken "a mutual oath to this purpose amongst themselves." Goring took it upon himself in March to ask Sir Edward Sackville "whether or noe he had never bin buisy in any underhand proceedinge with the Lords" to Buckingham's prejudice; to which Sackville answered "that he was soe far from it as to the contrary he was suspected to have revealed the persons and manner of theyre meetinge at Dorsset howse." [45] Southampton was arrested on June 16 as he left the council chamber and did not regain his complete freedom until the following September.

Coke and Southampton exemplify the ways in which the opposition was gaining strength. Coke illustrates the growth of procedure and of new ways of doing business which were taking power away from the councillors and placing it in the hands of

---

[45] Memoranda by Cranfield concerning Southampton, *Commons Debates 1621*, VII, 615–17; examination of the earl of Southampton, *P. and D.*, II, Appendix. Cranfield wrote "that however the Earl cannot be forced to make good the indiscretions of his friends, yet their affected miscarriage in this kind might well make his Majesty to suspect the Earl, it being impossible that those tongues should be silent under his roof which talked so licentiously in a more public theatre. That scarce one speech concerning any public grievance in England, Ireland, or the discipline ecclesiastical was uttered in Parliament by any other man than some bosom friend or ordinary guest at the least of the said Earl which cannot be noted in any other Privy Councillor of the kingdom." See also C. H. Firth, *The House of Lords during the Civil War* (London, 1910), 39. Sir Anthony Ashley to Buckingham, May 12, 1621, *Cabala*, 307–08. Goring to Buckingham, March 15, 1621, *Commons Debates 1621*, VII, 579–80.

Tillières wrote (March 11, 1621) that certain lords, angry at the precedence of the new Scottish viscounts over English barons, "have held several meetings at the houses of the Earls of Salisbury and Dorset." When James ordered Salisbury and Dorset to answer for this before the council, they replied that "during the sitting of Parliament they were entitled to hold assemblies and consultations of every kind." Raumer, *History of the Sixteenth and Seventeenth Centuries*, II, 250.

popular leaders. He typifies the successful though unhistorical
appeal to the past, the learning and debating powers of opposition leaders, and the violence of their assault upon abuses. He was
merely one among a number of leaders — Sir Edwin Sandys,
Sir Robert Phelips, Sir Dudley Digges, Edward Alford and John
Pym, Sir Francis Seymour and William Hakewill. These men
supported each other in their speeches; their tactics dovetailed
nicely; they were coming to be more of an organized opposition.
They were "the Pilots of the Commonwealth," who planned
their moves in the commons and "had an eye to the dangers that
lay in the way." [46] And the house was learning to follow their
lead. Southampton illustrates the fact that these men met outside
of parliament to shape a course of action in the house. They
could now count upon support from certain of the lords. The
lords had grievances of their own: the many new peerages of
the time and the question of precedence raised by Englishmen
created Scotch and Irish nobles. But fundamentally their opposition centered in their hostility to Buckingham and his position
in the state.

The government, however, had a following in the lords, and
opposition there was not a serious matter. The king, wrote Wilson, had a "strong party, especially in the House of Lords: All
the Courtiers and most of the Bishops steer'd by his Compass
and the Prince's presence (who was a constant member) did cast
an awe among many of them." Peers who spoke against the government were "snapt up" by the courtiers, and the number of
lay lords summoned in 1621 was ninety-two as against fifty-four
in the last parliament of Elizabeth. Yet there were some "gallant
spirits that aimed at the Publick Liberty more than their own
interest" and gave the courtiers many "stout encounters, . . .
among which the Principal were Henry Earl of Oxford, Henry
Earl of Southampton, Robert Earl of Essex, Robert Earl of Warwick, the Lord Say, the Lord Spencer, and divers others, that
supported the Old English Honour, and would not let it fall to
the ground." [47]

[46] Wilson, *History of Great Britain*, 161.

[47] Wilson, *History of Great Britain*, 161. Bacon wrote James, April 21, "Surely I con-
ceave, that your Majesty opening himself in this kind to the Lords Counsellors, and a
motion from the Prince after my submission, and my Lord Marquis using his interest with
his friends in the House, may effect the sparing of a sentence." *Spedding*, VII, 241. Chamberlain wrote that the prince attended almost daily in the lords. February 17, 1621, St. P.
Domestic, 14/119:103.

Opposition appears to have died out in the autumn meeting, perhaps because Southampton had been silenced. Cranfield reported that proceedings in the lords were "very respective and fair. Some few attempts have been made about privilege. . . . But those affected to those courses are so few, and the house in general so well affected to the King and his service, as I make no doubt but his Majesty will receive no discontentment in our house, but all satisfaction." Williams wrote that "in our house his Majesties servants are very strong, and increase every day, nor is there the least fear of any Malignant opposition." [48]

But if the court group in the lords grew stronger as the parliament advanced, we find an opposite tendency in the commons. Admitting that the court group had no party organization at any time during this parliament, we may at least point, at the time the parliament opened, to the largest number of councillors in any Stuart house of commons and to a fairly large number of other officials and courtiers from whom the government might reasonably expect support. [49] Bacon and the other judges associ-

---

[48] Cranfield to Buckingham, December 4, 1621, *Goodman*, II, 210–11. Lord keeper Williams to Buckingham, December 16, 1621, *Cabala*, 66.

[49] Serjeants and legal officials included Sir Thomas Coventry (solicitor, who forfeited his seat when he became attorney); Sir Robert Heath (solicitor); Sir John Walter (attorney to the prince); Sir Edward Moseley (attorney for the duchy of Lancaster); Sir John Bennet (a judge of the prerogative court of Canterbury); Sir Francis Ashley; Sir James Ley; Sir John Davies; Thomas Richardson; Sir Richard Weston (not the statesman); William Towse; Sir James Whitelocke (chief justiciary of Chester); Sir Richard Dyott (chancellor of the county palatine of Durham); Heneage Finch; John Finch; Sir Thomas Finch; Thomas Mallett; and Sir Thomas Trevor. Sir Edward Leech became a master in chancery in 1624. Sir John Hobart was the son of a judge. Minor officeholders included: William Beecher; John Coke; Sir Clement Edmondes; Thomas and William Fanshawe; Sir Miles Fleetwood; Sir William Harrington; Sir John Hippesley; Sir John Jepson (an Irish privy councillor); Inigo Jones; Sir Henry Mainwaring; Sir Humphrey May; Edward Nicholas; Robert and Walter Pye; Sir Benjamin Rudyard; and Robert Shute. John Boroughs, Sir George Hastings, and Thomas Meautys were connected with Bacon. Courtiers included: Sir Edward Barrett; Sir Francis Blundell (to whom Buckingham referred as "a man I take care of." Blundell's election was voided); Sir William Cavendish; Sir Edward Cecil; Sir Richard Cecil; Ralph Clare; Spencer Lord Compton; Sir Edward Conway; Sir Francis Crane; Sir John Danvers (a gentleman of the privy chamber to the prince); Sir George Goring; Sir Gilbert Hoghton; Sir Arthur Ingram; Sir Thomas and Robert Jermyn; Sir Robert Killigrew; Sir John Leeds (referred to as "the King's Servant." *P. and D.*, I, 31); Sir Henry Mildmay; Sir Giles Mompesson; Sir George More; John Murray (a gentleman of the bedchamber); Sir Thomas Roe; Sir Edward Sackville; Sir Edward Seymour; Sir Henry Spiller; Sir William Strode; Sir William Uvedall; Sir Henry Vane; Sir Robert Vernon (cofferer of the household); Sir Edward Villiers. Lord Zouch recommended to the Cinque Ports John Angell ("one of his Majesty's Pensioners"); Francis Fetherstone ("one of his Majesty's Pensioners"); Emanuel Gifford ("his Majesty's sworn servant"); Sir Robert Hatton; Sir Richard Young; Samuel More ("my servant"); Richard Zouch. James Bagg and George Chudleigh were also members.

ated with him in the work of preparation had considered "what persons were fit to be of the House" and how they could be placed "without novelty or much observation." For this purpose they listed "the privy councillors and principal statesmen or court-iers; the gravest and wisest lawyers; the most respected and best tempered knights and gentlemen of the country."[50] There is no evidence of widespread interference in elections by the govern-ment. Yet its efforts may have been greater than we know, and the obvious caution with which it acted may be partly responsi-ble for our lack of evidence.

Yet the erosion of discontent continued. In the autumn session the court group in the commons seemed to have all but disap-peared. Solicitor Heath and the recorder of London both sup-ported the petition that Charles marry a Protestant; and in the final debates on the Protestation of Liberties courtiers were strangely silent. "The king is exceedingly distasted with the Prot-estation," wrote Chamberlain, "and doth challenge and blame his servants, who all or the most part plead absence; and the Solicitor was in danger for not interposing himself more ear-nestly, howsoever he hath made his peace." A letter of Calvert shows clearly the bankruptcy of the royal group. "Wee finde so little helpe in our howse," he wrote on December 7, "or further-ance to bring to passe his Majesty's just and Princely ends, as I may not without wrong to their Meritt omitt to acquaint his Majestie . . . with the good services and endeavours . . . of Sir Edward Sackvile, Mr. Chancellour of the Dutchie, and Sir Henry Fane, who are the principall Men that upon all occasions stand up for the King. I doubt not but there are many other well af-fected Men, but they are no Speakers for the most part."[51] Thus the court group went to pieces.

It is perhaps further evidence of this disintegration that threats and punishments were taking the place of gentler methods in dealing with the disaffected and frightening the opposition. Bacon wrote Buckingham that he wished Sir Edward Coke "had some

---

[50] *Spedding*, VII, 116.

[51] *Commons Debates 1621*, II, 493–98; Chamberlain to Carleton, January 4, 1622, St. P. Domestic, 14/127:8. Calvert to Buckingham, December 7, 1621, *Commons Debates 1621*, VII, 625. "I know not what fatality there is in it, businesses go so crosse with us in the Parliament." Calvert to Conway, December 8, 1621, St. P. Holland, 84/104.

round *caveat* given him from the King; for your Lordship hath no great power with him: but I think a word from the King mates him." Goring accused Sir Edward Sackville of acting against the favorite, a charge which Sackville vigorously denied. Goring told Buckingham he had spoken to Sackville because he "loved not to see you loose any you may get, much lesse any already gaynd except proved by theyre misdemeanors to be unworthy of you." Early in the parliament Alford complained "there were Eyes over him to observe." Sir Francis Seymour said he had been threatened with questioning "after the Parliament in another Place." Both Sir Edwin and Sir Samuel Sandys were threatened by Cranfield, who said that "some would be questioned for some words spoken here in the House." Sir Edwin was arrested during the summer; in the autumn he remained away from parliament and Sir Samuel "stood mute." The dissolution was followed by a number of arrests, and other members were questioned.[52]

These methods might silence individuals but could not make them of any value to the crown, for the timorous lost all credit with the house. Sir Dudley Digges had attacked abuses vigorously during the early months of the parliament, but apparently he received a warning from court and drew back. In the autumn meeting he was "either silent or so little regarded when he spake that he had better have sat still. In truth I am sorry in his behalf," wrote Chamberlain, "for he is a proper (and I presume) an honest man, but he hath utterly lost the House, that hath a strong opinion of his halting, and the worst is he may chance hereafter stand straight on neither leg."[53]

[52] Bacon to Buckingham, March 7, 1621, *Spedding*, VII, 192. Goring to Buckingham, March 15, 1621, *Commons Debates 1621*, VII, 579–80. *Ibid.*, IV, 399, 405–07; *P. and D.*, I, 32; II, 55, 151–53, 259. The commons sent a committee to ask Sir Edwin Sandys why he absented himself and the cause of his commitment during the summer; his answer was burned by order of parliament at the end of the session. *Commons Debates 1621*, V, 245.

Williams wrote Buckingham, July 19, 1621, in behalf of Selden, "My Lord, The man hath excellent Parts, which may be diverted from an Affectation of Applause of idle People to do some good and useful Service to His Majesty." Selden was not a member of parliament in 1621. Hacket, *Williams*, I, 69. There is a strange letter from Lady Mary Jacob to Buckingham, April 28, 1621, in which she promises to pass on "to her friends the fathers of the Lower House" certain arguments in favor of supply with which Buckingham appears to have supplied her. Harl. MSS 1581, f. 240.

[53] Chamberlain to Carleton, December 22, 1621, St. P. Domestic, 14/124:73. "The most popular men, as soon as they wore the Court Livery, lost the love of the people; but those that suffered for them, were the more beloved and admired by them." Wilson, *History of Great Britain*, 192.

The opposition was thus better led and better organized than the courtiers in this highly important parliament, and the country party actually found leaders among the councillors of the king. The organization which Salisbury had created in James's first parliament and the party discipline and cohesion which he had sought to instill fell to the ground in 1614 and were not restored in the parliament of 1621.

6

The Duke of Buckingham and the Management of Parliament

When Charles's reign opened in 1625, the duke of Buckingham was in a position to do what Salisbury had done in the first parliament of James. The problem of dealing with the commons was now vastly more difficult. We are not concerned here, however, with the general causes of discontent, but rather with the way in which the crown's parliamentary business was conducted. Buckingham's personal relations with the sovereign gave him power and freedom of action that Salisbury had never known. His plans were accepted by the king and obeyed without question by the council. He might, at least, have conducted business in the commons in such a way as to reduce friction to a minimum, and he might have cemented the ties that bound certain members to the crown. But with criminal folly he threw away his chances and so abused the power in his hands that the commons turned against him, not only because of their hostility to the policy of the government but because of his reckless and inconsiderate tactics in dealing with the house. By 1626 he was bankrupt in parliamentary influence, and his opportunity for leadership was ended by his impeachment.

In his relations with parliament, as in his career as a whole, Buckingham's chances of ultimate achievement were diminished by early and easy success. He and the prince came to power during the parliament of 1624. They were able, on the one hand, to bend the king to their will and crush opposition when it raised its head in the council. For the moment they also found themselves in sympathy with the people and were able to form a temporary alliance with the popular party in parliament. Their position was one of great power, and the world appeared to be at their feet.

Charles and Buckingham, after they returned from the journey to Madrid, demanded that a parliament be summoned to dissolve the marriage treaties and to vote supplies for a war with Spain.

But the king and certain of the leading ministers strongly opposed a parliament, at least for the purposes that Charles and Buckingham had in mind. A struggle ensued in which it became perfectly evident that James's reign was about over and that the rulers of the country were now his son and his favorite. They remained with him constantly, keeping him almost a semiprisoner, excluding from his presence those who desired a policy different from their own. James was not in a position to resist for long. Physically he was now an old man. His policy of peaceful diplomacy was thoroughly discredited. His habit of yielding to his son and his favorite had become fixed. He held out for some time and did his best to prevent discussion in the council. But in the end he yielded and the parliament was called.[1]

When the commons assembled, James found that power had slipped from his hands. Charles and Buckingham encouraged parliament in its desire for a break with Spain; they were ready to concede many points in domestic policy if only money was voted to be used against the Spaniards; and for the moment they became the idols of the popular party. James could only stand aside in helpless horror at their sudden alliance with the opposition and their new sympathy with the popular cause. Emancipated from his father's authority, Charles became in the eyes of the court "a lytill more populare then was fitting for him."[2] The Spanish ambassadors in London told James that Buckingham was seeking popularity in parliament at his expense, and James's reply, pathetic in its weakness, showed clearly that he knew it to be true.[3]

Throughout the parliament the king's hand was constantly being forced. When his speeches did not please the commons, Charles and Buckingham explained away his meaning and were

[1] Chamberlain to Carleton, January 31, 1624, St. P. Domestic, 14/158:72. *Cal. St. P. Venetian, 1623–1625*, 210. Conway to Buckingham, December 20, 1623, St. P. Domestic, 14/155:65. Von Rusdorff, *Mémoires et négociations secrètes*, I, 156. This last reference I owe to *Gardiner*, V, 157.

[2] "The Prince his carriage at this Parlament hes bein from the beginning thocht be the wyseste sorte to be a lytill too populare, and I dout his father was a lytill of that mynd." "Their is not that harmonye betwyxt the Kings Majestie and the Prince as I culd wishe." Earl of Kellie to the earl of Mar, May 13, 22, 30, 1624, *Mar and Kellie MSS, H. M. C.*, II, 200–04.

[3] *Cabala*, 90–93. An anonymous letter to the king called Buckingham "a man that is ambitious of popular ayr, as plainly appeared in Parliament," where he was "stiled the redeemer of his countrie." He had procured the parliament "because he thought his plots would be most acceptable to the Puritans, not without great injury to your Councel of State," from which he had fled to the parliament as to an altar of appeals. *Ibid.*, 218–19.

able to obtain his sanction for their explanations. When James received very coldly the first offer of the commons for assistance against Spain, Charles and Buckingham "produced certain explanations of the king's mind, and told them [the commons] they found the king was misunderstood, and that they had been with him the night before and found that it was not so as some had conceived." Again later in the session the commons were told "that his Majesty had given full power to the prince both to declare and explain anything that was delivered . . . before by the king in his speech [of March 14]." Charles and Buckingham forced James, much against his will, to receive a deputation from parliament urging him to break the Spanish treaties; and Buckingham wrote a most astonishing letter in which he all but demanded that James accept parliament's advice, decide to trust his own subjects rather than Spain, and "resolve once constantly to run one way." On several occasions Charles and Buckingham made promises in the king's name. Thus James was being pushed out of the picture.[4]

Charles and Buckingham also crushed opposition in the council. Before parliament assembled in 1624, five of the leading ministers — Williams, Arundel, Cranfield, Calvert, and Weston — opposed its summons and voted for a continuance of the Spanish negotiations.[5] Their opposition sprang from various motives, and they were dealt with in various ways. Calvert and Weston, although they believed in the value of the Spanish alliance, could be trusted to mold their opinions to those of their superiors and to follow instructions, whatever they might be. Arundel was left alone for the time being. But Buckingham showed his displeasure with Williams in no uncertain terms. Williams began to hear ru-

[4] D. Carleton to Sir Dudley Carleton, March 17, 1624, St. P. Domestic, 14/160:89. After the speech of March 14 the prince and parliament proceeded to draw up a revised draft of the king's words; "and to make it good it was carried by the prince to the king who did evalwe the particulars and declared this to be his meaning." Edward Nicholas to John Nicholas, March 15, 1624, St. P. Domestic, 14/160:81. D. Carleton to Sir Dudley Carleton, March 5, 1624, *ibid.*, 14/160:33; Nethersole to Carleton, April 25, 1624, *ibid.*, 14/163:50; Buckingham to James, about March 15, 1624, P. Yorke, earl of Hardwicke (ed.), *Hardwicke State Papers* (2 vols., London, 1778), I, 466. James, of course, presented difficulties. At one point Buckingham in good faith told the commons that a dispatch breaking off the treaties was on its way to Spain but found later that James had recalled the dispatch. March 17, 1624, Holles, f. 102; Nethersole to Carleton, March 25, 1624, St. P. Domestic, 14/161:36.
[5] Salvetti Correspondence, January 5, 1624, Add. MSS 27962, Vol. III, f. 88. Tillières to Puisieux, December 21, 29, 1623, Paris Trans., 3/57.

mors that he was to be dismissed from his place and that Buckingham "intended to sacrifice him this parliament to appease" the commons. Williams was thoroughly alarmed; just before parliament met, he made a complete submission, promising never again to oppose the duke.[6] Cranfield was less yielding, and Charles and Buckingham determined upon his ruin. They soon produced charges against him in the commons, and his impeachment quickly followed.

In parliament Charles and Buckingham found ready backing. In the house of lords Charles employed to the full his position as future sovereign and his youthful appeal to the loyalty of the peers. "He never misses a day at the parliament," wrote Chamberlain, "and is so careful to have all things go well, that, if any good fall, we shall owe it to his care and solicitation." He openly showed his resentment against those lords who opposed his policy. On one occasion he rebuked Cranfield and Arundel so sharply that they waited on him later in the day to excuse their conduct, but they must have received cold comfort, for Cranfield took to his bed for several days thereafter. But opposition was slight and the vast majority of peers decided to "warm themselves in the Light of the Rising Sun." When James attempted to save Cranfield from impeachment, he found that his influence was gone. "He courted many to take the side of his Treasurer," but "prevailed little." James asked Williams to use his influence with the peers. But Williams replied, "I have attempted, among my surest Friends, to bring him off fairly. All shrink and refuse me; only the stout and prudent Lord Hollis adventured upon the Frowns of the Prince and Duke, and gave his Reasons why Middlesex to him appeared an Innocent." Williams' advice, as usual, was sound but unpalatable. He told James that the prince was "the main Champion that encounters the Treasurer" and that the impeachment was called the prince's undertaking. James, therefore, must dishonor either his son or his treasurer.[7]

[6] John Packer to Williams, January 21, Williams to Buckingham, February 2, 1624, *Cabala,* 86–90; see quotations from Laud's diary printed in J. Forster, *Sir John Eliot* (2 vols., London, 1864), I, 127 note.

[7] Chamberlain to Carleton, March 20, 1624, *Court and Times, James I,* II, 453; Kellie to Mar, March 11, 1624, *Mar and Kellie MSS, H. M. C.,* II, 196. "The prince is said to be very sensible of the proceedings of some, who, according to their custom in the last Parliament, have their intelligences and underhand combinations to hinder all good resolutions." D. Carleton to Sir Dudley Carleton, March 17, 1624, St. P. Domestic, 14/160:89. Hacket, *Williams,* I, 189–90.

The policy of Charles and Buckingham fitted nicely with that of the popular lords, and an alliance was easily arranged. One of the accusations of the Spanish ambassadors was "that the Duke had reconciled himself to all the popular men of the State, and drawn them forth out of prisons, restraints, and confinements to alter the Government of the State at this Parliament, as Oxford, Southampton, Say, and others, whom he met at Suppers and Ordinaries to strengthen his popularity." The ambassadors also said that "they knew of meetings between the prince and members of parliament at night." Southampton took a prominent part in attacking Cranfield. Abbot was the spokesman of both houses of parliament in urging James to end the Spanish treaties. Pembroke swallowed his mistrust of Buckingham and promoted the break with Spain. Williams overcame his aversion for Laud and cooperated to obtain the wishes of Charles and Buckingham in the lords. And there were many moderate peers, those whom Williams described as listening to the grievances of the people while maintaining their loyalty to the crown, who now saw their way to do both.[8] There was thus no difficulty with the lords.

Nor did Charles and Buckingham have serious trouble with the commons. It is clear that the councillors and other officials in the house obeyed the duke rather than the king. Councillors must have had some embarrassing moments. James sought to maintain his authority by private instructions. He wrote Conway in April that he was expecting a report from Charles on the progress of the subsidy but commanded Conway to make him a private report also. "I have commanded my son to acquaint you with what he can discover," James wrote, "yet knows he not of these my private directions unto you. All this I must commit to your secrecy, discretion and dilligence." In May James complained that he found himself "less informed at this parliament than at others from his privy councillors of the house, from whom he challengeth that duty." He commanded the councillors to "be watchful over the motions and proceedings of the house," to stop the com-

---

[8] *Cabala,* 91; *Cal. St. P. Venetian, 1623–1625,* 301. "The principal men who did persecute Cranfield were the prince and the Duke of Buckingham, while others gave their helping hand, as the Earl of Southampton and Sir Miles Fleetwood." *Goodman,* I, 325. D. Carleton to Sir Dudley Carleton, March 5, Edward Nicholas to John Nicholas, March 15, 1624, St. P. Domestic, 14/160:33, 81. Forster, *Eliot,* I, 127. Williams to King James, February 22, 1623, Hacket, *Williams,* I, 109–10.

mons, if possible, from discussing certain reforms, and, if they were discussed, to inform him at once. But councillors followed the commands of the prince and duke. James had asked the commons for the very great sum of six subsidies and twelve fifteenths; but certain of the councillors, seeing that the house balked at such a large amount, moved for exactly half the sum which the king had demanded. They would hardly have suggested such a radical reduction had they not had private instructions. The constant attacks of councillors upon Spain were certainly the result of instructions from the duke and not the king. Councillors made more use of the prince's name than they would have ordinarily done. The commons were constantly told "that the way to please and satisfy the prince" was to assure the government of financial support. Nor did councillors lift a finger in defense of Cranfield.[9]

Many of those who attacked Cranfield in the commons were minor officials, obviously acting under instructions from the duke. The first accusation in the commons came from Sir Miles Fleetwood, an official in the court of wards. One of Cranfield's servants, a certain Mr. Colbecke, who got into trouble for being too loyal to him, said during the impeachment that "Sir Miles Fleetwood had been often to speak with him," presumably to obtain evidence. Cranfield was also attacked in the commons by Sir Benjamin Rudyard, another officer in the wards, by Sir Robert Pye, an official in the treasury, by solicitor Heath, by Sir William Cavendish and other courtiers. The lords appointed serjeant Randall Crew and Coventry, the attorney, to make the charges against Cranfield, and these men did their work with unusual zeal. Crew constantly interrupted Cranfield while making his defense, pointing out the weaknesses in his case; and Cranfield, in desperation, flared out that he had "been baited all the day . . . by two mastiffs, meaning Sir Randolph Crew and the attorney." Moreover, some of the witnesses called by Cranfield, many of them officials, gave evidence which harmed him considerably. Carleton wrote that "the very first twelve that were examined, and should have testified something for him in the expectation of all his judges, deposed directly against him, as yf they had been currupted to do him mischief." Thus Buckingham used his influence over minor

[9] The king to Conway, April 22(?), 1624, St. P. Domestic, 14/163:30. Conway to Calvert and Weston, May 20, Calvert to Conway, May 21, 1624, *ibid.*, 14/165:4, 11. March 19, 20, 1624, Nicholas, f. 92–100; Holles, f. 103. March 12, 1624, Nicholas, f. 73v.

officials to aid the assault against Cranfield. The duke and "all his Party" were working against the treasurer.[10]

Finally, there was an understanding between Buckingham and the popular leaders in the commons. According to the Venetian ambassador, James consented to calling parliament only with the stipulation that certain opposition leaders — Coke, Sir Edwin Sandys, Phelips, and Digges — should be excluded by being sent to Ireland. This was opposed in the council by Pembroke and Hamilton, and since Charles and Buckingham agreed with them the suggestion was dropped. There may possibly be something in the assumption of Forster that Buckingham saved these men from exile as part of an agreement for cooperation in the coming session. Chamberlain wrote in March that Phelips, Sandys, and Digges had little credit in the house because the commons "suspected them to be favorites and held them for undertakers." Chamberlain wrote that Sandys "had made his peace by a promise of all manner of conformity." When Charles and Buckingham went out of their way in a conference to imply that Cranfield had neglected the government of Ireland, Sandys reported the matter to the commons "so punctually and cleerely as begott much admiration." We know that Buckingham was in correspondence with Phelips.[11] The meetings of Charles and Buckingham with members of parliament were not confined to the nobility. Buckingham urged James to come to a decision on the Spanish marriage because he wished "to assure some of them [the commons] . . . underhand" that the treaties would be broken. Buckingham's temporary alliance with the popular lords gave him ample opportunity to communicate and combine with the leaders in the commons. Rudyard

[10] C. J., I, 755, 758–69; April 5, 7, 8, 1624, Nicholas, f. 112, 121. "Sir Robert Pye is sayd to worke against him." D. Carleton to Sir Dudley Carleton, April 4, 1624, St. P. Domestic, 14/162:13. L. J., III, 336, 349, 360; Chamberlain to Carleton, May 13, 1624, Court and Times, James I, II, 455–56. D. Carleton to Sir Dudley Carleton, May 3, 1624, St. P. Domestic, 14/164:12; Hacket, Williams, I, 189.

[11] Chamberlain to Carleton, January 3, 1624, Court and Times, James I, II, 443–44; Cal. St. P. Venetian, 1623–1625, 182–83; reports of the Spanish ambassadors, January 2, 8, 9, 1624, Spanish Trans., 12/31. Forster, Eliot, I, 128. Chamberlain to Carleton, January 31, 1624, St. P. Domestic, 14/158:72; Sir Henry Goodere to Carleton, April 18, 1624, ibid., 14/163:2; D. Carleton to Sir Dudley Carleton, April 19, 1624, ibid., 14/163:16. Buckingham tried to obtain a seat in the commons for Sandys in 1626 and 1628, but failed in both instances. Sandys represented Penryn, Cornwall, in 1625 and 1626, a borough which usually responded to court influence. St. P. Domestic, 16/18:28; 16/95:67. In 1624 Digges was defeated in Kent because he was called "a royalist." Chamberlain to Carleton, January 17, 1624, Court and Times, James I, II, 447–48. Sir Robert Phelips to Buckingham, August 21, 1624, Cabala, 264–66.

was a close connection of Pembroke's, and Rudyard came in this parliament to be as much a government spokesman as any of the council.[12] Abbot, Southampton, and Williams all had connections with popular leaders and could help if they wished. Moreover, the mass of independent voters in the commons, charmed for the moment by Buckingham's anti-Spanish policy, willingly followed his lead. It must not be supposed that the commons forgot their suspicions of the government or abandoned the redress of grievances. Nevertheless, Buckingham's way was an easy one in 1624.[13]

The parliaments of 1625 and 1626, however, tell a very different story. Buckingham's alliance with the popular party was essentially ephemeral. It sprang from common hostility to Spain, before differences arose as to the form that hostility should take, and from England's sense of relief that the Spanish match was ended. It sprang also from Buckingham's dangerous disregard of the price he paid to attain an immediate objective on which he had set

[12] *Cabala*, 90–93; *Cal. St. P. Venetian, 1623–1625*, 301. Buckingham to James, about March 15, 1624, *Hardwicke State Papers*, I, 466. On March 19 Rudyard was called one who had "twice before happily led the House." Holles, f. 103.

[13] Legal officials and serjeants in this house of commons included: Sir Robert Heath (solicitor); Sir Thomas Crew (speaker); Richard Digges; Sir Heneage Finch; John Finch; Sir Robert Hitcham; William Towse; Sir Edward Leech; Sir Eubule Thelwall (master in chancery); Sir Edward Moseley; Sir John Walter (attorney to the prince); Sir Thomas Trevor (solicitor to the prince); John Bankes; Sir Richard Dyott. Sir Clipsby Crew, John Hobart, and Richard Hutton were sons of judicial officials. Minor officeholders included: Sir William Beecher; John Coke; Sir Francis Cottington; Thomas and William Fanshawe; Sir Miles Fleetwood (receiver of the court of wards); Thomas Gewen (auditor of the duchy of Cornwall); Sir John Hippesley; Sir Robert Harley; Sir Henry Holcroft; Sir John Jepson; Sir Robert Mansell; Sir Humphrey May; Edward Nicholas; Edward Pitt (teller of the exchequer); Sir Robert and Sir Walter Pye; Sir Benjamin Rudyard (surveyor of the court of wards); Sir John Suckling; Sir Isaac Wake. Sir Edward and Thomas Conway, the sons of the secretary, were members. Other courtiers in this parliament were: Sir Robert Carr; Sir William Cavendish; Sir Edward Cecil; Ralph Clare; Sir Robert Cotton; Sir Francis Crane; Sir Charles Glemham; Sir George Goring; Sir Arthur Ingram; Sir Thomas Jermyn; John Maynard; Sir George More; Sir Francis Nethersole; Roger Palmer; Sir Nathaniel Rich; Edward Roberts; Sir Edward Seymour; Sir William Spencer; Sir Henry Vane; Sir Edward Villiers; Sir William Uvedall. John Angell, Francis Fetherstone, Sir Robert Hatton, Samuel Moore, Sir Richard Young, and Richard Zouch were returned by the Cinque Ports. Western royalists included: James Bagg, Sir Richard Edgecombe, Sir Robert Killigrew, John Mohun, Sir William Strode, Sir William Wray, William Coryton, Sir John Eliot.

The earl of Exeter wrote Conway in behalf of Sir William Spencer, who had committed some errors in the parliament of 1621 but had "showed himself most forward in all things this Parliament which might tend to his Majesties service and best pleasing, with much greife that anything should fawle from him formerly which might be occasion of his Majesties displeasure." June 6, 1624, St. P. Domestic, 14/167:19. Just before the parliament opened in 1624, Carlisle wrote James of the complaints about grievances he had heard from "divers gentlemen of qualitie, who are Parliament men, none of those popular and plausible orators, but solid and iudicious good patriots who fear God and honour the King." February 14, 1624, Harl. MSS 1580, f. 193.

his heart. But by 1625 the fundamental questions separating king and people once more arose. There was the religious question, enhanced by the Catholic marriage of the king and by well-founded suspicion that the French marriage treaty, like the Spanish, contained provisions favorable to English Catholicism. Charles, moreover, was already leaning toward the Laudian school of churchmen. There was the question of where the war should be fought. The commons thought of Spain as the Elizabethans had done, but Charles and Buckingham envisaged a great European alliance and had made large commitments on the Continent. The commons presupposed that English arms would meet with success; yet the one military attempt since 1624 was the Mansfeld expedition, which proved a disastrous and shameful fiasco. The grant of the commons in 1624 had been largely for the defense of the realm, but it was clear that the seas surrounding England were not safe for English shipping. This naturally prompted the commons to ask for an accounting of the sums that had been voted. Moreover, administrative abuses and other grievances continued. Finally, the economic depression that was partly responsible for the bitterness in parliament had not lifted. It deepened momentarily in 1625 because of the plague. One may read in the acts of the privy council the devastating effects the plague was having on every phase of social and economic life. All these things combined to increase distrust of Buckingham. The parliament of 1625, in essence, passed a vote of nonconfidence in the king's principal minister. When that vote had no effect, a movement against the duke began which culminated in his impeachment the following year. His monopoly of the affections of the young king caused great heartburning among other courtiers; and the smoldering hostility of the nobility might blaze forth at any time. Thus the parliament of 1625 contained highly combustible elements and should have been handled with the greatest care.

But Charles and Buckingham approached the parliament of 1625 in a spirit of blind self-confidence and made the dangerous assumption that their success in 1624 would now repeat itself. They were most eager for parliament to meet. When Williams was called into conference on the day following James's death, he found Charles suggesting that the parliament of 1624 be reassembled despite the lapse of the commission for holding it. If that was impossible, new writs must go out at once and not a day be lost. To Williams' suggestion that courtiers be allowed more time to secure election Charles merely replied that money was essential and that it was high time that it be voted.[14] But delays occurred in Henrietta Maria's departure from France, and the government did not wish to face parliament before her arrival in England. As a result, the commons, first summoned for May 17, were kept waiting in plague-stricken London until June 18 before parliament finally began. This in itself showed lack of foresight and was a very bad start.

This blunder was followed by a far greater one. The councillors in the commons were left completely without instructions during the first days of the parliament. It seems almost incredible that Charles and Buckingham assumed that the commons would meekly vote large sums of money for extensive military operations on the Continent without an accounting for the past or an explanation for the future. But such was the case. In an important debate on June 22 the commons discussed the general problem of what they should do during the session, but no councillor took part in the debate. Sir Benjamin Rudyard made a plea for unity with the new king and asked the house to avoid dangerous topics, by which he meant that there should be no committee for grievances thus early in the reign; and at the end of the debate Heath, the solicitor, promised that an answer would be given to the grievances presented in 1624. But there was no leadership from the government in either of these speeches. "More was expected from Rudyard then from others," wrote Eliot, "as he was in use and estimation with some great ones . . . but his expression was thought languid as the conclusion was inept."[15] Thus the government let slip an opportunity to lay a program before the commons, and courtiers were helpless without clearer instructions.

The opposition naturally took advantage of the government's remissness. The government had hinted at the need for money but had done nothing more. Suddenly on June 30, "unexpected to the Courtiers," Sir Francis Seymour moved that the king be given one subsidy and one fifteenth, an absurdly small amount, perhaps a

---

[14] Hacket, *Williams*, II, 4. A new reign necessitated a parliament in any case, and the council advised Charles to call one as soon as he became king. March 28, 1625, *Acts of the Privy Council, 1625–1626*, 4.
[15] *Commons Debates in 1625*, 9–13. *Negotium Posterorum*, I, 68–69.

tenth of what the government needed. Councillors were taken completely by surprise and were without instructions. Rudyard said the sum was too small but did not name any larger amount. The rest of the courtiers were silent, "none of the King's Councell or servants speaking in it then." After some debate the commons voted two subsidies without fifteenths, which were thought to fall too heavily upon the poor. "The House began now to setle both upon this proportion and upon the tymes [of payment]; when divers courtiers came in, who were most of them absent in the beginninge of this motion, as not expectinge this would have fallen out a daye for that businesse. Soe, though divers were provided to have spoken and ment to have urged for a larger proportion, yet not knowinge how the debate had past, and seeinge noe likelyhood of prevailinge, they held their peace." The opposition had secured a snap vote on a vital issue. It smacked of trickery without doubt. "Some art ther was," wrote Eliot, "to extenuat the proportion." This was unfortunate, but the government had invited some such action by its laxness in stating its case.[16]

When Buckingham found that success in the commons did not drop into his lap, he turned to rashness and violence. His usual method of dealing with opposition was to beat it down by the brute force of his assault, and he was far too inclined to try some sudden coup, as if to snatch the success that was rightfully his. At first the government appeared to acquiesce in the very small supply granted by the commons on June 30. There was no immediate protest from the king. Sir John Coke was given provisional instructions to ask for a larger grant, but they must have been countermanded, for he never carried them out.[17] The small supply that had been voted was allowed to pass through the normal stages of legislation. Meanwhile members were slipping away from London and the plague. Then suddenly on July 8 Coke appeared with new instructions. He made, for the first time in the session, a fairly complete statement of the king's financial needs, he outlined the foreign commitments of the government, and appealed to the com-

[16] *Negotium Posterorum,* I, 75–76. *Commons Debates in 1625,* 30–33.

[17] Coke was ordered to make "the best questions . . . he could gett means to propound and to divyde the house"; but if these were "dasht," he was then to ask the house in the king's name not to deal with any other matter until the subsidies already granted were passed. Coke never made any such motion, probably because the government at first decided not to ask for more and because the house passed the grant already voted without urging. Provisional instructions to Sir John Coke, St. P. Domestic, 16/4:26.

mons to grant additional subsidies. This episode throws light upon Buckingham's relations with the court group, and we will return to it presently in that connection. From the standpoint of parliamentary management and its effect upon the bulk of the commons it was a gross blunder; it was regarded as a shabby trick to obtain a vote on supply in a thin house; and it fell so flat that the solicitor himself put an end to it. "The disposition of the House did so fully appeare, that Mr. Solicitor (desparate of bringinge it to effect) took care only to lay it aside quietly, which he did in a short speech." Buckingham's coup had failed.[18]

Then the commons were told that after a recess of two brief weeks they should reassemble at Oxford. This was a move almost inconceivable in its rashness. Members had been in plague-infected London since May, and their chief thought was to get safely home. The government now called upon them, as if to inflict a spiteful punishment, to assemble once more and incur new risk of infection. The commons imagined that they were to be worn down by traveling from place to place and by exposure to disease until they voted money to finance Buckingham's schemes. They held the duke responsible for the adjournment and said openly that he had procured it for his own designs, which the commons now separated from the legitimate policies of the state. When they assembled at Oxford, they were asked for a paltry £40,000, far too small a sum to justify a special meeting of parliament. It is little wonder that Eliot became convinced, though wrongfully, that Buckingham was asking for money merely to be denied. Altogether the adjournment to Oxford was regarded as an injury and an insult.[19] It amounted, indeed, to a reckless abuse of the prerogative of calling and dissolving parliament.

The commons discovered, moreover, that Williams and other councillors had opposed the adjournment but had been overborne by Buckingham. "Upon privat disgusts among the Courtiers," wrote Eliot, "the secret was let out . . . how the Lord Keeper with some others, when the proposition for the adiournment was first made, being but the daie before it was, had with much violenc oppos'd it to the King, with reasons both of honor and profit to perswade him, and yet were therin master'd by the Duke" with

[18] *Commons Debates in 1625*, 56–59.
[19] *Cal. St. P. Venetian, 1625–1626*, 141–43. *Negotium Posterorum*, II, 30–32, 48. *Commons Debates in 1625*, 154, 156.

threats that he would ruin them for their opposition. Williams, says Hacket, told Charles that the adjournment would greatly offend the commons, that a further grant of supply was highly doubtful, and that Charles should not risk the probable hazard of a denial. Williams also said that he knew through private sources that certain members planned to attack the duke if parliament should reassemble at Oxford. But Williams promised that if the next meeting of the commons was postponed until winter, he could, by his connections in the house, through which he always imagined he could do great things, prevent an attack. The adjournment to Oxford, however, was "a Proposition mainly favour'd by the Lord-Duke, so that he grinn'd at the Lord-Keeper, all the while he diswaded it." Buckingham declared that public necessity must overrule the lord keeper's jealousy and "bade him and his Confederates do their worst, and besought that the Parliament might be continued, to confront that Faction." [20] Thus Buckingham turned to rashness and violence; and these things became known in the commons.

At Oxford he committed new follies. Again the councillors and other courtiers were handicapped by lack of instructions. Buckingham knew that he would probably be attacked at Oxford, but when Sir George Goring told the commons that the duke would gladly appear and answer accusations, he was speaking without instructions. His speech "was not liked by the House, and as little by my Lord Duke, . . . although he could not be displeased with him that sayd it, being assured of his good intention." There was terrible uncertainty among the courtiers about the exact amount of money for which the king was asking. At the opening of the Oxford meeting Conway spoke of £40,000, but the next day Edmondes asked for two subsidies and two fifteenths, which would be four or five times that sum. Weston supported Edmondes' motion "rather as t'was thought to ioyne in some perticular then by instruction for the summe. For it was noted to varie from that speech, which was made before the King, wherin thirtie or fortie thousand pounds was talk'd of." Throughout the

[20] *Negotium Posterorum*, II, 78–79. Hacket, *Williams*, II, 13–14. Williams often speaks of his friends in the house but never says who they were. He once remarked that his position as lord keeper gave him great power over the lawyers in the commons and that he knew and understood Sir Edward Coke. But his influence with the lawyers in general and with Coke in particular could hardly have been great.

parliament councillors hinted at the need of far larger sums than those for which the government was asking. This created a bad impression and showed clearly that Charles and Buckingham dared not be frank about the extent of their commitments.[21]

Buckingham needlessly offended the commons by selecting Sir John Coke to make the principal speech from the throne at the beginning of the Oxford session. Parliament had opened on August 1. On August 4 Charles summoned the houses to appear before him and urged them in a short speech to grant supply. Secretary Conway outlined the condition of Europe in general terms. Then Sir John Coke "was called up to the Kinge, and privatly received from him some short instructions, and then returninge to the middle of the hall entered into a large discourse." But Coke was not yet a councillor, nor had the commons been asked whether he might be employed in this way. "The envy that I bear," wrote Coke, "is that it hath not been known nor is agreeable to the orders of the House (as some think) that a nether house man was ever employed to deliver the King's pleasure to both Houses of Parliament." Eliot wrote that Coke, "though yet noe publicke minister of the State, and a member of the commons, was without leave from them, and that never done by anie man before, in their presenc made a dictator for the King." The earl of Westmorland thought it "somewhat strandge" that Conway and Coke were selected as orators at a time when more important officials — the lord keeper, the lord treasurer, or the president of the council — were "noe fooles." [22] If the commons were easily offended, the government was tactless.

This minor error was the result of sheer bad management. As Coke wrote Lord Brooke, he had arrived at Oxford on Tuesday, August 2, and "that night received his instructions to deliver the present state of affairs to the nether House" by a message; "which on Wednesday night was changed and left doubtful whether the

---

[21] *Commons Debates in 1625*, 74, 89, 156–57. *Negotium Posterorum*, II, 17, 38. The same mistake was made in the early days of the 1626 parliament. The government offered neither excuses for the past nor a program for the future. In an important debate on impositions (February 15) no councillor spoke to explain the attitude of the government. Rich, f. 16–17. Such tactics drove the commons to the conclusion that they must seek information for themselves.

[22] *Commons Debates in 1625*, 74. Coke wrote, "For my part I neither had ambition nor thought of speaking in that place." Coke to Lord Brooke, August 4, 1625, *Cowper MSS*, *H. M. C.*, I, 208–09. *Negotium Posterorum*, II, 18–22. Earl of Westmorland to Sir George Manners, August 7, 1625, *Rutland MSS*, *H. M. C.*, I, 473–74.

Lord Conway or I [Sir John Coke] should relate it to both Houses in the presence of the King, and this morning even in the Hall where we met the counsel varied again, and the Lord Conway was required to say something and I to present the rest, so as a greater charge with so little warning and many changes could hardly have been laid upon so weak shoulders." The content of Coke's speech was also altered. His first instructions called for a brief narration of recent developments in Europe and a general statement of the need of money. But at the very instant Coke was about to speak, the king, as we have seen, instructed him privately "to show the importance of the Fleet, and that it could not proceed without a present supply. . . . [This] sudden change of counsel which gave not time to any other to be instructed for a speech of near an hour long" forced Charles and Buckingham to employ Coke as they did and thus offend the commons.[23] Such confusion and change of plan were unnecessary.

In other ways also, Buckingham showed astonishing tactlessness in dealing with the commons. He summoned them to appear before him on August 8, as if he were the king himself, and made a speech of self-defense which, in their eyes, was a compound of boasting and arrogance. He termed his speech a declaration from the king; yet it was chiefly a recital "of his own approbations and applauses" and made the king's name appear "a servant to his ends," which was thought insolent and presuming. He claimed credit for all he could, "turning fortuities into glorie." Williams was present, but his part was so small that he was made "subservient to the Duke," upon whom "the whole parliament was attendant." Buckingham's one concession dealt with religion; but this concession was regarded by the commons as a prostitution of sacred things for political ends and made religion itself "troope up with the rabble of his followers." [24] These are Eliot's impressions and are doubtless overcharged. But there is no doubt that Buckingham's manner gave great offense. Indeed, he never learned to

---

[23] Coke to Lord Brooke, August 4, 1625, *Cowper MSS, H. M. C.,* I, 208–09. "Instructions for a Message first appointed to be delivered in the nether howse: but afterwards by commandment delivered in the upper howse before the King, Lords, and Commons at Christchurch hall at Oxford." St. P. Domestic, 16/4:14. *Commons Debates in 1625,* 74; *Negotium Posterorum,* II, 18.

[24] *Negotium Posterorum,* II, 76–79. Williams certainly considered himself slighted at Oxford. He complained that he was "unemploy'd in the Duties of his Place," which were usurped by the duke or delegated to other councillors. Hacket, *Williams,* II, 18.

judge the effect his tactics might have among the commons. When the house voted five subsidies on April 4, 1628, Charles and Buckingham, in surprise and delight, spoke gratefully in the council of the action of the commons. On the following day Sir John Coke repeated Buckingham's words in the house in an effort to present their author in a favorable light; but he was sharply taken to task by Eliot for coupling Buckingham's name too closely with that of the king and for implying that the commons should be grateful for the approbation of the duke. Coke may have spoken ineptly. Yet he was carrying out instructions; Sir Francis Nethersole wrote that Buckingham had decided to have his speech reported to the commons, "wherein I think the Duke is ill-advised." [25]

Thus Buckingham's management of the crown's relations with the commons in 1625 could scarcely have been worse. Overconfidence, carelessness, rashness, and lack of tact combined to alienate parliament, and were not forgotten at the time of Buckingham's impeachment in 1626.

If we turn from his dealings with the commons as a whole to his relations with his own followers, or those who should have been his followers, we find a roughly parallel development. Buckingham was constantly alienating his own supporters. He was quarrelsome and easily offended. Partly because of his vanity and partly because he was an upstart who could not permit familiarity, he demanded a cringing subservience from his followers. His servants had to become his creatures. He never had a friend, wrote Clarendon, near enough in rank to give him candid advice; "nor was he very fortunate in the election of those dependents, very few of his servants having been ever qualified enough to assist or advise him, and were intent only upon growing rich under him." Independent judgment and frank advice were even less welcome at court than in the reign of James. The best men, therefore, either were excluded from office or refused to serve under the conditions Buckingham imposed. There was a growing sentiment that the state was not worth serving while he remained at the helm. Nor could his dependents be certain of his constant support. "His lord-

[25] Nethersole to the queen of Bohemia, April 6, 14, 1628, St. P. Domestic, 16/100:44; 16/101:3. Mead to Stuteville, April 12, 13, 1628, *Court and Times, Charles I,* I, 338–40. St. P. Domestic, 16/100:30. *Rushworth,* I, 525–27. Buckingham tried earlier in the session of 1628 to frighten the commons by telling them of the activities of a group of Jesuits found in Clerkenwell; but failed completely and the commons ignored the information placed before them. March 24, 1628, Harl. MSS 4771, f. 24.

ship was bred in a great Error," wrote Hacket, "he was so ready to cast a Cloud suddenly upon his Creatures, and with much inconstancy to root up that which he had planted, . . . quickly weary of those whom he had gratified, and apt to resume his Favours to make Trial upon others." The number of men who had held office only to lose it was constantly increasing, and Buckingham's path was strewn with those whom he had helped to ruin. Even such a patient and faithful servant as Sir John Coke might find himself in sudden disfavor. When Buckingham returned from the failure at Rhé, he tried to throw the blame on others and ungraciously accused Coke of neglect in sending supplies.[26] One could cite many cases in which Buckingham's servants felt his displeasure through no fault of their own. These things resulted in a constant drift of courtiers and offended officials into the ranks of the opposition. Disaffection among the courtiers had been serious under James; it now became a major cause of the government's failure in dealing with parliament. It was said in 1626 that the impeachment was begun by men who had been excluded from office or were the relations or dependents of those whom the duke had ruined. It is certainly safe to say that a large number of men formerly connected with the government joined, if they did not originate, the attack upon the favorite.

The way in which Buckingham tried the patience of his followers may be seen in the circumstances surrounding Coke's motion for increased supply on July 8, 1625. The commons had made a very small grant, as we have seen, on June 30, but the government had appeared to be content. Then suddenly came Coke's motion. There was much behind it. Buckingham had arrived from Hampton Court the night before, determined to make a fresh effort to obtain supply. He held a conference at his own house about midnight with his closest followers, his "privados" as Eliot calls them, who "were all sent for to receave instructions in the pointe." They agreed that a new attempt should be made. "But in the morning when it came to others [absent the night

---

[26] *Clarendon*, I, 42. For an excellent illustration of how courtiers were alienated, see Thomson, "John Holles," *Journal of Modern History*, 8:145–72. Hacket, *Williams*, I, 40. For the temporary disgrace of Coke, see *Court and Times, Charles I*, I, 297; *Cal. St. P. Venetian, 1626–1628*, 499; Sir James Bagg to Buckingham, May 24, 1628, St. P. Domestic, 16/105:4. While Charles was more faithful to his servants, he was easily offended and constantly thought in terms of their duty toward him rather than of his obligations toward them.

before], whose qualitie was more knowing and ingenuous," they besought the duke to abandon so reckless and dangerous a plan. Sir Humphrey May in particular, wrote Eliot, "travaild with much industrie in that service, but in vaine." The fact that May, Weston, and Heath were all passed over and the motion entrusted to Sir John Coke is proof in itself that Buckingham's ablest followers disapproved. When May's entreaties failed, he "came in haste" to Sir John Eliot, "whom he thought more powerfull with the Duke . . . and him he importund to a new attempt and triall for staie or diversion of that worke." Eliot agreed to go and talk with Buckingham, and May promised to hold back the motion in the house until the result of Eliot's efforts was known. Eliot found the duke still in bed but was admitted to his presence. He told him that the motion was dangerous and unseasonable because the king had apparently accepted the former grant and the house was now very thin; an attempt to obtain supply by "an ambuscado and surprise" would reflect upon the honor of the king, who should not give offense thus early in the reign. Eliot added that the commons would think of it as Buckingham's act and would dislike him for it and that it had small hope of success. But Buckingham would not be convinced. The commons themselves were to blame, he argued, if the house was empty; the king's honor was more engaged to fulfill his military commitments than to please the commons; and the attempt must be made if only to be denied. These last words, implying that the king was ready to turn to new devices for obtaining money, filled Eliot with consternation and increased his suspicions of the court.

Meanwhile in the house May had had great difficulty in re-straining Coke, "who was great, in his opinion, with that honor and imploiment, and labor'd, as a woman does with child, in desire to bring it foorth." Eliot's failure being known, the motion was made. It fell terribly flat, as we know. But what is surprising is that it failed, at least according to Eliot, largely through the opposition of the courtiers themselves. "Ther was noe deniall, nor noe question, it being never brought soe farr, which had almost a miracle within it; for ther were hardlie then three-score in the house, and of those, countrimen not the most. Anie support or agitation it had had must have needs driven it to a concession, or the contrarie; but as we noted, the Courtiers much disliking it, some as it came not in perticular by them, or that they were not preconsulted for the worke; others for the danger and preiudice it imported; the rest for the sudenness and strangeness of the thing, . . . all generallie abhorring it, . . . it vanish'd through it's own lightness and futilitie." All the duke's "privado's were condemn'd, as remiss and negligent in the service. His frindes were all complain'd of, thus to have fail'd his hopes." Buckingham had failed through the opposition of his own party.[27]

It may be that Eliot exaggerated the revolt of the courtiers. But certainly the episode was calculated to anger many of the duke's adherents. They regarded the motion for supply as a rash and foolish step, foisted upon them by the duke and his more irresponsible advisers. If the commons were irritated at the favor shown to Coke, the councillors and other officials in the commons must have resented it even more. It could hardly have aided cordiality between Coke and May. The episode shows clearly the difference between the two men. Coke is overflowing with blundering eagerness to carry out instructions, regardless of their consequences. With keener perception May reads the temper of the house more correctly and seeks to avoid mistakes. We have no direct evidence but a number of hints that the two men could not get on together, and an episode such as this must have left relations rather strained. May was himself a candidate for the office of secretary soon to be conferred upon Coke, whom he must have regarded as his inferior in every way. He remarked in the commons in 1626 that "the Lord Duke was knowne better to him for injuries than benefitts." [28] May continued to render able service to the crown, but he and other courtiers must have felt profound disgust for the way in which affairs were run.

During the session at Oxford another type of disintegration is seen in the court group. Buckingham was soon in trouble with the commons, and a break appeared inevitable. About August 6 a group of men who were Buckingham's friends without being

[27] *Negotium Posterorum,* I, 110–19. The opposition of Williams and other councillors to the adjournment to Oxford became known, wrote Eliot, "upon privat disgusts among the courtiers." *Ibid.,* II, 78.

[28] May had been a candidate for the secretaryship in 1617. But the office was given to Naunton. Chamberlain wrote that they "both presume upon the Duke of Buckingham's favour." In 1625 Chamberlain wrote regarding the office of secretary, "Sir Humphrey May is come in as a pretender or competitor to Sir John Coke." *Court and Times, James I,* II, 46, 508. March 24, 1626, Whitelocke, f. 84–85.

his creatures urged him to make concessions to the commons. "The advise he had," says Eliot, "was much to indeavor an accomodation with the parliament." The concessions suggested to him were far-reaching. He was to blame minor officials for mistakes in naval administration, to admit new men to the council, to follow the commons in religious policy, and, above all, to dissolve parliament until the plague had abated. If these things were done, there was hope of some better accord in the next session. These ideas appear in the speeches (August 6) of Sir Henry Mildmay, master of the jewel house, Eliot, William Coryton, Sir William Strode, and Sir Nathaniel Rich. The next morning Sir Miles Fleetwood argued for supply at some later date but opposed it for the present. "These and the like counsells were presented to the Duke," says Eliot, "which wrought an inclination for the instant that gave his friends some hope: but those that were about him gave it an alteration in the cabinet." Buckingham refused concessions except on religion and determined to make a last personal appeal to the commons for money. This was, of course, a complete failure.[29]

The men who urged Buckingham to yield to the commons were men connected with the government. Eliot, Coryton, Mildmay, and Fleetwood all held office at this time. Williams wrote, perhaps with some exaggeration, that Eliot, Saye, Strode, and Rich were "never out of my Lord-Duke's Chamber, and Bosom."[30] What became of these men? Mildmay, Fleetwood, and Strode remained with the government. But Eliot, Coryton, and Rich moved into the opposition.

The court group in the commons was deeply affected by hostility between Buckingham and certain leading members of the house of lords. These men became a nucleus for opposition in

[29] *Negotium Posterorum*, II, 53–55; *Commons Debates in 1625*, xiii–xx, 90–91; *C. J.*, I, 811. "The duke is guided by the private counsels of individuals, who are partly inexperienced in affairs, partly malicious." *Cal. St. P. Venetian, 1625–1626*, 298. See also Hacket, *Williams*, II, 15.

In the debate in the council when the decision was taken to throw over the Catholics, "all agreed in advising the king to satisfy parliament in everything. The Lord Keeper stood apart, protesting that he was a good Protestant, but they must consider that the king had pledged his word of honor about the Catholics over the marriage. The duke and Carlisle, who managed the affair, said there was nothing in that to prevent, and so the Lord Keeper came round to the general opinion. With this decision the king sent the duke to parliament, with various expedients." *Cal. St. P. Venetian, 1625–1626*, 143; *Commons Debates in 1625*, 93–105.

[30] Williams to the king, August 14, 1625, Hacket, *Williams*, II, 18.

the upper chamber. They also joined forces with the popular leaders in the house and used their influence among members to increase the strength of the opposition. Thus Buckingham found members of both houses working in close cooperation against him, while certain men in the commons who would ordinarily have been counted among the supporters of the crown were drawn away into opposition through their connections with the nobility. This development became apparent in the last days of the Oxford session and was of great importance during the impeachment proceedings of 1626. It was a final blow to any hopes that Buckingham had concerning the house of commons.

Buckingham believed that the attack upon him at Oxford was due in large measure to a group of hostile lords. He "was possessed" that Abbot, Williams, Pembroke, and Arundel, all privy councillors of great importance, were ready to push any accusation that came against him in the house of lords and that they combined and consulted with many in the lower house to attack him in the commons.[31] He also suspected Bristol of plotting with the commons. Sir James Bagg, in an interesting letter written in 1626, attempted to analyze the faction that was attacking the duke. He found a widespread combination of lords and commons and believed that this combination was forming at the end of the Oxford parliament.

Before turning to the commons, let us look at the noblemen whom Buckingham suspected. From Bristol we have an emphatic denial. "I hear my Lord Duke should be informed," he wrote in 1626, "that I should plot and combine with some Parliament-men that seemed adverse to his Grace at Oxford . . . I take God to record, I never would have to do, since I came into England, with any thing belonging to Parliament, nor never attempted any thing to the Duke's prejudice."[32] This, from Bristol, is conclusive.

[31] Buckingham "was, and is possessed, that there were four in the higher House, that upon any Complaint that should come up of him to them, that they with all their Strength would set it forwards there. He is likewise possessed, that there was divers combined against him in the lower House. For them in the higher House, it was my Lord's Grace of Canterbury, my Lord Keeper, my Lord Marshal, and my Lord Chamberlain. For them of the lower House, he doth conceive, there were many, who had their Conferences with these four Lords and others, that were depending upon them; among which, you are not altogether free." Sir Arthur Ingram to Sir Thomas Wentworth, November 7, 1625, *Strafford's Letters*, I, 28. There was a rumor that these four lords would be questioned after the dissolution. Kellie to Mar, August 15, 1625, *Mar and Kellie MSS, H. M. C.*, II, 233.
[32] Earl of Bristol to Sir Kenelm Digby, February 6, 1626, *Goodman*, II, 397–99.

If ever a man had reason to hate Buckingham, it was he; and in the parliament of 1626 his charges of treason against the duke paralleled the accusations of the commons. But we must believe his statement that he did not combine with the opposition leaders in the house.

Williams also denied the charge. In a letter to the king written in August, 1625, he declared that at Oxford he had never spoken "with any of the stirring Men, . . . excepting once with Philips, with the Privity, and for the Service of the Duke." Again and again, he declared, he had asked the king and Buckingham for instructions for the part he was to play and for the use to be made of his influence among the commons. But no instructions were ever given him. Those members who were ready to vote supply, wrote Williams, came as often to him as to any other lord and could vouch for his zeal to promote the interests of the duke. As the presiding officer in the lords, he had actively opposed many of the commons' desires. But since he knew that his position at court was most precarious and since he had no assurance of royal support for anything he did, he durst not be more "active and stirring by his friends in that House" than became the ordinary duty of a privy councillor. Williams was doubtless telling the truth. He was not the man to cut off hope of reconciliation with the duke by intriguing against him with the leaders of the commons, and his fear of dismissal would make him more cautious than usual.

Williams added that it was Buckingham who stirred the commons against him rather than he who stirred the commons against the duke. He had been told that he would be complained of in the commons in 1625 and justly suspected Buckingham of instigating some such move. Buckingham told him that he knew the men who planned to produce charges but would not reveal their names; when Williams send confidential agents to the duke to make inquiries, they were answered with insolence. As members gathered at Oxford, one of Buckingham's followers told Sir Francis Seymour that if the commons would "set upon the Lord-Keeper, they should be backed by the greatest Men in the Kingdom"; but Seymour answered sharply that he found nothing against the lord keeper "but the Malice of those great Men." Williams wrote that the members who spoke against him in the commons at Oxford were known to be intimate with the duke. And several lords told Williams that "his Grace's Agents stirred all their Powers to set the Commons upon him." Thus Buckingham imagined that the commons might rid him of Williams as they had of Cranfield. The attack upon Williams did not materialize at Oxford; but he was dismissed from his place as lord keeper in the following autumn and ordered to remain in his bishopric during the parliament of 1626. Thus he took no part in public life during the impeachment of the duke.[33]

Arundel had opposed Buckingham both in the council and in the house of lords, and the relations of the two men were certainly bad in 1625. Ingram wrote in November that Arundel "had the Hand of the Great Duke upon him, who by his Means had brought the King, that he would hardly speak with him." Before the opening of the parliament of 1626 Arundel was placed under arrest, and his restraint raised a question of privilege between the king and the upper chamber. But while the lords eventually secured Arundel's release, he did not take his seat until the closing weeks of the parliament of 1626, which makes any combination between him and the commons practically impossible. Nor is there any evidence of his combining with them in 1625. We know, however, that in that year he obtained a seat at Thetford for Sir Robert Cotton, who circulated among the commons a paper containing medieval precedents in support of the advanced views of the constitution held by opposition leaders. This paper came to Buckingham's knowledge, and Cotton fell into disfavor at court. Cotton was an intimate friend of Arundel, and the connection between them may well have been the basis of Buckingham's suspicions.[34]

[33] Williams declared that during the last parliament he had shown his loyalty to the king by urging in council that the crown should not yield to the commons regarding religion, by "lingering and staying the Bill against Recusants," by opposing Lord Saye in stopping the bill of tonnage and poundage, "which was the Darling of the Active part in the House of Commons." Williams to King Charles, August 14, 1625, Hacket, *Williams,* II, 17–18, 68–71.

[34] Ingram to Wentworth, November 7, 1625, *Strafford's Letters,* I, 28. Cott. MSS Julius C III, f. 284. "Sir Robert Cotton's books are threatened to be taken away, because he is accused of imparting ancient precedents to the lower house." ———— to Mead, April 28, 1626, *Court and Times, Charles I,* I, 98. See also *D. N. B.* under Cotton. Arundel secured the return of John Wilson and Robert Spiller from Castle Rising in 1621 and the return of Spiller from the same borough in 1624. Arundel to the mayor and citizens of Castle Rising, 1623(?), St. P. Domestic, 14/135:42. The Venetian ambassador spoke of Arundel's "followers" in the parliament of 1626. *Cal. St. P. Venetian, 1625–1626,* 512.

Buckingham had better cause for suspecting Pembroke and Abbot. Pembroke's hostility to the duke at this time is well known, and he was in a position to indulge it more freely than others. He was the wealthiest peer in the kingdom, and his power and prestige were very great. He was able to influence elections in a number of constituencies. He had at least a dozen friends and dependents in the commons during the parliament of 1625[35] and as many in that of 1626. The chief interest of Bagg's letter, to which we have referred, lies in its assertion that certain of the seats at Pembroke's disposal were filled in 1626 with men, many of them formerly connected with the government, who now led the attack upon Buckingham.

Bagg's letter was written in March, 1626, and addressed to Buckingham.[36] "Taking the end of the Oxford parliament and the beginning of this into consideration," he wrote, it was clear that a plot had been laid "maliciously withoute cause intendinge your ruine." Bagg found a number of elements combining against the duke; and Pembroke was a prime mover. But Pembroke, Bagg asserted, was not acting through his obvious adherents, such as Sir Benjamin Rudyard or Sir William Herbert, who were Buckingham's "owne ministers," but rather through strangers who might be thought to be acting independently, though Pembroke knew them to be the duke's enemies and for that reason had provided them with seats in the commons. It is true that neither Rudyard nor Sir William Herbert took a prominent part against the government. Rudyard, though normally following Pembroke's lead, was always moderate during this parliament; he was appointed to assist the managers of the impeachment proceedings, but he was not active against the government. Nor was Sir William Herbert. On the other hand, Edward Herbert, later the attorney-general, took a prominent part in the impeachment.

[35] Violet A. Rowe, "The Influence of the Earls of Pembroke on Parliamentary Elections, 1625–41," *English Historical Review,* 50:242–56. Miss Rowe finds the following were Pembroke's friends and dependents in the parliament of 1625: Sir Benjamin Rudyard (Portsmouth), John Thoroughgood, Pembroke's secretary (Shaftesbury), Michael Oldsworth, another of Pembroke's secretaries (Old Sarum), Sir John Stradling (Old Sarum), Edward Herbert, later attorney, and Sir Clipsby Crew (Downton), Sir Thomas Morgan and Sir Thomas Harrington (Wilton), Sir William Herbert (Montgomeryshire), William Price (Cardiff), William Coryton (Liskeard), and Richard Pooley (Queenborough, Kent).

[36] Sir James Bagg to Buckingham, March, 1626, *Notes and Queries,* 4th series, 10: 325–26; *Cal. St. P. Domestic, Addenda, 1625–1649,* 112–13. Bagg is not the best of witnesses, but his letter, when tested against other evidence by Miss Rowe, appears to be substantially sound. I am indebted to Miss Rowe's article for several suggestions.

Bagg began by declaring that Sir Robert Mansell had been placed at Lostwithiel through Pembroke's influence, Pembroke taking elaborate precautions that the fact should not be known. Mansell had long been connected with the administration of the navy, in which he had amassed wealth by notorious peculation; but he had quarreled with Buckingham in 1621 and became in 1625 and 1626 a most troublesome member of the opposition. His declaration in 1625 that though he was a member of the council of war, he had never been consulted about Buckingham's military plans so embarrassed the government that it produced an elaborate defense by Heath. The earl of Kellie wrote of this episode, "Then Sir Robert with sume violence and more heate then judgement did showe a great deall of spleen and anger against my Lord of Bukkinghame." Mansell was reprimanded by the council after the dissolution. In 1626 he continued his attack upon Buckingham's military policy, and the government feared he would disobey instructions issued to the council of war not to answer questions in the house of commons. As a matter of fact, Mansell obeyed his instructions; but he declared in the commons that in his opinion the council of war should answer the questions of the house. He added that he would like to go to the king for permission to answer freely. He is a good example of a former public servant now violently opposed to Buckingham's administration.[37]

Mansell's election had been secured through Pembroke's vice-warden of the stannaries, William Coryton, whom Pembroke had instructed to find seats for Mansell, Sir Francis Stewart, Sir Clipsby Crew, and William Murray. Sir Francis Stewart was a courtier whom James had loved and to whom Charles had also shown favor. But he took a very independent tone in 1626. His opposition may have been known before the parliament met, for he had been backed against Sir Thomas Edmondes by the more independent voters in the election at Oxford University. A story

---

[37] *Commons Debates in 1625*, 115–16, 122–24, 161–62; *Negotium Posterorum*, II, 97–98; *Mar and Kellie MSS, H. M. C.*, II, 233. February 24, 1626, Rich, f. 34v. Conway wrote Buckingham, March 8, 1626, that he had asked the members of the council of war to come to his house for instructions about what they should say in the house. "I am confident that, except it be Sir Robert Mansell, we shall all make the same answer as we formerly did, and if Sir Robert come hither we will inform him sufficiently to keep him from flying out, or to leave him inexcusable if he do." *Cal. St. P. Domestic, Addenda, 1625–1649*, 107; March 9, 1626, Whitelocke, f. 34v; Rich, f. 65v. Mansell was said to be in danger in 1626 of losing his patent for the manufacture of glass "if his great enemy may prevail against him." ———— to Mead, November 4, 1626, *Court and Times, Charles I*, I, 165. See *Goodman*, I, 56–57.

was told in 1626 of a conversation between him and Buckingham "when they came forth of the house." Buckingham reproached Stewart for his opposition and declared that Stewart himself was not "so clear from pillaging as his flourishes persuade the world." Nevertheless, said Buckingham, he had not attacked Stewart; to which Stewart replied, "My Lord, you had best to begin with me by times, for to-morrow, in the morning, I mean to fall upon you." As a result of his independence Stewart was dismissed from court in April. Pembroke pleaded with Charles to spare him, but the king refused. At the same time two other courtiers, Sir Ralph Clare and Sir William Croft, were also dismissed from court because of their behavior in the commons.[38] Of the other men for whom Coryton was told to provide, Sir Clipsby Crew was the son of Sir Randall Crew, speaker in 1614, who was dismissed as chief justice of the king's bench late in 1626; and William Murray was a gentleman of the bedchamber. These were men from whom the government might have expected support.

Bagg also suggested that Dr. Turner owed his seat at Shaftesbury to Pembroke's influence. A Mr. Thoroughgood, Pembroke's secretary, had been elected there but relinquished the seat upon a double return and was succeeded by Turner. There is also other evidence of Turner's connection with Pembroke. Turner spoke boldly and sharply against the duke and was the first member to bring formal charges against him. He appears to have been a person of force and character and not the mere tool that Gardiner depicts him.

Bagg suspected, though he could not prove, that Sir James Fullerton had been placed at Portsmouth by Pembroke. Pembroke was captain of the castle at Portsmouth, and Rudyard had been elected there to the parliaments of 1621, 1624, and 1625. In February, 1626, Rudyard wrote: "I am not yet certayne that I am of the Parliament, havinge delivered my usuall place of Portsmouth to my Brother Harrington Lieutenaunt theare, whoe desyred it of me soe late, that all my Lordes letters weare sent out before."[39] Sir

---

[38] For Stewart's election at Oxford, see page 76 above. Mead to Stuteville, April 15, ——— to Mead, April 28, 1626, *Court and Times, Charles I*, I, 95, 97–98; *Cal. St. P. Venetian, 1625–1626*, 416.

[39] Rudyard to Nethersole, February 3, 1626, St. P. Domestic, 16/20:23. Rudyard had married Sir William Harrington's sister, who was a kinswoman of Pembroke. Harrington was also elected at Hertford; he relinquished the seat at Portsmouth, which was then obtained by Fullerton.

James Fullerton was a Scot who had long held places of importance in the household of Prince Henry and later in that of Prince Charles. It is possible that the secret correspondence between James and Sir Robert Cecil before the death of Elizabeth had passed through his hands. "I observe," wrote Bagg, "that Sir James Fullerton speakes nothinge, but with that thect the Lord Cavendishe while he was of that House, was the abettor of all that faction; his nearness to Fullerton you knowe." Fullerton was the stepfather of Lady Cavendish. Sir William Cavendish, or Lord Cavendish as he was styled, was the son of the earl of Devonshire, whom he succeeded early in 1626. He was a leader of court society and had been a personal friend of James. He had long been in the house of commons, where he had consistently supported the government. But he attacked Buckingham bitterly in the commons during the opening debates in 1626 [40] and continued his hostility after he became a member of the lords. He was a close associate of Pembroke.

William Coryton, Bagg continued, was a close connection of both Pembroke and Cavendish. He was Pembroke's vice-warden for the stannaries, his deputy lieutenant, and custos rotulorum for Cornwall; and he told Bagg that if he lost Pembroke's favor he was undone. He was also an associate of Cavendish, with whom he was closely connected by marriage. "With that familye," wrote Bagg, Coryton "is well esteemed, . . . and to that house he often resorts. A word of direction from a person so near in attendance on his Majesty will give much encouragement to their ill intendements." [41] Coryton was a close friend of Eliot and became a leader in the commons although his tone was always moderate. Bagg also connected Sir John Eliot with Pembroke. Eliot, he wrote, "was in a distraction how to divide himself betweene your Grace and the Earl of Pembroke. But to whom he hath whollie given himself your lordship can judge." Here Bagg allowed his dislike of Eliot to warp his judgment. If Eliot looked to Pembroke, as he may well have done, he was not prepared to give himself wholly to the earl any more than he had formerly done to the duke.

So much for Pembroke's connections in the house. Bagg found other elements also in the combination against the duke. Sir

---

[40] February 22, 24, 1626, Whitelocke, f. 72v, 66v.
[41] For the family relationship of Cavendish, Fullerton, and Coryton, see Miss Rowe's article, 249 note.

Thomas Lake, the old secretary of James, and his two sons, Sir Thomas and Sir Arthur, were members of this parliament and joined in the attacks upon the favorite. The younger Sir Thomas Lake, wrote Bagg, "doth not weekely assiste this faction, and he is thought to be an inward man with the Earl of Kelly." Meddus wrote in May that Lake was in danger of arrest; and Hippesley besought his patron in 1628 to persuade Pembroke not to give seats in the commons to "Sir Thomas Lake and Doctor Tourner and such like that for their owne endes neither care for the Kinge nor common wealth, these are the men that bringe all to utter Ruen." An anonymous letter to Charles in 1626 stated that much of the attack upon the duke came from "malcontents censured or decourted for their deserts, as the kindred and dependents of the Earl of Suffolk, and of Sir Henry Yelverton [whose son Sir Christopher was a member of this parliament], Coke, Lake, and Middlesex." [42] Thus Buckingham was paying for the long series of dismissals which he had helped to bring about.

Bagg next mentioned two connections of archbishop Abbot: "For Sir Dudley Digges, beinge pryvately more dangerous than publique, is thought wholly my Lord of Canterburies. Sir Morrice Abbott, cheiffe of the East India Companye, maye be thought the plotter of that accusation." The archbishop's hostility to Buckingham is well known, as is also his close connection with Sir Dudley Digges. Digges is not an easy man to place. He was obviously extremely loath to lose the good opinion of the court and sought to keep it while opposing the government in the house of commons. His constitutional ideas were drawn from the reign of Elizabeth. A letter of advice which he wrote to Charles at the opening of the reign in 1625 bears a striking resemblance to the advice which Bacon had bestowed so lavishly upon Charles's father.[43] Digges represented that conservatism, so universal among

---

[42] Meddus to Mead, May 22, 1626, *Court and Times, Charles I*, I, 105. Hippesley to Buckingham, February 2, 1628, St. P. Domestic, 16/92:12. *Cabala*, 224–27. "Some say, my Lord of Suffolk having given his proxy to my Lord of Walden, his eldest son, and now, finding him ducal, hath revoked it, and given it to the Earl of Berkshire, his younger son, being the duke's professed opposite." ——— to Mead, May 26, 1626, *Court and Times, Charles I*, I, 106.

[43] Chamberlain wrote in 1622 that Digges was then at court "in hopes somewhat would fall to his lot." Abbot said that Digges was for a time in Buckingham's service but left it because of "some unworthy carriage" toward him on Buckingham's part. Abbot wrote, "He called me father and I term his wife my daughter." See *D. N. B.* under Digges and Abbot. Digges to the king, January, 1626, St. P. Domestic, 16/19:107.

members, which regarded the acts and policies of the Stuarts as new and dangerous departures from established Tudor custom. Thus he was forced into opposition. He was one of the managers of Buckingham's impeachment, and his arrest in the very midst of the session shows clearly how he was regarded at court. Sir Maurice Abbot, an eminent merchant, who may have been alienated by the duke's demands upon the East India Company, was the archbishop's brother.

"Sir Walter Earle," Bagg continued, "is not soe great with any man as with the Lord Sea [Viscount Saye and Sele]." Sir Walter Erle took a prominent part in the commons. Lord Saye was a puritan peer who had been in opposition in 1621. Buckingham, as part of his approach to the popular party in 1624, "resolved to embrace the friendship of the Lord Saye, who was as solicitous to climb by that ladder." Saye was spoken of in 1625 as Buckingham's friend; but in 1626 he was again in opposition and there was a bitter passage in the house of lords between him and the duke on May 15. An anonymous letter to Charles, to which we have already referred, declared that certain men attacked the duke "because they were not preferred, as they did imagine that they deserved, as the Lord Say, Earl of Clare [formerly Sir John Holles], Sir John Eliot, Selden, and Glanville, Sir Dudley Digges, and the Bishops of Norwich and Lincoln [Williams]." [44]

Finally, Bagg mentioned Henry Sherfield and Walter Long as leading opponents of Buckingham. "Shervill of Salisburie hath formerly beene the creature of the Lord Treasurer [Cranfield?], violent and no less ignorant. Long is his sonne in lawe, and by him altogether guided, his carriage to all noted. Knowe the instruments your enemye, and judge whether the principalls be your friends. I could name more of their party, . . . if I were not conceited more able servants of yours gave it to you in full." It is certain that there was a widespread combination of forces working against the duke in 1626, and much of it came from men who might normally have supported the government.

It is possible to point to other officials whose support of the government was only halfhearted. Sir Henry Marten, a judge of the admiralty, normally supported the government and was chosen in

[44] *Clarendon*, VI, 409; Hacket, *Williams*, II, 18; S. R. Gardiner (ed.), *Debates in the House of Lords, 1624 and 1626* (Camden Society), 194–95. *Cabala*, 224–27.

1625 to make a last-moment appeal for supply. But earlier in the Oxford session he had blurted out that when the state employed older and more experienced ambassadors, mistakes in diplomacy had not been so common, a speech "which caused a sharp reflex upon him from the envie of the State, . . . wherof he had not long after a full taste." In 1626 he was angered to find his rulings altered in the case of the French ship, *St. Peter,* and this resulted in an open quarrel in the house with Sir John Coke.[45] Even courtiers whose loyalty could not be questioned occasionally criticized the duke. The insinuation made in 1626 that Buckingham had hastened James's death by administering a plaster was received by the courtiers with horror; but one of them, Sir Thomas Jermyn, confessed that the plaster had been "a great indescretion and rashness" on Buckingham's part. Sir Walter Pye declared in the commons that in his opinion the council of war should answer the questions put to it by the house.[46]

But the court group in the commons could not stand such widespread disaffection. It was small enough at best in comparison with the total membership of the house. If large numbers gave only a grudging loyalty or deserted to swell the strength of the opposition, it was lost. And this is what took place during the parliaments of 1625 and 1626. The loyalty of courtiers as a group was gone. Sir Dudley Digges wrote Charles in 1626 that little obligation to the crown was now felt in the commons except from the king's household officials. The Venetian ambassador wrote in 1626: "I may say that this kingdom is divided into two: the king, Buckingham, and a few individuals, who being near at hand sun themselves in the rays of royal favour; the other party consisting of all the rest of the country."[47] These words described the country as a whole, but they could also be applied to parliament. Buckingham had caused discontent of so many different kinds and in so

---

[45] *Commons Debates in 1625,* 68–69, 120–21. *Negotium Posterorum,* II, 11–13, 96–97. Marten's speech for supply was thought to be an act of atonement for his former indiscretion. Eliot wrote: "Some did imagine that an act of expiation to the Court for the former trespass he had done, not a will offering, and what properlie was his owne, and in that regard gave the less credit to it. More it did lose the Advocat, then anie waie made advantage for his Client, whose fame was not better by that act, the others worse." *Ibid.* February 22, 1626, Rich, f. 23v, 25.

[46] April 28, March 8, 1626, Whitelocke, f. 166, 34v. Brooke wrote Conway, "God make my Lord Duke's undertakings and employments prosperous to himself, for they are painful to mention." October, 1625, *Cal. St. P. Domestic, Addenda, 1625–1649,* 60.

[47] Digges to the king, January, 1626, St. P. Domestic, 16/19:107. *Cal. St. P. Venetian, 1625–1626,* 511–12.

many different quarters that courtiers and countrymen found themselves united in opposition. Thus he destroyed the possibility of a royal group in the commons.[48]

Buckingham attempted to stem the tide of desertion and discontent by a revival of lobbying among the commons. But it was done rather crudely. The court made little effort to persuade its opponents, as Salisbury had done; that had become impossible. Sordidly material rewards were now the only inducements likely to carry weight, and they were used freely by the government during these early parliaments of Charles.

It is clear that agents of the duke were working among the commons. Their efforts on August 5, 1625, the crucial day of the session at Oxford, are described by Eliot. He explains how sharply, even passionately, the two camps were facing each other and then adds: "Either part in the remainder of that daie labord the strengthening of their side. Infinit was the practise us'd with all men, to sound and gaine them, wherein the Courtiers did exceed. Noe promises or perswasions were too much to make one proselite in that faith. Whom ambition had made corruptible, their offerings did allure, and, what reason could not, hope did then effect." Williams wrote that he approached Sir Thomas Wentworth at Oxford "at his [Wentworth's] first coming to Town, and before his coming to the House, Who promised (and I verily believe he perform'd it) to carry himself advantageously to his Majesty's

[48] Serjeants and legal officials in the parliament of 1625 included: Sir Robert Heath; Sir Francis Ashley; Sir Thomas Crew; Richard Digges; Sir Heneage Finch; Sir Robert Hitcham; William Towse; Sir Henry Marten; Sir Ralph Freeman (master of requests); Sir Edward Leech; John Keeling (crown attorney of the king's bench); John Bankes; Sir Richard Dyott; Nicholas Hyde; and Thomas Mallett. Robert Caesar, Thomas Coventry, and Richard Hutton were sons of legal officials. Minor officeholders included: Sir William Beecher; Edward Clarke; Sir John Coke; Sir Francis Cottington; Sir Henry Wotton; Thomas Fanshawe, father and son; William Fanshawe; Sir Miles Fleetwood; Sir John Jepson; Sir Henry Mildmay; Sir Robert and Sir Walter Pye; Sir George Rivers; William Russell (treasurer of the navy); Sir William Uvedall; Sir John Hippesley; Sackville Crow; Thomas Fotherley; Sir George St. Paul; and Sir George Hastings. Other courtiers included: Sir Francis Annesley; Sir Robert Carr; Sir Arthur Ingram; Sir George Goring; Sir Charles Glemham; Sir Thomas and Henry Jermyn; John Maynard; Sir George More; Sir Francis Nethersole; Sir Roger Palmer; Edward Roberts; John Sackville; Sir Henry Vane; Sir Edward Villiers; Sir Henry Whitehead; Sir Edward Deering; Sir John Franklin. James Bagg, John Drake, Sir Reginald and John Mohun, Sir Edward Seymour, Sir William Strode, Sir Robert Killigrew, Sir Thomas Cheke, and Sir George Chudleigh were also members.

Serjeants and legal officials in 1626 included: Sir Richard Shilton, Sir John Finch, Richard Digges, Sir Heneage Finch, Sir Robert Hitcham, William Towse, Sir Henry Marten, Sir Eubule Thelwall, John Keeling, John Bankes, Sir Richard Dyott, Thomas Mallett. Robert Caesar, Thomas Coventry, Sir John Hobart, Sir Richard Hutton, and Sir Henry Ley were sons of judicial officers. Minor officials included: Sir William Beecher,

Service, and not to joyn with any that should fly upon my Lord Duke." "At the dissolved Parliament in Oxford," Wentworth later wrote Weston, "you are privy how I was moved from and in behalf of the Duke of Buckingham, with Promise of his good esteem and Favour." Before parliament met again in 1626, the Venetian ambassador wrote that "the duke's dependents are bestirring themselves by enquiry and other means to secure a strong party"; and again that "the duke has approached many members with various proposals and inducements to help his cause." Salvetti reported that the practical object of the Easter recess (April 4 to 13, 1626) was "to give time to win Members over to the Duke's side." Conway asked Sir Fulke Greville, Lord Brooke's heir, to talk with certain men likely to be elected in 1626 and to persuade them to "go well in the King's business." Sir George Goring was at work among the commons in 1626; he wrote Conway on April 1 that he could not attend him that morning, "being to meete divers presentes upon appointment touching the great worke this day in agitation." [49]

Before the parliament of 1628 Sir James Bagg wrote Buckingham that "Wright, the Clerk of Parliament, of all men sithence my being of that House hath done worst service to his Majestie. And it is much in his power to doe good; he is either to be made serviceable by faire, or enforced by violent wayes, to doe his dutie. Conferre with some of your servantes about him, he is the most usefullest man of the house." We find Sir John Coke trying privately to persuade Pym not to report from a certain committee be-

Sir Sampson Darrell, Thomas Fanshawe and his father Sir Thomas, Sir Miles Fleetwood, Thomas Gewen, Sir Robert Harley, Sir John Hippesley, Sir Robert and Sir Walter Pye, Sir George Rivers, Sir William Russell, Sir John Savile, and Sir William Uvedall. Other courtiers included: Sir Thomas Badger, William Carr, Sir Edward Conway, Sir Walter Devereux, Sir George Goring, Sir Gilbert Hoghton, Sir Henry Hungate, Sir Arthur Ingram, Sir Thomas and Henry Jermyn, Sir George More, Sir Roger Palmer, Edward Roberts, John Sackville, Sir John Skeffington, and Sir Henry Vane. Thomas Fotherley and Emanuel Gifford were two of Buckingham's servants; captain Thomas Brett, Basil Dixwell, and Sir Edward Hales were men whom Hippesley called Buckingham's friends. Sir George Hastings and Thomas Meautys were also members. Sir James Bagg, John Chudleigh, John Drake, father and son, Reginald Mohun, Sir Richard Strode, Richard Oliver, and Sir Robert Killigrew were members.

[49] *Negotium Posterorum*, II, 48. Williams to King Charles, August 14, 1625, Hacket, *Williams*, II, 17; Wentworth to Weston, 1626, *Strafford's Letters*, I, 34–35. Wentworth was approached again in 1628. Speaker Finch, in writing to him about other business, managed to insinuate a plea that he do more for the royal cause. May 29, 1628, *Strafford's Letters*, I, 46. *Cal. St. P. Venetian, 1625–1626*, 311, 390. Salvetti Correspondence, *Skrine MSS, H. M. C.*, 56. Sir Fulke Greville to Conway, December, 1625, *Cal. St. P. Domestic, Addenda, 1625–1649*, 81. Goring to Conway, April 1, 1626, St. P. Domestic, 16/24:3.

cause the king was not satisfied with the committee's decision. In June, 1628, Sir John Maynard defended himself from the charge of attacking the duke and of setting "others under hand upon him," by reminding Buckingham that before the parliament he was given "commission to converse with his [the duke's] enemies and write what he pleased." [50]

The inducements offered by the court were material in nature. Thomas Alured suggested to secretary Coke that some of the knighthoods about to be conferred at the coronation should be distributed with an eye to the coming session of parliament. He also wished that Sir Edward Coke might again become chief justice of the common pleas, "which would not only avail *ad faciendum populum,* but would win him (if there be anything won by him)." Sir Fulke Greville wrote Conway that he had made some inquiries why a certain Mr. Hopkins, member for Coventry, was "always so cross and violent in Parliament against the king's affairs and what was the way to take him off." Greville learned "that there was no way to alter him but by his father, Sir Richard Hopkins," a serjeant who was very angry because he had not been made a judge. If the elder Hopkins were advanced to the bench, "he would not only make his son go right in the king's business, but several others of his friends who went in the house of commons as peevishly as his son did." Hopkins, however, was not made a judge. Goring wrote Conway that it would be wise to satisfy Ingram's wish to be a member of the council in the north; "upon my credit," wrote Goring, "Ingram hath donne and is now a doing his Majesty faythfull service by all his true indeavours this parliament," and the appointment would "inlighten his hart to

[50] Bagg to Buckingham, March 17, 1628, St. P. Domestic, 16/96:36. When Coke asked Pym not to make a report, Pym "asked him what he should do if the house called for it; he answered he might absent himself or go out of the house." May 10, 1628, *ibid.,* 16/102:57. Sir John Maynard to Buckingham, June, 1628, *ibid.,* 16/108:71.

Sir Allen Apsley wrote to Dorchester, March 20, 1629, denying a rumor that his son Allen was connected with the opposition. "I conceive [the rumor] springs out of this ground my son being affiliat with Mr. Harry Percy. They were bred together at a common school Thithellworth and afterwards 4 or 5 years at the University of Oxford. The Lord Lester (as I take it) got a burgesses place for Mr. Percy presuming he would have run the same way as they did that hated the Duke. But my son being his bedfellow perswaded him the contrary for his best little strength and his voice was ever for the King and against the enemies of the Duke for which they yet do not abide Mr. Percie. My son was by Mr. Alford (one of the faction) offered a burgesses place provided he should have given his voice against the Duke which he detested to do or accept. My son was a continual companion with Mr. Asburnham and others near the Duke and the Duke himself made much of him, so far as he had gone the voyage with him if his Grace had lived, and upon Mr. Ashborn-

persevere as he had begun." Sir James Bagg, in urging that Mohun be made a peer in 1628, stressed his service in the commons and his potential value as a member of the house of lords.[51]

Shortly after the dissolution in June, 1626, Sir John Savile was made a privy councillor "for his service in parliament"; and soon after his son Sir Thomas also received office. Early in James's reign the elder Savile had joined the opposition and had been punished after the parliament of 1614 for his attacks upon the government. In 1624 he was said to be "still the same man," and Wilson called him a powerful influence in the house. But soon afterward he "was taken off by the King, made Comptroller of the Household, a Privy Councillor, and not long after a Baron." Wilson contrasts this treatment with the punishment of other members sent to Ireland: "The King found out two ways of silencing those that were able to do him mischief. Active Spirits that come too near him, must either come nearer to him, or be sent further from him, which he doubts not will take off the edge, and bate the sharpness of the Humor another time. And these preferments and punishments were also practised by his successor." James had, as we know, tried to exclude certain members from the parliament of 1624; and in 1626 Charles excluded the leaders of the opposition by naming them sheriffs. The Venetian ambassador was probably referring to this device when he wrote, "They are dealing with all those who at one time or another have displayed independence in the parliaments in order that they may not oppose their plans when parliament meets again." Bagg suggested a somewhat similar scheme in 1628.[52] But the experiment of 1626 had produced new leaders in the commons, less skillful but even more violent; and it was not tried again. Lobbying and similar devices, it need hardly be pointed out, were useless in these parliaments.

ham's preferment, he indeavoured to have served the Duke in his stede. Had I conceaved his heart had been opposite to his Majestys ways or disaffectionate to the Duke, he should have been to me illegitimate and as a bastard, I would never have given or left him a penny and hated him more than any other. He is not 23, I do not think that ever he medled with any thing serious, his wit lying a contrary way." St. P. Domestic, 16/139:19.

[51] Thomas Alured to Sir John Coke, January 9, 1626, *Cowper MSS, H. M. C.,* I, 248. Sir Fulke Greville to Conway, December, 1625, *Cal. St. P. Domestic, Addenda, 1625–1649,* 81. Goring to Conway, April 1, 1626, St. P. Domestic, 16/24:3. Bagg to Buckingham, March 17, 1628, *ibid.,* 16/96:36.

[52] Rudyard to Nethersole, August 3, 1626, St. P. Domestic, 16/33:30; *Court and Times, Charles I,* I, 198. *Court and Times, James I,* II, 452. Wilson, *History of Great Britain,* 191. *Cal. St. P. Venetian, 1625–1626,* 254. Bagg to Buckingham, March 17, 1628, St. P. Domestic, 16/96:36.

Thus in 1626 Buckingham found himself surrounded by a sea of difficulties. "The pallor of his face," wrote the Venetian ambassador, "betrays his deep uneasiness at the embarrassments in which he finds himself." [53] The commons were violently hostile, and his followers among them had melted to nothing. In the lords he was faced by the accusations of the lower house and by the equally embarrassing charges of Bristol. And while he had a certain following in the upper chamber, which he sought to increase in various ways, [54] the majority of the lords were now against him. He naturally concentrated upon his own defense; and the best brains at the service of the government were devoted, not to the advancement of the general policy of the crown, but to the duke's protection. Sir Robert Heath, as able an adviser on parliamentary affairs as the government possessed, drew up the defense offered by Buckingham to the lords. Heath was assisted by Nicholas Hyde and bishop Laud, and together they produced a very able document. Edward Nicholas was busy collecting evidence favorable to the duke in the administration of the navy. Conway saw to it that the council of war made no embarrassing revelations in the commons; he carefully watched events and personalities in the house of lords and quickly reported all developments of opinion and policy. [55] The king sought to shield the favorite by personal intervention in both houses. Charles took a more active or

[53] *Cal. St. P. Venetian, 1625–1626*, 425.

[54] Three of his followers were made lords during the parliament, and four sons of living earls were called to the lords in the right of their fathers' baronies. Buckingham also had a number of proxies, "in addition to which his adherents in the House comprised nearly all the Bishops"; but the lords passed an order that no single peer could use more than two proxies at one time. When Wimbledon complained of a broken promise to make him a lord lieutenant, Buckingham replied that the appointment would anger several of the lords and he dared not "distemper a vote." "About this Time, the Duke had used all possible Endeavors to gain the Earl of Clare, to his Party; to which End, he had procurred two or three meetings with him in the Strand, at the Countess of Banburie's; but never could obtain him." Salvetti Correspondence, *Skrine MSS, H. M. C.*, 56, 64–65. Wimbledon to Buckingham, September 8, 1626, *Cal. St. P. Domestic, Addenda, 1625–1649*, 159. A. Collins, *Historical Collections of the Noble Families of Cavendishe, Holles, Vere, Harley, and Ogle*, 91, cited by Thomson in "John Holles," *Journal of Modern History*, 8:169. *Cal. St. P. Venetian, 1625–1626*, 390. An anonymous letter to Buckingham suggested that the king call six prominent lords to him in private and explain to them his reasons for defending the duke; these lords, being convinced, would then persuade others. *Cabala*, 228–32. It was said in the commons that Buckingham created new peers "to make a party." June 3, 1626, Whitelocke, f. 212.

[55] See *Gardiner*, VI, 116–17. Heath to Buckingham, June 13, 1626, *Cal. St. P. Domestic, Addenda, 1625–1649*, 133–34. For the council of war, see St. P. Domestic, 16/22:2, 19, 56, 60, 68; Conway to Buckingham, March 8, 12, 1626, *Cal. St. P. Domestic, Addenda, 1625–1649*, 107–08. The Venetian ambassador wrote, "All this affair has been managed by Conway and Grandison, a dependent of the duke." *Cal. St. P. Venetian, 1625–1626*, 358.

at least a more public part in dealing with parliament than he had in 1625; and Buckingham, where he could, prudently remained in the background. It cannot be said that Charles's intervention did much good, for his rashness and impetuosity paralleled that of Buckingham in 1625. "As for your proceedings in Parliament," Sir Ferdinand Gorges wrote secretary Coke, "I behold with fear a certain confusion in all our courses, and from thence a wonderful irresolution." [56] The councillors in the commons obeyed instructions and did what they could. But there was a certain hopelessness about the government's approach to the lower house. Its influence there was a thing of the past.

The parliament of 1628, so far as management by the court was concerned, was little more than an epilogue to what had gone before. The opposition was in full control of the commons, and its policy was ultimately accepted by the lords. The most skillful parliamentary management in the world could not have saved the crown from defeat. Charles and Buckingham were paying not only for their highhanded actions since 1626 but for their long accumulation of errors in dealing with former sessions.

This parliament, however, had certain distinctive features which must be briefly mentioned. They arose from the new desperateness of the crown's relations with the commons. Buckingham had full warning in 1627 from men who wished him well — May, Weston, Goring, Sir Robert Pye — that affairs in England were reaching the breaking point and that changes in policy must soon be made.[57] He also had full warning that the parliament of 1628 would be a highly dangerous affair and that it would have to be handled with the greatest tact and caution. "I heare there is a Parliament shortly," wrote Sir John Hippesley, "in the which give me leave to tell you that you have the part of a wise and discreet man to playe, in which all your servantes" must exert themselves to the utmost. "At the next meeting of Parliament," wrote the earl of Suffolk, "as I conceive, it will be the time for all your friends and servants to show themselves worthy of that title." [58] The parliament of 1628 saw a new caution and judiciousness in the duke's

[56] Sir Ferdinand Gorges to Sir John Coke, February 15, 1626, *Cowper MSS, H.M.C.,* I, 256.

[57] See *Gardiner,* VI, 190–94, 335.

[58] Hippesley to Buckingham, February 2, 1628, St. P. Domestic, 16/92:12. Theophilus, earl of Suffolk, to Buckingham, May, 1626, *Cal. St. P. Domestic, Addenda, 1625–1649,* 131.

approach to parliament, a caution which, to some extent at least, gradually communicated itself to the king.

The privy council was consulted more frequently on parliamentary affairs than had been the case for many years. That parliament was called at all was a victory for the council. Early in the session councillors were asked how the king's financial needs might best be laid before the commons; and when five subsidies were voted on April 4, the king at once directed Sir John Coke to make a full report to the board. There were long debates in the council upon the answer to be given to the Petition of Right. On the day before Charles accepted the petition and gave it the force of law, "the King and Lords were in counsell from two till past eight of the clocke at night, in which they say the debate was whether his Majesty should presently dissolve the Parliament." Again in June a long debate in the council preceded the prorogation. Before the commons met again in 1629, a consultation took place in the council which outlined the entire approach of the government for the coming session and fixed upon tactics to be employed by the councillors who were members of the lower house. The Venetian ambassador complained he could not see any of the ministers "because they were constantly occupied, at one time in parliament, at another with the king, in consultation for its good guidance." [59] This new activity of the council in directing parliamentary affairs must, of course, be viewed with caution. The council was now composed so completely of Buckingham's dependents that, at least until the summer of 1628, when certain changes were made, its decisions were largely his. The answers it proposed to the Petition of Right were far less satisfactory to the commons than the answers made by the judges when they were consulted by the crown; and this in spite of a number of recent dismissals from the bench. At least one new councillor, bishop Laud, who was admitted in 1627, was certain to offer bad advice upon parliamentary affairs. It is clear, moreover, that Charles and Buckingham did not always consult the council as a whole but

[59] Minute of advice of the council to the king, March, 1628, St. P. Domestic, 16/98:52. Sir John Coke's report to the commons, April 7, 1628, Harl. MSS 4771, f. 64–65. Nethersole to the queen of Bohemia, June 7, 1628, St. P. Domestic, 16/106:55. *Court and Times, Charles I*, I, 370. *Rushworth*, I, 642–43. *Cal. St. P. Venetian, 1628–1629*, 493, 550. "It is certain that the king by consulting the best persons, assiduously advances these affairs of the parliament, to render it useful to the kingdom and his friends, restoring the good understanding, which has not existed hitherto, between him and his subjects." *Ibid.*, 531.

asked the advice of certain selected councillors.[60] Yet even so, the council's share in the direction of parliamentary affairs had considerably increased.

A more cautious policy on the part of the government is also apparent in the careful and exact instructions issued to councillors and other courtiers in this parliament. Councillors prepared their speeches with the greatest care. There are among the state papers a large number of drafts of speeches delivered in the commons at this time by Sir John Coke and Sir Thomas Edmondes. A speech delivered by Edmondes on March 24 may serve as an example. There are two drafts of the speech among the state papers, both in Edmondes' hand. One is a first draft, with many corrections, additions, and marginal notes; the second is a fair copy with the corrections and additions included. Both drafts are endorsed "Parliament Notes" in the hand of Sir John Coke. It is possible that Edmondes and Coke worked upon the speech together to secure the exact phraseology they desired.[61] This speech and similar ones bear sufficient resemblance to the accounts of the same speeches in the diaries to indicate that they were given substantially as they were written. They were the result of careful planning by men who saw the necessity of giving their words the precise tone and emphasis desired by the court. Messages were framed with equal care. A number of Rudyard's speeches were obviously inspired at court. Solicitor Shilton had exact instructions; he was, indeed, so feeble a parliamentarian that he floundered miserably when he had not been told exactly what to do. The speaker, Sir John Finch, was more completely the agent of the government than any speaker since Phelips in James's first parliament. "It joyeth my heart that this day's work is so acceptable to His Majesty," he wrote on April 4 when the commons voted supply. "My prayers and endeavours shall be His Majesty may receive all satisfaction." "Sir John Finch must not insinuate with the House," wrote Bagg, "he must endure their frownes and hazard his credit with them for his Master's Service."[62] He performed many unpleasant duties as best he could for the advantage of the government.

Before the commons met in 1629 Charles "consulted with a

[60] *Rushworth*, I, 642.
[61] St. P. Domestic, 16/98:39, 40.
[62] Sir John Finch to Sir John Coke, April 4, May 3, 1628, *Cowper MSS, H. M. C.*, I, 342–43. Bagg to Buckingham, March 17, 1628, St. P. Domestic, 16/96:36.

select Committee of his Privy Councillors, what probably the Parliament at their next sitting would insist upon, and how the Privy Council (who were members of the Parliament) should demean themselves in such cases." It was decided that the bill of tonnage and poundage should be prepared in advance and presented to the house by the councillors in the commons on the first day of business. The councillors should explain that the bill was presented thus early "to cut off all Questions and Debates, and to persuade them to a dispatch thereof." If the commons asked that the goods taken by the government from merchants who refused the duties be returned before the bill of tonnage and poundage was passed, the councillors should answer that if the commons intended to pass the bill "it would end all Dispute." If the commons refused to pass the bill, Charles should declare to them that once the bill was passed he was ready to acknowledge that he collected tonnage and poundage only by will of parliament; but that if they persisted in their refusal, the parliament would be dissolved and the breech would be one "not sought by the king." The council also decided that if the commons insisted upon bringing up dangerous points or attacking the king's ministers, the councillors in the commons were to "intimate that these debates would tend to a breech, and would not be admitted of, and the king thereupon to declare himself presently, that he would not suffer such irregular courses of proceeding." [63] Thus the councillors in the commons in 1629 had very exact instructions.

Yet the temper of the house was such that the most careful instructions to councillors could not avoid misunderstanding. When Coke brought in the bill of tonnage and poundage as he was commanded, Eliot accused him of offering it "in his Majesty's name," as if the king commanded the house to pass it. Charles added to the embarrassment of his minister by quickly declaring that "this bill was not to have been offered unto you in my name." Coke defended himself in the commons by saying, "Indeed I used many arguments in speaking of his Majesty. I said it much concerned him, and that his Majesty much desired it; but this was mistaken, as if his Majesty had commanded it; and I had required it in his name, which I did not intend but to avoid dispute." Eliot returned to the attack: "Sir, I apprehend a difference between his

[63] *Rushworth*, I, 642–43.

Majesties expression and the expression of his Ministers; for, Sir, that bill was tendered here, and again professed, in his Majesties name, and now we find that his Majesty disavows it, and that he did it not. What wrong is this done to his Majesty and to this House, to press things in the Sovereign's name, to the prejudice and distraction of us all? I think him not worthy to sit in this House." "But on a little dispute this mocion of Sir John Elliotts was lett fall." The fault was that of Eliot, who read more into Coke's words than was meant. But the episode shows how easily Charles repudiated the actions of his minister.[64]

The cautious attitude of the government in 1629 may be seen in another way. The commons had met on January 20, but difficulties developed so rapidly that the house was adjourned from February 25 to March 2, which proved the final day of the parliament. During this week of adjournment the king endeavored by private negotiations with leading members of the opposition to reach some compromise that might prevent a rupture. Charles said that the adjournment was planned in the hope "that in the meantime, a better and more right understanding might be begotten between us and members of that house." But the leaders of the commons were determined to punish the customs officials for collecting tonnage and poundage, a point on which the king could not yield. "It was thus impossible to assuage either side," and the negotiations came to nothing. Yet for the king to treat with the leaders of the house was in itself a token of a new earnestness to compromise.[65]

The condition of the court group in the commons was one of utter weakness. There was neither leadership nor a following worthy of the name. Only three councillors — Coke, Edmondes, and May — were members of the commons. During most of the session Coke acted as the principal representative of the government, but about the middle of May he was sent down to Portsmouth on naval business and Sir Humphrey May became the chief agent of the crown. May, however, was less in sympathy with the policy of the government than he had been in 1626. He had warned Buckingham in 1627: "Make not your designs too vast; lay all your energies for the Citadell. That being compassed,

[64] *Commons Debates for 1629,* 12, 31–33, 121.

[65] *Cal. St. P. Venetian, 1628–1629,* 579–80; *Parl. Hist.,* II, 502 (cited in *Gardiner,* VII, 66–67).

provide for the safety of it, and then at leisure, *de novo consultendum est,* what is further to be done." May delivered many messages and spoke continually, but his attitude was wholly different from Coke's. He was less unctuous and complimentary in speaking of the court; he appeared more detached and noncommittal; his carriage seemed to imply that he was placing the wishes of the king before the commons but was not demanding compliance. This did not go unnoticed at court. Coke was told that Sir Robert Pye, in a conversation with Buckingham, "perceived the Duke both thought and now found (perhaps the more in your absence and upon trial of others) that you were both honest and wise." [66] There are other indications of dissension and discontent among the courtiers. A heated dispute took place in the commons on June 21 between Sir Miles Fleetwood and Sir Robert Pye over proposals by Fleetwood to save money for the king. Heath was in temporary disgrace at court in 1629 for pleading the command of the king when accused by the commons of leniency toward a group of Jesuits.[67]

Yet such dissensions and disputes were not the fundamental cause of the government's weakness in this house of commons. The great exodus of members from the ranks of the courtiers to those of the opposition had already taken place in 1625 and 1626, and only those few remained who were ready to support the crown in all contingencies. The weakness of the government sprang from the fact that its candidates were so widely defeated in the elections to the parliament of 1628; it had few new adherents to take the place of those who had deserted.

"All the counties," wrote the Venetian ambassador, "have uniformally rejected candidates who had even a shadow of dependence upon the Court, electing members who refused the late subsidies, who are now everywhere called good patriots." Buckingham made a great effort to obtain seats for his followers. "The duke stays in London," wrote the Venetian ambassador again, "negotiating and working with all his might, so that the members

---

[66] May to Buckingham, October 7, 1627, St. P. Domestic, 16/80:60. Thomas Alured to Sir John Coke, June 21, 1628, *Cowper MSS, H.M.C.,* I, 353.

[67] Alured to Sir John Coke, June 21, 1628, *Cowper MSS, H.M.C.,* I, 351; June 21, 1628, Borlase, f. 276. For dissensions among leading councillors at court, see *Cal. St. P. Venetian, 1626–1628,* 571–73; *1628–1629,* 432, 580. Heath to Dorchester, February 7, 1629, St. P. Domestic, 16/135:17; Heath to Carlisle, February 7, 1629, *Cal. St. P. Domestic, Addenda, 1625–1649,* 329–30; *Cal. St. P. Venetian, 1628–1629,* 551.

returned for the Lower House may be on his side." But his efforts were largely failures. At Westminster, where he was high steward, he was unable to obtain the return of Sir Robert Pye.[68] Of the privy councillors, one was defeated in Essex and another in York. Conway failed completely in attempts to control elections in the Isle of Wight, where his position as captain had given him considerable influence in the past. He recommended four men by name to the three towns on the island, but not one of them was returned. Conway had not only underestimated the hostility toward the government but offended the local magistrates by asking them to vacate the seats they had formerly held to make room for men from distant London. His attempt to place his candidates at Southampton was also a complete failure, and again he offended a well-wisher of the crown by his interference. After several rebuffs he obtained a seat for his son Ralph only with the greatest difficulty, and he could not place his son Edward at all. When he asked the town of Evesham, which he had represented in 1621 and 1624, to return his son-in-law, Sir Robert Harley, the town at first refused, though Harley eventually secured the place.[69]

Shortly after the dissolution of parliament in 1626 Buckingham had patched up his quarrel with Pembroke. Pembroke became lord steward and his brother, the earl of Montgomery, lord chamberlain; and a marriage contract was arranged between Buckingham's infant daughter and Montgomery's young son, who was Pembroke's heir. Before the elections began in 1628, Hippesley begged Buckingham "to geat my Lord Steward [Pembroke] to make such as shall complye with the King's occasions." But if Buckingham approached Pembroke, as he very likely did, the re-

[68] *Cal. St. P. Venetian, 1628–1629,* 10, 21; *1626–1628,* 605. Mead to Stuteville, March 8, 1628, *Court and Times, Charles I,* I, 327. Williams wrote Cotton that he had recommended him for election at Westminster. Williams began by saying, "I have used heretofore to recommend to the town of Westminster one of their burgesses only, and none other than was recommended unto me by my lord duke of Buckingham, our high steward. I have no desire, nor is it any safety for me to endeavour any alteration in that custom, and peradventure as the case now stands it is not feasible [since] his grace will do it immediately, without moving me at all therein." February 12, 1628, Cott. MSS Julius C III, f. 171.

[69] St. P. Domestic, 16/92:4, 5, 6, 15, 16, 17; 16/93:60; 16/94:9, 10, 48. Conway wrote Sir Thomas Jervoise, "I am in some distress where to provide a burgesse place for my sonne Ralph. And understanding of the power you have in that kind both at Andover and in some places in Shropshire, I doe make it my earnest request to you to accomodate him in some of those places." February 2, 1628, *ibid.,* 16/92:14. See also *ibid.,* 16/93:47, 48. Ralph Conway was returned from Andover. Fulke Reed to Conway, February 14, 1628, *ibid.,* 16/93:32.

sult was disappointing. Three of the men whom Bagg had pointed out as Pembroke's agents in attacking the duke in 1626 — Turner, Fullerton, and Sir Clipsby Crew — now disappeared from the house. And Buckingham was able to secure the return at Portsmouth of two men connected with the naval administration. But the bulk of Pembroke's friends — including Sir William Herbert, Edward Herbert, Rudyard, Sir Francis Stewart, Mansell, and William Murray — retained their places in the commons. Pembroke apparently was willing to exclude a firebrand such as Turner, but unwilling to desert the rank and file of his friends. The Venetian ambassador, in two separate dispatches, declared that certain councillors, "pointing out the necessity of calling parliament, offered the king their guarentee, in case he consented, that nothing should be said about Buckingham." This is almost certainly a reference to Pembroke; it shows that while he was ready to drop accusations against Buckingham in the light of recent events, he nevertheless remained in touch with the opposition.[70]

The government met with rather better fortune in the Cinque Ports. By sheer negligence in 1626 Buckingham had forfeited the customary privilege of the lord warden to name one member from each of the towns. When parliament was summoned in 1628, Hippesley warned him of the necessity of "making as many Burgesses as he could," and offered practical suggestions regarding candidates whom the Ports would be likely to accept and the tactics to be employed in securing their election. As a result, at least six of the members returned from the Ports were royalists who could be counted upon to aid the cause of the government.[71] A number of courtiers were also returned in Cornwall, where the government's great influence was fortunately augmented by an active and powerful group of loyal gentry.[72] Yet even in the Cinque Ports and Cornwall the crown met with reverses. There was much doubt about the outcome of the election at Dover, and Buckingham's candidate, Sir Edwin Sandys, was defeated at

[70] Pory to Mead, July 1, ——— to Mead, July 21, 1626, *Court and Times, Charles I,* I, 123, 132. The marriage contract was referred to as a move "to gain the Lord Chamberlain's faction." *Cal. St. P. Venetian, 1625–1626,* 512. Hippesley to Buckingham, February 2, 1628, St. P. Domestic, 16/92:12. *Cal. St. P. Venetian, 1626–1628,* 584, 588–89.

[71] For the elections in the Cinque Ports in 1626, see St. P. Domestic, 16/18:28, 37, 58, 60, 61, 97. For those in 1628, see *ibid.,* 16/91:91; 16/92:12; 16/94:38, 45; 16/95:67; *Rye MSS, H. M. C.,* 189–90.

[72] See, for example, Bagg to Buckingham, March 17, 1628, St. P. Domestic, 16/96:36.

Sandwich. In Cornwall three boroughs, Launceston, Newport, and St. Germans, which normally returned courtiers, now responded to other influences and elected opponents of the crown.

These elections may be regarded as typical. Courtiers could be returned only from close boroughs, and even there they suffered many defeats. The king's supporters in the commons were certainly very few. On several occasions during the parliament the councillors in the house opposed a division on important questions because they foresaw defeat for the crown.[73]

The opposition, on the other hand, was more numerous and better organized than ever before. New procedures in the commons had now reached a high stage of development and were working with smoothness and precision. The leaders of the opposition had learned to integrate their efforts and subordinate personal inclinations to the dictates of a common policy. Before the parliament opened, a group of them, including Wentworth, Denzil Holles, Phelips, Eliot, Pym, Selden, Kirton, and Sir Edward Coke, met at Cotton's house to decide their course of action in the coming session. In this meeting Eliot proposed to attack grievances and abuses upon a wide front by renewing impeachment proceedings against the duke. But other leaders believed that protection of the liberties of the subject was now of paramount importance and that grievances in general, including the attack upon Buckingham, must wait. Eliot, in spite of his preponderating influence in

[73] Mead to Stuteville, May 17, 1628, *Court and Times, Charles I,* I, 353–54; May 6, 1628, Mass., f. 151. Nethersole to the queen of Bohemia, June 11, 1628, St. P. Domestic, 16/106:1.

Legal officials in this house of commons included: Sir Richard Shilton, Sir John Finch, John Hoskyns, Sir Edward Leech, Thomas Eden, Sir Ralph Freeman, Sir Henry Marten, John Bankes, and Sir Richard Dyott. Thomas Coventry, Sir John Croke, and Sir Richard Hutton were the sons of important judicial officers. Sir Thomas and Sir Heneage Finch and Thomas Meautys were also members. Minor officials included: Sir William Beecher, Sir Francis Cottington, Edward Nicholas, Sir Sackville Crow, Sir Thomas Fanshawe, Sir Miles Fleetwood, Sir Henry Holcroft, James Howell, Sir Henry Mildmay, John Packer, Sir Robert and Sir Walter Pye, Sir Thomas Savile, Sir Edward Sawyer, Sir William Uvedall, and Hannibal Vyvyan. Other courtiers who secured election were: John Ashburnham, Sir Thomas Badger, Sir Robert Carr, Ralph Conway, Sir Walter Devereux, Sir George Goring, Sir Edward Howard, Sir Arthur Ingram, Sir Robert Harley, Sir Thomas and Henry Jermyn, Sir Thomas Jervoise, Sir John Maynard, Sir Francis Nethersole, Sir Roger Palmer, Sir George St. Paul, Henry Percy, Sir Henry Spiller, and Sir Henry Vane. Owen Jennings, William Towerson, Sir John Hippesley, captain Thomas Brett, Thomas Fotherley, Thomas Godfrey, Sir John Jepson, and Sir Henry Mainwaring were connected with the naval administration. Sir James Bagg, Sir Richard Edgecombe, Pierce Edgecombe, Sir Richard Grenville, Sir Robert and Sir William Killigrew, Sir John Chudleigh, and Thomas Wise were members. Sir Henry Whitehead, Philip Mainwaring, and Sir Edward Osborne were scattered supporters of the crown.

1626, agreed to follow the course marked out by other leaders, though he reserved the right to revert to his own policy at a later date. When, on June 3, he applied his reservation and denounced the government in violent terms, he explained "that himself and others had a resolution to open these last mentioned Grievances, . . . and only stayed for an opportunity." His explanation was "attested by Sir Thomas Wentworth and Sir Robert Phelips." Thus the leaders of the opposition worked together.[74]

In 1628, as in 1626, Buckingham turned to the house of lords, where he did everything in his power to halt the Petition of Right or render its meaning innocuous. But the more moderate lords, who formed a middle group between extreme parties, eventually sided with the commons. They were undoubtedly voting against Buckingham's tactics as well as against the general policy of the government. In an earlier period Buckingham had obtained peerages for his friends and relations, but in 1626 and 1628 he was deliberately packing the upper chamber. And this was even more bitterly resented.

We have come a long way since Buckingham was hailed as the savior of his country in 1624. His alliance at that time with the popular elements in both houses was based on little more than a common dislike of the pro-Spanish policy of the old king. Such an alliance could not last. But Buckingham assumed that it would and treated the commons in 1625 with astonishing arrogance and folly. The reaction against him was swift and terrible and ended his hopes of leadership by destroying the only group in the commons which, in the long run, he could hope to lead.

[74] Forster, *Eliot*, II, 114–15; *Rushworth*, I, 592–93. This debate contained an interesting defense of private consultations among members. Courtiers charged that Eliot's speech sprang "from private councels and conference, rather peradventure [than] from public causes." Mr. Strode replied, "I heard one say that these propositions might be occasioned by private councells and conference. I hope there is no new othe, like the othe for Iones amongst us, to forbid us to confer. I knowe private conference is not only fit, but necessary to the service of this House, and hath advanced much the business of it." June 3, 1628, Borlase, f. 212. Laud had advised Charles that the commons should "sitt lesse time, that they may not understand one another too well." St. P. Domestic, 16/94:89.

7

The Loss of Influence in the House

While the council was seeking to redress such grievances as it might, while councillors were placed in the house when opportunity served, while Salisbury and Buckingham were managing the crown's parliamentary affairs and were seeking to build a following in the house, the former influence and power wielded by councillors in the daily debates and decisions of the commons were rapidly disappearing. One has merely to compare the pages of D'Ewes's journals for the early years of Elizabeth's reign with the diaries and debates of the parliaments of 1626 or 1628 to see that a fundamental change had taken place. The deeper causes of that change must be found in the general evolution of England. But in the house of commons itself three things stand out. In the first place, councillors came to be regarded with an ever increasing hostility, which in itself rendered their former leadership impossible. Secondly, the growth of parliamentary procedure, now developing with great rapidity, was calculated in a host of ways to lessen the influence of councillors and give power to other members who had the confidence of the house. And finally, a group of popular leaders arose, ready and eager to seize the power offered them by new circumstances and new procedures. This last point is beyond the scope of these pages; the first two must be examined in some detail.

Superficially, the councillors were treated in the early Stuart period with formal respect and deference. They were still the "members of the House of Principal note and quality," "those honorable gentlemen of the King's council neere the Chaire"; they were called "noble gentlemen" in contrast to other members. "If we differ from our superiors," said a member in 1621 when opposing a motion of the council, "it should be with reverence."[1] The electors of Middlesex excused their rejection of two councillors as members in 1621 with the plea that ordinary persons

[1] March 22, April 11, 1628, Borlase, f. 11–12, 70. *Commons Debates 1621*, II, 21. See also *C. J.*, I, 667, 671; *Commons Debates for 1629*, 92.

could not have easy access to such great officials as privy councillors.[2] Councillors continued to perform certain formal functions which distinguished them from other members and emphasized their close connection with the crown. They nominated the speaker and administered the oaths required of members at the beginning of the session; they carried important bills and messages to the upper house; they constantly brought messages, letters, and commands from the king. They had constant access to the sovereign and could place the wishes of the commons before him more quickly and easily than any other agency at the disposal of the house. They knew, or were supposed to know, the secrets of the state. They represented the king in the house, said Bacon in 1614, as other members represented the commons of the realm.[3] These formal functions and important connections gave them a unique position of which the house made constant use, although councillors received small credit for their services. And councillors had behind them the prestige of their importance in the Tudor house of commons and, stretching further back, an even greater tradition as the core of the medieval parliament.[4]

But beneath this outward respect there was a growing hostility which flared out more and more easily as councillors came by necessity to share the mounting opprobrium with which the government was regarded. This became apparent during the first two parliaments of James in the determination of the commons that councillors should be treated as ordinary members without special rights or privileges. Yelverton told the commons to decide the case of Goodwin vs. Fortescue on its merits and "not to fear the greatness of Sir John Fortescue." [5] The expulsion of Parry in 1614 is another example. If the house saw fit to question Parry at the bar, said a member, it should do so, were he "Ten Counsellors." "The

---

[2] Locke to Carleton, December 16, 1620, St. P. Domestic, 14/118:30. Tate wrote in the reign of Elizabeth that a councillor should not be speaker because other members could not have "bould and familiar accesse and conference" with him, and hence he would not know enough about the temper of the house. Harl. MSS 253, f. 32–33.

[3] C. J., I, 478.

[4] Councillors won occasional approbation when their actions fell in with the wishes of the house. We have seen how Sir Edward Coke was praised in 1621. Cranfield was praised for attacking abuses in the courts, Weston for denouncing Spain in 1624, Sir John Coke for reproving Phelips openly in 1628 rather than carrying tales to court. *Commons Debates 1621,* II, 44. D. Carleton to Sir Dudley Carleton, March 5, 1624, St. P. Domestic, 14/160:33. March 22, 1628, Borlase, f. 11–12.

[5] March 30, 1604, Lansd. MSS 486, f. 11v. In 1621 Mallory said that "hee feared not those that sit in thrones and chayres." *Commons Debates 1621,* V, 283.

greater the Person," said another, "the more the Offence." "A good Precedent for future Ages," said a third, "that this shall be punished, in any, how great soever." Parry was "not here as a Counsellor, but as a Knight of a Shire" and should answer his offense "as another person." Councillors, said Sir Samuel Sandys, had before this answered for their offenses at the bar, and there was no precedent of a delinquent answering in any other way. Since councillors were as ordinary members, the house was perfectly competent to handle cases concerning them without aid from any other quarter. When James added a further punishment to that inflicted by the house upon Parry, the commons told the king somewhat rudely that they considered their own punishment sufficient, though James might do as he pleased.[6] Nor was the presence of councillors in any way necessary to the house in conducting business. When James excused his sudden adjournment of the commons in June, 1621, by saying he had need of his councillors for his own service, Sir Robert Crane replied, "We can spare the Lords of the Council. We have company enough of ourselves." "Here are other honest Hearts besides to go on with the Businesses here in Hand."[7]

Rules of procedure must be binding upon all alike. In debate, wrote Eliot, "the meanest burgess has as much favor as the best knight or counsellor, all sitting in one capacitie of Commoners." Sir Edwin Sandys told Cranfield in 1621 that when he entered the house he must lay aside his greatness.[8] When Sir Edward Coke was named as chairman of a committee of the whole in 1621, a member objected because Coke was a councillor, but it was answered that all members were equal and therefore Coke could be chosen. Calvert was reproved in 1621 for "forgetting the orders

---

[6] *C. J.*, I, 477–81. To the argument that a servant of Parry's was to blame, members said it was "lamentable that this state governed by a councillor that governed by his man." *Ibid.* "That the Privy Counsellors here, Knights and Burgesses." All members sit "in the like relation to their Countries." *Ibid.*, I, 508; *Negotium Posterorum*, II, 52. Sir George More said Bacon must be punished in 1621 were he "never so great, never so dear." *P. and D.*, I, 186.

[7] May 30, 1621, *Commons Debates 1621*, II, 410 note; *P. and D.*, II, 128. Eliot spoke of the king's "councillors and great officers, wherof ther are never wanting in the Commons house too manie." *Negotium Posterorum*, I, 113. A member remarked in 1614 that in an earlier age no privy councillor had sat in the commons. *C. J.*, I, 456.

[8] *Negotium Posterorum*, II, 52. Sir Edwin Sandys said, "Lett every man that coms in heear lay downe his greatness at the doore, and so the meanest lay downe his meanness." *Commons Debates 1621*, III, 376. See also *ibid.*, IV, 399. Sir Samuel Sandys remarked, speaking apparently of Sir Edward Coke, "No Man here to think himself so great, as to oppress any Member of this House with his Greatness." *C. J.*, I, 557.

of the House"; and May was called to order in 1626 because it was thought he wandered from the point at issue.[9] The rule that members could not refuse a service required of them by the house was strictly applied to councillors, although these services were often most distasteful. Carleton took messages to the lords in 1626 concerning the impeachment of his patron Buckingham; and when he asked to be excused from carrying a message to Charles about Montague, one of the royal chaplains, his request was denied.[10]

As a matter of fact, the house was far from fair in these matters. The special position of councillors was to be used when it suited the convenience of the commons but denounced when employed in the interests of the court. Free speech was to be allowed in abundance to popular speakers, but councillors might be refused the floor. Hoskyn's violent words in 1614 passed without censure and Sir Henry Wotton was attacked when he objected to them; Eliot's blasting denunciations were approved, while Clarke was called to the bar for saying the house used "bitter invectives" and May was silenced when he objected to Eliot's words.[11] But, on the other hand, councillors might be denied the right to speak. In the spring of 1621, when the house was angry at the impending adjournment, "Sir Lionel Cranfield, Master of the Wards, would have spoken (the House being in this Passion, and ready to rise) . . . ; whereupon all the House cried out . . . and would not hear him: Then Sir Henry Vane, an intimate Friend of the Master of the Wards, moved, that we should hear the Master of the Wards, but yet the House would not: then the Chancellor of the Dutchy, Sir Humphrey May, moved, that we did overthrow the Liberties of the House, if we would not permit every Man to speak; but for all this the House [refused] . . . and rose in a great Passion and Confusion." In 1626, when Weston wished to move the hastening of the subsidy, "in two hours [he] could not get leave to speak." In 1628 May sought to stop a speech by Eliot but could not get the floor: "Mr. Chancellor of the Dutchy desirouse to speake was forbidden, and making as if hee would go

---

[9] *Commons Debates 1621*, IV, 16–17. Alford "had not knowne in his tyme a young Counsellor [Calvert] so much forgett the orders of the Howse." Locke to Carleton, February 16, 1621, St. P. Domestic, 14/119:99. April 27, 1626, Whitelocke, f. 165.

[10] April 19, 1626, Whitelocke, f. 140.

[11] Chamberlain to Carleton, June 9, Lorkin to Puckering, September 11, 1614, *Court and Times, James I*, I, 320–22, 345. *Commons Debates in 1625*, 91, 139–40. June 3, 1628, Borlase, f. 212.

out of the howse was forbidden, and Sir John Eliott bidden to go on." Again in 1626 Sir Robert Pye, in defending May from an attack by Eliot, asked "that there may be freedom of speech on both sides." In the same parliament Carleton begged the commons to remain silent until he had finished his speech.[12] Thus the commons could forget their rules in dealing with the king's ministers.

Insistence by the commons that all members were equal and owed an equal loyalty[13] left the councillors in an unfortunate position, for they were primarily servants of the king and owed him their first allegiance. There are constant indications of their embarrassment as a result of this divided duty. When Cranfield tried to explain the adjournment in the spring of 1621, he began by saying that "he was in a great Strait between his Duty to the King, and his Duty to this House." In defending the government in 1625 Heath first made "a protestation for himself, that having two capacities, one as a member of that house, the other as a servant to the King, he would without partialitie express himself." In 1629 Sir John Coke said "that he hath used much dilligence and care in performance of the commands of this house and findeth he goeth in a slipery way betweene his Majestie and his people." [14] Councillors and other courtiers protested solemnly that their speeches were dictated by conscience and not by their connections with the court. "I have no other interest then the publique," said Coke in 1628. Sir Robert Pye "was afrayd of none, or did so much care for his office as to neglect his duty to the publicke"; he welcomed criticism of the duke, who would, he knew, profit by it. In 1624 Sir Henry Mildmay said that he spoke for supply not because he was a courtier but because of love of country, and declared that in spite of his place he would vote against a grant of money if it did not contain provisions which he considered necessary.[15] Such

---

[12] May 29, 1621, *P. and D.*, II, 121–22. ——— to Mead, May 26, 1626, *Court and Times, Charles I*, I, 105. June 3, 1628, Borlase, f. 212. June 12, 1626, Whitelocke, f. 235. May 12, 1626, *ibid.*, f. 189; Rich, f. 87v.

[13] "Such of the House as are of the Kings privy Council or of his Council at Law ought nevertheless in debate of Matters in the House as ought all others to speak according to that which they shall think in their Conscience may be most for the good of the Common Wealth, tho' it do perhaps cross the King's desire in that particular." Add. MSS 36856, f. 48–48v.

[14] May 29, 1621, *P. and D.*, II, 122. *Negotium Posterorum*, II, 45. February 3, 1629, *Commons Debates for 1629*, 121.

[15] April 25, 1628, Borlase, f. 105. *Commons Debates in 1625*, 113. March 19, 1624, Gurney, f. 133, 143. Serjeant Hoskyns said in a debate in 1628, "As for myself I am neither for flattery nor for fear, for I have had my part of sufferings." May 2, 1628, Borlase, f. 126.

protests merely emphasized the difficulties of the court faction. The dilemma was insuperable and grew more awkward as king and commons drifted apart. When May was asked point-blank to tell of something that had happened in the council, he naturally refused. And Coke told the commons that though they passed a law against imprisonment without cause shown, he, as a councillor, would be forced to commit men as before.[16] May might beg the house "to think it is not I that speak this day"; and Edmondes might declare that he found no conflict between his duty to the king and his duty to the commons.[17] But neither carried conviction. By insisting that councillors were commoners first and courtiers second, the house was striking at the very foundation of the council's former influence in parliament.

Councillors were often treated with studied discourtesy.[18] In the parliament of 1614 Winwood had to ignore many affronts. When in 1621 Edmondes told Sir Edward Coke that a certain bill read "Oxford and Cambridge" rather than "Cambridge and Oxford," Coke answered rudely that Edmondes need not trouble himself since he had attended neither university. Again Coke told Cranfield that he displayed a spirit of contradiction in a conference with the lords; and when Cranfield objected, Coke said he had not directed his remarks at any one but implied that if they fitted Cranfield he had no one to blame but himself. Calvert was frequently treated with discourtesy. The Venetian ambassador wrote in 1621 that "various signs of contempt and various ways of mortification have been shown in the assembly against the said secretary of state on various occasions when he has uttered many important particulars in the name of his Majesty." When on one occasion Calvert and Alford rose to speak at the same instant,

[16] When May was asked to give some information, he said he did not know anything about it, "nor if he did would he declare or discover matter of Councell." February 17, 1629, *Commons Debates for 1629*, 154. Earlier, on June 7, 1628, May said, "You do not expect from mee anything, though I did know it concerning excise that I should tell itt you. Wee are servants to Princes to execute there commands." Borlase, f. 225. For Coke's speech, see May 1, 1628, Nicholas, p. 123; Holles, f. 10; Harl. MSS 1721, f. 200v.

[17] June 11, 1628, Borlase, f. 237. Speech of Edmondes, February 5, 1621, St. P. Domestic, 14/119:73. Cf. *C. J.*, I, 461.

[18] Councillors were treated with some discourtesy in the last years of Elizabeth's reign. In 1593 the lord keeper told the commons that the queen "misliketh also that such irreverence was shewed towards Privy Councillors, who were not to be accounted as common Knights and Burgesses of the House." *D'Ewes (Elizabeth)*, 466. An anonymous writer to Charles said that the puritans first began to spit out their venom against the councillors in the parliament of 1580. *Cabala*, 225.

Alford began with great vehemence in order to obtain the floor. When Calvert objected to a violent speech by Coke aimed at pro-Spanish ministers, the house assumed that Calvert was speaking "idly." Calvert was flatly contradicted on more than one occasion.[19] The blundering earnestness of Sir John Coke exposed him to the constant snubs of the commons; and Carleton was reminded quite unnecessarily, when he became a lord, that he had no property from which to take a title.[20]

Councillors found their arguments answered with bitter sharpness. When secretary Coke explained a plan for the defense of the Thames in 1626, he was told that his proposal was "nothing." When in 1628 he sought to frighten the commons by telling them of some Jesuits discovered in Clerkenwell with a commission from Rome to open an "anti-Parliament," "Sir Dudley Digges answered he could not believe it; that it was not the Jesuits, but some malevolent persons about the court, who wished ill to the Commons, that disturbed our parliaments." When Coke in 1629 begged the commons to act with moderation, he was answered, "We have moderation preached unto us in Parliament. I would others did the like out of Parliament." When in 1628 Coke told the commons that they were accusing the king of breaking the laws, Wentworth answered sharply, "I say there hath been noe violacion in the King; but this I say and will say it againe that there hath beene violacion in his ministers." [21] Admissions by councillors were quickly turned against them, weak points in their arguments were seized upon and exposed, and not uncommonly, instead of answering, the commons turned upon them with bitter personal attacks.

These attacks became increasingly savage. The arrest of Sir Edwin Sandys in the summer of 1621 produced an explosion against the council when the commons met in the autumn. The excuses of councillors were swept aside because they themselves had been parties to the arrest. "If we shall suffer the Council Table

[19] Chamberlain to Carleton, April 14, 1614, St. P. Domestic, 14/77:7. The same to the same, May 2, 1621, *ibid.*, 14/121:5. May 12, 1621, *P. and D.*, II, 63. *Cal. St. P. Venetian, 1621–1623*, 185. February 5, 1621, *C. J.*, I, 508; *Commons Debates 1621*, II, 18 note, 39 note, 70; IV, 12.

[20] Notes of Sir Thomas Barrington, June 3, 1626, St. P. Domestic, 16/29:12.

[21] February 25, 1626, Rich, f. 42. ——— to Mead, March 21, 1628, *Court and Times, Charles I*, I, 330–31 note. *Commons Debates for 1629*, 7–8. May 2, 1628, Mass., f. 145. Other instances abound in which the councillors were answered sharply. See February 22, March 6, 1626, Rich, f. 23v, 59; May 9, 1626, Whitelocke, f. 183.

to call in question such as sit here for parliamentary business," said Sir William Spencer, "then farewell England." Mallory pushed the accusation home: "Let us not look upon ourselves only but upon our posterity also. These honorable persons that sit about the Chair know not whether their posterity shall be Privy Councillors or no. Neither are they sure their children shall not be so served." When Cranfield sought to persuade the house to go on with bills after the news of the adjournment in June, 1621, he was interrupted by Sir Edward Cecil, who was sorry to hear him "in such Manner go between the King and us, and to say, that that which we intended for the Honour of the King is only to delude and abuse the King; and to tax the whole House in such a Fashion, of Inconstancy and Pettishness." Sandys wished that those who had advised the adjournment "did love their king and his honour better." [22] In 1625 Phelips declared that Sir John Coke "deserv'd to render an accompt" for asking for additional supply when the house was very thin. Eliot told Coke in 1629 that he had acted "to the prejudice and distraction of us all" and was not worthy to sit in the house. [23] In 1626 Coke was accused of disobeying an order of the council concerning the navy and of pressing into service for the Cadiz expedition a ship so unseaworthy that it was lost with all on board. Carleton's speech about new counsels was heard "with horror," and he was saved from punishment only by his elevation to the upper house. Councillors were told that they dared not speak their minds in council for fear of Buckingham's displeasure; and in 1629 Coryton declared that the king was surrounded by wicked ministers. [24]

This suspicion and hostility extended to all members of the commons who were connected with the court. "The King's Livery hindereth the Sight," said Sir Roger Owen in 1614, and rendered men unfit to serve in the commons. When the attorney of the duchy defended Sir Thomas Parry, Owen again remarked that

[22] *P. and D.*, II, 142, 259. *Commons Debates 1621*, II, 398–99, 483–86; III, 375–76; V, 411.
[23] *Negotium Posterorum*, II, 31. *Commons Debates for 1629*, 33.
[24] March 6, 1626, Rich, f. 59; Whitelocke, f. 17–18. June 3, 1626, *ibid.*, f. 212; Rich, f. 88; Add. MSS 22474, f. 146. June 6, 1626, Whitelocke, f. 219. February 12, 1629, *Commons Debates for 1629*, 61, 197–98. See also Sir Edward Coke's speech about "evil counsel" in *Commons Debates in 1625*, 115. During these years the commons were groping their way toward ministerial responsibility, though it was long before that goal was reached. It was very difficult in the early Stuart period to fix responsibility upon any one minister. This produced suspicion of all of them.

the eyes and understanding of the attorney "may be sealed up by his Place." In the same parliament, when the commons sent forty members to an audience with James concerning the violent speech of bishop Neile in the lords, an order was made "that none of the King's servants should be of that number." [25] Eliot wrote that many of May's speeches in 1625 were effective but that "his intentions had a preiudice as comming from the Court." [26] Courtiers protested in vain against this hostile attitude. When, in 1625, exception was taken against the solicitor as the chairman of a committee of the whole "because hee was sworne to the Kinge and of his fee," May "dislikt that exception, as tendinge to division by settinge markes of distrust upon the King's servantes." In 1629 May protested against the sharp distinction made in the commons between courtiers and other members.[27]

The house was determined that offenders should be punished irrespective of their connections with the government. When the commons were about to punish Sir John Leeds in 1621, "it was alledged he was the King's servant"; but members answered that they "were not to take notice thereof, but proceed to the punishment of the offence." In 1625 Charles sought to shield his chaplain, Montague, by saying he was his servant; but Alford put the house "in mind of the Danger to exempt the King's Servants from questioning in Parliament," and Parry's case was cited as a precedent to be followed.[28]

The hostility of the commons fell especially upon the learned counsel and upon the speaker. The commons resented the presence of the learned counsel in the house for a number of reasons. Members of the learned counsel represented the interests of the crown in an especially intimate way and tended to criticize all legislation

[25] *C. J.*, I, 456, 478. *Portland MSS, H. M. C.*, IX, 135. Owen declared that in ancient times none who "took Livery of the King" were members of the commons.

[26] *Negotium Posterorum*, II, 28. See also April 11, 1628, Borlase, f. 71.

[27] June 23, 1625, *Commons Debates in 1625*, 16. "Sir Humphrey May: I wish we heare noe more of the distinction betwixt Courtiers, and country gentlemen: nor orators, and reasonable men: but know, that good counsell hath bene given you out of reason." *Commons Debates for 1629*, 236. Eliot said, February 10, 1626, that perhaps courtiers might take it amiss that he attacked the government so early in the session. "At which worde Sir George Goring tooke exception howe the name of Courtyer was a woyrd of faccion and howe he thought that Courtyers were as honest men as any were in the house and did interest themselves as much in the good of the State." John Millington to his brother, February 11, 1626, St. P. Domestic, 16/21:2. Goring protested, "He knowes not so well Courtyers as Courtyers doe him: prayes that name be omitted." Rich, f. 8.

[28] *Commons Debates 1621*, V, 447. *Negotium Posterorum*, II, 13–15; *C. J.*, I, 809; *Commons Debates in 1625*, 69–70.

from the point of view of its effect upon the financial and legal position of the crown. As the king's legal advisers, they were held partly responsible for the numerous attempts of the early Stuarts to free themselves from restraints imposed by law. They passed upon the legality of many of the patents of monopoly. They drafted much of the legislation desired by the crown, including the bills of subsidy. In 1607 some of the commons objected to placing a member of the learned counsel in the chair for the act of union with Scotland because "his hand was in the penning of the bill." [29] Moreover, the attorney acted as legal assistant to the lords, along with the judges, and thus attended in the upper house. The commons during these years were constantly reminded of the presence of the learned counsel; for it contained two men of outstanding ability, Bacon and Sir Robert Heath, who were far more prominent in defending the crown than was the average privy councillor. The attitude of the commons was expressed in 1606 by Hoby, who, noting that the attorney was not a member of the house, remarked, "It were good the rest of the Kings Councell were in like Case." In 1615 Sir Edward Coke advised that none of the learned counsel should be members of the next house of commons, where their presence was not well taken. [30]

The commons displayed their hostility in two ways. They strictly applied the doctrine that all members were alike without special place or privilege, a doctrine emphasized in the case of the learned counsel by the claim that all members, as component parts of the high court of parliament, were judges and legal advisers to the king. One of the learned counsel asked permission to defend the king's interests in a debate on a bill for assart lands in 1604 "in respect of the Place he held." But he was told "that every Man here was as much of the King's Counsel as he that spoke; that the King's Counsel in this House was never heard at the Bar, or within the Bar, as in other Courts, because the whole House is of the King's Counsel." Bacon had spoken a few days earlier on the same subject, but he had spoken not as king's counsel but as "One of the Members of the House (thereby holding the Place of a Judge)." Sir Robert Heath in 1624, when asking permission to defend the king's right to certain customs duties, promised to re-

---

[29] Wilson's notes for May 8, 1607, printed in *Spedding*, III, 343.
[30] *Bowyer*, 186. *Spedding*, V, 200.

member he was a member of the house and "soe carry himselfe in this busines." [31] Thus the learned counsel could speak in the commons only as ordinary members, subject to the give and take of debate and to the usual rules of procedure. Doderidge was called to the bar in 1606 for speaking "over bitterly"; and when the speaker offered to excuse him, "the howse called out Lett him excuse himselfe," which Doderidge was obliged to do. Shilton had to meet the arguments of Sir Edward Coke and other members during the parliaments of 1626 and 1628 and often floundered badly. Even when he made a telling point against Sir Edward Coke, Wentworth remarked, "Mr. Solicitor hath done that which belongs to his place, but not so ingeniously as he might." [32]

A second and far more potent means employed by the commons was their exclusion of the attorney. The question first arose in the autumn of 1606. Sir Henry Hobart, already a member and one of the learned counsel as attorney of the wards, was appointed attorney-general in the summer of 1606. The question of his eligibility to serve in the commons arose as soon as the house met in November. The committee of privileges reported that there was no precedent of an attorney's serving in the commons; but upon the question of whether Hobart should retain his seat the committee was divided, some thinking he should do so and some being "of an other minde," and the matter was therefore referred back to the house. The speaker put the question, but the vote by acclamation was doubtful; and when the speaker wished to divide, neither side was willing to leave the chamber. "Herein the House would not agree, and so without concluding any thing in the Point a Silence followed." Then Sir William Morrice made one of his idle speeches on an entirely different matter, which was followed by further silence, and then the house arose. Obviously there was much difference of opinion and the commons were reluctant to decide. On the following day the attorney came into the house with the speaker and continued to attend for the rest

[31] *C. J.*, I, 197, 226. "In the 2nd. Session of the first Parliament of King James one of the House being of the King's Council at Law desired he might be heard to speak as Council for the King; for which he was reprehended, and told that there was no such difference to be taken of the members of that House, as if some of them were Council for the King and some against him, but that they were all Council with the King and Common Wealth indifferently." Add. MSS 36856, f. 48v. See also April 13, 1624, Gurney, f. 212.

[32] *Bowyer*, 80–81. March 29, 1628, Mass., f. 50. Shilton confessed his own incompetence by replying to questions in the house with the remark that he could not answer until he had consulted the attorney. See June 13, 1628, Borlase, f. 245–46.

of the parliament "by connivance," the question of his eligibility not being raised again.[33]

In 1614, however, the house took a much firmer tone. Bacon was now attorney, and the question of his eligibility arose at once. In the debate which followed opinion was against the attorney's serving in the commons. It was pointed out that except in the last parliament no attorney had ever been a member; and that Hobart had been permitted to serve only because he had been elected long before his appointment as attorney, an argument which I do not find in the records for 1606. It was clear that Bacon would be excluded if a vote was taken. The speaker therefore sought to evade the question and suggested a committee to look for precedents, for which he was sharply rebuked. But his suggestion found support and the search for precedents was agreed upon. Two days later the king suggested a compromise: that Bacon, since he was elected and sworn a member, should be retained in the house, but that in the future the commons should do as they pleased. After a debate in which it was pointed out that both privy councillors and king's counsel were often valuable members, the commons adopted James's suggestion. Bacon was to remain, but in the future no attorney should serve in the commons.[34]

James may have been making the best of a bad business. But it is far more likely that his instinct for compromise and meddling had betrayed him into making a much larger concession than he realized. It was in reality the commons who were innovating. It was true that no attorney had happened to be a member of the house in the past, but the commons had admitted the king's serjeant, who took precedence over the attorney and performed much the same function. Here was a point upon which James might well have stood firm, for he was certainly as much in the right as the commons.[35] By yielding so easily he deprived himself of the services in the commons of one of his most valuable officials

[33] *Bowyer*, 186–89; *C. J.*, I, 323–24. "Hereupon Mr. Attorney finding that upon Debate thereof the Opinion of the House was like to sway that he ought still to serve amongst them, Did of his own accord without any express order in the Case come into the House and serve there." Cott. MSS Titus F IV, f. 93v.

[34] April 8, 11, 1614, *C. J.*, I, 456–60. Sir John Bennet to Carleton, April 10, 1614, Add. MSS 34079, f. 29. Sir Roger Owen told the house that he had been informed by some persons in authority that there were special reasons why Bacon should be retained as a member, doubtless referring to the fact that Bacon had charge of the bills of grace.

[35] See notes of Sir Edward Montagu, 1606, *Buccleuch MSS, Montagu Papers, H. M. C.*, III, 108.

216

and materially weakened his chances of future success. To obtain a temporary point at the cost of an order that he should not have it again was to employ the worst of tactics and to place in the hands of the commons a device which might prove very dangerous to the crown. James had done much the same thing in the case of Goodwin vs. Fortescue, which proved a complete victory for the commons. An extension of this device was proposed in 1621, when a member, citing the case of the attorney in 1614, wished to apply the same solution to the case of Henry Cary, Viscount Falkland, a councillor who had been created a Scottish peer. Falkland was to remain in the house, but in the future no peer of Scotland should be admitted. Although this order was not passed, it suggests possibilities.[36]

The order of the house excluding the attorney was not forgotten. It was applied with promptness and vigor in 1621 when Sir Thomas Coventry was excluded and again in 1626 when Sir Robert Heath became attorney. In each of these cases the order of 1614 was cited and at once enforced.[37]

The speaker won the special hostility of the commons because, although in theory he was elected by the house and was its servant, in practice he was chosen by the king and normally did everything in his power to promote the interests of the court. A study of the speaker in the Tudor period would reveal how constantly he used his unique position to serve the crown. But in the latter years of Elizabeth's reign his power began to decline; and in the early Stuart period it shrank very rapidly, partly because of the enforcement of rules and orders which restricted him in many ways and partly because of the growth of the committee system. Thus the speaker exemplifies both the hostility of the commons toward an unpopular official and the way in which rules of procedure could be employed to diminish his authority.

With a single exception the speakers from 1604 to 1629 served the interests of the court and were correspondingly disliked by the commons. Sir Edward Phelips was the ablest and the most successful, and some of his activities are described in other connections.[38] But there were many occasions when, as he wrote Salis-

[36] February 7, 1621, *Commons Debates 1621*, II, 36–37.
[37] *P. and D.*, I, 21; *Commons Debates 1621*, V, 249. February 9, 10, 1626, Rich, f. 5, 7v. The same rule was applied in the Long Parliament. See *D. N. B.* under Sir Edward Herbert.
[38] See pp. 111–14, 272–73, 296–97.

bury in 1607, he achieved his ends "not without the distaste of many who misliked that myself should so often oppose their propositions." Sir Randall Crew, speaker in 1614, acted in the same way but was much less successful and was frequently reproved by the house. The speaker in 1621, Thomas Richardson, was most unpopular, not only because he served the court but because he lacked sufficient acquaintance with the rules of the house to fill his office properly. He had never been a member of the commons before. He was, wrote Chamberlain, "not very gracious in the House, having had divers bruske incounters and reprehensions, for matters perhaps proceeding rather of ignorance than craft or cunning." [39] Sir Thomas Crew, the speaker in 1624 and 1625, was of a very different type. He had opposed the crown in earlier parliaments, and his selection as speaker was a concession to popular opinion. He apparently caught something of the true spirit of his office as that of an impartial moderator. He was "the most able Speaker and one of the honestyest behavior and Carriadge betweene the House and the King, that hath held that place in many yeres before." Eliot regarded his selection as speaker in 1625 as a good omen for the success of the parliament, "making againe as t'were a new marriage and coniunction betweene the King and people." Eliot spoke in the highest terms of Crew's ability, knowledge, and eloquence, "nature and art concurring to make him equall to the place." [40] But Sir Heneage Finch, speaker in 1626, was of the more ordinary type and was disliked; while Sir John Finch, speaker in 1628, was a subservient courtier, bitterly opposed in the commons, where, perforce, he endured the frowns of the house for his master's service. [41]

The speaker continued to be nominated at court, and his election in the commons remained an empty form. There was an occasional murmur of discontent. Phelips's nomination in 1604 was followed by "some Silence" and "the Names of others were muttered, . . . but the more general Voice ran upon Sir Edward Phelips," who was thereupon elected. In 1621, when Richardson

---

[39] *Bowyer*, 54 note, 331 note, 345. For the speaker in 1614, see *C. J.*, I, 456, 499–500; *Portland MSS, H. M. C.*, IX, 134; *Commons Debates 1621*, VII, 633, 646. Chamberlain to Carleton, March 28, 1621, St. P. Domestic, 14/120:52.

[40] Edward Nicholas to John Nicholas, May 29, 1624, St. P. Domestic, 14/165:61. *Negotium Posterorum*, I, 47–48.

[41] Henry Manners to Sir George Manners, June, 1626, *Rutland MSS, H. M. C.*, I, 477–78. Bagg to Buckingham, March 17, 1628, St. P. Domestic, 16/96:36.

made the usual deprecatory excuse of the newly elected speaker, a member "served him right in the lower House by stepping up when he went about to disable himself and said they would proceed to the choice of another." [42] But opposition went no further than this. The crown, in fact, did less to maintain the fiction that election was at the discretion of the commons than it had formerly done. Tate, writing in the reign of Elizabeth, had warned that councillors must use the greatest tact and caution in nominating the speaker. But Edmondes nominated Richardson as one "whome the King liked," and said in 1624 that the king had "ever used to interpose his Judgement, whom he thinketh to be the meetest person to be employed in that service." [43] Thus the crown made no secret of its right.

The speaker continued to receive instructions from court, and these instructions came in such natural and informal ways that the commons could do little to prevent them. The time was not ripe for any extended control of the actions of the speaker outside of parliament. The commons, for example, could not keep the speaker from waiting upon the king, and these personal interviews became a symbol of the speaker's close connection with the court. Theoretically the speaker attended the sovereign only when sent by the commons. Elizabeth had been careful to summon the speaker only occasionally in exceptional circumstances, but James during his first parliament made the mistake of calling the speaker to him habitually for reports and instructions. "Mr. Speaker, by a private Commandment, attended the King this Morning at Eight a Clock," runs a typical entry in the *Journals,* "and there stayed till Ten." [44] There were protests in the commons. A member declared in 1610 that "Mr. Speaker is not to go to the King but by Leave"; and Phelips was told that "it hath grown into too much Custom, that the Speaker should bring Messages from the King" and that "he was the mouth of the House to the King and not from the King to the House." [45] But the speaker continued to wait upon the king, though the practice appears to have diminished in later parliaments or, at least, to have become less obvious; and he continued

---

[42] *C. J.,* I, 141. Locke to Carleton, February 5, 1621, St. P. Domestic, 14/119:67.

[43] Harl. MSS 253, f. 32. January 30, 1621, *Commons Debates 1621,* II, 14. St. P. Domestic, 14/159:60.

[44] April 5, 1604, *C. J.,* I, 166.

[45] *Ibid.,* I, 427; Lansd. MSS 486, f. 141–41v. See also (1614) *C. J.,* I, 500; *Portland MSS, H. M. C.,* IX, 134.

to receive instructions from court. Things being as they were, the commons could do nothing.

The speaker's attendance upon the king was part of a larger question: whether the speaker was the servant of the king or of the commons. And here the commons became more and more insistent. Richardson was told sharply in 1621 that he was "neyther master nor masters mate but a servant to the house." A climax was reached in 1628–29 when the commands of the king ran directly counter to the determination of the commons. On June 5, 1628, Finch stopped a speech by Eliot, saying he was commanded by the king to do so. "I protest before God," he added, "I meane all well, if you Knewe what I have donne you would not blame mee, for I am sure I have used all my best facultyes to do you service." On March 2, 1629, the house commanded the speaker to put Eliot's resolutions to the question, but Finch refused. "The Speaker with abundance of tears answered, I will not say, I will not, but I dare not; desiring that they would not command his ruin therein; that he had been their faithful servant, and would gladly sacrifice his life for the good of his country; but he durst not sin against the express command of his Sovereign." "I am not lesse the Kinges Servant for being yours." But he was answered, "You have protested yourself to be our servant, but if you do not what we command you, that protestation of yours is but a compliment. The Scripture saith, 'His servants ye are whom ye obey.' If you will not obey us, you are not our servant." [46] Thus the speaker was caught in the dilemma of divided allegiance.

In the house itself the commons went far in curtailing the speaker's power. They did this in part by refusing to do as he asked. In 1614, 1621, and again in 1625, the speaker wished to put the question for supply but was prevented.[47] The commons on several occasions, in protest against the actions of the king, refused to go on with business and ignored the efforts of the speaker to continue the work of the session. In June, 1621, the anger of the commons at their sudden adjournment "was exprest by a generall crye, Rise, Rise, which Mr. Sollicitor began to temper by a fayre and mild speech. And the Speaker offred to Restrayne by calling for the Keyes, for which he was thus reproved by Sir Samuel

---

[46] *Commons Debates 1621*, V, 285. June 5, 1628, Borlase, f. 217. *Commons Debates for 1629*, 104–05, 240–41, 255–58; *Gardiner*, VII, 70–71.
[47] *Commons Debates 1621*, VII, 656; V, 438. *Commons Debates in 1625*, 115.

Sands: That he was our Speaker and not our Goaler, and like a wise man should rather labour to moderate mens passions than to imitate them." In the autumn, after a sharp message concerning privilege, the commons "rose in some confusion, insomuch as the Speaker hearing the cry of the House to rise would have persuaded them first to read a Bill or do somewhat but the cry was redoubled, still rise, rise." On the morning after the arrest of Eliot and Digges in 1626 the speaker wished the house to proceed with business as usual and "put the House in minde where they left yesterday. The House cried, no . . . After long silence Mr. Speaker rose and said, I am sorry to see this so general sadness and silence. The House cried, sitt downe, but the Speaker went on and repeated the motion." The answer of the house was to go into a committee of the whole. On March 2, 1629, the speaker, having delivered a message from the king, said he was commanded to leave the chair "but was by force drawn to it again by Mr. Denzil Holles, son of the Earl of Clare, Mr. Valentine, and others. And Mr. Holles, notwithstanding the endeavour of Sir Thomas Edmondes, Sir Humphrey May, and other Privy Councellors to free the Speaker from the Chair, swore, Gods wounds, he should sit still until they pleased to rise." The speaker in great distress pleaded the command of the king. "Yet notwithstanding the Speakers extremity of weeping and supplicatory oration quaintly eloquent, Sir Peter Heyman (a gentleman of his own country) bitterly inveighed against him, and told him he was sorry he was a Kentish man, and that he was a disgrace to his country, and a blot to a noble family, and that all the inconveniences that should follow, yea, their destruction, should be derived to posterity as the issue of his baseness, by whom he should be remembered with scorn and disdain. And that he for his part (since he would not be persuaded to do his duty) thought it fit he should be called to the Bar, and a new Speaker chosen in the meantime, since neither advice nor threats would prevail." The resolutions were put to the question by another member as the officers of the king knocked on the door to announce the dissolution of the parliament.[48] Thus the commons refused to do the speaker's bidding and forced him to their will.

[48] *Commons Debates 1621*, IV, 390; III, 345. Locke to Carleton, December 8, 1621, St. P. Domestic, 14/124:22. May 12, 1626, Whitelocke, f. 189. Meddus to Mead, May 12, 1626, *Court and Times, Charles I*, I, 102. March 2, 1629, *Commons Debates for 1629*, 104–05.

The commons also curtailed the activities of the speaker by new orders of procedure, by the enforcement of old orders, and by new practices and ways of doing business. A few examples must suffice. An attempt of the speaker in 1604 to reverse a decision of the house by voting upon it a second time produced at once an order that "a Question, being once made, . . . cannot be questioned again, but must stand as a Judgement of the House." The speaker was quickly rebuked in 1606, 1614, and again in 1621 for attempting to defer a vote desired by the house. He had been accused in 1580 of putting the question before the house was ready for it, and in 1621 he was reminded that he must state the question clearly before putting it to a vote, so that "Men might prepare themselves to answer." Later in 1621 Richardson was roundly rated for his awkwardness, real or feigned, in framing questions. He was told that "sometimes [he] neglecteth his Duty to the House, in intricating or deferring the Question," "that he hath been the Cause that many good and plausible Motions have become abortive, and hath made them perish as soon as they have been born," "that he doth not carry himself well in putting Things to the Question, nor frameth the Questions according to the Sense of the House." Thus the time was passing when the speaker could with impunity "over-reach the House in the subtile putting of the Question." [49] Rules governing debate were carefully enforced. In March, 1621, the house claimed its right of deciding by question who should have the floor when two members rose to speak at the same instant. A week later the speaker twitted the house for its interference. Two members rising together, the speaker, instead of deciding the precedence, said that he hoped the wiser would sit down first. To this Noy objected "as a Jeast unfitt the gravitye of this Assemblye, And desired the Speaker might be punisht, which was likely to come to Question" had not Glanville intervened with a modest and discreet speech. The speaker could no longer interrupt a member's speech. This point had been raised by Peter Wentworth in 1586. It was driven home in 1621 when Phelips declared that privilege must precede supply; "here the Speaker beginning to interupt him, Sir Thomas Roe replied that the Speaker was not to have any voice but when the House was divided." And

[49] C. J., I, 162, 456. Bowyer, 54 note. D'Ewes (Elizabeth), 306, 499–500. C. J., I, 527, 546; Commons Debates 1621, II, 318; P. and D., I, 135.

on another occasion in 1621 the speaker was reminded that in debate "he must respect the meanest, as well as those about the Chair." [50]

The speaker could no longer use his own words in phrasing his speeches to the sovereign but was forced to submit his speech beforehand to a committee of the commons. "Yow must forbeare your prefaces," Richardson was told in 1621, "for yow are toe large in them." An address of the speaker to the king in 1624 was to follow certain points which the house set down in writing; and Sir Heneage Finch noted that a speech which he delivered in 1626 "was penned by a select committee and allowed by the Howse, and ordered to be so delivered to the King." In 1621 the speaker was not allowed to address an offender brought before the house until he had received instructions. [51]

In 1604 James asked the speaker to show him a bill that was in process of passage through the house. When the speaker obeyed, James kept the bill in his own possession, claiming it was unfit to be debated in the house. The commons were deeply annoyed and ordered "that no Speaker from henceforth should deliver a Bill, whereof the House standeth possessed, to any whosoever, without Allowance." [52]

An episode in March, 1621, produced an order that the speaker could rise, thus adjourning debate, only at the pleasure of the house. Interruptions of this sort had caused much friction in the past. In a well-known incident in 1571, when debate was running along rather dangerous lines, "the Council whispered together and thereupon the Speaker moved, that the House should make stay of any further Consultation thereupon." Wentworth had asked in 1586 whether the speaker could rise at will. The speaker was rebuked in 1614 for rising during a report from an important committee. On March 8, 1621, he rose as the house was preparing for a conference with the lords. When the house met on the follow-

---

[50] *C. J.*, I, 547, 564; *Commons Debates 1621*, II, 18; IV, 173, 196–97. *D'Ewes (Elizabeth)*, 411. *Bowyer*, 345.

[51] *Commons Debates 1621*, II, 40; III, 370. March 1, 1624, Winchilsea, f. 12. March 15, 1626, *Finch MSS, H. M. C.*, I, 45–46. See also *Commons Debates 1621*, IV, 295–96; June 14, 1626, Whitelocke, f. 239; April 10, 14, 1628, Holles, f. 40, 42; April 11, 1628, Harl. MSS 1721, f. 166v; May 5, 1628, Harl. MSS 2305, f. 208v.

[52] *C. J.*, I, 223–24. The commons ruled, however, that the speaker might show a copy of a bill to the king. For other instances in which the speaker showed documents to persons in authority, see *D'Ewes (Elizabeth)*, 411; *C. J.*, I, 500; *Portland MSS, H. M. C.*, IX, 134; *Commons Debates 1621*, III, 121.

ing morning, the speaker was hotly denounced. Sir Henry Withrington said that "the greatest indignity yesterday was offered by Mr. Speaker in rising that ever I saw offered in parliament, to rise at 10 of the clock." Mr. Mallory "would spare none, though they sat in Chairs; whereof Mr. Speaker likely to have a Share." It was said "that the Speaker came out of his Chair without the consent of the House . . . when he was required by the greatest voice of the House to sit still." An order followed "that hereafter he should not rise at anie unusual hower But by the direccion of the howse uppon Question, Nor at an usual hower if any did contradict it, but uppon Question." [53]

The speaker was rapidly losing his former control over the order of business. In 1601 he had clashed with the house when the commons demanded that a certain bill be read and he had wished another. The commons had finally had their way, and in the Stuart period the speaker could select the bills to be read only when the house expressed no preference. His power in regulating the order of business was even more curtailed by new rules and practices. Thus at the opening of parliament in 1621 orders were quietly passed that no bills should be read before nine o'clock except private bills, which might be given a first reading, that the hour from nine to ten should be devoted exclusively to reading bills of all kinds, and that notice should be given a day in advance when any bill was to be passed. [54] Such rules as these left little discretion in the hands of the speaker. The growth of the committee system, with large committees assigned to meet on certain days each week, forced the commons to arrange the order of business well in advance. In the committee of the whole, where the most important decisions were coming to be made, the order of business was in the hands of popular leaders; and the reports of this committee were being passed in the house itself more and more as a matter of course. By the end of James's reign the speaker was

[53] D'Ewes (Elizabeth), 176, 411. C. J., I, 499. Commons Debates 1621, VII, 633; II, 202; IV, 139; C. J., I, 546–47. A larger question was involved: whether the speaker, at the command of the king, could adjourn the commons for a number of days. On May 20, 1607, "Mr. Speaker came early to the howse before the company was in anie sort full and adiourned the court untell that day senight." Bowyer, 297–98; Lansd. MSS 496, f. 32. The commons claimed the right to adjourn themselves. They enforced this right against the crown on March 2, 1629.

[54] D'Ewes (Elizabeth), 677. Commons Debates 1621, II, 34; VI, 356; C. J., I, 511; Add. MSS 36856, f. 36v.

all but powerless to arrange the order in which business should be taken up.

In the committee of the whole the speaker was eliminated altogether and was forced to sit in an adjoining room while the house elected a temporary chairman. In the 1620's this committee was in constant use, and thus the speaker was excluded day after day. The committee of the whole had many other advantages. But certainly one reason for its popularity was that it disposed so easily and naturally of the speaker. It first appeared at a time when the crown was making more than ordinary use of the speaker in attempting to control the house. In 1621 a member moved that the house go into a committee of the whole "that we might not be troubled this day with the Speaker; and that it might not be permitted him to speak, till the House call him up." Again in 1626, when the house was determined to do no business and the speaker was trying to carry on as usual, the house went into a committee of the whole for the obvious purpose of being rid of him.[55] Thus in many ways the speaker found himself shorn of his former powers, forced either to do the will of the house or to sit by completely impotent; and councillors were deprived of the most useful of their allies in the commons.

The history of conferences between the two houses provides another illustration of how new rules of procedure could undermine the position of the council. Conferences formed a normal and useful method of procedure; but there was the inherent danger in them that the councillors in the lords and other important peers might overawe the commons and persuade them to accept decisions which the house as a whole would not approve. This danger became much greater in James's first parliament when Salisbury, excluded from the house, made great use of conferences to place his program before the commons. He was supported by other councillors from the lords' committee, and, for all practical purposes, many of these conferences became meetings between committees of the commons and the most important councillors of the crown.[56] This continued in later parliaments. In many a con-

---

[55] *P. and D.*, II, 330. May 12, 1626, Whitelocke, f. 189. In 1621 the speaker was reproved for remaining in the house during a committee of the whole. *Commons Debates 1621*, V, 352.

[56] See pp. 123–25 above.

ference in the 1620's the commons, addressed by one councillor after another, felt the full impact of the council's weight and authority.[57]

The commons naturally became suspicious of conferences. That suspicion was not a new thing in the Stuart period. "There is noe one thinge that hathe soe shaken the true Libertie of the Howse as often Conference," wrote Tate in the reign of Elizabeth, "sometimes by withdrawinge the attendance of the best membres amonge us, sometimes by terrefieinge of mens opinions. I meane not that the Lordes doe terrefie men, butt men of the Common Howse cominge up amonge them at conference espie their inclinacions, and knowinge that in the common Howse nothing is secrett, they gather other advisements." This suspicion came to a head in the first parliament of James, and during that parliament the commons rapidly developed rules that protected them from the crown. Many things combined to bring the crisis at this time. There was as yet no popular party in the lords, who were dominated by Salisbury; and the commons felt that the lords might well be too much for them. In 1604 Hoby objected to a conference because he thought the lords had already made up their minds on the point in question and "being resolved, they are over-weighty for us." A few days later, when the commons wished to end a conference because Salisbury introduced new matter, the lords "overruled that they should proceede," which the commons reluctantly did.[58] There was thus real danger that conferences might result in decisions unfavorable to the house.

The lords treated the commons with less respect and deference during this parliament than in later sessions and assumed a certain superiority which the commons were quick to resent. In a conference in 1606 the commons presented a long list of grievances growing out of purveyance. But the lords, "replying little more than that they would make relation to the House," brushed aside the subject of grievances and began a long account of the king's need for money. Again when the commons asked for a conference on religion, the lords replied that they wished to con-

[57] On November 21, 1621, the commons were addressed by lord keeper Williams, Digby, and lord treasurer Cranfield; on March 3, 1624, by the archbishop of Canterbury, Buckingham, Prince Charles, and Pembroke. *Commons Debates 1621,* II, 433–39; VI, 312–14. Winchilsea, f. 15–17; Gurney, f. 89–90.

[58] Harl. MSS 253, f. 35. April 19, 28, 1604, *C. J.,* I, 177; St. P. Domestic, 14/7:74.

fer about the union with Scotland and would take up religion "in due Time." In a conference in February, 1606, a member from the commons, Mr. Hare, spoke with some violence against purveyors and was sharply rebuked by the lords. This was resented by the commons. Sir Maurice Berkeley desired "all reprehension at Conferences to be forborne, for, quoth he, if we meete uppon such disadvantage I could wish our conferences should not be so frequent as they have ben this cession." "The Lords," said Mr. Hyde, "ought not to taxe us nor wee them." And Bacon added that "if reprehension shoulde be used it woulde hinder the service of this howse . . . [and] make the howse unwillinge to crave or admitt conference, which woulde be to the hinderance of the service of both howses." In a series of conferences during the autumn on the union with Scotland, the commons were treated rather roughly. "The Lords at the beginning of owr Conferences were very milde; but ended like the month of March in storme and tempest." The commons were told that "perforce they must yeald to many conditions though they forsaw they should be loosers"; a committee of merchants from the city was "roundly shaken up by my Lord Chancelor"; and Mr. Fuller, who indiscreetly remarked that the Scots were more like peddlers than merchants, was "shrewdly chidden." In 1610 the lords sent a message telling the commons "to goe roundly about their busines; and to use no more delayes than of necessity they must." [59] This sort of thing naturally irritated the commons.

The lords occasionally asked for conference on matters already determined in the lower house, and this caused much resentment among the commons. The commons "took it somewhat derogative from their House" that the lords sought to modify the decision in the case of Goodwin vs. Fortescue and replied to the lords that "it did not stand with the Honour and Order of the House, to give Account to any of their Proceedings and Doings." In 1607 the lords asked for a conference on a point in the union upon which the commons had already taken their stand; the commons replied that they were willing to confer but that their opinions remained unchanged. In 1610 the commons, having been asked by the lords

[59] Sir Edward Hoby to Edmondes, March 7, 1606, *Court and Times, James I*, I, 60. April 30, 1604, *C. J.*, I, 193. *Bowyer*, 50–53, 208–09. June 8, 1610, *Parl. Debates in 1610*, 50.

why a certain bill had been passed, refused an answer. The same point arose occasionally in later sessions. In 1621, when the lords asked for a conference on a bill passed by the house, "Mr. Alford saith, that it behoveth us to have a great Deal of Care, and to be very wary of our Proceedings herein; for we are at this Conference to justify a Bill which we have sent up to the Lords, as having past us for a good Bill." In the case of Floyd in 1621 a member of the commons warned that "we should not submitt to the Examinacion of the Lords the vallidity of our act, as if they were Judges of our Jurisdiction." [60]

The commons were also fearful lest they find themselves in the conference chamber unprepared. In 1606 the commons asked for a conference on ecclesiastical grievances, and the lords after several days' delay suddenly replied on April 8 that they would confer that same afternoon. "This appointment," said Sir Robert Wingfield, "of so Suddaine a tyme by the Lords did, he feared, not proceed from their Allacrity to conferr, but it is rather to surprise us of a Suddaine." He therefore moved that the house debate the matter before the conference was granted.[61] Many other conferences were postponed by the commons because they did not feel themselves prepared. In James's first parliament it was the lords who took the initiative in urging the union with Scotland in 1604 and 1607 and the Great Contract in 1610; and the commons therefore, playing as they did a game of obstruction, would not have conference until they were ready for it.

James, in his early ignorance of the rules of parliament, increased the commons' dislike of conferences. He interfered at once in the case of Goodwin vs. Fortescue, first by commanding the commons to confer with the lords and secondly to confer with the judges. The commons demurred. James then sent them a third message, much more peremptory in tone, in which "he desired and commanded, as an absolute King, that there might be a Conference" with the judges and that the privy council be present. "Upon this unexpected Message, there grew some Amazement,

[60] Cecil to Parry, April 14, 1604, St. P. Domestic, 14/7:27; *C. J.*, I, 156. *Bowyer*, 211, 239. Lansd. MSS 486, f. 155. *P. and D.*, I, 277; *Commons Debates 1621*, IV, 309.
[61] *Bowyer*, 107–08, 190–97. For more general suspicion of the lords, see *ibid.*, 178; *Cal. St. P. Venetian, 1607–1610*, 2. When the commons were about to confer on Floyd's case in 1621, a member moved "not to venture such a great Question of our Libertye upon suddayn answere." *Commons Debates 1621*, IV, 309.

and Silence; but at last One stood up, and said, The Prince's Command is like a Thunder-bolt; his Command upon our Allegiance like the Roaring of a Lion. To his Command there is no Contradiction." The conference was therefore held "in the presence of the king, the Counsel, and Judges." [62] But such interference would not be forgotten. Again, in 1604, James told the commons how they should conduct themselves at conferences on the question of union with Scotland; and in the same year he summoned before him at Whitehall a committee of the commons about to confer with the lords and told them what he wished to have done. He asked the commons to confer with the privy council on the abuses of purveyance and with Convocation on ecclesiastical affairs. The councillors in the lords anticipated the objections of the commons by saying they would come to the conference "not as Privy Counsellors, but as Committees" of the upper house. At first the commons refused to confer with the bishops but later agreed to meet them, not as bishops but as lords of parliament.[63] Such actions by the crown were certain to arouse deep suspicion about conferences.

The commons also looked askance at conferences because of the position of the judges and the attorney as assistants to the lords. The lords had the advantage of expert legal opinion in preparing for conference and could bolster their arguments before the commons by quoting the rulings of the judges. The judges, moreover, frequently attended conferences as legal assistants to the lords and might be called upon to state their opinion in the presence of the commons upon any legal point that arose; while the attorney was allowed by the lords to speak in conference in the interest of the king. To all this the commons found serious objection. When the lords in asking a conference in 1604 said that on one point they would intimate the opinion of the judges, a member said he thought the commons, as well as the lords, should know the opinion of the judges before the conference took place. In 1606 the lords asked the commons to appoint a committee of lawyers to debate the right of the king to purveyance; but "divers in this howse did thincke that wee shoulde dispute the question of right uppon greate disadvantage, first for that our warning is veary short: and the matter requiereth greate study, and no doubt but their

[62] C. J., I, 156, 158, 166; Cecil to Parry, April 14, 1604, St. P. Domestic, 14/7:27; Cal. St. P. Venetian, 1603–1607, 147.
[63] C. J., I, 172–73, 175–76, 179–80, 183–84, 193, 197.

Lordships have had good advise. And perhaps they understand the opinion of the Iudges already, which saied one for my parte I had rather rely on when they give it setting in court then otherwise at conference." In 1607 the commons refused to be bound by a ruling of the judges concerning the post- and ante-nati. The commons argued that "though the Iudges were alwaies and in all places Reverend, yet were not their words so Weighty when they were but Assistants to the Lords in Parliament, as when they sat Iudicially in Courts of Iustice; For in the latter Case they had an Oath to tie them" and had heard both sides of the case. The objections of the commons were epitomized by Fuller in 1606: "The Lords both conferr, and set as Moderators, for when they please, the Kings Counsell and Iudges over-rule us with their Censure, and when we desire the Opinion of the Iudges it is denied." [64] In April, 1621, Alford objected to a conference on the ground "that then the young Lawyers, Members of this House, should be put to debate with the learned Judges there, and with the King's Attorney, who are no Members of that House, but only Assistants there." In the case of Floyd, in which the jurisdiction of the commons was involved, Sir Edward Coke declared that the commons should not confer with any who were but assistants in the lords, "for that we are all Judges, and so are not Assistants." [65] Yet in most of these cases the lords held the conferences as they wished. The commons could only refuse to confer, and that might have serious consequences, as did the refusal of the lords to confer on impositions in 1614.

Finally, conferences imposed a considerable amount of physical discomfort upon the commons. They were required by custom to stand throughout conferences and to remain bareheaded, though these regulations did not apply to committees from the lords. Conferences were now much longer than in the past, and the number of members employed in them had greatly increased. "Conferences growe so long and wearisome," said a member in 1606, "it were good that we should require Seates, for we staie long before their Lordships come; And if we departe before the Conference be ended, we offend, and many of us that are old, cannot stand so

---

[64] *C. J.*, I, 193. *Bowyer*, 57, 158, 218–19. In 1610 Caesar told the commons not to dispute what the law was on impositions but to go to the judges and find out. *C. J.*, I, 430.
[65] April 24, May 7, 1621, *P. and D.*, I, 312–13; II, 35–36. *Commons Debates 1621*, III, 72, 191; IV, 253–54.

long but we shall fall downe." Divers ancient gentlemen of the house, said Alford in 1607, who were those necessarily employed in conferences, could not endure such long and unseasonable meetings and found themselves sick and lame long after. The lords, however, did nothing to make the commons more comfortable.[66]

The commons, thus suspicious of conferences, protected themselves in two important ways. They began, in the first place, to make careful preparations for meetings with the lords and refused to confer until those preparations were complete. This development was foreshadowed in the reign of Elizabeth; in 1571 a committee about to confer with the lords was instructed to meet and decide what line it should take in the conference.[67] But in the first parliament of James preparations became much more elaborate. This tendency was greatly accelerated by the legislation upon union with Scotland, in which the commons were impelled to place long and elaborate arguments before the lords. Thus on April 27, 1604, Bacon reported from a committee appointed to prepare for a conference on the union. He said that the committee had debated long and thoroughly, taking into account the directions of the house, and had divided the subject of the conference into several heads, "assigning several Parts to several Persons, of several Qualities, as they conceived fit." Of five main points to be placed before the lords Bacon was to deal with the first, Sir Edwin Sandys with the second, three of the serjeants in the house and the attorney of the wards with the third, and twenty other members with the fourth and fifth. In preparation for another conference on the union in 1607 parts were assigned to fifteen members of the commons, who were to lay seven heads or divisions of the subject before the lords. Similar preparations were made in later parliaments. In 1621 the commons, about to confer on patents of monopoly, appointed six members or "managers" for the conference, each to speak against certain patents.[68] Thus each speaker in these conferences knew exactly what he was to say, basing his words

---

[66] *Bowyer*, 158, 233–35. St. P. Domestic, 14/26:83, 84. See also *C. J.*, I, 189, 352.

[67] *D'Ewes (Elizabeth)*, 183. I owe this reference to Joseph R. Starr, "Communications between the Lords and the Commons" (Ph. D. thesis, University of Minnesota Library).

[68] St. P. Domestic, 14/7:76; *C. J.*, I, 188–89, 349–52; *Bowyer*, 223–24, 232. *P. and D.*, I, 123–24; *C. J.*, I, 540; *Commons Debates 1621*, II, 170–71. See also May 10, 1626, Whitelocke, f. 98.

upon preparatory discussion in the committee and upon arguments made in the house upon the point in question. As early as 1604 we find Sandys telling the house that he and others were about to confer and asking for instructions. Members were sometimes required to rehearse before the house the speeches they planned to make in conference so that the commons, if they wished, could suggest alterations. Such measures protected the commons not only from the lords but from irresponsible words by their own members. In 1610 Sir Edwin Sandys, in speaking of various kinds of conference, said that one type allowed "every man to speake his owne opinion without direction from the Howse, whearin the Howse received often greate disadvantage"; but in a second type of conference the commons first debated and resolved "and then devided to certayne men theyre parts." [69]

The commons found a second and most effective method of protection by carefully limiting the power of the members sent to conference. In the first weeks of James's first parliament the commons began to stipulate that what took place in conferences should not bind the house. In a conference on April 11, 1604, the committee from the commons "had no Authority to consent." In another on April 21 the committee had power "to treat and debate . . . as Occasion offers itself; but not to conclude of anything." In a third conference on April 27 the committee was to "treat and debate but not conclude." On April 30 the lords asked the commons to give their committee authority to conclude a certain matter, and the commons refused.[70] Thus suddenly did a change come over conferences. It came to be assumed that no conference would bind either house unless the committees were given special permission and authority to make a final decision; and the number of cases in which such powers were given was extremely small.

The conference chamber was thus left as a place where arguments might be exchanged and members from either committee might take part in seeking to persuade the committee from the

---

[69] *C. J.*, I, 227. *Parl. Debates in 1610*, 45. "Our strength stands not in the dexterity of any singular man's wit or abilities but in our multitude. We ought therefore first to debate, then to resolve of a committee, next to hear their report and so allow it or disallow it. And having resolved upon the parts and matter to proceed to a conference upon that and not to leave it to any man's discretion to speak what he list. But let him that is appointed speak out of the resolution of the House . . . That none speak at the conference but what shall be set down." *Commons Debates 1621*, II, 355; IV, 143–44.
[70] *C. J.*, I, 168, 179, 193; St. P. Domestic, 14/7:74.

other house. No decision could be made. But even so, since the committees were now large (sometimes including as many as eighty or a hundred from the commons, who normally sent twice as large a committee as the lords) and since they contained the most important members of both houses, the lords still had an opportunity of convincing and exerting pressure upon a substantial portion of the commons. The commons therefore took a further step in restricting their committees. A new type of conference arose in James's first parliament, in which the commons merely gave an audience to the lords, heard what they had to say without making any reply whatsoever, and reported back to their own house, where answers were formulated and decisions made. It was this type of conference that rendered any control from the lords impossible. It became far more frequent than any other type and was referred to by the commons in the 1620's merely as a "conference," while a conference in which arguments were exchanged was called a "free conference" to distinguish it from what was coming to be the more ordinary type. In 1640 Pym said, "At a conference wee only bring our Eares, at a Free conference there is liberty to speake." This restricted conference, sometimes called an audience, or a meeting, or a reference, had become the norm. It first made its appearance in James's first parliament. On April 23, 1604, Bacon reported a conference in which the commons had had authority only to listen. "More Silence than was meant," said Bacon, "for Want of Warrant"; and he advised the commons that in the next conference "there might be free Mandate and Commission to debate." This the commons permitted, but a week later in another matter they again resolved to do no more than listen to what the lords had to say. In 1606 and 1607 conferences of this kind, in which the commons listened to the lords without replying, were constantly employed, especially in the question of union with Scotland. The restricted type of conference thus became well established; and it continued in later parliaments much as it appears in the parliament of 1604–10.[71]

[71] *D'Ewes (Long Parl.)*, 75 note. Terminology was, of course, vague. Thus in 1626 the lords granted "a meeting but not a conference, because they will only lend us their ears." April 8, 1626, Whitelocke, f. 182. *C. J.*, I, 182, 193. St. P. Domestic, 14/7:74. *Bowyer, passim.* See *Bowyer*, 24–25, for a debate on the question whether a committee should answer in a coming conference or merely listen. In 1610 Sir George Carew said there were three kinds of conference: "Ad audiendum et referendum. Ad Communicondum et tractandum. Ad tractandum et Concludendum." Lansd. MSS 486, f. 147v. The com-

This development naturally met with opposition and resentment among lords and councillors. The commons were constantly urged to allow their committee members more freedom. In 1604 Bacon urged that the commons in a conference "should not be the objectors only, but to make the case indifferent betwixt the two houses." In this same session James urged the commons to "prepare themselves to speak freely" at a conference. In 1606 Bacon urged the house "to authorise the Committees for the conference to propose as well as to heare, and to direct them what and how to propose, for said he otherwise if they shall only heare what the Lords will saie this is no conference." In November, 1606, the lord chancellor said in a conference, "Silence in Consultations effecteth nothing: Wherefore he wished that our Commission had extended to speake as well as to heare." On March 14, 1607, a committee from the commons told the lords that unless a certain point in the union was dealt with as the commons wished, the committee was instructed to give an audience to the lords but not to answer. "This spoken, the Chief of the Lords at the upper end bending their bodies, and putting their Heads together over the boarde did conferr long in that sorte together; And then the Earle of Salisbury spoke to this Effect, It was resolved by my Lords, That more should speake, and better able then he that had spoken; But now wee have resolved to give the Lower House no such Conference as shall beare the Title of an Audience, for there is much difference: Wherefore since this day is rather a Narrative, then a Conference, therefore wee will shut it up without giving reasons untill wee may meete on a Conference, not an Audience." A few days later Dudley Carleton complained that business was hindered "by the Strict Commission" given to the committees from the commons. But in spite of the disapproval of

mons used the restricted type of conference when the subject to be discussed was not known or when the lords introduced new matter. When members of the commons spoke in conference, they were permitted only to repeat arguments and propositions made in the house. See *Parl. Debates in 1610*, 45. Free conference had a revival in 1628 because the commons wished to persuade the lords to accept the Petition of Right. Glanville said that the meetings with the lords were "justly stiled Free Conferences, either Party repairing hither disengaged to hear and weigh the others Reasons, and both Houses coming with a full Intention, upon due consideration of all that can be said on either side, to join at last in resolving and acting that which shall be found most just and necessary for the honour and safety of his Majesty and the whole Kingdom." *Rushworth*, I, 569.

This paragraph is based in part upon a thesis by Joseph R. Starr, "Communications between the Lords and the Commons" (University of Minnesota Library), Chaps. IV and V, from which I wish to acknowledge a number of suggestions.

the council and its adherents in the commons, conferences of this type continued; and a motion to grant the committees more discretion in an important matter in 1607 was firmly denied.[72]

In 1610, when Salisbury was seeking to implement the Great Contract through a series of conferences, he found the restrictions of the commons most embarrassing. He had to report to the upper house on May 7 that the lords found a recent conference did not "answer their expectations" because the commons had no authority to do more than present a written message, "whereby a free Dispute, by way of Questions, Answers, and Replyes, and Change of Arguments, as was by this House desired," was prevented. As late as May 26 he complained that "there hath not yet been so much gained of the Commons as to have a free Intercourse of Arguments, but only by Messages." He therefore suggested that a conference be held for the express purpose of showing the commons the necessity of freer conferences in concluding the Great Contract and to explain to them the great difference between "a free Conference" and a "dry Meeting." He thought that a conference might convince the commons where messages from the lords had not. In the next conference Salisbury told the commons that "Exchange of arguments [was] desired by way of question and answer tending to mutual satisfaction . . . The upper house trust their committee better than the lower house do theirs who had only to deliver a message . . . Conference ripens and hastens dispatch of business. We are not to use caution as if we were to deal with strangers, especially seeing our conference did not bind . . . Out of jealousy you will empound us [the lords] into a narrower roome then is for the good of the realme. The upper house hath interest in the Commons of the Realm as well as the lower house. We must not use too strict observations in the punctilios of conference . . . The higher house hath dealt better with the lower house than the lower house with the higher. . . . What tempest is come amongst us that we can not clear our meanings by conference? . . . This distance and separation may make us repent when the Parliament is done that we dealt not more freely."[73] But the commons were unconvinced and restricted conferences continued. Thus the trend of the times was for the commons to

---

[72] St. P. Domestic, 14/7:74. C. J., I, 183–84. *Bowyer*, 24, 191, 239–40, 245.

[73] *L. J.*, II, 589, 601–02. Collections (by Dudley Carleton) out of divers speeches at conferences of the two houses, June(?), 1610, St. P. Domestic, 14/55:58.

bring conferences more and more under their control and to allow a minimum of latitude to the men sent to confer. The logical conclusion of this development was to reduce conferences to an exchange of written documents. The passage quoted above mentions a written message delivered by the commons in a conference. But conferences were not reduced to this last stage of empty form until a subsequent period.

But more than anything else, the rapid growth of the committee system lessened the influence of councillors and other royal officials in the commons. When committees were small and comparatively few in number, as in the earlier years of Elizabeth's reign, they had played into the hands of the councillors, who found them easier to dominate than the whole body of the house. But when committees became more numerous, when their membership increased and their functioning became more complicated, councillors found that their former advantage disappeared and that the system worked against them. The use of committees was developing rapidly in the latter years of Elizabeth's reign, and in the reign of James their growth was even faster. They dealt with an increasingly large number of bills, which were committed after the second reading in the ordinary way. They were now used for all sorts of other purposes: for drafting remonstrances, letters, and replies to the king, for deciding what action the house should take in an emergency, for investigating abuses and complaints, for conference with the lords, and for planning the general course of business during the session. In James's first parliament there were large standing committees for religion, for grievances, for continuance and repeal of statutes, for privileges and returns, for conference with the lords on the act of union; and these committees were dealing not with individual bills but with larger questions of policy and great fields of legislation. Some of them were of a type known in the later years of Elizabeth as a "general committee," in which an important matter was referred to a large committee, but other members, not of the committee, might attend and "inform" the committee though they had no vote in its proceedings.[74] Cecil said of a committee on supply in 1601 that the attendance was "little inferiour to our Assembly" in the house it-

---

[74] Sir George More said in 1621 that the "ancient course" was that all members might attend "to inform the Committee; but only they to have Voice, who [were] named Committees." *C. J.*, I, 616.

self.[75] This general committee developed into the committee of the whole house, which first appeared about 1607 and became of the greatest importance. In the parliament of 1621 there were four important committees of the whole — for grievances, courts of justice, trade, and wool — each with assigned times for meeting and many subcommittees; as well as many other committees of the whole for more restricted topics. Grievances played so large a part in the parliaments of the 1620's that the committee of the whole for that subject tended to become a sort of committee of ways and means and directed a large share of the commons' activities.

But quite apart from the committee of the whole, to which we will return presently, the development of committees was disastrous to the position of leadership formerly held by the council. There were now many committees on which no councillors served and many more on which they were so weakly represented, one or two councillors on committees of perhaps thirty or forty members, that their influence must have been very slight. It had become physically impossible for them to attend all committees, for committees were now so numerous that several met at the same time, sometimes in the City as well as at Westminster. In Elizabeth's reign, at least in the earlier portion of it, councillors had served on all committees of any consequence; and in any committee of importance the list of members normally began with the phrase, "all the privy councillors who are members of the house." This phrase became less and less frequent during the early Stuart period and by 1629 had all but disappeared. It disappeared in part because the clerk was now required to name members of committees individually instead of using single words or phrases to indicate a number of members. But there was more to it than that. When a committee was about to be named, members no longer thought instinctively of councillors but rather of those whose special knowledge or interest deserved representation. The vast majority of committees during James's first parliament contained no councillors, though the most important committees still did.[76] Miss Keane has compiled some figures that show the great increase in

---

[75] D'Ewes (Elizabeth), 632.

[76] Committees for privilege, for religion, for grievances, and for conference on the act of union contained councillors.

committees upon which councillors did not serve.[77] And many of the committees on which councillors served contained so few that their presence was of small significance. A list of committee members for seventeen bills between November 20 and December 5, 1621, shows that seven committees contained no councillors at all, nine included one councillor, and only one committee more than one councillor. The size of these committees ranged from twenty to forty members.[78] Thus the strength of the council on many committees was negligible.

This exclusion of councillors was partly due to the fact that the house was growing more careful in nominating committees. The Elizabethan method was most haphazard. Members called out names at will, and the clerk wrote them down as best he could, including those who had spoken in a debate on a bill without objecting to it in principle. His list when complete formed the committee.[79] The clerk sat close to the councillors and doubtless listened more attentively to their nominations than to others from the floor. The same men tended to be nominated again and again, and they were, for the most part, connected in some way with the government. This slovenly method of selection was not discarded in the Stuart period; but it came to be regarded as unsatisfactory and a number of modifications were introduced which tended to correct its faults. In 1604 Mr. Martin moved "that some course

[77] Dorothy A. Keane, "The Function and Influence of Privy Councillors in Parliament in the Early Seventeenth Century," M. A. thesis, London. Miss Keane's figures may be tabulated as follows:

	Committee lists beginning with the phrase "all the privy council in the house"	Committee lists in which one or more councillors are mentioned by name	Committee lists containing no councillors
1604–1607	30	27	over 150
1610	41	21	about 90
1614	14	3	33
1621	20	52	62
1624	1	19	46
1625	0	2	13
1626	0	28	86
1628	2	23	56

[78] St. P. Domestic, 14/124:15.

[79] The clerk should write down names as he hears them, "at leastwise of such whose names in that confusion he can distinctly hear. And this he ought to do without partiality, either to those that name or to the party named." He should then read out the list "in a loud voice." Add. MSS 36856, f. 34. The noise in the house was often very great. In 1628, when the subsidy was about to be discussed, a member said, "I desire silence, wee that sitt heere at the lower ende Knowe not what you above doo, wee heare nothinge, you may give 10 subsedyes for ought I knowe." May 31, 1628, Borlase, f. 203.

might be thought on, for more Certainty and less Confusion in Naming of Committees." He proposed that three urns be provided, one containing the names of knights, one of citizens, and one of burgesses; and that, when a committee was to be chosen, a small boy should draw as many names from each urn as the house should direct. "This Project was not generally approved; but it was thought fit presently to name a committee to consider of this, and to bethink themselves of any other, likely to give satisfaction to the House in this point." But no report of this committee is recorded in the *Journals*. In 1610 Martin wished the house to add new members to the committee for a private bill because the original committee was not impartial. This motion caused much dispute, and thus again the system of naming committees was subjected to criticism. In 1614 Sir James Perrott moved "for the Choice of Committees; for that most chosen about the Chair; the lower not heard, or not respected; moveth for the indifferent naming of Committees." [80] These motions show the faults of the system: that it caused too much confusion, that it might not provide an impartial committee, and that most committee members were named from the upper part of the house nearest the clerk.

The parliaments of 1621 and 1624 produced a number of corrective measures. The speaker was reminded that he could not take part in nominating committees. An order was passed that no member should name more than two for a committee.[81] There were many motions adding new members to committees in order to make the committee better balanced or more impartial. The rule that no member could be nominated for a committee unless he was present in the house at the time of nomination was applied rigorously to the council; when the clerk used the phrase, "all the privy councillors of the house," that phrase should apply only to councillors then present in the commons. When the clerk included in a committee for a bill all members who had spoken in the debate on the bill, they must be noted by name and not as a group. Committees, when they met, displayed new care in excluding those who were not members of the committee.[82] Sub-

[80] *C. J.*, I, 172, 404, 461. Again in 1626 a member moved "for a select Committee to consider of an indifferent Course for Naming of Committees." March 3, 1626, *C. J.*, I, 829. The principal object seemed to be to avoid confusion. Whitelocke, f. 45v; Rich, f. 57v.

[81] *C. J.*, I, 616. *Commons Debates 1621*, IV, 357.

[82] March 24, 1624, Gurney, f. 159. *Commons Debates 1621*, VI, 349, 354, 357; V, 490; II, 39–40. March 9, 1624, Nicholas, f. 60–61v.

committees of the committee of the whole were nominated in a new way: a motion for a subcommittee regularly included a list of the members of the proposed subcommittee, and thus the house in voting on the subcommittee voted also on its membership.

A practice became common in 1621 which appears at first glance to run counter to these developments, though in reality it did not do so. After the clerk had completed the list of the membership of a committee, another phrase was occasionally added: "that all that come may have voice." In these committees any member who appeared at the committee meeting might take part as fully as if he had been nominated in the house. The significance of this practice may be gathered from a debate on May 11. Certain members objected to it because it was new, because it made the original members of the committee careless about attendance (since they could assume that the committee would go on without them), and because it raised the point whether, if a sufficient number of members were present but not a sufficient number of those on the original committee, the committee could then proceed with business. But it was answered that the practice was a valuable one. It was "the Remidy to prevent the Inconvenience of not putting in those which sit far off from the Chair." Many committees did not include those members "best acquainted" with the business in hand and "therefor best all to have voyces." Sir Peter Heyman said that he had seen "committees furnished by that [practice] and for want of it many unfurnished." He mentioned a meeting of a committee for courts of justice at which, if other members besides the original committee had not attended, the officers of the court in question "would have overborn" the decision of the committee.[83] Thus this type of committee was liked because it avoided the awkward manner in which committees were nominated and assured that persons could attend committee meetings in which they were especially interested. It also undermined the power of councillors to determine the membership of committees and to dominate them when they met. The practice continued during 1621. But an attempt in 1624 to make the committee for privileges

---

[83] *C. J.,* I, 616–17; *Commons Debates 1621,* III, 221–22; IV, 324–25. A member objected (March 16, 1621) that a committee meeting was so crowded by persons who were not members that the original members could not hear. *C. J.,* I, 557. An example of this type of committee is found in 1610. "Any that will come by Special Order may have their voices in the Committee for wards." March 22, 1610, Lansd. MSS 486, f. 137.

a committee of this type was voted down,[84] and the practice gradually became less frequent, doubtless because the development of the committee of the whole rendered it unnecessary.

The influence of councillors in committees naturally declined. This was due primarily to the fact that there were now so many committees and so few councillors. What chance would a lone councillor have to sway a committee of thirty or forty members? In all probability, very little. In a committee meeting in 1621 Edmondes found himself opposed by all the other members of the committee and unable to prevent them from carrying out their wishes.[85] Members were more assiduous in attending committees than they had formerly been, and a far larger percentage of the membership of the house was taking part in its work.[86] The committee of the whole fostered speeches by obscure members; and once members began to speak, they also began to serve on committees. The work of the house had broadened and deepened and now encompassed a widening sphere of activity, in which knowledge of local conditions and specialized information of all sorts could be employed. This meant that time and time again councillors were snowed under in committees. It is significant that so many committees on which councillors were serving were reported back to the house by other members. The chairman of a committee, who normally made the report, was not necessarily the dominating personality of the committee. Yet the virtual exclusion of councillors from the chairmanship of committees means, at least, that the suspicion with which they were regarded in the house was carried into the committee chamber. In 1625 the solicitor was permitted to take the chair at a committee of the whole only for the reason that "whomsoever wee imploye, wee are too many witnesses to suffer wronge." [87]

An episode in 1624 shows how little the councillors were regarded in committees. Edmondes came into a meeting of the committee for privileges, although he was not a member, and, finding the room rather crowded, called upon the chairman, Mr. Glan-

---

[84] February 23, 1624, C. J., I, 671; Gurney, f. 8–9; Holles, f. 81.

[85] C. J., I, 619; Commons Debates 1621, V, 373.

[86] In 1621 a member objected to business being done in the house at times "when the most part of the House is absent at other committees for public businesses." Commons Debates 1621, II, 331.

[87] June 23, 1625, Commons Debates in 1625, 16.

ville, to adjourn the committee to some other place. But Glanville and the committee did not wish to move. When Edmondes continued to press for an adjournment, "Mr. Glanville said he was not of the committee and therein read over the names of all the committee, and then stoutly told the treasurer that he had no voyce nor was of the Committee." At this Edmondes told Glanville that if he were out of the chair he would be less insolent. The committee was so angry that it determined to report the matter to the house. "But about an howre after Sir Thomas Edmondes (having retired himself and advised with his friends) came again into the Committee, and there made an apology," saying that he had imagined that he was a member of the committee and, being crowded, had moved an adjournment, whereupon he had been "slighted" by Glanville and was "very tender of it" since he regarded it as derogative to the dignity of his office. He asked that the episode might not be reported to the house. Glanville then also asked to be excused if, in his irritation, he had offended either the committee or Sir Thomas Edmondes. "And upon this descreete and submissive mocion of Sir Thomas Edmondes and Mr. Glanville" the committee resolved to let the matter drop.[88]

It would be erroneous to assume that councillors played no part in committees. In 1626 the committee for privileges contained five councillors and in 1628 three (all there were in the house). In 1624 Weston was placed on a committee to draw up the commons' reply to James upon the negotiations with Spain. In 1626 instances may be found of committees for bills of some importance containing three and four councillors. Committees might still at rare intervals be dominated by the council. In 1610 a committee meeting was adjourned through the influence of the councillors, who saw that since the committee was divided in opinion, "they could procure a better answer for the King's satisfaction" at a later meeting.[89] But their power was insignificant compared to what it had formerly been, and they were far less influential than many other members of the house.

The committee of the whole lessened the influence of the council even more. It appeared about 1607. By 1610 it was in common

[88] March 9, 1624, Nicholas, f. 61–61v.
[89] C. J., I, 816, 819, 821, 873. March 25, 1624, Winchilsea, f. 43v. See also C. J., I, 874, 906, 922. Parl. Debates in 1610, 33.

use and its essential features were fully developed.[90] During the 1620's the most important work of the house was done through it and its many subcommittees. It had many advantages for those who opposed the king and many disadvantages for his adherents. The speaker, as we have seen, was eliminated, and membership of subcommittees was completely controlled. Moreover, the informality and democratic spirit of debate in small committees were here transferred to debate in the whole house. An order of the house, though one occasionally broken, required that a member speak but once during the debate on a single bill and but once a day in a debate upon a general proposition.[91] When speaking in the house, therefore, members tended to crowd all they had to say into a single speech, and hence speeches were frequently long and somewhat formal. They were prepared in advance and attempted to cover the whole subject of the debate. Eliot, whose best speeches were often extemporaneous, was constantly sneering at the prepared harangues of the council. In the committee of the whole, as in other committees, a member could speak as often as he could catch the eye of the chairman. Hence the style of debate was completely altered. Short, pithy speeches, dealing with single points and small details, were made back and forth across the floor. "In Committees," said Sir Herbert Croft, "by short Arguments many times truth is beaten out." Long, set speeches were out of place, and a livelier and more penetrating tone was given to debate. Members could answer criticisms of their speeches. In 1606 Sir Edwin Sandys wished to prepare for a conference in a committee rather than in the house, "because there a reply is admitted, which is not here." In other ways, also, debate was more informal. Members need not rise when they spoke, and they could refer to one

---

[90] A committee of the whole for impositions in 1610 is thus described: "The Committee for this great business was the whole House sitting in the Parliament House, Mr. Speaker sitting by upon the Lower seat next on the right hand of the Chair. And when any thing Resolved by the Committee was to have the approbation of the House Mr. Speaker came presently up into his Chair and then a Short Report being made by the Moderator of the Committee who during the Committee sate in the Clerks chair, but when he made his Report came and took his place upon one of the Seats, the matter was Resolved by a Question put by the Speaker, and then Mr. Speaker, as occasion was, left his Chair againe and the Moderator took his place in the Clerks Chair and so by several changes the Same Company was sometimes the Parliament House and sometimes a Committee divers times in one day, which had not been Seen in former Parliaments." Lansd. MSS 486, f. 144v–45v. See also *C. J.,* I, 429–30.

[91] For an ampler statement of this rule, with refinements and exceptions, see Add. MSS 36856, f. 52–53. See also *Bowyer,* 66–67, 69, 72.

another by name, which was not permitted in the house.[92] Obscure backbenchers who had nothing to say in the house itself[93] were encouraged to make short speeches on matters with which they were familiar and to take their share in the progress of the debate. One can easily understand what Digges meant when he moved for a committee of the whole "where we might speak at pleasure."[94]

All this bore heavily on the influence of the councillors in the commons. They lost their ally, the speaker; they could not so easily prepare their speeches in advance and were more exposed to the give and take of debate, debate faster in tempo and sharper in tone. They were placed more completely on a basis of equality with other members and forced to defend their position with more exactness and detail. Since the great work of the committee of the whole came to be the investigation of grievances and the formulation of corrective measures, councillors were constantly on the defensive, and their arguments were often buried under an avalanche of detailed and hostile criticism. In the early days of the committee of the whole these things were doubtless not so true. In 1607 Sir Herbert Croft preferred debate in the house because he had observed "that in Committees when every man may reply, some speciall Persons of Place by speaking often, and countenance, doe prevaile more then by their reasons."[95] But this soon ceased to be true, and we find councillors and courtiers objecting to the increased use of committees and especially of the committee of the whole. "Wee are not attentive enowgh to bills," said Sir Edward Montagu in 1621, "not endureinge debate, which is more proper and proffitable in the Howse then in a Committee." "An Hour spent here, better than Ten at a Committee."[96] Councillors contended that the committee of the whole wasted time, and this was true when the king desired immediate action while the commons wished investigation and debate. Bacon said in 1615 that there were too many committees of the whole, "which hindereth

---

[92] *Bowyer*, 197, 246. The house went into a committee of the whole in 1610, "that if occasion were, there might be often replies." Lansd. MSS 486, f. 144v. *Commons Debates 1621*, VI, 347.

[93] In 1624 Pym wished that the bill for monopolies (carried over from 1621) might be recommitted because "some that with goode deliberation can and would alter this bill are loathe to speake in soe great an assembly suddenly." February 26, 1624, Gurney, f. 32.

[94] March 1, 1624, Winchilsea, f. 10v. See also May 3, 1628, Borlase, f. 131.

[95] *Bowyer*, 246.

[96] March 10, 1621, *Commons Debates 1621*, IV, 141. *C. J.*, I, 548.

all business." Weston in 1626 objected to a committee of the whole for supply because "the state of the question is known and the king expects performance and not delay"; Carleton objected to "long harangues" in the committee of the whole, and Sir John Coke said that "debate in committee is great losse of tyme." Another drawback was that in the committee of the whole objections and criticisms tended to pile up and lessened the chances of success for measures desired by the crown. "The nature of a Committee is to admitt of interlocutions," said Carleton in 1626, "but instead of interlocutions now contentions." It was also said to be more honorable for the king if great questions involving direct dealings with the sovereign were discussed in the house and not in a committee. And the inevitable criticism was made that the practice had not existed in former times.[97] But such arguments went unheeded.

The growth of committees combined with the aggressiveness of popular leaders to alter fundamentally the manner in which legislation was introduced and passed in the commons. These new leaders, full of grievances needing investigation and reform, found in the committee system a means of carrying through their program. Eagerly on the first days of a session they pressed forward to have the proper committees appointed and the work of reform begun. This may be seen as early as 1604. As soon as prayers were over on the first day of business, Sir Robert Worth offered seven important topics for the consideration of the house — confirmation of the book of common prayer, grievances and abuses in wardship, in purveyance, in monopolies, in dispensations upon penal statutes, in exportation of iron ordnance, and in the dealings of the exchequer. Worth was followed by Sir Edward Montagu, who, by listing the complaints of his own county, touched upon grievances common to all. Two large committees were appointed to consider these topics and report on the possibilities for action.[98] Thus within a few moments of the opening of business a course was charted for the session and committees set to work upon ways and means. This may be compared with a later parliament, 1624 for example. The moment business began Sir Thomas Hoby moved the house to survey the bills it had dealt with in the previous parliament of 1621 (when no bills had become statutes) before

[97] *Spedding,* V, 190. April 25, June 12, 1626, Whitelocke, f. 157v, 231. May 6, 1628, Nicholas, p. 140; Grosvenor, III, f. 56. See also *C. J.,* I, 430.
[98] March 23, 1604, *C. J.,* I, 150–51.

any new bills were taken up. Sir Henry Poole urged that those bills that had passed both houses in 1621 be considered first; and Sir Edward Coke wished first the bill against informers and then the bill against monopolies. These two bills were introduced the next morning, and within two days a number of the bills passed in 1621 were again before the house. Thus the work of one session was continued into the next. At the same time committees of the whole — for grievances, for courts of justice, and for trade — were appointed to carry on the work of reform. A special committee for abuses in the exchequer was appointed a few days later.[99] Thus quickly did the commons set to work, not under the leadership of the council but under that of other members.

It was out of the work of these committees that legislation emerged. Private members, councillors among them, still introduced legislation in the ordinary way. But suggestions for new laws naturally arose in debates in the committee of the whole, especially the committee of the whole for grievances. These suggestions came most frequently from the new leaders of the commons. A subcommittee would then be appointed to frame the law in question, and it was the popular leaders who were placed on the subcommittee. The committee system was thus partly responsible for the loss of the initiative by councillors. Later in the 1620's suggestions for new laws might come, not from individuals, but from subcommittees appointed to investigate the need for legislation in special fields. Other subcommittees might be appointed to frame the measures in question. Thus, with the committee of the whole as a guiding committee, suggestions for legislation came from one subcommittee and the bill itself from another. The bill would be criticised by the committee of the whole, then reported to the house, where it might be further revised or committed in the ordinary way. The same process was employed in other business.[100] Thus was the work of the commons, especially in legislation, organized and managed by its own leaders. These men, using new procedures, ended the control of the council by substituting their own leadership and reduced councillors to a position in which their influence was only that of private members.

[99] *C. J.,* I, 671–73, 716–18. Cf. *Commons Debates 1621,* II, 34; *C. J.,* I, 874.
[100] This paragraph is based on Notestein, *The Winning of the Initiative by the House of Commons,* 38–41.

8

The Defense of Government Policy

A new leadership, hostile to the government, had arisen in the commons, but the direction of policy, foreign and domestic, remained in the hands of the crown. It was, therefore, more necessary than ever that that policy be properly set forth, interpreted, and justified in the commons by responsible ministers of the crown. This task became the most important function of councillors. They had many qualifications to perform it well. The council was still the crown in action, and councillors, even where they had had small share in determining what policy should be, were intimately acquainted with the way in which it had been carried out. Except for the personal intimates of the king, councillors were closer to him than anyone else. Their knowledge of what went on behind the scenes, of which ordinary members were of course ignorant, gave them a great advantage. They could reveal or keep hidden many acts of the crown, as best suited their purpose; and they knew enough of the motives and objectives of the government to give events a plausible shading and interpretation. Diplomatic relations with foreign states normally passed through the hands of the two secretaries, who were usually members of the commons; and occasionally councillors could describe negotiations which they themselves had conducted abroad. The knowledge of foreign affairs possessed by the commons was, on the other hand, extremely meager.

Yet in spite of these advantages, the councillors' defense of government policy was very weak and became progressively weaker. It was weak primarily because the government became so terribly vulnerable on so many counts and the cause of the crown became so bad a cause. Councillors were forced to defend actions that were all but indefensible. Any adequate parliamentary defense, moreover, presupposes a certain confidence and cooperation between the two parties in the house. But this was lacking, and councillors were not believed even though they told the truth. As a result of these things, their speeches tended to abandon logical argument and fell into an often repeated pattern of excuses, protests, and pleas for loyalty and moderation that could hardly hope to convince. The defense of the council, moreover, displayed a steady deterioration as the period advanced.

The parliaments of 1621 and 1624 illustrate well the councillors' defense of domestic policy. The government was faced by an attack on a wide front against economic, judicial, and administrative conditions. Even James admitted that his kingdom had become an unweeded garden. Councillors, nevertheless, were not swept aside by the rush of the opposition, as they were in later parliaments, but stood their ground and defended the government more adequately than at any other time in the early Stuart period. Moreover, these parliaments not only indicate the more customary methods of the council in meeting opposition, but contain a striking departure from those methods.

That departure was the work of Cranfield. Partly because he was thoroughly convinced that administrative corruption was a principal source of the government's difficulties and that many abuses, such as patents and monopolies, were harmful to trade, partly because he believed that parliament must be conciliated, and partly because of his dislike of Bacon and his quarrel with the court of chancery, he actively promoted the exposure of corruption and gave his support to corrective measures. His attitude may be seen in a speech of February 15, 1621. The debate concerned supply, but he waved aside the question of money, saying that he knew the house was prepared to make a grant, and turned to grievances, of which he made three divisions, justice, trade, and monopolies. The courts of the kingdom must be prevented from infringing upon one another's jurisdiction, and suitors must not be tossed about from one to another. Fees must be just and equitable. Trade must not be crushed by customs and excessive taxation nor injured by patents and monopolies. The balance of trade with foreign countries must be maintained, or England would be denuded of money. And these reforms were so obvious that the king would willingly yield to them. "If . . . the subject is prejudiced thirty shillings where the King hath but one shilling, no doubt but he will reform it." As for monopolies, they were harmful. But they could not be blamed upon the king. They had been referred to various officials, the so-called "referees," who advised the king concerning their legality and expediency. If the referees had been at fault, could the king "do himself more honor than to call them to account"? This applied also to patentees who had abused their rights.[1] The king received a scant £400 a year from all the monopolies combined and would gain infinitely more by winning his subjects' hearts.

When Cranfield's own court, the court of wards, was under fire, he confessed at once that some things were amiss; he welcomed, or pretended to welcome, investigation and offered to make amends for any wrongs that had been done. He sought to enlarge the scope of the inquiry "and moved withal that the corruptions of other courts of justice might likewise be considered." Later he presented eight heads of abuses and corruptions in various courts; though it was noted that they touched the chancery much more than the court of wards. Subsequently he made a violent attack upon bills of conformity in the chancery, which protected insolvent debtors, and bade the commons "be bold to proceed," for he was sure the king was with them.[2] Cranfield's answer to complaints about the condition of trade was again to seek reform. At the same time he defended the interests of the government in commercial matters. When a member declared that the town he represented was being ruined by the customs, Cranfield replied with figures showing that the trade of that particular town had doubled in the last twenty years. When wild charges were made that the East India Company was ruining the country by draining it of coin, he showed that other companies sinned even more deeply in that respect. At the end of the session he acknowledged with regret that the program of the commons was unfinished but added that trade was not as bad as members supposed and promised that the government would take adequate measures for its promotion and recovery.[3]

This does not mean that Cranfield was one of the leaders in 1621 who made investigation and reform the work of the session.

[1] *Commons Debates 1621*, II, 89–90; Chamberlain to Carleton, February 17, 1621, St. P. Domestic, 14/119:103. These ideas, especially the idea that corruption was a chief cause of the king's difficulties, are found in many of Cranfield's papers. See Sackville Transcripts (Public Record Office), 6770, 6773, 6774, 7503. "In good faith (my lord) the privy councillors are as forward as any of us." Sir Dudley Digges and Maurice Abbot to Carleton, February 15, 1621, St. P. Holland, 84/99.

[2] *Commons Debates 1621*, II, 44, 154; VI, 274. *P. and D.*, I, 44, 110–11, 157; II, 111. Locke to Carleton, March 3, 1621, St. P. Domestic, 14/120:6.

[3] *Commons Debates 1621*, II, 212–13, 217. *P. and D.*, I, 106, 150–51; II, 133, 140.

His part was small compared with that of Coke or Noy, Hakewill, Phelips, or Alford. But at least he parried opposition by frankly admitting that things were amiss and gave the impression that the government was ready to cooperate in a program of reform. He believed that wiser and more honest administration, coupled with increased prosperity, would be followed by a reconciliation of king and people. He did not touch the deeper constitutional difficulties; but as far as his policy went, it bore the mark of statesmanship. Certainly, if the Stuarts had set their own house in order, other problems would have found an easier solution.

Cranfield's defense had one glaring fault. It shielded the king by blaming his ministers and led directly to attacks in the commons upon those held responsible for abuses. Cranfield did not dodge this result of his policy. When other councillors sought to excuse two courtiers of the bedchamber who had obtained a patent from the king, Cranfield said bluntly, "I see not how you can exempt any except you mean to overthrow the whole business." Twice in the commons he made the demand that all officials to whom patents had been referred for approval be examined by the house. "We have a projector and a patent," he said; "the projector had had no patent if the referees had not certified both the lawfullness and the conveniency." Bacon, the most important of the referees, spoke of Cranfield as the trumpet in this business.[4]

It was a dangerous and shortsighted game, as Cranfield found in the parliament of 1624. He was then himself in difficulties; and the councillors in the commons, joining in the cry against him, found it a simple matter to defend the government by throwing the blame for unpopular measures upon the falling minister. Old impositions had been continued and new ones added since 1621, and an attack upon them was inevitable. On March 26 Weston had defended new impositions upon wines by saying that the council had determined to levy them only until the next meeting of the commons. But on April 9, after the attack upon Cranfield had begun, a report from the committee on trade showed that the new impositions on wines were now to be permanent. Weston rose to clear himself, protested he had not seen the new book of rates and did not understand how the change had come about. The

---

[4] *Commons Debates 1621*, II, 123, 147. *P. and D.*, I, 89, 103, 137. *C. J.*, I, 530. Bacon to Buckingham, March 7, 1621, *Spedding*, VII, 191–92.

book of rates was Cranfield's province, and Weston's implication was clear. Calvert drove the matter home. He declared that the council had levied new impositions on Cranfield's advice. The council, Calvert said, was in desperate need of money and "knew not what way to supply their wants." Then "the Lord Treasurer proposed the laying of that new impost and therein the Lords, having an implicite faith" that Cranfield knew what he was about, "did ioyne in the advice thereof to the king." Calvert therefore asked that investigation be confined to the "projectors and advisers" of the imposition and not be aimed at the council as a whole. The accusation against Cranfield on this point, when presented to the lords, was carefully worded to lay the blame on Cranfield alone and to cast no slur on the rest of the council. In these debates May had asked the commons to drop impositions altogether. He had no wish to defend the lord treasurer, but he considered impositions so dangerous a topic that it might wreck the entire parliament. Impositions, he said, must be treated "with a very tender Hand," "lest the king mislike the rest [of the accusations] for the company of this." Thus the commons might "open a Gap" for Cranfield "to lay hold on the Horns of the Alter." The house included impositions in its charge against the lord treasurer. But the matter was clearly presented as a fault of Cranfield, and the commons made no assertion of any kind regarding the right of the crown to levy impositions. This was an important victory for the council.[5]

These tactics appear both blind and sordid. When for a moment there was danger that Williams might also be attacked in the commons, the solicitor said, "Let us not be too hasty to iudge [the lord keeper], lest through his sides we stryke into his master's honor for putting him into that place."[6] It was an argument overlooked by councillors in attacking Cranfield.

Occasionally other councillors followed Cranfield's lead by pointing out abuses and supporting reform. But for the most part he played a lone hand, and at times he was opposed by other coun-

[5] March 26, 1624, Erle, f. 112b. April 2, 1624, Harl. MSS 159, f. 96v; Winchilsea, f. 45. April 9, 1624, Erle, f. 128a; Nicholas, f. 131. April 14, 1624, Nicholas, f. 155v; Holles, f. 134v; Gurney, f. 223–24. April 12, C. J., I, 764; Winchilsea, f. 61. For further evidence of the councillors' attitude toward Cranfield, see April 5, 9, 10, 1624, Winchilsea, f. 49v, 57; Holles, f. 127v, 129.
[6] May 2, 1624, Holles, f. 140v.

cillors.[7] In other respects the defense of the government during these years took a more normal and conservative course. The first instinct of the crown and of councillors as well was to silence criticism wherever possible and stop discussion of grievances. In 1624 the councillors in the house were directed "to gainsay and endeavour to depresse" debate in the commons concerning impositions, privilege, or other matters trenching upon the prerogative. This might be done in various ways. In April, 1621, Cranfield avoided an investigation of Irish affairs by asserting that the king had begun a reformation there and wished the honor of completing the task alone. "The King wisheth to have this left wholly to himself, that he may make it his masterpiece." In the same way Calvert prevented a discussion of the new order of baronets by arguing, as Winwood had done in 1614, that the king was the sole fountain of honor and that his hands must not be tied.[8] Thus the prerogative was made an excuse for avoiding inquiry or action. The plea was often advanced that investigation might anger the king, with the result that other concessions upon which the house had set its heart would be endangered. Discussion of grievances was sometimes avoided by prompt assurances from the council that the government had taken or was about to take action upon the point in question. To complaints, in 1621, of the poor quality of many justices of the peace Calvert replied that James had already given instructions to drop unworthy justices from the commission. Cranfield assured the house in the spring of 1621 that the government would make every effort to improve trading conditions.[9] In 1625, when the commons discovered that a Jesuit had been released from prison, the councillors at once promised

[7] *Commons Debates 1621,* II, 149, 480; IV, 69; V, 511. *P. and D.,* I, 303, 305, 342. For speeches of Cranfield at variance with those of other councillors, see *Commons Debates 1621,* II, 123, 332–33; *C. J.,* I, 550, 597.

[8] Conway to Calvert and Weston, May 20, 1624, St. P. Domestic, 14/165:4. *P. and D.,* I, 356–60, 364; *Commons Debates 1621,* IV, 283. *C. J.,* I, 494. See also *P. and D.,* I, 318; *Commons Debates 1621,* IV, 256.

[9] *Commons Debates 1621,* II, 432. *P. and D.,* II, 140, 167. See also *Commons Debates 1621,* II, 332; V, 254; *P. and D.,* II, 362.

"Charges of Sheriffs in passing accounts. Touching which for preventing of complaint to his Majesty a note was brought into the House by Mr. Chancellor of the Exchequor Vizt of the Fees in passing Sheriffs accounts, which is much less than the Fees usually taken almost by one half, with promise that the note should be observed hereafter. This promise was made in private to some principal gentlemen of the House, of which many standing by were witnesses and he delivered the Note indorsed with his own hand to Sir Jerome Horsey, of which I have taken a Copy." 1610, Lansd. MSS 486, f. 151.

there should be no repetition of such leniency.[10] Assurances of this kind occasionally proved effective.

If investigation or debate could not be avoided, councillors sought to minimize the evil of which the commons complained. A monopoly that prevented ten men from engaging in a single venture, said Cranfield, was no injury to the nation as a whole. Trade was far better in 1621 than was commonly supposed and the merchants more prosperous than they told the world. Certain types of enterprise had to be carried on through monopolies, and if old ones were destroyed, new ones, perhaps more objectionable, would necessarily appear. When the commons attacked proclamations in 1621, Calvert pointed out that the proclamation under discussion was a most innocuous affair, a command to the butchers of London about selling meat during Lent.[11] Councillors also minimized attacks upon privilege. The privileges of the house were perfectly safe, councillors contended, and the fears of the commons grossly exaggerated. Calvert told the commons early in 1621 that a petition to the king for freedom of speech would merely ask for what was already granted; he assured them that a recent proclamation forbidding licentious speech was directed against loose talk in taverns and alehouses and not against the speeches of parliament men. In the autumn of 1621 Weston told the commons not to raise questions of privilege until they had real occasion to do so, and Calvert replied to an objection of Alford by saying "that Mr. Alford hath expressed more Fear than he seeth Cause for him to do." The commons should not strain the words of the king "more to their disadvantage than he meant them." To define privilege too closely was detrimental to the commons rather than to the king. "Let us not urge so curious a definition of so nice a point," said Edmondes, "whereby we may make ourselves more subject to lose ground, than to advantage ourselves." Councillors also argued that the commons were too impatient and that many matters would straighten themselves if time were only given. In 1628 the commons complained that although Charles had promised to release certain merchants from prison, nothing had been done. "These men are too impatient," said May, "they press too earnestly for that which will not be de-

---

[10] *Negotium Posterorum*, II, 10–12, 36–37. On August 10, 1625, Weston promised satisfaction on religious questions.

[11] *P. and D.*, I, 309; II, 140. C. J., I, 529. *Commons Debates 1621*, V, 259; II, 119–22.

nied them. My Lord Treasurer told mee he desired respite but of one day and they shall have satisfaction." [12]

Councillors at all times defended the personal acts of the king and protected his honor. When the commons bitterly assailed a royal license to export iron ordnance in 1621, Calvert explained that James had promised the license as a favor to the Spanish ambassador and could not now go back upon his word. A similar excuse was given in 1625 for the release of a Jesuit from prison. Cranfield's attack upon other ministers was partly motivated by his desire to clear the king; he carefully pointed out to the commons how angry James had been when he discovered that his confidence had been abused. Other councillors joined Cranfield in clearing the king of any responsibility for bills of conformity. Councillors also pointed out that many patents were both legal and advisable in the form in which they had been presented to the king and that the faults of which the commons complained were a result of the subsequent activities of the patentees. Measures of reform should cast no slur upon the sovereign. Cranfield asked that a bill against excessive fees in the courts "reach further than since the King's Time, that it may not lay a Stain on the King's Honor, as though Exactions of Fees had only been since his Reign." [13] Councillors also had the task of defending the honor of foreign princes. When the Spanish ambassadors complained to James in 1624 that words had been spoken in the commons derogatory to the rulers of Spain and Austria, Kellie wrote Conway that the king did not believe the report; "yet if it be true he can not think but either yourself or Secretary Calvert or some other of his servants had answered them, and the sother because his Majesty had specially sent to yourself to have a care, that no such thing should pass, and not answered." [14]

[12] *Commons Debates 1621*, II, 25; VI, 333. *P. and D.*, II, 197–98, 308, 333. Speech of Edmondes, December 15, 1621, St. P. Domestic, 14/124:42. On December 17, 1621, May begged the house not to raise the point of privilege because it would result in heated discussion. *Commons Debates 1621*, VI, 335. When pressed, councillors had to descend to very weak arguments concerning privilege, such as that the arrest of Sandys in 1621 and that of Eliot and Digges in 1626 were punishments for offenses that had nothing to do with parliament.
May 25, 1628, Borlase, f. 190.
[13] *Commons Debates 1621*, V, 254. *Commons Debates in 1625*, 68. *Commons Debates 1621*, II, 221–22; IV, 154; *P. and D.*, I, 137, 157; II, 12.
[14] Kellie to Conway, March 2, 1624, St. P. Domestic, 14/160:15. Conway replied, "I sought information from his Majesties Servants of the House, from the most Eminent gentlemen, and the best observers, from my particular and familiar friends of that house,

Councillors also defended the financial interests of the crown. On March 20, 1621, Heath pointed out a number of ways in which a proposed bill against monopolies would reduce the royal revenue. If no monopolies were granted, said Cranfield, repeating the words of James, how could the king reward his servants? Heath also objected to a bill against purveyance because it would diminish James's income. In 1624 he told the commons that the new impositions "concerned the king's revenue in many thousands of pounds" and asked permission to defend them at some length. Later in the parliament he assured the commons that a certain patent, formerly held by the earl of Nottingham and recently bought by James, would be continued only until it repaid the crown the amount given for it.[15]

In 1624 the councillors could answer criticism in the house by pointing out that the government was doing a good deal to remove grievances and improve trade. A number of royal commissions had been appointed since 1621, and the work of these commissions was explained to the house on several occasions.

Finally, councillors sought to keep discussion of grievances within decent limits of moderation and to have them presented to the king in a respectful and becoming manner. In 1621 the commons wished to call two courtiers to account for their part in securing a patent from the king. May and Edmondes begged for caution. "If we proceed rashly it might bee a meanes to spoyle our intended desire in the busines, which otherwise might take good effect . . . Sir Thomas Edmondes very discreetly desired us that if wee would needs run that Course, yet that we would observe soe much good manners to his Majestie (for we could not send to take them oute of his beddchamber) as to send to his Majestie first about it." Cranfield warned the commons not to question the king's right to issue proclamations; "but if there be any grievance in any proclamation, let us seek to remedy it by humble petition to the king." That redress of grievances be secured, not by legisla-

---

but could not discover that there had bene any words uttered to that Sence." He and Calvert then waited on the Spanish ambassadors and expressed polite doubts that offense had been given in the commons. If it had, they said, James would have been extremely angry. Calvert and Conway to Kellie, March 3, 1624, *ibid.*, 14/160:17. See also Nethersole to Carleton, March 29, 1624, *ibid.*, 14/161:50.

[15] *P. and D.*, I, 200, 309. For an able defense of purveyance, partly on financial grounds, see *ibid.*, II, 103; *Commons Debates 1621*, IV, 372–73. April 13, May 22, 1624, Nicholas, f. 150v, 215v–16; April 16, 1624, Winchilsea, f. 67.

tion, but by petition, was a constant theme of councillors. Nor should petitions specify too categorically the course to be followed by the crown. In 1624 the commons wished to insert in a petition for better enforcement of recusancy laws a request that the king issue a proclamation promising to do as they wished. But councillors objected. A proclamation, they said, would imply the king's connivance in past laxity of enforcement, make the commons appear to chalk out a line of action for the crown, and embarrass the government in its quest for Catholic allies against Spain.[16]

As a matter of fact, councillors rendered an important service in the commons by their pleas for moderation. The reforming zeal of members could easily run away with them. In 1624, for example, they wished to inflict an absurdly severe penalty upon an undersheriff for a minor fault in an election return. May argued "that moderation may bee used in Courts of Justice, and greate counsells: that often nothing is made something: something an error: an error a crime and consequently a great punishment imposed on that which at first was nothing." Councillors also pointed out the unfortunate consequences of hasty action, especially in commercial matters. If the monopoly of the Merchant Adventurers was dissolved, May argued in 1624, many more English ships would be captured by the enemy in time of war, and foreign competition would be greatly increased in time of peace. New navigation laws restricting the activities of foreign merchants in England were certain to bring reprisals abroad.[17] Sobering admonitions such as these were much needed in the commons.

The impeachment of Buckingham rendered the task of councillors impossible. Here was an attack that could neither be silenced nor sidetracked, nor would the crown protect itself by sacrificing its minister. The issues dividing king and commons were more obvious, more clearly defined, and more passionately followed than in former parliaments. The defense of the government was far more difficult. Councillors must vindicate a minister hated by all but his own dependents; they must extenuate military failure that stung the nation to fury; and they must explain a series of administrative and diplomatic blunders that called forth

[16] *Commons Debates 1621*, II, 119–24; VI, 285–86. April 7, 1624, Gurney, f. 183; Holles, f. 121–21a.

[17] March 16, May 26, 1624, Gurney, f. 118, 244–45. May 10, 1624, Nicholas, f. 199–200. See also February 26, 1624, Gurney, f. 30; March 4, 1624, Holles, f. 90.

the deepest resentment. The house grew less amenable to reason; its language grew more violent; its attack on the duke contained a venomous and desperate hostility with which councillors simply could not cope.

Their defense of the crown was necessarily feeble. Even so, it is surprising to discover the utter weakness to which they were forced to descend. A speech by solicitor Heath, a very able parliamentarian, may serve as an example. If places of importance in the government were held by persons of small experience, Heath said, the public must not be made to suffer for it. If faults had been committed, all the more reason to grant a large supply. The disasters of the past were the work of God and could not have been prevented. Dangers from abroad demanded immediate attention, while domestic grievances could wait. A similar speech was prepared by Edmondes in the opening days of the parliament of 1626. To inquire into the failures of the past, he said, would accomplish nothing. If corruption could be discovered in Buckingham's administration, exposure might have some justification, but the commons would find nothing beyond errors. Errors there had been and they were to be deplored. But all human activities were subject to failure and the greatest captains of history had had their defeats. The great services that Buckingham had rendered in the past should not be forgotten. His intentions were excellent, and if he had been too self-confident and fond of his own way, these faults were often found in young men admitted early to royal favor. Time and experience would rectify such blemishes and the future would more than compensate for the deficiencies of the past. Buckingham, moreover, was so entrenched in the favor of the king that the commons could not hope to tear them asunder. Disrupting investigation of the past would merely dim the prospects of future success.[18] Speeches such as these, which abandoned all pretense at logical and intelligent argument, stand self-condemned.

To many accusations councillors made no reply at all. In a speech on August 5, 1625, Sir Edward Coke listed many mistakes of the government and in conclusion demanded why, if the fleet

[18] *Negotium Posterorum,* II, 45–46. St. P. Domestic, 16/23:38. Edmondes said of Buckingham's willfullness, "I am so far from excusing him from blame that waie as I will express the Judgement of myne owne heart that I think he had been happier in his greatnesse if he had been more cautious not to exceede therein."

was not to sail till autumn, soldiers had been pressed in the spring. "To all which, except the last," wrote Eliot, "the King's Sollicitor gave an answear, but that he baulkt, for to denie the argument he could not, the inference being soe cleare." In the early days of the parliament of 1626, when member after member from the port towns spoke of the frightful conditions resulting from the Cadiz expedition, the ravages of pirates, and the decay of trade, there was no adequate defense by the council. These accusations reached an early climax in a long debate on February 27, but in that debate no councillor spoke except Weston, who made a short and rather aimless reply.[19] A certain hopelessness may be seen among councillors. They felt their task impossible.

Occasionally councillors made a telling point. They defended Buckingham with some success against the charge that he favored and gave office to Catholics. "Know what ye doe," warned May, "att the Council Table no man gives sharper and swifter counsel against Papists than he." Here councillors could point to the break with Spain and to concessions offered by the government in enforcing the recusancy laws. By concealing much that the commons did not know Heath was able, on March 11, 1626, to clear Buckingham from blame in the detention of a French ship, the *St. Peter,* although this charge was later revived by the house. Perhaps the soundest argument of the council was that the government could not act without money. Buckingham had done all that was possible to defend the Channel, said Sir John Coke, but ships could not be sent without funds to pay for them. Members unreasonably pointed to the grant of 1624 and to money collected for tonnage and poundage. They suggested that unnecessary expense had been incurred by loaning English ships to France. May at once declared that "the ships sent to Rochelle cost not the king or state one penny." He asserted that the figures of expenditure, to which members referred so glibly, were entirely erroneous and that the house was utterly ignorant of government finance. Sir Robert Pye, an official of the exchequer, said the same thing.[20]

[19] *Negotium Posterorum,* II, 45. See also *Commons Debates in 1625,* 147–48. February 15, 16, 27, 1626, Rich, f. 16–18, 43–48; Whitelocke, f. 22. Buckingham, as far as I know, was never defended against accusations that he held too many offices, that he sold honors, or that he bestowed offices upon his relatives.

[20] March 11, 24, May 4, 1626, Whitelocke, f. 18b–18b v, 33–36, 84–85, 178–78v. *Lowther,* 15. *C. J.,* I, 835. May told the commons that in their speeches on finance they "were daily deceived in generals."

When the commons proposed a remonstrance against the collection of tonnage and poundage without grant by parliament, councillors pointed effectively to the fact that both Elizabeth and James had levied these duties in the early months of their reigns before a vote in the commons had been taken. But councillors did not appeal to the past as often as one might suppose. They doubtless found it a sword that cut both ways. Councillors were also effective when they complained that the debates and investigations in the commons greatly increased the difficulties of the government in conducting its foreign policy.[21]

But much of the defense of the duke was the merest protest and expostulation. To the charge that Buckingham had loaned ships to France for use against the Huguenots, Coke loudly protested that the negotiations had contained no word of La Rochelle. He was willing, he said, to suffer utter ruin if ever a scrap of evidence to that effect should come to light. "When this House seeth what will be the end of this," said May, "I thinke they will be sorry they have spent so long time about it." To the accusation that Buckingham had given a plaster to James in his last illness Weston replied, "The Duke cares not whether in this any man speaks for him or not, but relyes wholly upon his own innocencye." Councillors protested that an act which was perfectly innocent, a matter of course between the king and his intimates, had been distorted by the commons into a presumptuous crime. When accusations were made that the duke excluded other advisers from the king, Weston replied, "Out of my experience in parliament, I believe such an unreasonable proposition as this might be made, but I cannot believe such an assembly will agree to it." [22] Replies such as these did not answer the accusations of the commons but merely protested the innocence of the duke. They did not carry conviction and their effect upon the course of events was negligible. Councillors fell back upon pleas for moderation in wording the articles of impeachment. "I doe not except against the matter of this charge," said Carleton, referring to the stay of the *St. Peter,* which councillors earlier had defended, "only desire some of the

[21] March 18, April 27, May 1, 2, 1626, Whitelocke, f. 57, 163v, 169–70, 173. To the objection that accusations against Buckingham did harm abroad Eliot replied, "The question is fixed on our justice here."
[22] April 21, 28, June 9, 1626, Whitelocke, f. 148, 166–66v, 219. *Lowther,* 8–9. "This business [of the plaster] will but adde to the bulke of the charge butt not the weight of it."

words may be altered . . . The recitall . . . goes farre beyond the intention of the House." Councillors also besought the house to modify its demand that Buckingham be imprisoned during his trial.[23] But pleas for moderation formed a very weak defense.

At the same time councillors made increasing use of threats in dealing with the commons. The threat of abrupt dissolution was employed upon a number of occasions during the parliament of 1626, and the commons were told that if they remained recalcitrant the king would turn to "new counsels" in obtaining funds. These threats failed utterly of their object.

Councillors found that their defense of the duke drew upon them constant attacks from other members, some of them men connected with the government. These attacks and dissensions have already been discussed, but it may be noted here that they seriously marred the effectiveness of the councillors' defense. On March 24, 1626, Eliot reported from a subcommittee a long list of charges against the duke. When secretary Coke, in defending Buckingham, asked members to "consider how unjustly these things were laid upon the Lord Admiral," Eliot at once took exception to Coke's words as a slur upon the subcommittee and pushed his point so far as to demand that Coke be punished. Coke answered mildly enough that he "had no intention or meaning to lay any imputation upon the subcommittee." But the effect of his defense had been lost in Eliot's attack.[24] The explanations given by councillors concerning the *St. Peter* were greatly weakened by a quarrel in the commons between Coke and Sir Henry Marten, a judge of the admiralty. Each charged the other with advising the stay of the *St. Peter*. The house sided with Marten and a member demanded "that Sir John Coke may proove that Sir H. Martyn did give this advise." The affair made a very unfortunate impression, and it was said that "the act was ill when the advise was not acknowledged." Coke's close connection with the navy exposed him to attack, and there were frequent demands that he explain events and policies, demands so hostile in tone as to indi-

[23] May 6, 9, 1626, Whitelocke, f. 181–83. *Lowther,* 16–21. Efforts of the council to have the charges against Buckingham presented to the king rather than to the lords in the form of an impeachment were surprisingly weak. They doubtless regarded the attempt as hopeless. May 2, 1626, Rich, f. 84–85v; Whitelocke, f. 173.

[24] March 24, 1626, Whitelocke, f. 18b–18b v. See also March 18, April 21, 28, May 6, 9, 1626, *ibid.,* f. 57–58, 148, 166, 181–81v, 183; *Lowther,* 9, 16–21.

cate in advance the reception his explanations would receive.[25] Attacks and interruptions of this kind came most frequently from Eliot and show that his noble rage could easily betray him into unfair and unreasonable conduct. His tactics, nevertheless, were effective.

Much the same story may be told of the parliament of 1628. Occasionally councillors were able to make telling speeches, especially where the Petition of Right trenched upon the prerogative; but normally their defense was weaker than ever. It consisted very largely of pleas for moderation, with no attempt to justify the actions of the government, about which councillors made very damaging admissions.

In opposing the Petition of Right councillors had a better cause than they had had for some time. May made an excellent speech on March 31, when he showed that in certain kinds of cases and in times of emergency it was essential for the crown to commit men to prison without showing cause. Matters of great importance would otherwise become public and untold damage would be done. If dangerous political prisoners were allowed a trial when the state could not make public its side of the case, the judges, forced to act upon the evidence presented to them, would by necessity declare the prisoners innocent. Within seven years, said May, he had known of four such cases. It was an argument that could not be answered. In a debate on March 29 solicitor Shilton, though ordinarily a poor parliamentarian, greatly embarrassed the opposition and Sir Edward Coke by citing a case in 1613 in which the judges had stated that the king could commit without showing cause. Sir Edward Coke's concurrence in the judgment was absolutely clear. He floundered terribly in his reply, saying that that opinion was justified by the Gunpowder Plot, which, of course, had occurred some time before. But the house was with Coke even in his embarrassment. Councillors also made effective speeches on the necessity of martial law. It was absolutely essential for military discipline. "If a soldier draw a weapon against an Officer," said May, "the Common law will not give any remedie for it." Martial law, said Coke, was necessary in dealing with the militia and infinitely more so when armies were sent abroad,

[25] March 1, 1626, Rich, f. 52–54; Whitelocke, f. 55v, 52v. For demands for explanations from Coke, see *Commons Debates in 1625*, 138; February 25, March 6, 1626, Whitelocke, f. 63v, 18a v; Rich, f. 39v–42v, 58v–60.

when the delays of the common law would be fatal to military success. Recent debates in the commons were already doing much harm in the army. Coke therefore begged that, while abuses might be pointed out, the principle of martial law be left untouched and the debate be ended at once.[26] Members answered these arguments very weakly. The most radical members had to agree with Shilton that the expedient of pressing men for military expeditions could not be interfered with. Shilton was also effective when he told the house it must not touch the king's prerogative of sending persons abroad on the service of the crown.[27]

Generally speaking, however, the defense of the council was very weak. As in former parliaments, many points raised by the opposition remained unanswered. In the early days of the parliament this was the result of deliberate policy. Councillors sought to obtain a vote of supply early, while members still held themselves under some restraint and while the sentiment prevailed that, whatever the faults of the government, a vote of money was now essential. Councillors therefore said as little as possible about the past, allowed attacks upon the government to go unchallenged, and promoted at all costs a spirit of conciliation. When Sir Edward Coke attacked forced loans, secretary Coke replied, "I hope you do not expect I should answere sutch learning as you have heard. My desire is to quiett, not to provoke any." "Wee have had too mutch experience of late miserable distractions of Parliaments," said Edmondes; "if wee meete with the like now, wee are to expect nothing but ruyne . . . Heere lett us bury all former ill passages." "Let us forgett all former Unkindnesse and provide speedily to prevent future mischeefes," begged councillors. "Let us deale gently by our King." "Lett us bee as kind to him as to conclude this business [the subsidy] and in handling of grievances lett us avoyd asperitie and gall." "I speake to the younge gentlemen of this howse," said May, "that may remember it when I am dust and ashes. Mildness, sweetness and gentleness are the fairest ways with princes. Cold-

[26] March 29, 31, 1628, Harl. MSS 4771, f. 45–46v; Borlase, f. 34; Holles, f. 13–20. The debates on martial law took place on April 11, 15, and 22. Harl. MSS 4771, f. 76v, 87–90, 103–04; Borlase, f. 70, 81, 98; Holles, f. 86; Harl. MSS 1601, f. 29v.

[27] March 25, April 3, 1628, Harl. MSS 4771, f. 28v, 60; Holles, f. 28–30. Shilton warned the house not to debate the practice of pressing soldiers; "What a noyse will this make in the Countrey. Let us take care that we enter not into this point." See a number of excellent speeches by councillors showing that the government's actions between the sessions of 1628 and 1629 had been both legal and moderate. Commons Debates for 1629, 60–61, 197–98.

ness and hesitations do no good. If wee have the King's heart lett us keepe it, and lett him have ours. Lett nothing walke betweene us but confidence and assistance." [28] Thus councillors pleaded for conciliation and hoped that the past might be forgotten.

But in seeking to bury the past and conciliate the commons councillors undoubtedly went too far and made very damaging admissions. They acknowledged that the government had acted illegally. "Illegal courses have beene taken," said Coke on March 22, ". . . but withall add the law of necessity. Necessity hath no lawe." Again in May he confessed that the actions of the government had been illegal and excused them on the ground of "extremity" when England was at war with both Spain and France. Such admissions were dangerous and rendered the defense of the crown more difficult. When Coke told the commons in the debates preceding the Petition of Right that they were charging the crown with a violation of the laws, he was naturally answered that councillors themselves had admitted as much and more than was contained in the words of the commons. Coke got himself into fresh difficulties by saying that as a councillor he must commit without showing cause despite legislation of the commons. Thus he first confessed that the king had broken the law and then assured the house that it would be done again. He was answered by Sir Harbottle Grimstone, who remarked, "I doe rely on the Kinges word but what shall I say of his Ministers, when after it was voted in this Howse that none could committ without shewinge cause, one of them sayes here that hee had and must committ without shewinge cause, therefore I looke ere longe to bee in the Fleete agayne." May was more wary than Coke but also used the argument of necessity. "Necessity hath binne a pressing Councelor," he said on May 17, "I hope hee is upon his departure." [29]

The awkwardness and weakness of Coke's admissions may be seen in a debate upon the decay of shipping, which was said to be partly due to the methods of the government in obtaining ships for the navy. Coke wished to stop the debate on the ground that it would disclose England's weakness to foreign countries. "Con-

[28] March 22, 24, April 2, 16, 1628, Harl. MSS 4771, f. 16–24, 53; Borlase, f. 9, 85. See also March 25, 26, 1628, Harl. MSS 4771, f. 27–27v, 31v–34; Borlase, f. 19–21.

[29] March 22, 1628, Harl. MSS 4771, f. 22. May said, "I shall desire you to forbeare asperitie of words. I will not justify things amisse. I pray to God that they are no worse. Necessitie is a dangerous Counsellor." Borlase, f. 9. May 1, 2, 6, 17, 1628, Nicholas, p. 123; Borlase, f. 128, 141, 173; Holles, f. 10; Harl. MSS 1721, f. 200v; Mass., f. 150.

sider the laiinge open and discovering our owne weakness. Let us shewe desire rather to recover strength then make knowen our wants." Alford replied that the purpose of the house was to justify a petition to the king "and this decay now confessed by the honourable gentleman we need not look any further." [30]

These admissions were accompanied by pleas for moderation which grew more desperate and more abject as the parliament advanced. Councillors begged that the Petition of Right be worded moderately. "Is not this too harsh to a Kinge?" asked Coke; "lett the Committee so qualifie it that it may bee sweet in the Kinges eare." "Penn it so as it may tend to your desires." After Charles addressed the house in a harsh and bitter speech on May 5, councillors begged the commons to interpret the king's words with temper and "sweetness of sense." They also begged the commons not to name the duke in a remonstrance prepared at the end of the session. "The King will take it as a great testimony of your loves and a token of your toleration . . . to forbear particulers." May added that Charles was now well acquainted with the evils of his administration and was determined upon alteration. "If an Angel from Heaven tell you otherwise he would deceive you." When the councillors in the house were accused of giving false reports to the king, May replied, "I protest before God that since the Conquest never any of the Council have better deserved of this howse then those that sitt in it now. Take heed of provocation, for god knows what may fall out." [31]

Councillors were forced to protest more than ever before against the violence and disrespect of many speeches. In the first debate of the session May begged the commons to "forbeare asperitie," and Coke rebuked Phelips's bitterness in speaking of religion. Four days later Coke again deprecated Phelips's language when he compared the methods of the government in collecting money to the Inquisition in Spain. The difficulties of councillors were greatly increased when Charles asked the commons to rely upon his prom-

[30] April 25, 1628, Borlase, f. 105a; Holles, f. 58–60.
[31] May 2, 5, 22, June 11, 1628, Harl. MSS 4771, f. 129–36; Borlase, f. 128, 137, 185a, 237; Holles, f. 21; Mass., f. 232, 238a. On June 11 an attack was made upon a commission to the council for raising money. May said, "I desire this house to believe that this is the second time I have seene this commission or heard it read. Neither was there any time spent in the debate of it at the Counsell board more then once and uppon that wee all resolved there was noe way but a parliament to raise money." Thus the commons were told only half-truths.

ise to respect their liberties in the future. To raise this point in debate seemed in itself a violation of decorum and loyalty; yet the king himself had caused the difficulty. Coke protested with a redundancy born of his embarrassment, "I feare wee growe too peremptory when wee come so farr as to approach neare a question whether wee shall rely upon the Kinges word or no." His difficulties were increased when Pym declared that the king's promise would add no strength to existing law. "I desire you to consider," Coke appealed to the House, "whether it bee fitt such speeches should passe that the Kinges word adds not strength to lawe. I pray lett us have an interpretation and forbeare theis negatives uppon the king's honour." But Pym in his reply was quite impenitent. Thus a question had been raised by the crown itself which placed the councillors in an impossible position. To permit the debate was to allow unbecoming words.[32]

In conclusion, a word may be added concerning the defense of foreign policy. This first became of importance in the commons in 1621. But the object of councillors in 1621 was merely to stop discussion. Early in March the commons wished to debate foreign affairs, "but the Secretary Calvert boldly interrupted the proposal, doubtless by the king's command, saying loudly that the consideration and decision of such matters belonged to his Majesty's prerogative and that Assembly had nothing to do with them." Councillors were horrified at the petition asking that Charles marry a Protestant, a matter "of so high and transcendant a Nature," said May, "as he never knew the like within the Compass of these Walls." Weston warned "lest we, instead of a Remedy, provoke his Majesty's Displeasure, by dealing with Things of so high a Nature, without some Warrant first received from his Majesty." James declared that the commons had discussed "Matters wherewith never any Parliament had presumed to meddle be-

[32] March 22, 26, May 6, 1628, Harl. MSS 4771, f. 16–16v, 19–23, 32v–34; Borlase, f. 9, 20–21, 141–42. On March 26 we find councillors objecting to an overvehement statement of their side of the case by one of their own supporters. A newsletter thus described Coke's rebuke of Pym: "Secretary Coke taxed him doubly, saying, how dishonourable would it be for the king, if the question should go against him, for then it would be said in foreign parts the people of England would not trust their king. Besides, he hoped the House would call Mr. Pym to account for upbraiding the king's oath unto him, and would make him expound himself. Whereunto Mr. Pym answered, 'Truly, Mr. Speaker, I am just of the same opinion I was, viz., that the king's oath was as powerful as his word.'" Mead to Stuteville, May 17, 1628, *Court and Times, Charles I*, I, 353. See also May's attempt to silence Eliot on June 3, 1628, Borlase, f. 212; *Rushworth*, I, 609; Forster, *Eliot*, II, 242 note; Thomas Fuller (ed.), *Ephemeris Parliamentaria* (London, 1654), 195.

fore, . . . nay, not befitting Our Privy Council to meddle with without Our special Command and Allowance." [33]

The ban, however, was lifted in 1624, and in the parliaments of 1624, 1625, and 1626 the exposition and defense of foreign policy by councillors became of great importance. Buckingham opened the parliament of 1624 with a long recital of the deceits and enormities of Spain, and an exposure of Spanish trickery became the theme of councillors throughout the session. They also kept the commons informed of the steps taken by the government against Madrid.

To defend foreign policy in 1625 and 1626 was much more difficult, but councillors did their best. May made a very skillful speech on August 5, 1625. Despite the failure of the Mansfeld expedition, he said, the situation abroad had greatly improved since 1624. France and Spain were then united, with the pope doing his utmost to keep them working together. The German princes were at variance and beaten by the emperor. The king of Denmark was showing himself "a warie prince unlikelie to ingage himself in warr for the benefit of others." Now, said May, France and Spain were separated and the French were marching armies against the Valtelline and Genoa; "the Germans reunited; the Dane prepared for war." Toward these results the policy of James and Charles had greatly contributed. At this point May passed naturally to the need for granting supplies. In the parliament of 1626 councillors did their best to defend the loan of ships to France. It had been done only after long deliberations in the council, said May, and should not be censured until the reasons for it were more fully known. Nor should its wisdom be judged by the event. The commons, said Weston, seemed more anxious to arouse anger at home against the government than to improve the situation abroad. If they could see the text of the marriage contract with France, said Coke, they would be convinced that Charles was most anxious to defend the French Protestants. The Dutch had loaned ships as well as the English, and subsequent events arose from the deception and trickery of the French. Later, on April 18, Carleton gave the house a long and detailed account of relations with France. Thus councillors interpreted and defended foreign policy.[34]

---

[33] *Cal. St. P. Venetian, 1619–1621,* 590. *P. and D.,* II, 267, 270, Appendix.

[34] *Negotium Posterorum,* II, 26–29. March 18, 1626, Whitelocke, f. 57–58. *Cal. St. P. Venetian, 1625–1626,* 381. April 18, 1626, Rich, f. 76–78.

But here as elsewhere councillors met with great difficulties both at court and in the commons. At court they were often excluded from the inner circle controlling foreign policy; and thus did not know everything, though they knew a good deal. In 1624 they were embarrassed by conflicting commissions from the king and Buckingham; and Buckingham usurped their function by himself relating and explaining foreign affairs from the lords. In the commons the councillors had to face a growing conviction not only that England's foreign policy was rash and dangerous but that she was being outwitted in negotiations with foreign powers. In 1625 a member spoke "of the disadvantage which wee have ever received by Treatyes and Ambassages"; and Carleton was told in 1626 that the government placed too much confidence in its diplomacy. Weston tried to turn this argument to Charles's advantage by blaming the pacific policy of James. "For the councells, he [Weston] excused them with the long time of peace, that had bred some errors in the State by a dependance upon treaties, which followed the inclination of King James." But members placed the blame squarely upon the duke; and councillors were told that England was more successful abroad when older and more experienced men handled her foreign affairs.[35] These things made the defense of foreign policy most difficult. In 1628 foreign affairs were overshadowed by the domestic crisis.

The defense of government policy in the commons included the defense of the crown's request for subsidies. This, however, is a large subject and deserves treatment in a separate chapter.

[35] *Commons Debates in 1625,* 68–69. *Negotium Posterorum,* II, 37. April 20, 1626, Whitelocke, f. 141.

9

The Councillors and the Subsidy

The quarrel of king and parliament, reduced to its simplest terms, consisted on the one hand of a struggle by the commons to secure redress of grievances, a struggle gradually broadening into a demand for sovereignty, and on the other of a continuous effort by the king to obtain money. There would have been few parliaments in the early Stuart period had it not been for the financial needs of the crown. The one effective check of the commons upon the king was their power over taxation, and they therefore held up supply, though they confessed it was needed, because they disapproved of the actions of the government. When the king raised money by extraparliamentary means, he piled up new grievances which the commons, when they met, insisted upon probing before they turned to further grants. Finance was thus at the very center of the quarrel.

Another word may be added by way of introduction. It is customary to think of James and Charles as wasteful and extravagant. James certainly wasted money in the early years of his reign, not so much by his gifts, large as they were, as by his neglect of personal supervision over expenditures. The moral tone of the court was low in matters concerning money, and if the sovereign was not on his guard, officials spent freely and filled their own pockets where they could. If the king did not watch the pennies, why should they? Charles might have done better than his father had he not plunged into military ventures which threw his finances into utter chaos. Yet in two important respects James and Charles were the victims of circumstance. Prices were constantly rising. They were more than three times as high under Cromwell as they had been under Henry VII. The rapid rise in the cost of government would in itself account for great financial stress and would justify James and Charles in asking for larger sums from parliament than the Tudors had received. But the situation was greatly complicated by another factor. During the Tudor period England had been getting better government than she was paying for in taxation. The Tudors never risked their popularity by making large demands upon the commons. They preferred to plunder the nobility, the church, Catholic recusants, and Spanish shipping rather than to assume the thankless task of teaching the people that government was growing more costly and must eventually be paid for in taxation. Thus the commons in the early Stuart period had not learned the unpleasant lesson that taxes were bound to increase. The king, except in emergencies, was still to live off his own. In asking the commons for money the councillors had a good case, perhaps even better than they knew, but they had an audience unaccustomed to face the facts.

It was the duty of councillors to present and justify to the commons the financial needs of the crown, to secure a vote in the house granting supply, and to pilot the subsidy bill through its subsequent stages of legislation. But these things merge into one another, and distinctions between them are rather artificial. It is better to approach the subject from a somewhat wider point of view and to consider the ways and means employed by the government in attempting to obtain supply. Such a discussion makes perfectly clear the position and functions of councillors in respect to subsidies.

The grant of 1606, which was the first that James obtained, showed clearly that skillful manipulation of the commons was still of great importance and still might bring results. Parliament and the king were, to be sure, on fairly cordial terms. They were drawn together by the common danger of the Gunpowder Plot, and no great issue was, for the moment, causing friction. The crown obtained a grant of two subsidies and four fifteenths. But the government wanted more and Salisbury set out to obtain it. His success was due to the good will of the commons but also to his own tact and skillful management. Bacon wrote that the commons made an additional grant "chiefly out of their own good affections," but also "upon conference with the Lords touching the occasions of the King and by persuasion of some good servants of the King's which were gracious with the House." [1]

Salisbury was, of course, behind the original grant. James wrote him on February 10, the day the grant was made, to use all his influence to obtain subsidies from the house rather than a smaller

[1] Bacon to the king, 1615, *Spedding*, V, 178.

annual supply which could not be used to retire outstanding debts. The motion for a grant was made by Sir Thomas Ridgeway, a minor officeholder, who must certainly have had his instructions. Salisbury may have thought that the motion would appear more spontaneous if it came from a minor official than from Sir John Herbert, the only councillor then in the commons. Ridgeway dwelt upon the blessings enjoyed by England since James's accession and upon the extraordinary expenses of recent years. He then moved for a committee, such as those of Elizabeth's reign, to frame a grant to the king. Another member, however, Sir Edward Montagu, who was not a courtier, made a direct motion for two subsidies and four fifteenths. This was passed and a committee directed to frame the bill. Bacon, writing in 1615, said of this motion: "After the Parliament had sitten a good while, an honest gentleman (by name Sir Edward Montague) stood up and in a plain and familiar manner moved for two subsidies and four fifteens; concluding with these plain words, that so much he thought would content, and less would not be well accepted; whereupon the two subsidies passed upon question the same day." [2]

Thus a grant had been easily obtained. But Salisbury wrote that the government wished "if it be possible to gett somewhat more than two Subsidies." [3] He began to prepare the ground for another vote. In a conference on February 14 lord treasurer Dorset presented to the commons a long and detailed account of both normal and extraordinary charges since James's accession. He described the large demands made upon the treasury by temporary and unusual expenses, such as the burial of Queen Elizabeth, the journey of James and his family from Scotland, the coronation and formal entry into London, entertainment of foreign ambassadors, erection of new buildings, and changes in the wardrobe and elsewhere necessitated by the accession of a male sovereign. He described the king's debts, showing how Elizabeth had left a deficit and how that amount had necessarily increased since James came to the throne. He showed that sources of revenue long enjoyed by the crown were now on the decline, while many items

[2] Dirleton to Salisbury, February 10, 1606, St. P. Domestic, 14/18:77. *Bowyer*, 31. *C. J.*, I, 266. *Spedding*, V, 178.
[3] Salisbury to Mar, March 9, 1606, St. P. Domestic, 14/19:27. Sir Edward Hoby wrote Edmondes that the two subsidies "came short to expectation and necessity." March 7, 1606, *Court and Times, James I*, I, 60. See also *Winwood*, II, 198; M. de la Fontaine to M. de Villeroy, February 26, 1606, Paris Trans., 3/41.

of expenditure at court and elsewhere had greatly increased. He admitted that James in his "good and princely disposition was apt and inclinable to give even where small desert was, upon mere insistance." But this was to be expected at the beginning of a reign, and many persons had rendered James such important service that their requests were hard to deny. He ended by answering a number of objections likely to be raised in the house. Thus the commons were furnished with a full account of past expenditures presented in an orderly and plausible manner. This in itself was something new; Tudor parliaments had not been offered such detailed information concerning the expenditures of the crown. Dorset's speech was repeated in a second conference on February 19.[4]

In the commons Salisbury instructed government officials to work for further supply and assigned to each his part. He made every effort to conciliate the commons. They were debating the grievance of purveyance, and Salisbury appeared to be listening sympathetically, although he wrote in private that the crown had no intention of parting with its rights. A violent attack upon purveyance by Hare, which might have caused much unpleasantness, was mildly deprecated. The commons were allowed to pass a law against purveyance, although it was later stopped in the lords. But the house was reluctant to make an additional grant. In spite of the promptings of the courtiers, subsidies were not seriously debated for over a month; and then forceful speeches were made against an increase. The solicitor was called to the bar for speak-

---

[4] *Bowyer*, 42–45, 371–75. In 1610 Salisbury began the session with a long account of the king's finances, which he reviewed since the accession. He showed how extraordinary expenses had kept the crown in poverty and how recovery had been prevented by charges in Ireland. Nevertheless, the debt had been reduced. While this account glossed over the king's extravagance, the commons were given a fairly clear account of how money had been spent. In the commons Sir Julius Caesar explained and amplified Salisbury's speech and "offered to give full satisfaction to any of the Howse that would come unto hym, in any thinge whearin he was willing to be resolved." *Parl. Debates in 1610*, 1–9, 12; St. P. Domestic, 14/52:69.

When the council was debating preparations for a possible session of parliament in 1615, Sir Edward Coke suggested that an exact statement of the king's expenses for some years be laid before the commons to impress them with the fact that the poverty of the crown grew from necessary expenses and not from the prodigality of the king. Coke spoke as if this was a most unusual thing to do. *Spedding*, V, 200.

During the 1620's the commons were not normally given such detailed accounts. But this was because there were so many unusual expenses, such as those of war and diplomacy, that the councillors confined themselves to these topics. In 1628 the council decided as a matter of policy that the general headings of expenses should be presented to the commons but not the exact sums required by the crown. St. P. Domestic, 16/98:52, 53, 58.

ing "over bitterly" in favor of supply. Decision was postponed from day to day. Hobart wrote Salisbury on March 13, "It is hard if the backwardness of the House should be turned upon my blame, that was most desirous to discharge it. Direct what you please and I will follow it presently." [5]

Salisbury therefore determined to force a vote. This was to be done by the speaker, Sir Edward Phelips, who should first deliver a message from the king urging haste and follow it immediately by putting the question for supply whether members liked it or not. Phelips felt his responsibility; he wrote, "I have prepared my poore strengthe, unto to morrowes work, and doe much hope of the good success thereof." He asked for discretionary power in case of emergency. On March 18 he delivered the message as Salisbury had planned. It thanked the commons for what they had already granted, pointed out the need for additional supply, offered redress of grievances, and asked that the commons come to a decision. There is a draft of this message in Salisbury's hand among the Cecil papers. The speaker offered to put the question. "But Sir Henry Savile moved that it might be deferred and first considered of: Notwithstanding Mr. Speaker moved the question thus: Whether according to the Kings desier the howse woulde grow to the question: which question prevaled in the affirmative." A dispute arose, however, as to the form the question should take. Phelips cleverly suggested that there were two questions which might be put, one a general question whether the house would give more than it had already given and the other a particular question concerning the amount. Courtiers preferred the first of these since it would be more difficult to deny. Bowyer wrote that "they which studied to please required the generall question and such as continued according to their first opinion moved only out of conscience called for the particuler question." Finally a vote was taken as to which of these questions should be put. This was a vital point, and the house divided, the government winning by a single vote, 140 to 139. After this, victory was easy. The general question was carried and was followed by a vote for one subsidy and two fifteenths. Apparently the speaker helped here also by wording the question in such a way that members hesitated to

[5] Sir Henry Hobart to Salisbury, March 13, 1606, Hatfield House MSS. Salisbury to Mar, March 9, 1606, St. P. Domestic, 14/19:27. *Bowyer*, 38–42, 79–81.

vote against it.[6] Thus the government had won, though by a slim majority. As Bacon said, success came largely because of the good will of the commons themselves. But skillful manipulation had certainly done its part.

Never again during the period, however, was a grant obtained by these means. This was due, of course, to the increased determination of the commons that grievances must precede supply and to their deepened suspicion, often quite unreasonable, of anything approaching management by the crown. But it may also be noted that the tactics of the crown became less skillful.[7]

Attempts at management by the government tended to degenerate into trickery. The subsidy in 1624 had been carefully worded by the commons to exclude the Palatinate as a sphere of military operations "in regard of the infinite charge." But when the bill was brought from the committee for its final reading in the house, which should have been a mere matter of form, the government attempted to slip in the recovery of the Palatinate as an objective to which the subsidies might be applied. In reporting the bill the solicitor "did tender to the house by direction (as he said) some alterations in the preamble." When asked from whom he had received authority for these changes, the solicitor "said it was the prince's intreaty as from the king. This was utterly disliked by the house." It was said that the king's name should not be used in a matter of this kind, that the proposal was most untimely, "not in the committee but in the house at the instant of passing, . . . in a thinne house and late in the afternoone," that it was a breach of order "to interpose it betweene the report . . . and the Speaker's proposall," and that "that which was proposed was clean contrary to the intent of the house, . . . it being otherwise resolved upon debate before that the Palatinate should not be named." Some members wished to recommit the bill, others to defer the debate until the next day. "But the House overruled it

---

[6] Phelips to Salisbury, March 17, 1606, printed in *Bowyer*, 82 note. *Ibid.*, 82–85; *C. J.*, I, 286.

[7] Part of this mismanagement lay in not telling the commons how much money the government needed. Early in 1626 it was actually proposed in debate that the financial condition of the king be discussed. Sir John Savile wished "that the privy Counsell may lead the way." But no councillor rose and Mr. Coryton said he saw "no reason to call up men when they have no mind to speake." At the end of the debate Weston said weakly that he was confident the king would allow an investigation of past expenditures but that the permission of the king must first be obtained. February 24, 1626, Rich, f. 34v–38v; Whitelocke, f. 64v–65v; *C. J.*, I, 824.

and it passed by the question to ingrossing, without such addition or alteration." [8] Such dubious tactics deserved to fail.

The adjournment to Oxford in 1625 was also regarded as a trick by the commons, a trick to wear them out until they voted money. "To give mony is the end of Parliaments," said Phelips, "but to give mony upon a catche, wilbe the shame of Parliaments." [9]

Again in 1625, as we have seen, the government appeared to accept a small grant of subsidies, and members left London in large numbers to escape the plague. Then suddenly on July 8 Sir John Coke came forward with a renewed demand for money. His motion fell very flat and was "laid aside quietly" by the solicitor himself. [10] But the commons believed that the government was trying to trick them into voting more money. A somewhat similar episode occurred in 1628. The commons were expecting an adjournment over Easter, which fell on April 13. On Tuesday, April 8, however, Charles sent a message to the lords asking them to forego their recess, to which they consented. But no such message came to the commons. Members assumed that they were to have their usual holiday, and many slipped away to the country. Then on Thursday, April 10, the message arrived in the house. "This stirred a strange jealousy in our House that there was some dessein in it, and the rather because the Councillors of the House having beene employed to intreate his Majesty to give us leave to make a recesse brought back a fayre denyall." Some of Buckingham's friends, according to Nethersole, hoping to do their patron a good turn, had spread a rumor that Buckingham had asked Charles not to send any such message to the commons and had prevailed. The councillors in the house had had an opportunity to deliver the message on April 8, for an adjournment had been spoken of in the house on that day; but the message had been delayed. Meanwhile "many skores were gone into the countrey." It was known how eager Charles was for a vote on supply, and it appeared likely that the government was about to force a vote when its supporters might form a majority in a small house. The commons turned upon the councillors. "It puts feare in mee that wee heard not of this sooner," said Kirton; "had this been intimated yesterday wee

[8] May 14, 1624, Erle, f. 184.
[9] *Commons Debates in 1625*, 82.
[10] See pp. 169–71 above.

had yielded, but an emptie howse may make a prejudiciall cause." "It may be there is some misprison or plot intended," said Eliot; "it was expected that this message should come Tewsday last. They say the Lord Keeper spoke it in the upper howse and then should I have received it with all joy. But when I perceived the silence of those Councillors yesterday and the day before when this recesse was motioned how they held their peace and took no notice of it, what shall I saie or what shall I thinke." He wished that no more members be allowed to leave and that no vote be taken on the subsidy until the house was full again. May deprecated Eliot's suggestion and gave what may well have been the true explanation: "This gentleman is too apprehensive and foreruns the king's meaning. The king thought the message should have been delivered yesterday and the Speaker was to have gone to the king; but coming by in the morning the king was not ready and the howse expected him." Councillors asked pardon of the house. "I would take away if I could all imaginations of suspicions," said Coke, "and freely confess unto you twas our faults, desiringe you to forgive us." "I ever scorned secrett feares," said May; "this message should have been given yesterday. The King gave order for it. It was our fault and the King was angrie that it was not delivered." Kirton seconded Eliot's motion that no action be taken on the subsidy till after the holidays. The motion was rejected; but if a trick had been intended, it was soon snuffed out.[11]

For the councillors to force a vote on supply would appear to modern eyes a perfectly legitimate parliamentary maneuver. But the commons did not so regard it. They disliked very much to vote directly against supply. An adverse vote for the crown created a situation that was awkward and, in the minds of the commons, unjust to their true sentiments toward the sovereign. It brought a certain dishonor to the king, cast a slur upon the loyalty of the commons, and placed popular leaders in some danger of reprisals from court. Councillors could rely upon these things and knew that if they could precipitate a vote they had won a very

[11] Nethersole to Elizabeth, queen of Bohemia, April 14, 1628, St. P. Domestic, 16/101:4. Borlase, f. 65–67; Mass., f. 83; Holles, f. 77; Nicholas, p. 50–53. Mead to Stuteville, April 19, 1628, *Court and Times, Charles I*, I, 343. On the other hand, the king without doubt regarded certain actions of the commons as trickery. Seymour's sudden motion for a small supply in 1625 and the resolution of the commons in 1626 and 1628 to vote supply but not to pass the bill were considered tricks.

real advantage. The commons, on the other hand, held that the question for supply could not properly be put until it was clear that the response of the house would be favorable and the passage of the subsidy a foregone conclusion. Thus on a number of occasions the councillors sought to force a vote and the commons sought to avoid it.

The commons' dislike of a vote on supply when they were determined not to grant money is well illustrated by an episode in 1610. On June 11 Salisbury had suggested that the commons vote supply at once and that other questions concerning the Great Contract, including a presentation of grievances, be deferred until another session in the autumn. This was followed by a motion in the house for two subsidies and two fifteenths. But the commons opposed a grant until their grievances were presented and answered. Sir Julius Caesar, "finding the Howse bent against subsidies," delivered a message offering to receive and answer grievances at once if supply was granted first. "But the Howse, distasting Mr. Chancelor's motion, agreed to defer the debate till the morning." Caesar then repeated his message, and a motion for supply was made once more. "Divers assented, but the moste denyed to give any before wee had received an answer to our greevances. So that the matter was debated *pro et contra* in the Howse from nyne of the clock till after one. And in the end the moste thought it fitt that no question should be made that day concerning any subsidy at all. And so the question being putt whether any question should be putt, the negative voyces prevayled." [12]

In the autumn, Salisbury, having learned his lesson, protested against James's wish to force another vote on supply. James argued that it was as great a disgrace not to put the question as to have it denied. But Salisbury managed to evade James's suggestion, and there was no attempt to force a vote.[13]

Three times in 1614 the councillors sought to force the question, and each time the house refused to vote. Early in the session the courtiers "were so confident of their own strength, as they called upon Mr. Speaker to have it put to voices." But other members "quieted that motion, and drew the House to a resolution to do nothing in matters of that nature, till they had ordered something

[12] *Parl. Debates in 1610*, 55–58. A month later, grievances having been presented and some of them answered, the commons voted one subsidy.
[13] Lake to Salisbury, November 23, 1610, St. P. Domestic, 14/58:31.

for the good of the public." On May 5 Lake "moved to put it to the Question, whether the King shall be supplied." But Sir Anthony Cope answered, "Not fit to proceed to the Question now. He, if it may be respited, resolved to give; if now pressed, will deny it." Other members agreed. "Not to hazard the giving upon the Question now . . . Those that press this now, shall do the King worst Service . . . A putting of the Question, to strain too far for the King; which, instead of good, may do him hurt . . . If he should now gain divers Subsidies, with so many negative Voices, not honourable." The question therefore was deferred. On the last day of the session "the speaker woulde have put it [the subsidy] to the question but was prevented." [14]

Again in 1625 the council attempted without success to force the question. The commons were resolved not to give. In an important debate on August 10, subsidies were urged and attacks upon the government answered by Naunton, May, and Weston. Weston began mildly by pointing out the great hopes entertained of the young king; if Charles needed a small sum to send out the fleet, it should not be denied him. "But finding by the inclination of the house that that way could not serve, he [Weston] concluded in another for the question of supplie, and prest to have a resolution in that pointe. That rocke was seene betimes, and therefore as speedilie avoided; for the negative the wiser sort did fear, the affirmative all generallie did abhorr." Members opposed putting the question. Glanville drove the point home by declaring that a denial would be dishonorable to the king while a reluctant consent would betray the position of the commons. The king, he added, should not force the question of supply until it was seen that the house was ready to consent. The commons had liberty to conduct business as they saw fit, and this liberty was infringed if they were forced to vote upon a matter against their will. "Upon this all color was removed from those that sought the question. No such question could seeme proper, wher ther was noe reason for supplie." Even Sir Robert Killigrew, an ardent supporter of the crown, now opposed the question, "for it is a greater disgrace to be denyed by a fewe then by all." [15]

[14] Lorkin to Puckering, May 28, 1614, *Court and Times, James I,* I, 315–16. *C. J.,* I, 474. *Commons Debates 1621,* VII, 656.

[15] *Commons Debates in 1625,* 107–16, 120–22, 161; *Negotium Posterorum,* II, 84–93. Glanville said the commons had liberty of action but "to be putt upon that question, was

Since the commons could not be maneuvered into granting money, the crown had to rely upon the persuasions of councillors and other courtiers in the house, upon speeches in conference by councillors who were members of the lords, and upon the pressure that could be applied by the intervention of the king. These things could be coupled with such concessions as the crown might be willing to offer.

The chief defense of supply fell naturally upon the councillors in the house. One could cite scores of debates in which councillors pleaded for money. The same arguments were constantly repeated: increased cost of government and mounting debt, extraordinary expenditures, the great value of concessions offered by the crown, the dangers of an empty exchequer and the advantage it offered to the enemies of the country at home and abroad, the impossibility of waging war without funds, the promptings of loyalty and patriotism, and, finally, the danger that the crown might turn to more despotic methods of government. These and similar arguments were made again and again.[16]

I propose to illustrate the work of councillors by following the subsidy through a single parliament, that of 1624. There is a certain advantage in studying a session in which the councillors had real concessions to offer and had some success in the commons. The parliament of 1624 also illustrates the extreme caution of the commons, even where they were willing to make a grant. They had to be convinced that the promises of the government were becoming realities and that progress with the subsidy was being paralleled by concessions from the crown. Supply and grievances must proceed together.

The first mention of subsidies in 1624 came from the king himself. James had asked the advice of parliament on foreign policy and was answered by a joint declaration of lords and commons asking that the treaties with Spain be ended and intimating strongly that this should be followed by war. James showed in his rather peevish reply on March 5 that he was thinking much more about the recovery of the Palatinate than of a war with Spain. He

---

preiudice to that libertie." "The wisedome of this House hath not in this case usd to rush so farr, as to a question, till it be sure to be graunted; for as it wilbe a dishonor to the Kinge if it be denyed, so to pass with difficultye by numbringe of voyces will take away the merrit from us."

[16] An important duty of councillors was to correct erroneous impressions among the commons as to how money was being spent. See p. 258 above.

did not promise to end the Spanish treaties. He added that war could not be waged without funds and that he needed money for his own support as well as for military charges. Thus the commons saw at once that their plans differed radically from those of the king and that subsidies must be voted in such a way as to secure their desires and to preclude designs of which they did not approve.

The commons set March 11 for a debate on supply. On that day Weston gave the house a detailed account of the extraordinary expenses of the crown in foreign negotiations since 1619,[17] and lord treasurer Cranfield made a similar declaration in the lords. Weston's exposition was at once followed up by other councillors. Conway explained that James could not declare what his policy would be until money had been voted. If the commons wished the king to declare the Spanish treaties at an end, they must first vote supply. Perhaps partly to avoid this point, members began to denounce the Spanish and called loudly for war. Heath then pointed out that the question of war or peace could not properly be debated in the commons; the present objective of the house was to persuade the king to end the treaties. Heath urged the commons to declare that if the treaties were broken and if war should result, they would be ready to assist the king with money. This suggestion found general support and the declaration was drawn up.

On the following day councillors attempted to convert this declaration into an immediate grant. They were able to report a speech Charles had just made in a conference. Charles boldly contradicted his father's words in asking money for himself. Every penny voted by the commons, Charles declared, would be used for war; the personal needs of the sovereign could wait. Charles added that his honor was at stake, that Spain was both angry and powerful, and that if the commons yielded now he would not forget their action in the years to come. Calvert's report of this speech greatly impressed the house. Edmondes "took the oppor-

---

[17] Weston described the cost of special embassies abroad, of the prince's journey to Spain, of entertaining foreign ambassadors in England, and of expenses incurred in the defense of the Palatinate. He showed that there had been extraordinary expenses in the navy and explained that there were large debts owing to the king of Denmark and to various moneylenders. For these extraordinary expenses James had disbursed £661,671, while his extraordinary receipts through a contribution for the defense of the Palatinate amounted to a paltry £12,500. Weston assured the commons that the navy was in good condition and was costing less than it had formerly done and that in Ireland revenue was rapidly approaching current expenditure. Erle and Gurney give his figures.

tunity of these affections" to urge the commons to make a more substantial rejoinder than their declaration of the day before. "Secretary Conway perceiving that out of this general [declaration] there could not be realities enough extracted to satisfy the King, dealt plainly with us. That there was no way in that resolution which we took yesterday, to give satisfaction . . . As our former resolution doth not bind us to particulars so will it not satisfy the King. We must offer him somewhat real and individual, but under those conditions to which he hath bound himself. This only, without other ceremony will give the Prince real satisfaction and produce the King's declaration." But the house would not yield. An immediate vote would leave the king free to wage war or not as he pleased, and the treaties with Spain were still in force. James must prove more conclusively that the wishes of parliament would be followed.

The hesitation of the commons was increased by a speech of James on March 14 in which he objected to the reflections made in parliament upon the honesty of Spain and showed that he was still thinking in terms of the Palatinate. He wished the commons to declare how much money they would give and asked for five subsidies and ten fifteenths for the war and an additional subsidy and two fifteenths for his own needs. This speech caused the greatest dissatisfaction among the commons. But under pressure from Charles and Buckingham James again allowed his words to be explained away. The commons were told the next day that James was now convinced of the justice of war with Spain and would spend all that the commons granted for that purpose.

Thus encouraged, the commons again debated supply on March 19. They now assumed that the treaties would be broken and were ready to make a grant. But the sum of six subsidies and twelve fifteenths was rather appalling. Courtiers scarcely dared ask for such a sum. Rudyard urged that the subsidies be voted in principle but that the times of payment be stretched over a long period and not determined for the present. Edmondes went further. He was sure, he said, that the commons wished to vote subsidies but that "the vast sum deterred them." He therefore asked that an amount be voted sufficient to take care of immediate military needs; and suggested three subsidies and six fifteenths, to be augmented as the war progressed. Thus he cut in half the amount asked by the

king, and he would scarcely have made such a motion had he not
had some sort of discretionary instructions, doubtless from the
prince or Buckingham. Weston and Conway urged the full
amount. "The sound indeede of 6 subsidies is fearful," Weston
said, "but the greatnes and goodnesse of the cause, the King's
honour, and our safetye require it." But Weston offered a number
of conditions. The commons should grant the entire sum in principle and engage themselves for it "as farre as particular men
may." But only a portion of the amount should be made available
for immediate needs and the rest referred to later consideration.
Payment should end at once if peace was made with Spain, expenditures should be authorized only by treasurers appointed by
the commons, and parliament should be consulted about the terms
of peace at the end of the war. Conway supported Weston. But
Pym, Perrott, Sir Edward Coke, and Mallory all spoke against so
large a grant, the last of them wondering "to see so much Importunity put upon us at this time." Sir George More suggested with
perfect tact that "he would have us follow his Majesty as Peter
followed Christ, a farre off." It was obvious that the government
was asking for more than it could hope to obtain. On the following morning, March 20, Edmondes repeated his motion for three
subsidies and was supported by Calvert. This sum was then voted
by the commons; and James, in return, declared verbally that he
would follow their advice and annul the treaties. Thus the commons voted a sum sufficient to carry out their program as they
conceived it, but insufficient for larger plans of war on a Continental scale. Nor did they make their grant until they were convinced that the treaties would be ended.[18]

But the vote of March 20, in the minds of the commons, was
far from ending the question of supply or its power to secure concessions from the crown. The subsidy bill had still to be introduced and pass through the normal stages of legislation. The
commons would go no faster than the king. More than a month
elapsed before the bill received its first reading. When on April 9

[18] March 11, 12, 19, 20, 1624, Gurney, f. 100–12, 123–51; Winchilsea, f. 24–28, 32–35;
Erle, f. 68–73, 76–77, 92–100; Holles, f. 95v–99, 103–10; Harl. MSS 159, 29v, 75–78,
82v–89v; Nicholas, f. 68v, 73v, 90–100. Nethersole to Carleton, March 20, 1624, St. P.
German, 81/30. The grant of 1624 was accompanied by an address to the king which
clearly stated the purposes for which money had been granted. They were: the defense of
the realm, the security of Ireland, aid to the Dutch, and the expenses of sending out the
navy. L. J., III, 275.

the solicitor urged that some progress be made, members raised the question whether James had declared with sufficient finality that the treaties were to be broken. Councillors answered that the king had made a verbal declaration, that this had been repeated by the prince, and that a public proclamation was being prepared. But the commons were not satisfied. Twice again, on April 15 and 20, the solicitor urged action and councillors dwelt upon the evils of delay. The commons agreed to a debate in a committee of the whole on the afternoon of April 20. But in this committee serious difficulties arose, and the commons were reluctant to complete the subsidy until concessions were made on a number of new points. They had heard nothing as yet about the general pardon. They had prepared a petition for more rigid enforcement of anti-Catholic laws, but James had set no date for its presentation. There was still some doubt about breaking the treaties. Nethersole wrote of this debate, "The Bill of Subsidy is revived, but it was feared these subsidies might go the same way as the two given last Parliament, if the subsidy bill came on winged feet, and bills of grace on leaden ones. It was objected that the petition against priests and recusants stood still, and that the declaration of the dissolution of the treaties was only by word of mouth, and should be made and inserted in the body of the bill. Those spirits of jealousy were coniurd down not without some ado. Thus we passed out of that fitt, but had not done it so easily, nor so soone had not Mr. Secretary Conway allayed much of the distempered humors by declaring at the Committee" that English ambassadors abroad had been instructed to inform foreign governments that the treaties with Spain were at an end. Councillors pointed out that the first reading of the subsidy was merely a preliminary matter which did not bind the house. As a result, the subsidy was read for the first time on April 22.[19]

On the same afternoon Buckingham told the commons that he and the prince had obtained, after several refusals, the consent of the king to receive the petition against Catholics. James had been won over by the news that the subsidy bill was about to be read. He had then declared "that he would not be backward" in advancing the wishes of the commons "if they were not backward in

[19] April 9, 15, 20, 1624, Nicholas, f. 131–32; Winchilsea, f. 56v, 66v, 74v; Erle, f. 152. Nethersole to Carleton, April 25, 1624, St. P. Domestic, 14/163:50. *C. J.*, I, 771–72.

his; and therefore appointed to-morrow for the audience." Heath reported Buckingham's speech to the commons and at once moved that a day be set for the second reading of the subsidy. This took place on April 24, and Heath then revealed the contents of the general pardon. The commons did nothing more concerning supply until May 1, when they were again urged to action by Heath and Calvert. Calvert showed that James was acting upon the petition on religion, that the attorney was drafting a proclamation against priests and Jesuits, and that English Catholics were being prevented from attending mass at the house of the Spanish ambassadors. This statement produced an order that the subsidy go into the committee stage on May 4. It was reported back to the house on May 14 and finally passed.[20] Thus concessions and subsidies progressed together.

Even in 1624, when conditions were favorable, the councillors had had to work for the subsidy. In later parliaments, when opposition was very strong, their pleadings were useless. They were faced by the fixed resolve of the commons that redress of grievances must precede supply; and grievances arose which the king was adamant in refusing to redress. In this situation the councillors could do nothing. Their speeches in 1625, Eliot wrote, were "pressing and patheticall" and appealed to the fears of the commons but not to their intelligence, "moving more in apprehension then in iudgement." The arguments of the council, Eliot added, were confounded rather than answered by the opposition.[21]

The pressure exerted in conferences by councillors who were members of the upper house need not detain us, for it was almost invariably futile. Salisbury had employed conferences with some success in 1606, when the needs of the king were emphasized and explained by various councillors from the lords. But conference, as a method of dealing with the commons in money matters, was vastly overworked in 1610 and fell into disrepute among the commons. It was used, however, in later parliaments, though less extensively. And many speeches from the lords, while they did not ask directly for money, were designed to impart information or

---

[20] April 22, May 1, 1624, Winchilsea, f. 77v, 86; Nicholas, f. 168, 188–89; Erle, f. 156, 166. *C. J.,* I, 772–74, 782, 789. May 14, 1624, Erle, f. 184. Sir Henry Goodere wrote that the commons "intended" the petition against recusants "as a touchstone to deserne cleerely his Majestyes reality." Goodere to Carleton, April 18, 1624, St. P. Domestic, 14/163:2.

[21] *Negotium Posterorum,* II, 81, 85.

bring forward arguments that might show the commons indirectly the need for voting supplies. Such speeches were usually ignored. If the commons were pressed, they fell back upon the principle that money grants could not originate in the upper house. To Salisbury's request for money early in 1610 the commons replied with a message to the lords explaining that money grants originated in the commons and could not properly be initiated by the lords in conference. In 1626 the government opened its campaign for supply by a conference in which leading councillors urged the need of money upon the commons. But this conference brought the retort in the house that members had "never heard that the lords did put us in mind of supply." Again during the Short Parliament a resolution of the lords that supply should precede redress of grievances was regarded by the commons as a breach of privilege.[22] Conferences were less than useless for obtaining supply.

As other methods failed, the king was tempted to fall back upon personal intervention and the stark force of his own authority. James, for all his meddling in the work of the commons, had for the most part left financial dealings with the house in the hands of his ministers. The parliament of 1614 forms an exception; James threatened dissolution unless subsidies were voted and was as good as his word.[23] Charles, however, prone to violence in dealing with the commons and exasperated by lack of funds in time of war, quickly resorted to more personal and direct de-

[22] *Parl. Debates in 1610*, 14. March 8, 1626, Whitelocke, f. 37v. *Gardiner*, IX, 108–11.

[23] Another exception occurred in 1610. About the middle of November "his Majesty called thirty of the Parliament House before him at Whitehall, among whom was Sir H. Neville: Where his Majesty said, the Cause of sending for them was to ask of them some Questions, whereunto he desired they would make a direct Answer." James first asked whether they thought he was in want. Bacon began to answer but did so in such an elaborate style that James cut him short and asked Sir Henry Neville to reply upon his conscience. Neville said he thought the king was indeed in want. James then asked whether it was not the duty of parliament to relieve him. Neville replied that it was truly the duty of parliament to relieve the king when his expenses grew from affairs of state, but that in this parliament the commons had already granted four subsidies, which was a great sum, and yet had no relief from their grievances. James asked what the grievances were. Neville replied that he did not know all of them but would name those he knew. He spoke of abuses in the courts of justice and was about to speak of the council of Wales when Sir Herbert Croft, who was much interested in that grievance, interrupted and explained it. "Otherwise, it was thought, Sir Henry (being charged upon his Conscience) would have delivered his Judgment in all, in what respect soever it might be taken." This was a direct attempt at lobbying by the sovereign, and the news of it threw the house into an uproar. So far as I know, it was not tried again during the early Stuart period. More to Winwood, December 1, 1610, *Winwood*, III, 235. See also *Rutland MSS, H. M. C.*, I, 424–25; *Parl. Debates in 1610*, 137 note.

mands. Councillors were reduced to a position in which their principal function was to deliver the messages sent by the sovereign.

The parliament of 1626 provides an excellent illustration. Since the commons made no move toward supply, Charles began to urge them through messages. On March 10 Weston delivered a message asking for funds to meet a number of military charges soon to fall due. The commons resolved to consider this message on March 13, and at that time an important debate took place. Councillors and courtiers urged an immediate supply, but no decision was taken. Nevertheless a start had been made, and it was highly unfortunate that Charles quarreled with the commons at this point over speeches by Dr. Turner and Clement Coke. Again on March 20 Charles sent a message asking for supply. The commons debated when they should take this message into consideration. March 27 was suggested, but Weston declared, "It is necessary to begin sooner." May urged March 23; Coke said that military preparations were at a standstill until the commons acted and "that we should not lose a day." The commons decided upon March 23, as May had wished. On that day Coke gave a detailed account of military expenses; he dwelt upon the power of Spain and Austria and made the king's needs "very great." He was supported by other courtiers and councillors. May spoke of the cost of administration in Ireland. Weston brought a gracious word from the king promising permission to investigate past expenditures. Rudyard, Pye, and Savile spoke for supply. Decision was postponed until March 27. On that day a grant was made of three subsidies and three fifteenths. But the commons resolved that they would not convert their grant into a bill until their grievances were redressed. Coke, Weston, and many courtiers opposed this condition, but it was carried.[24] Thus the king, through his messages, had obtained a grant. But the condition was hard; redress of grievances was coming to mean the removal of Buckingham and to this Charles would hardly give way.

Charles continued to urge the commons through messages to increase the size of their grant and to convert their former vote into a bill. On April 13, the day on which the commons reassembled after their Easter recess, Weston delivered a message urging

[24] Sloane MSS 1710, f. 283, 286; Add. MSS 18016, f. 4, 8; *Rushworth,* I, 215. March 13, 20, 23, 27, 1626, Whitelocke, f. 38, 61, 77–78, 89. March 27, 1626, Rich, f. 72–72v. *C. J.,* I, 840, 842. *Finch MSS, H. M. C.,* I, 49. St. P. Domestic, 16/23:52, 53.

them to lay aside small things for great and to proceed with supply. But the commons ignored this message. It was again brought to their attention on April 18. At that time Carleton gave a report on recent relations with France and held out the hope that the French might still enter the war against Spain in an effective manner. Weston then "revived" Charles's message for supply. He warned the house that "delay was denyall and therefore prayed to proceed." "We have heard a renewed Message," said May, "and the order of the house [is] either to give answer presently or els to appoint a time to take it into our consideration." He asked that a day be fixed to consider the message. Weston begged the house to show that it valued the king's message. The necessity was very great and immediate action essential. Other courtiers urged the commons not to offend the king. They pointed out that once a matter was raised in the house it was never left *sine die*. But opposition was very strong. The commons were being asked to abandon the condition upon which they had made their grant, a condition that the king chose to disregard. No day was appointed to take the message into consideration, and the house continued its collection of charges against the duke. This produced an extremely sharp message on April 20. "The king hath moved us by Messages," said Weston, "for the expediting and speeding of the great and weighty affaires, but nothing hath proceeded but losse of time." The message of April 13 had been laid aside. Charles, therefore, could not exercise his wonted patience. If the commons did not act on supply within four or five days, their sittings would be terminated and the king would turn to new counsels. Weston then moved that supply be considered on April 25. He was supported by May and Carleton, who warned of the disastrous consequences of ignoring the king's message and of the necessity of making a grant. The commons determined to deal exclusively with grievances until April 25 and then take up supply. On that date the commons yielded to the extent of adding a fourth subsidy to what had been granted. But it, like the others, was not to be made into a bill until grievances had been answered.[25]

Charles, however, continued to send messages. On May 2 Weston brought a message thanking the house for its recent vote and

[25] Sloane MSS 1710, f. 289 (message of April 13). April 13, 18, 1626, Whitelocke, f. 126, 137–39; Rich, f. 76–79; *C.J.,* I, 845–47. Add. MSS 22474, f. 39 (message of April 20). April 20, 1626, Whitelocke, f. 141–44; St. P. Domestic, 16/24:78; 16/25:67.

urging that it be converted into a bill at once. On May 5, although there had been no move by the commons, serjeant Hitcham brought the subsidy bill into the house and offered it to be read. But Mr. Kirton declared "that we should remember the order of the House. Wonders that Serjeant Hitcham would break it." Hitcham defended himself by saying that he had been ordered by the attorney to bring in the bill. This maneuver failed as it deserved, but councillors seized the opportunity to urge action. "I would be very glad to hear a sound reason," said Weston, "why the bill should not now be brought in." He had another message in which Charles told the commons that if they passed the subsidy their grievances would not be forgotten. On the other hand, Charles said, he would consider further delay a neglect not only of public affairs but of his own person. Weston was answered that the subsidy was the gift of the commons and they could pass it as they pleased. May and Carleton spoke also. In the end the commons set a date to consider the preamble. But this was a very halting step, and councillors found the preamble slow work. On May 22 Weston "moved to proceed on the King's revenue and to bring in the preamble of the subsidy." This was ordered for May 24, but for over two hours on that date Weston could not get the floor to report the preamble, and then it was merely recommitted. The preamble was read on June 3 and again the bill was offered to the house; but the commons reread and confirmed their order which forbade bringing in the bill till grievances were answered. Thus no action was taken.

On June 9 Charles sent a most peremptory message that if the subsidies were not passed the parliament would be dissolved. Coke urged that the commons consider this message on the following day, but it was postponed until June 12. On that date a most important decision had to be taken. The commons had begun a general remonstrance against Buckingham. They had either to turn to subsidies or to continue the remonstrance. To do the latter would almost certainly end the parliament. Compromise was no longer possible. In the debate that followed, May, Coke, and Weston begged that the bill be read. May put the issue squarely: "The beginning with the bill of subsydyes will conclude no questions, the conclusion of the declaration will conclude your councells I am afrayde." But the house would not put the question for reading the subsidy. It voted to proceed with the remonstrance, and as a consequence parliament was dissolved.[26]

The story of subsidies in 1628 was much the same and would have had a similar ending had not Charles consented to the Petition of Right. One point may be noted. On April 12 Charles sent an extremely sharp message demanding action on the subsidies. The commons, believing that they were about to be dissolved, determined to justify their stand. They prepared a document to be presented to the king by the speaker. They maintained that they were not refusing to deal with supply but were, on the contrary, proceeding with it cheerfully and rapidly. They pointed out that it was the "ancient right of Parliament to dispose of matters there debated in their own methods," that grievances normally came before supply, but that nevertheless they had postponed most of their grievances, debating only those that were absolutely fundamental, and had gone as far with the subsidy as was possible in the committee of the whole. Thus the reply of the commons was that the time and method of passing the subsidy were things to be determined as they saw fit and that, considering the state and number of their grievances, they had been doing a great deal toward supplying the king.[27] Thus king and commons approached the question from entirely different points of view. To the gulf between them the interference of the king had undoubtedly contributed. Pressure from the crown, if skillfully employed, might have accomplished much. But Charles's insistence merely made matters worse.

In conclusion, two other points may be made. This chapter has described a number of means by which the crown attempted to secure supplies. It should perhaps be emphasized that normally the crown made simultaneous use of a large number of devices. During the short session at Oxford (August 1–12, 1625) Charles

[26] May 2, 5, 24, June 9, 12, 1626, Whitelocke, f. 174, 179–80, 206, 227, 231–34. *Lowther*, 16, 29. *C. J.*, I, 863, 866, 869. ——— to Mead, May 26, 1626, *Court and Times, Charles I*, I, 105. June 12, 1626, Harl. MSS 1601, f. 1–9.

[27] Harl. MSS 1721, f. 166v. The subsidy had been voted in the committee of the whole but had not been reported to the house. When secretary Coke urged on May 7 that the subsidy be reported, he was answered by Pym, who said that to report the subsidy, after the resolution of the commons not to proceed further until grievances had been answered, would be to bring it in "in force and is to the disservice of his Majestie." Borlase, f. 146. After Charles had accepted the Petition of Right, the commons held up the subsidy until the petition was enrolled among the statutes. After the subsidy had been passed, the commons at once asked to know the contents of the general pardon, but Charles refused their request.

urged supply in person and sent a number of messages, leading councillors in the lords addressed the commons both in a royal audience and in conferences, the councillors in the commons argued and pleaded, lobbying was used for all it was worth, and, finally, an attempt was made to force a vote. In the second place, while the record of the councillors in obtaining supply was undoubtedly a very poor one,[28] they were not in a position to exert influence that could hope to sway the issue. Finance was too vital a factor in the quarrel, too much an integral part of all that king and parliament were striving for, for its success or failure to be determined by a small and comparatively unimportant group of ministers. Councillors did what they could. But they were pawns on a larger chessboard.

[28] Four subsidies were obtained in the parliament of 1603–10, two in 1621, three in 1624, two in 1625, and five in 1628, when the king agreed to the Petition of Right. Four subsidies voted in 1626 were lost because the king quarreled with parliament and the subsidies could not be legally collected. The commons refused to make any grant in the parliament of 1614. In 1625 they voted two subsidies and refused to increase the amount.

10

The Councillors as a Means of Communication between King and Commons

Councillors had served as a means of communication between commons and king long before they became elected members of the commons. In medieval parliaments they constantly addressed the commons both in the parliament chamber and in the chapter house. They served on deputations to attend the commons in their private sessions and give them advice, and at times the commons met in the palace to be near councillors in case that advice was deemed desirable. During the Tudor period those councillors who were members of the commons brought messages and instructions from the king and regularly reported the doings of the lower house to the sovereign. These reports by councillors, natural and quite inevitable though technical infringements of parliamentary privilege, were accepted by the commons as long as crown and parliament worked in essential harmony. The commons, indeed, saw a certain advantage in the close proximity of councillors to the king and habitually employed councillors, accompanied by other members, in sending communications to the ruler. Thus councillors were a connecting link and performed a beneficial function desired by both king and commons. But as time advanced there were occasional murmurs of disapproval. In the Stuart period, when king and commons had ceased to cooperate with each other, councillors found their position as intermediaries a most difficult and uncomfortable one. To bring messages from the king was one of their formal duties, and when discharging formal duties they were treated with a certain respect in the house. But the commons came to regard messages with such dislike and suspicion that they vented their disapproval upon the heads of the messengers. Councillors were suspected of advising the king to send harsh messages and of changing messages to suit their own ends. Their reports to the king of what took place in the commons were under even greater suspicion, and they were openly accused of making false reports. In this respect, as in so many others, the position of councillors was becoming untenable.

There were many reasons why the commons in the Stuart period looked with dislike and suspicion upon messages from the king. Fundamentally, this was caused by the growing opposition to the sovereign and to his words as they came to the house in messages. But there were other reasons. The mere frequency of these communications, the commons complained, was a serious interruption to business and a constant loss of time. Elizabeth's messages had been few, but all the more effective for that reason. She avoided them where she could and relied upon more subtle methods. Peter Wentworth spoke in 1576 of rumors that ran through the commons, quietly conveying to members the attitude of the queen on many matters. But James and Charles had much to say to the house of commons. Royal communications of every kind — speeches, messages, letters, informal announcements by courtiers in the house — all vastly increased. Admitting that the Stuarts had more occasion to communicate with the commons than Elizabeth, it is nevertheless true that many of their messages might have been avoided and some of them dealt with trifles. James's constant messages were calculated to irritate and provoke rebuttal without accomplishing their purpose, and were apt to raise new issues that might otherwise have remained dormant. In 1621 there was constant protest by the commons. Members wished "to moove the King that ther may not be so many interpositions, which interrupt the business of the house very much"; "to declare to his Majesty that his Majesty's messages have been the cause of our interruptions," "so that wee cannot dispatch business"; "to request him not so often to interpose." In 1626 a member complained of "many intervenient messages"; and at the end of the parliament the commons said they had accomplished little because of the many interruptions of the king. In 1628 there were constant complaints of this sort: "We have had many interruptions by messages from the king"; "we shall goe on readily if we be not hindered by messages"; "so many messages so many interruptions to our business." [1]

---

[1] *P. and D.*, I, 365; *Commons Debates 1621*, III, 112; VI, 234; II, 536; V, 236. March 31, 1626, Whitelocke, f. 116; *Rushworth*, I, 400. Sir Richard Harrison to Francis Windebank, May 8, 1628, St. P. Domestic, 16/103:51; April 12, 1628, Nicholas, p. 57; May 3, 1628, Grosvenor, III, 33.

The commons also objected to messages because they formed an obvious part of the parliamentary tactics of the court. Messages became surprisingly gracious just before a vote on supply or when some other decision affecting the crown was about to be made. In 1628 the council advised Charles that since the commons were debating arbitrary imprisonment and taxation and were about to lay these matters before the lords, the king should send a message promising to "yield such demands as were just and reasonable and might stand with his prerogative," which might prevent the commons from "possessing the Upper House with this business and might quicken them . . . to give more subsidies than otherwise they may be any way induced to do: to-morrow being the day appointed for consideration of the King's supplie." But the king's promises, once they had accomplished their purpose, meant very little. In 1621 James had ended a debate on free speech by a message promising in general terms that free speech would be respected. Yet the question arose again in far more violent form before many months had passed. Glanville then "remembered the former Message about Freedom of Speech; and how [the commons were] taken off it by a general Message; yet this questioned already before the End of this Session of Parliament." Messages were constantly used to persuade the commons to lay aside this or that subject of debate and to divert the house from matters under discussion. In 1621 Mr. Mallory urged that members connected with condemned patents should be declared unworthy to remain members of the house; and this involved Sir Edward Villiers, Buckingham's brother, who had had a part in the patent of gold and silver thread, though investigation had shown him innocent of misconduct. "Whilst this Cause floated in the Variety of debate, it was rather diverted then determined by the volluntarye departure of Sir Edward Villers And by the riseing of the Chancellor of the Exchequer, who intimateinge that hee had a Message from his Majestie withdrewe the attencion of the Howse to the Expectation of newe matters." [2] We have seen how in 1628 the councillors, either by design or mismanagement, delayed a message telling the commons there was to be no Easter recess, and how this was regarded as a trick to win a vote on supply in a thin

[2] April 3, 1628, St. P. Domestic, 16/100:25. *Commons Debates 1621*, IV, 55, 290; *C. J.*, I, 667. A gracious message could, of course, be highly effective. See *Court and Times, Charles I*, I, 339.

house. Messages, then, might be used as cards in the political game.

A far more serious objection was that messages appeared to the commons infringements upon their liberty of action. In the reign of Elizabeth, Peter Wentworth had objected to messages "either of Commanding or Inhibiting, very injurious to the freedom of Speech and Consultation." And Tate had warned against messages containing a command, "for soe would by and by be raised by some humerous bodie some question of the libertie of the Howse, and of restraininge their free consultacion." But James began his reign by commanding as an absolute king that the commons confer with the lords and judges on the Fortescue case. Thus messages made the commons jealous of their privileges. A message of December 12, 1621, commanding the commons to leave grievances and proceed with bills, was answered thus by Glanville: "By beinge commanded to billes, wee are restrained from grievances; if we now go on with this Message, and proceed hereupon with Bills, then next we shall have Command to go on with Grievances, and then with this and that Bill, and then with that Grievance; and so hereafter we shall do nothing, but what the King commands, and proceed with no Business, but we shall have a Command for it from the King."[3] At least twice during this period the commons, having yielded to the wishes of the king as expressed in messages, decided not to record their action in the *Journals* for fear of creating a precedent. On many occasions councillors had to explain as best they could that messages contained nothing which cut into the liberty of the commons.[4]

As a result of these things, messages became less and less effective as a means of imposing the royal will. When James commanded the commons in 1604 to confer with the judges on the Fortescue case, he was obeyed. But as early as 1606 he was complaining that a message of his "hath laytlie produced no other effect but the multiplicity of Arguments." During the 1620's the

[3] *D'Ewes (Elizabeth)*, 237. Harl. MSS 253, f. 33. *P. and D.*, I, 365; II, 312; *Commons Debates 1621*, V, 236. See also *ibid.*, VI, 234; VII, 628. "This message is a restraynte," said a member when the king ordered the house to leave other matters and proceed with supply. April 13, May 3, 1626, Whitelocke, f. 126v, 175. In 1625 Alford pointed out how the commons, to their great disadvantage, had dropped investigation of grievances in the past as a result of messages from the king. *Commons Debates in 1625*, 69–70.

[4] *Bowyer*, 15. Nethersole to the queen of Bohemia, June 7, 1628, St. P. Domestic, 16/106:55. See also *Parl. Debates in 1610*, 33–34; *C.J.*, I, 430. February 14, 1626, Rich, f. 13; April 13, 1626, Whitelocke, f. 126v.

commons often postponed consideration of messages or ignored them altogether. We have seen how the councillors begged the commons to set a day for the consideration of Charles's messages regarding supply. In 1629 a member moved for a committee to consider an answer to a message "that we may not seeme to neglect wholly his Majesties Messages." In the same session a message asking for action on the bill of tonnage and poundage fell to the ground because the commons had decided that religion should take precedence over all other business. Indeed, it was said in 1628 that the constant messages of the king were a chief cause of opposition, for messages then inflamed moderate men "in soe much they grew into heate and joined with those few violent spirits which before they perpetually opposed." "I think theis Messages rather hinder his Majesties service then further it," said Seymour, "and therefore theis honourable personages [the councillors] may certifie his Majestie so much." "Did ever Parliament rely on Messages?" asked Sir Edward Coke when Charles wished the commons to trust his word that liberties would be respected. "Messages of love never came into a Parliament."[5]

Suspicion of messages transferred itself to those who brought them. The commons feared, in the first place, that councillors might alter messages in delivering them and that messages did not exactly reproduce the thoughts of the king. This may have been more of a hope than a conviction, but the result was the same. Messages normally came to the house in oral form; the words spoken in the commons were those of the messenger. But messages were carefully drafted before they were delivered, and councillors had the wording of the draft well in mind though they did not read it to the commons. The state papers contain a very large number of these drafts, especially of messages delivered by Sir John Coke in 1626 and 1628. Many are corrected in the

[5] April 5, 1604, *C. J.*, I, 166. Message of James, March 18, 1606, St. P. Domestic, 14/19:57. *Commons Debates for 1629*, 113, 247. Sir John Maynard to Buckingham, June, 1628, St. P. Domestic, 16/108:71. A message in 1628 "intended to take the house off the remonstrance (as was conceyved) on the contrary set them on to proceed therein with more earnestness." Nethersole to the queen of Bohemia, June 7, 1628, *ibid.*, 16/106:55. Another indication that messages were neglected is the greatly increased use of the king's name in messages after 1625. Before that date a mere hint had been sufficient, but after 1625 councillors were forced to reiterate the name of the king in order to gain attention for messages. April 12, 1628, Mass., f. 90; *Rushworth*, I, 558. For examples of the commons' ignoring messages, see *Commons Debates 1621*, V, 412; June 4, 1628, *C. J.*, I, 908; Borlase, f. 216.

handwriting of the king. And it must be supposed that councillors were given very little discretionary power in the words to be employed in delivering messages.[6] There were instances in which the wording was left to councillors. In moments of crisis instructions for messages might come to councillors while they were sitting in the commons, and at such times, it may be supposed, the wording was left largely to their discretion. But such instances were rare. Councillors had much more freedom in timing the delivery of messages. Not infrequently messages entrusted to them were to be delivered only in case a crisis arose in the commons. But this did not affect the wording of the message.

Calvert was accused of inserting a falsehood in a message in 1621. In defending the export of some iron ordnance at Gondomar's request, Calvert declared that the Trinity House had been consulted and had seen no reason to stop the shipment. This was later denied by the Trinity House. Members at once assumed that Calvert had lied to them. Calvert said "that he fownd himself traduced to have made a false Report of the Kings answere . . . yet he must mayntayne it to be true. That the Kinge saide soe, whose word he was sure we would not suspect of falshood." The king declared, said Calvert, that the Trinity House had made the statement in question, the Trinity House denied it; and therefore "it resteth between the king and them." The matter was referred to a committee, which, as far as I know, never made a report. Again in the autumn Calvert was accused of delivering a message without authority from the king.[7]

The commons became more exacting about the form in which messages came. They demanded that messages of any importance, after being delivered orally, be reduced to writing and inserted in the *Journals*. There were many reasons why the commons should wish this, but one was the fear that messages "might suffer some alteration when delivered verbally." It could be assumed that messages thus reduced to writing would be submitted to the king for approval before they were brought back to the house. In 1628 Sir John Coke delivered a message confirming the privileges of the house; "to which the House willing him to set his hand, he said, he would if the king would give him leave. So after he had spoken

[6] In 1604 the speaker of his own accord read a message "because he would not miscarry it." *Buccleuch MSS, Montagu Papers, H. M. C.*, III, 87.
[7] *Commons Debates 1621*, IV, 206–07; V, 326–27, 329; VI, 88; VII, 628.

with his Majesty, he penned the same message, and thereto set his hand." Again in 1628 Coke was asked to write down a message asking for supply. The next day he brought it in in writing and said "that he, having set it down in Writing, shewed it to the King; who perused and allowed it; so as now it is the King's Message." Councillors were glad to do this for their own protection.[8]

The fear that messages might be altered before they reached the house may be seen in other ways. During James's first parliament many messages were delivered by the speaker. An incident occurred in 1610, however, which rendered the commons suspicious of messages coming in this way. On May 1 the speaker brought a message commanding the house to drop its discussion of impositions. It was the type of message to which the commons objected most and was certain to be received with some irritation. But the attention of the house was first directed to the form in which the message came. James had been out of London for a week, and the speaker was asked how the message had come into his possession. "Sir William Twisden moved that Mr. Speaker should declare or no whether he had that message immediately from his Majesty or from some other, for that it was well known his Majesty was not in town since the occasion of the message was given, being but the day before." The speaker declared that he had delivered fifty-six or fifty-eight messages since the parliament began and that there was no precedent for pressing the speaker to say whether he had a message directly from the king or not. But the attack continued. It was said the speaker was the mouthpiece of the house and not of the king and should not deliver messages from the king without the permission of the commons. Elizabethan precedents were cited in which speakers had acknowledged that it was not their office to bring messages from the queen.

The speaker finally confessed that he had not received the message from the king or from any one person, but from the privy council. This raised a much more serious question. The council was doubtless acting under instructions left by the king. But if messages came from the privy council in the name of the king, the

---

[8] *Cal. St. P. Venetian, 1621–1623,* 184. The commons frequently asked councillors to repeat messages. The king's letter of December 17, 1621, was read in the house three times. *C. J.,* I, 666. Sometimes the councillors objected to repeating messages so often. See March 15, 1626, Whitelocke, f. 47. Mead to Stuteville, May 3, 1628, *Court and Times, Charles I,* I, 350; *C. J.,* I, 892. See also *Commons Debates 1621,* II, 83–84; March 10, 1626, Whitelocke, f. 28.

house would be in constant danger of deception. "It might be much to the prejudice of the House that the Lords should be Mediators or Messengers between the king and the Commons, for so the House might be abused with false messages." The house therefore refused to accept the message as a message from the king, appointed a committee to pen an order "to prevent the like for times to come," and declared that henceforth the speaker should deliver no message from the king without first asking permission of the commons.

This produced a brusque message from James asking whether the commons intended in the future to refuse a message delivered by the speaker "upon declaracion by hym made that it cometh by warrant from his Majesty by worde or wryting, or from the body of his Privie Counsell." A committee, appointed to consider a reply, quickly concluded that the house "would receave no messages coming from the Counsell as messages sent from His Majesty." To the first part of James's question the committee drew up a conciliatory answer that the house had no intention of refusing messages from the king. But the phrasing of this statement was disliked, and the councillors on the committee "seeing they could procure a better answer for the King's satisfaction, rose sudainly up." Before the committee came to an agreement and reported to the house, James sent word that he expected no answer to his question and did not wish the commons to trouble themselves further about the matter. The incident was closed several days later by a conciliatory message to the king, doubtless procured by the councillors on the committee, that the commons had had no intention of refusing messages and that their purpose had merely been to regulate the conduct of the speaker. They decided not to enter the report of their committee in the *Journals*.[9] Thus both king and commons drew back from the position they had originally taken. Henceforth, however, the speaker brought messages far less frequently, and never again were the commons given grounds to suspect that messages came from the council.

During James's first parliament, especially in 1610, the commons occasionally received messages through the house of lords. This was largely due to a temporary situation. Salisbury wished

[9] Lansd. MSS 486, f. 141–43. *C. J.*, I, 427, 429–30. *Parl. Debates in 1610*, 32–34. See also Bacon's defense of the government, *Spedding*, IV, 177–79.

to explain policy to the commons in person and did so through conferences. In these conferences he fell into the practice of imparting information in the form of messages from the king. But the commons had serious objections. Matters came to a head on June 11, 1610. The lords asked for a conference "to impart such things to the House as by the King's Commandment they were to make known to them. Whereupon it was moved by Sir Edward Montagu that it was against Precedent and dangerous to the liberties of the House to receive messages from the King's Majesty by the Lords." A committee appointed to consider this question resolved to make a statement to the lords before the conference began. This was done by the solicitor, who informed the lords "that if their Lordships have desired this meeting upon intent only to communicate something with us which it hath pleased his Majesty to impart to them, we are there to receive their pleasures; but if their Lordships be employed as Messengers to our House, we are commanded by our House to signify to their Lordships that this course we conceive to be contrary to the ancient Orders and Privileges of the House, and therefore the entertainment thereof must be left to the consideration of the House." Salisbury at once replied that no message was intended and that the information which the lords wished to impart came from themselves alone. The lords remembered this warning, for in a later conference Salisbury took pains in imparting information "to avoyd a scruple, lest wee [the commons] should conceive it as a message from the King." [10]

As a matter of fact, this situation was repeated to a certain extent in the parliament of 1624, when the prince and Buckingham reported to the commons in conference information from the king concerning the Spanish treaties. But here the commons made no

[10] Lansd. MSS 486, f. 149; *Parl. Debates in 1610*, 51, 132. On March 14, 1610, the commons were about to send a message of thanks to the king in return for a message of his which had come through the lords. The question arose whether the commons should thank the lords also or at least tell them of the message of thanks. Both proposals were objected to as "a Kind of Dependence." *C. J.*, I, 411. Neville, as we know, advised James not to send messages through the lords. St. P. Domestic, 14/74:44. In November, 1610, a message from the king was brought by justice Croke, who was presumably acting as a messenger from the lords. This was regarded by the commons as "a dangerous president as trenching into the Priviliges of the house causinge us to receyve messages at the second hand from the king." *Rutland MSS, H. M. C.*, I, 424. On May 8, 1610, the commons objected because the lords sent them a message by messengers whom they had sent to the lords. This was not a message from the king. Lansd. MSS 486, f. 140v.

objection because they approved of the policy which Charles and Buckingham were forcing upon James.

The principal cause of suspicion by the commons sprang from the fear that they were misrepresented at court; that councillors and other courtiers carried tales about parliament to the king; and that these misrepresentations produced the king's harsh messages. The commons knew, of course, that information about their doings might come to the king in any number of ways and that councillors could not be held solely responsible for false reports. The house was full of men connected with the government or the court only too happy to win notice from their superiors by supplying information. The king's wishes often came to the house in roundabout ways: in 1606 Sir Francis Hastings said that the lord chief justice had told him that he had been informed by Lord Kinloss that James would be glad to see a certain bill pass the house; and it must be supposed that news might come to the court in even stranger fashion. In 1621 the commons realized that a piece of misinformation about their church policy had come to the king through the upper clergy. Charles's information about the speeches of Digges and Eliot in 1626, for which they were put in prison, was drawn from notes taken by certain peers.[11] And we have seen that in many parliaments, especially those of James, there were men at court who deliberately set out to bring about the dissolution of parliament by angering the king. But if information came from all sides, the privy councillors in the house formed the recognized channel through which the king heard of happenings in parliament, and the suspicions of the commons inevitably fell upon them. "We aboute the chaire have a heavy burthen," said Cranfield, "for we are Questioned for all the things in the house by the King."[12]

There was an occasional attempt to draw distinctions between what could and what could not be reported by councillors. In 1621 two subsidies were voted in the committee of the whole, and councillors at once informed the king. "I was one of those," said Calvert, "who with other of my fellow Councillors did attend his

---

[11] *Bowyer*, 104. *Commons Debates 1621*, II, 334. May 13, 1626, Whitelocke, f. 192–94; May 13, 19, 1626, *Lowther*, 24–27. Carleton first said that the king heard of Eliot's speech from four or five nobles. Then he corrected this, saying that the king, having heard rumors of the speech, asked four or five nobles to let him see the notes they had taken.

[12] *Commons Debates 1621*, III, 135. Certainly the king protested if he thought that he was not sufficiently well informed by the councillors in the house.

Majesty after the breaking up of the Committee the last night, and acquainted him with the loving and generous resolution of the House." But Alford pointed out that the vote in the committee had not as yet been reported to the house. "It was delivered by way of caution that the Privy Counsellors should not have related unto the King what was done for granting of the Subsidies at the Committee, till they had been past in the House, because it might have been over-ruled in the House, notwithstanding the Opinion of the Committee." This speech of Alford's "was approved of and well liked, and [declared] to be the order of the House." "The King," said Sir Thomas Hoby in 1628, "is misinformed by those that carry the disputes but not the resolutions of this House . . . He desires that those which carry the businesses of the House to the king that they would report the bill when it is drawen and not report propositions for a bill before the bill is drawen." "The Kinge," said Alford in 1621, "ought not to be acquaynted with the debate of any matters till after they be determined." [13] In other words, councillors might report the resolutions of the house but not the debates or other proceedings leading to those resolutions. But councillors could not abide by such distinctions.

Nor in reality could the commons. They assumed that reports were made by councillors on all that took place in the house. Indeed, councillors were often encouraged to report events to the king and were asked to place matters before him in a light favorable to the commons. After Coke brought a message on April 3, 1628, thanking the house for supply and inviting the presentation of grievances, it was moved "that this honourable gentleman may sitt in the chair this afternoon, hear our grievances, and knowingly report them that we may be the more fit for our great business." After rather heated words had passed between secretary Coke and Phelips in 1628, Sir Henry Mildmay said, "I desire all my Fellowes that have relacion to the Court to make a true presentation of this dayes business to his Majestie." After a debate on supply in the same parliament, Phelips said, "I humblie move that noe mistakes may be made of this dayes service, but that good reports may be

<hr />

[13] Speech by Calvert, February 16, 1621, St. P. Domestic, 14/119:98; *Commons Debates 1621*, V, 467. "What is done in a Committie there ought noe speech of it to be made by any to the kinge, before after the report of it to the house, [and] the house resolve of it." *Ibid.*, VI, 351; Locke to Carleton, February 16, 1621, St. P. Domestic, 14/119:99. May 3, 1628, Borlase, f. 132; Harl. MSS 1601, f. 36v. *Commons Debates 1621*, IV, 433.

made to his Majesty to the general advantage of all our affairs."
Again in 1628 it was said, "Let those Gentlemen near the Chair
see that we have endeavoured to apply ourselves to his Majesty's
service."[14]

Yet the cry that the king was misinformed was a constant one
in the commons. Occasionally this meant that the king was in
error, but far more often it was an honest expression of belief that
the king was deceived by those who reported the doings of parliament. In 1614 the commons debated how to prevent misinformation from reaching the king and "how to restrain these talebearers, be the information true or false." In May, 1621, a similar
debate took place. Sandys moved that when the commons believed
the king was misinformed, the speaker should be sent to explain
the truth. Sir Henry Poole was "sorry that the King was so often
misinformed" and suggested that James be asked to value at their
true worth "those busy Men that misinform him." "This Message
proceedeth from a Misinformation," said Glanville in December,
1621, when the king ordered the commons to continue with business. Glanville wished the protestation of December 12 sent to the
king the moment it was complete "lest we give Opportunity to
the Adversaries of this House to suggest to his Majesty some Misinformation or Misinterpretation." "It is thought some privie
whisperers and tale carriers do misinform his Majesty," wrote
Chamberlain about the same time, "and so annimate him to the
prejudice of the House . . . There cannot be a good understanding whilest . . . whisperers misinform and exasperate his Majesty." In 1628 Eliot spoke of "those misreports which begett so
many messages"; Sir Edward Coke said "there is error and misinformation in messages"; and even the secretary admitted that the
king was misinformed. A few days earlier Rich had denounced
whisperers. On more than one occasion a law of 2 Henry IV was
cited which aimed at talebearers who told the king of the doings
of the commons.[15]

It was difficult to tell the king he was misinformed without

[14] April 3, 1628, Borlase, f. 41a. March 22, 1628, Harl. MSS 4771, f. 22v. May 7, 1628,
Borlase, f. 146. *Rushworth*, I, 539.

[15] *C. J.*, I, 500; *Portland MSS, H. M. C.*, IX, 134. *Commons Debates 1621*, IV, 284; III,
374; *P. and D.*, I, 365; II, 312, 354; Chamberlain to Carleton, December 15, 1621, St. P.
Domestic, 14/124:40. May 3, 1628, Harl. MSS 1601, f. 26v; Borlase, f. 132–33; Mass.,
f. 147; April 12, 1628, Borlase, f. 75. For citations of 2 Henry IV, see *P. and D.*, I, 365;
May 3, 1628, Borlase, f. 132–33; November 23, 1621, *Commons Debates in 1621*, IV, 433.

giving offense. When in December, 1621, the commons told the king that his actions arose from misinformation, James replied very tartly, "Now whenas . . . you tax Us, in fair Terms, of trusting uncertain Reports, and partial Information, concerning your Proceedings, We wish you to remember, that We are an old and experienced King, needing no such Lessons; being, in our Conscience, freest of any King alive from hearing or trusting idle Reports; which so many of your House, as are nearest Us, can bear Witness unto you if you would give as good Ear to them, as you do to some Tribunitial Orators amongst you." Councillors naturally opposed messages to the king telling him he was misinformed. In 1628 secretary Coke begged the commons not to send Charles such a message; it would reflect upon the king to imply that he gave credence to idle reports and was carried away by them. At times the commons asked the councillors to advise the king privately not to believe information coming to him through unofficial channels.[16]

What the commons objected to most strenuously was the report of single words or speeches. Such reports lifted phrases from their context and made them sound worse than they actually were. Speeches, said Sandys, could only be understood in the light of what had gone before. "There are some amongst us," said Sir Edward Cecil, "who do pick out the worst of every Man's Speech and Words."[17] Here the connection between reports and the harsh messages of the king was very clear; and reports of this kind might lead directly to serious infringement of free speech and freedom from arrest. Nothing brought the councillors under more suspicion than the knowledge that they made such reports, and bitter things were said of those who "did ill offices between king and commons" and poisoned the king's ear. The fault, in reality, lay largely with the king for demanding these reports from his councillors, who certainly gave them with reluctance. At the end of James's first parliament he wished to punish certain members who had spoken too freely. The council demurred and said they did not know the names of the offenders, to which

---

[16] December 14, 1621, *P. and D.,* II, 318. May 3, 1628, Mass., f. 147. April 12, 1628, Harl. MSS 1601, f. 24.

[17] "Speeches both by naturall and Artificiall Construction are to be referred to that which was last in question." *Commons Debates 1621,* IV, 406. "If speeches may be devided and the beginning and ending taken away, straunge sence may be made therof." March 15, 1626, Whitelocke, f. 48. *P. and D.,* II, 137.

James replied sharply that he had three privy councillors in the house who could easily supply the necessary information. In the autumn of 1621 James asked Calvert the name of the member who had spoken certain words, and Calvert, with some reluctance, named Glanville.[18]

Councillors were accused of making false and misleading reports to the king. In May, 1621, a speech of Cranfield was interrupted by Sir Edward Cecil, who said "he was sorry to hear him in such Manner to go between the King and us . . . He had heard, that there were some of this House, who did the House ill Service by Misinformations; and we might justly suspect it, since here openly our Speeches and Intentions were wrested to the worst Construction." In 1628 Eliot remarked that if the king truly understood the intentions of the house his messages would be more gracious. "Some there are of this House near about him, whose conscience, mee thinks, should call upon them to take care of that work." In 1629, when a series of messages urged the house to pass the bill of tonnage and poundage, a member remarked, "I cannot but much sorrow to see how we are still pressed to this point. I hoped those near the Chair would have truly informed his Majesty of our good intentions. But we see how unhappy we are, still some about his Majesty make him diffident of us." Misreports, in the minds of the commons, amounted in effect to a denial of the right of access to the sovereign. "There have been ill Offices done to this House by some Members of this House," said Sir Edward Cecil in May, 1621, "for at first Sitting, while the King's Ear was open to us, there was a good Harmony between his Majesty and us; but by the Carriage of some ill Messages the King hath been misinformed." [19]

These accusations were, generally speaking, unjust to councillors. Such reports as have come down to us appear, on the whole, fair and judicious accounts of what took place in the commons. Doubtless there were councillors who colored their reports

---

[18] Lake to Salisbury, December 2, 1610, St. P. Domestic, 14/58:54. Calvert to Buckingham, December 17, 1621, *Commons Debates 1621*, VII, 628. In 1628 Phelips thanked secretary Coke for reprimanding him in the house itself for the language he had used instead of reporting it to the king behind his back. Mildmay added, "If any word have fallen from any let it be fairly presented to his Majestie." March 22, 1628, Harl. MSS 4771, f. 22, 23.

[19] May 31, 1621, *P. and D.*, II, 142; *Commons Debates 1621*, III, 375–76. June 6, 1628, Borlase, f. 222. *Commons Debates for 1629*, 22. *P. and D.*, II, 129, 131, 281. See also *C. J.*, I, 500, where the speaker "cleareth the Counsellors" of making misreports.

in such a way as to make the actions of the commons appear more antimonarchical than they were. But the real difficulty lay not in the reports of councillors but in the interpretation placed on those reports by the crown. And it must be added that the commons were demanding a good deal of the king when they asked him to regard many of their actions as expressions of affection and loyalty. There is a touch of hypocrisy about their protestations that they were pushing supply as fast as they could and that they had no intention of diminishing the power of the crown.

To the attacks and insinuations of the commons the councillors replied surprisingly little. They apparently assumed that their position would be an unpleasant one and did not wish to cause more bitterness by answering accusations too sharply. They occasionally defended themselves by saying they were merely following instructions, and doubtless they could have done this more often than they did. When Eliot attacked Coke in 1628 for delaying the delivery of a message, Coke said, "Touching my long silence, it was his Majesty's directions." "He that gave me the message gave me the time, and appointed me how I should carry myself." [20] And councillors at times served the house well by delaying messages in the hope that conciliation would make their delivery unnecessary. Councillors frequently protested that they were innocent of making false reports. Carleton told the commons in 1626, "I will undertake that all good offices are done by those that are members of this House neare the King"; if the king was misinformed, it was through other channels. When James was informed of the commons' petition of December 6, 1621, through some unauthorized source, "Sir Edward Sackville said it was none of our House that did misinform the King but a stranger." When the rash words of Clement Coke in 1626 produced a sharp message from the king, Weston remarked, "He should not need, knowing the good opinion of the House, to say he knew not where the king had these words." In 1621 Calvert said, perhaps to forestall attack, "It is not strange that the Business of the House (which is so commonly spoken of abroad in the Town) doth come to his Majesty's ear." The accusation was made in 1626 that councillors did not dare tell the truth to the king for fear of offending Buckingham; and that as a result "the poisonous in-

[20] May 1, 1628, Harl. MSS 1601, f. 35; Borlase, f. 122; Holles, f. 11.

formations of those vipers" who misinformed the king were not contradicted. Weston replied, "I doe not think you will have such an opinion that those officers about the king dare not doe their dutyes were the Duke tenn Dukes. I will end with an entreaty that no calumneys may be suffered agaynst those that serve the king wisely, feythfully and honestly." If the actions of the commons were not liked at court, it was the commons who were to blame and not the councillors. "I rejoice," said May, "when I can go to Court able to justify your proceedings." [21]

Councillors might also have pointed out that their reports to the king were often of great value to the house and that occasionally they played the part of true mediators between king and commons. This was certainly the role of Cranfield during the parliament in 1621. Undoubtedly the messages he delivered regarding the court of chancery had been obtained from James through his influence. Thus a councillor might persuade the king to send messages that met the desires of the commons. Again in April of 1621 Cranfield did the house good service. The commons had censured a patent which the king had previously withdrawn by proclamation, and the action of the house seemed to James an indication that the commons did not trust his word. James was very angry. But Cranfield explained in the commons "that he told the King, that the House did in this but prosecute what they had in Hand before the Recess; and that the King, being at Length rightly informed, was satisfied. He told the King further that the House had done nothing but what was for his Majesty's Honour; wherto the King said, he thanked the House for it, but wished that we should not be so careful for his Honour, as to destroy his Service." Thus Cranfield had appeased James's anger by his report of the doings of the house; and in all probability he

[21] May 13, 1626, Whitelocke, f. 193. *Commons Debates 1621*, II, 508. "The Petition of the Lower House . . . was so long in debating that the King was informed of all the particulars of it before it was sent (which will prove no good office in them that did it)." Locke to Carleton, December 8, 1621, St. P. Domestic, 14/124:22. March 15, 1626, Whitelocke, f. 47; Rich, f. 71v. *P. and D.*, II, 341. June 6, 1626, Whitelocke, f. 219. *Commons Debates for 1629*, 92.

On June 5, 1628, the speaker asked leave to go to the king. On the next day he said, "I did you no ill service. Should I not make true relations I might justly deserve your censure. But let my tongue cleave to the roof of my mouth if I did deliver anything to the disadvantage of any man. I hope you will have no other thoughts of me." June 6, 1628, Borlase, f. 222. On December 8, 1621, councillors assured the commons that a message entrusted to them to be taken to the king would be faithfully delivered. *P. and D.*, II, 300.

softened the king's reply in reporting the matter back to the commons.[22]

The suspicions of the commons placed councillors in a most awkward position. They had to deliver messages, of which they might themselves disapprove, to a hostile and suspicious assembly that showed its resentment by sullen silence or angry expostulation. The discontent of the house vented itself upon the messengers. They were accused of falsehood and trickery, and the slightest irregularity in their conduct was at once interpreted in the worst possible light. The way of the mediator was hard. "We which have the happines to sitt in this house, being Counsellors of State to his Majestie, do find our selves reduced to a great strait, in regard that what wee speak out of zealous Intent to preserve his Majesties good opinion of the proceedings of this house, is subiect to exception and misconstruction."[23] Councillors did not relish their part. When Sir John Coke was away from London in the spring of 1628 and complained to Conway of his difficulties among the shipyards at Portsmouth, Conway replied, "To comfort you in that worke . . . I will tell you that you have escaped the deliveringe of manie messages, in which you would have had noe delight nor for which you would have received thankes." At the end of the parliament of 1621 we find Buckingham encouraging Calvert to remember that he is serving the king and not to bewail his unpleasant work in the commons.[24]

Nevertheless councillors did their best. They labored to obtain a sympathetic hearing in the house for the king's messages. Sometimes they began on a note of apology, saying that the king "desired not to interrupt our Business with Messages" or that "his Majesty was sensible of the loss of an afternoon" occasioned by a message. Councillors could find a benign and gracious meaning in messages where the commons saw only harshness. Thus in 1626

---

[22] Locke to Carleton, March 3, 1621, St. P. Domestic, 14/120:6. At the end of the session Cranfield said "that he had been charged before the King, that he did first set on Foot the Business of the Chancery; and yet he shall still desire to have it finished, and that the Committee may consider of the Heads that he himself and others at first laid down." *P. and D.*, II, 111. April 24, 1621, *ibid.*, I, 308–10; *Commons Debates 1621*, III, 67–68.

[23] Speech of a councillor, February, 1629, St. P. Domestic, 16/136:80. Cranfield said in the commons, April 30, 1621, "A tickle Matter, to bring a Message between the King and his People." *C. J.*, I, 597. Sir John Coke said in 1629 that he "findeth he goeth in a slippery way betweene his Majestie and his people." *Commons Debates for 1629.* 121.

[24] Conway to Coke, June 9, 1628, St. P. Domestic, 16/106:71. Calvert to Buckingham, December 4, 1621, *Commons Debates 1621*, VII, 621–22.

councillors pointed out the magnanimity of Charles in allowing the commons themselves to punish Clement Coke for rash words in the house.[25] If the king took the commons to task, said councillors, he was speaking as a father to his children. "How unwillingly the king came to this message," said Carleton in 1626, "I being present cann witness." Councillors at times added words of their own in the hope of making messages more palatable. In the autumn of 1621, May had the task of delivering a very curt message rejecting a petition of the commons; but he added that "the King seemed well pleased and said that our Petition was a mannerly and well penned Petition." A sharp passage in James's letter of December 14, said Calvert, was not an attack upon privilege but "only the Slip of a Pen in the End of a long Answer." In 1628, when the commons requested the king to allow them a recess at Easter, Charles "expressed his denyall in some anger, though that was suppressed" in delivering the message to the commons. Councillors begged the house not to put too harsh an interpretation upon messages. In 1621 the solicitor besought the commons to avoid any "curious construccion" of a sharp letter from the king. "Shall wee desire him favourably [to] interprett our words and shall wee tye his so strictly?" Again in 1628 Sir John Coke, in delivering a sharp message demanding a vote on supply, "humbly desired this honourable assembly not to undervalue nor to overstrain this message." Messages were to be obeyed, councillors explained, and not to be answered, for replies brought more messages and caused more time to be lost. "As messages from the King retard our business, soe ours begett replies; and that hinders as much; the King expects no answer."[26]

An incident of 1626 may be cited to show that councillors sometimes softened the effect of a message when they saw that it could not possibly win obedience from the house. On March 15 Charles sent a sharp message asking the commons to punish Clement Coke for using words in debate which the king claimed were seditious. But after councillors had delivered the message, they did not press the house to follow it too closely. Rather they seemed

[25] May 19, 1628, C. J., I, 900; May 3, 1628, Mass., f. 147. March 15, 1626, Whitelocke, f. 47–50. See also April 28, 1628, Harl. MSS 1721, f. 196v.

[26] April 20, 1626, Whitelocke, f. 142. P. and D., II, 338, 362. Nethersole to the queen of Bohemia, April 14, 1628, St. P. Domestic, 16/101:4. Commons Debates 1621, VI, 335–36. April 12, 1628, Borlase, f. 73. May 3, 1628, Grosvenor, III, f. 31–35.

to deprecate the message and to imply that they were willing to treat Coke leniently if a quarrel with the king could be avoided. May suggested a committee to examine Coke's words and either to punish him or to tell the king he had been misinformed. Sir John Finch, Weston, and other courtiers said they had been offended by Coke's words but had not considered them seditious. In the end the commons accepted this interpretation. They declared that Coke had displeased the house and that his words were open to a sinister construction but that they had not been seditious. Councillors doubtless felt that this was as far as the house would go and hoped that it was far enough to satisfy the king. Again in 1621 Calvert softened a message commanding the house to go on with bills by saying that in his opinion the commons were not precluded from proceeding with other business along with bills.[27]

It is clear that councillors sometimes modified messages or added words of their own as a result of instructions from court. If unpleasant words or phrases which the king wished to convey to the commons, but for which he did not wish to take the blame, were omitted from the message and spoken by the messenger, acting apparently on his own responsibility, the crown perhaps might escape opprobrium. Thus on April 12, 1628, Coke delivered a message commanding the house to take up supply. The message was a sharp one, but Coke added words of his own that were still sharper. "There is notice taken," he said, "as if this House should trench, not on the abuses of power, but on power itself." We have two drafts of this message in Coke's hand, and both drafts are carefully corrected by Charles himself. But neither draft contains the additional words spoken by Coke. It is clear, therefore, that these words were not in the message. Yet when Coke was asked to explain what his words meant, he said he could not do so because he had them from the king. "I cannot descend to particulars. I have no leave nor power. I only deliver you these words thus committed to my trust by his Majesty." Thus Charles had wished these words to be spoken in the commons but did not wish them to be a part of his message.[28]

[27] March 15, 1626, Rich, f. 70–71v; Whitelocke, f. 47–50. *Commons Debates 1621*, VI, 335.
[28] St. P. Domestic, 16/100:88, 89. April 12, 1628, Borlase, f. 73; Nicholas, p. 56. Nethersole to the queen of Bohemia, April 14, 1628, St. P. Domestic, 16/101:4. Nethersole wrote (June 7, 1628) that the speaker, after delivering a message, added a comment "as of himself, but without doubt by direction." Nethersole to the queen of Bohemia, *ibid.*, 16/106:55.

If the government decided to retreat from a position it had taken, it could do so with a minimum of embarrassment by instructing councillors to interpret former messages in a new way. Thus in 1621 the house had imprisoned Goldsmith for bringing a suit against Sir Edward Coke. On December 7 Calvert delivered a message demanding Goldsmith's release; this message the house ignored. On December 11 Calvert brought a second message commanding the house to proceed no further against Goldsmith. Calvert then explained that the king's instructions could be obeyed if Goldsmith was kept a prisoner and no further action was taken against him. Calvert suggested that the commons detain Goldsmith in prison while they made a declaration to the king justifying their proceedings. This interpretation strained the meaning of the second message and absolutely contradicted the former one. It is impossible to imagine Calvert taking such liberties with the royal word unless he had instructions to do so.[29]

It must not be supposed that councillors had any great discretionary power in modifying or adding words to the messages of the king. Unless they had instructions from court, they were on very dangerous ground. In 1621 Calvert begged Buckingham to excuse him to the king for delivering a message for which he had general but not specific instructions. And, even with instructions, councillors had to act with the greatest adroitness and skill if they were to avoid complications with the commons. Normally councillors delivered messages exactly as they received them and refused to enter upon explanations unless they were certain of the crown's approval. When Coke was asked to interpret a message in 1628, he replied "that the message was delivered him so, can neither add nor detract to nor from it." In 1626 a message told the commons that Eliot had been imprisoned for matters "extrajudicial" to the house. But councillors would not comment on the meaning of that phrase until they had gone to the king and obtained his definition and permission to repeat it to the house.[30] Sir John Coke, whose additions to messages were always laborious and forced, constantly took refuge in refusals to explain the words he had used.

Councillors found their position all the more exasperating be-

---

[29] *P. and D.*, II, 294, 306–09.
[30] *Commons Debates 1621*, VII, 626. May 1, 1628, Holles, f. 11. May 16, 17, 1626, Whitelocke, f. 196–97; *Lowther*, 25–27.

cause they were constantly employed by the commons to carry messages and other information to the king and to the house of lords. The commons, in fact, found the councillors highly useful. It was an enormous advantage to be able to communicate with the sovereign through persons who were certain of a cordial reception, who were liked and trusted by the crown. When the commons sent a deputation to James in 1621, he called for stools for the ambassadors, as if the commons were a foreign power. But councillors were received more kindly. Moreover, they could obtain immediate access. It was probably this more than anything else which made them valuable to the commons. If access was requested through the speaker or other means, it might easily be delayed or postponed by the king. But speed was often essential. In 1621 the commons suddenly learned that Gondomar was about to export some iron ordnance and that the ordnance was to be placed on shipboard the very day on which the news of it reached the house. Councillors were sent at once to James with a protest. This could hardly have been done through any other means. There were also many matters on which the commons felt deeply and yet hesitated to place their opinions before the king in a formal way. But councillors could be employed to explain these things to the king informally. At times they were asked to do this not as members of the commons but as advisers of the crown. In 1621 the house wished the king to suspend a certain patent, but it was suggested that a formal request to the king might perhaps weaken the power of the commons to end patents themselves. It was therefore ordered "that Mr. Secretary (taking Notice of the Inclination of the House) should move the King, as from himself, to suspend the Execution" of the patent in question. On another occasion the commons ordered "that Mr. Treasurer as from himself (yet taking knowledge of the desire of the House therein) should move his Majesty for stay of the further execution of the glass patent." Again in 1621 the commons decided not to send word to the king on a certain matter because "it was enough that there had been something of it intimated here, in the Presence of the Privy Counsellors and of the King's Council." [31] Thus coun-

[31] December 19, 1621, *P. and D.,* II, 362–63; I, 119. St. P. Domestic, 14/124:58. See also *P. and D.,* I, 293; II, 171. The solicitor might be used in the same way. "When there is occasion of access to his Majesty the use is to appoint the Privy Councill Members of the House to pray access. 16 Martii 1609." Lansd. MSS 486, f. 136v. In 1604 Sir John Stanhope was sent privately to the king with a request of the commons. Harl. MSS 6283, f. 154.

cillors were used not only to place requests before the crown but to influence the king in favor of those requests. The commons had an opportunity of communicating with the ruler in a way utterly impossible through ordinary channels. Such intimate connections, if rightly employed by the commons and correctly understood by the king, might have led to very important and far-reaching developments. But these possibilities were destroyed for the time being by suspicions and hostilities.

Councillors were also employed to carry bills and messages to the house of lords. Here their function was more formal and of little real importance. It is possible that when councillors were sent to the lords, they lent some added authority to the communications which they brought and helped to convince the lords that the commons were in earnest. But this was a function that steadily declined in significance as the period advanced.

Councillors, though they were under suspicion when they brought messages from the crown, were thus expected to do very similar things for the commons. They were often most unwilling messengers. In May, 1621, Greville, Sir John Coke, and Calvert were sent to the king on the thankless mission of telling him that he was misinformed. Greville protested, "I am your servant and to be commanded to doe your appointed service, but I desyer that you will impose no difficultyes on me." In 1628 the councillors were asked to show the king a petition from some wine merchants in trouble over tonnage and poundage. "Sir Humphrey May excused him self and his fellows, by saying that they were ill carryers of a petition that had sett their hands to the contrary." But the commons held that since councillors had been present in the house when the petition had been approved, they were "now converted" and "the fittest Instruments to present such a message." [32] It is little wonder that councillors occasionally reminded the commons of the value of their services. In 1629 May warned the commons, "If you be too quick to except against the Ministers of his Majesty that serve his Majesty and this House, it will discourage and stop our Mouths, whose service you daily command." Earlier in 1626

[32] May 1, 1621, *Commons Debates 1621*, III, 113. April 11, 1628, Borlase, f. 69. Councillors began to ask that the messages they carried to the king be written down. Putting these communications in written form relieved councillors, to some extent, of personal responsibility for the content of messages and emphasized the formal character of their function. See June 7, 1626, Whitelocke, f. 222.

May had said that sharp words in the commons "discouraged men from dooing service." [33]

In brief, the Tudor arrangement by which councillors formed a connecting link between king and commons had broken down. The men who formed this link were the servants of the king, and they were repudiated by the commons when parliament and the sovereign no longer formed a harmonious constitutional entity.

[33] February 3, 1629, *Commons Debates for 1629*, 33. May 6, 1626, Whitelocke, f. 181.

Index

Index

Abbot, George, archbishop of Canterbury, leads anti-Spanish faction, 18; speech in council, 39; Bacon uses in parliament, 151n; spokesman for parliament, 164; connection with popular leaders, 167, 187–88; suspected of working against Buckingham, 180; in conference, 226n; restored to favor, 51

Abbot, Sir Maurice, attacks Buckingham, 187–88; letter of, 249n

Aiton, Sir Robert, letter of, 51

Alençon, Francis of Valois, duke of, 25

Alford, Edward, 250; private meeting with Salisbury, 118; leader of commons, 155; clashes with councillors, 87–88, 208n, 210–11, 264, 300; praises Sir Edward Coke, 90; says he is watched, 158; warns commons, 213, 228, 230–31, 253, 293n; offers seat to Allen Apsley, 192n

Alienation office, 108

Alured, Thomas, suggests ways to win votes, 192; letters of, 97n, 200

Andover, election at, 201n

Angell, John, 156n, 167n

Anne, queen of James I, attorney to, 106; vice-chamberlain of, 107

Annesley, Sir Francis, 190n

Apparel, law concerning, 38

Apsley, Allen, defended by his father, 192n

Apsley, Sir Allen, lieutenant of the Tower, interferes in election, 72; defends his son, 192n

Apsley, Sir John, defeated in election, 72

Arches, dean of court of, 107

Armory, master of, 143n

Army plot, 68

Arundel, earl of, *see* Howard, Thomas

Arundel, members for, 81n, 99

Ashburnham, John, 192n–93n, 203n

Ashley, Sir Anthony, letter of, 154

Ashley, Sir Francis, 143n, 156n, 190n

Ashton, Devon, 79

Assheton, Sir Richard, 108

Aston, Sir Roger, gentleman of the bedchamber, 108

Attorney-general, 106, 135, 143n, 156n; in Goodwin vs. Fortescue, 57; excluded from commons, 144, 215–17; assistant in

house of lords, 214, 229–30. *See also* Bacon; Coventry; Heath; Hobart; Learned counsel

Austria, 254, 285

Bacon, Sir Francis, solicitor, attorney, lord chancellor, 18, 26, 71, 106, 143n, 144n, 156n, 207n; used by Salisbury in commons, 111–12, 114–15; reports conferences, 231, 233; advice on conference, 227, 234; describes vote, 269–70, 273; statement to lords, 298; on party organization, 120–22; criticizes Salisbury, 29, 104, 118–19, 126, 127n–28n; eligibility to serve in commons, 214, 216–17; candidate for secretary, 131–32; political philosophy, 132–35; on financial reform, 39n; warns against dissension, 116, 141n; on undertaking, 32, 35, 136, 142–43, 145–46, 148; preparations for parliament in *1621*, 40–45, 60, 156–57; on Sir Edward Coke, 89, 157–58; on Naunton, 93n; urges reform, 46; obstructs work of commons, 151n; impeachment, 47n, 86, 150, 155n, 248, 250; advises James to speak less often, 14n; accepts presents, 23; on councillors in commons, 59, 206; opposes committee of the whole, 244–45; private meeting with James, 248n

Badger, Sir Thomas, 191n, 203n

Bagg, Sir James, 156n, 167n, 190n, 191n, 203n; analyzes opposition, 180, 183–88; suggests means to obtain votes, 191, 193; letters of, 176n, 197n, 202n, 218n

Banbury, countess of, 194n

Bankes, John, 167n, 190n, 203n

Barker, Robert, 107, 143n

Baronets, debate on, prevented, 252

Barrett, Sir Edward, 143n, 156n

Barrington, Sir Francis, election of, 74; motion by, 112

Beaulieu, John, letters of, 50n, 51n, 74n

Bedchamber, 250, 255; gentlemen of the, 108, 156n, 185

Beecher, Sir William, 67n, 143n, 156n, 167n, 190n, 203n

Beer Alston, Devon, letter to mayor of, 105n

315

INDEX

INDEX

Fiennes, William, Viscount Saye and Sele, in opposition, 155; courted by Buckingham, 164, 179; attacks Buckingham, 188; opposed by Williams, 182n

Finch, Sir Heneage, 107, 156n, 167n, 190n, 203n; reviews penal statutes, 44; recorder of London, 157; speaker, 218, 223; letter to, 53n

Finch, Henry, 143n

Finch, Sir John, 143n, 156n, 167n, 190n, 203n; in debate, 308; speaker, 191n, 197, 218, 220–21, 305n

Finch, Sir Thomas, 156n, 203n

Fines and forfeitures, grievances concerning, 31

Fishing, 36

Fleet prison, 263

Fleet Street, 154

Fleetwood, Sir Miles, receiver of the court of wards, 143n, 156n, 167n, 190n, 191n, 203n; attacks Cranfield, 164n, 165; urges Buckingham to make concessions, 179; quarrels with Sir Robert Pye, 200

Fleetwood, Sir William, receiver of the court of wards, 107

Fleming, Sir Thomas, solicitor, chief baron of the exchequer, 106; son of, 143n; letter of, 26n

Fleming, Sir Thomas, 143n

Flemyng, Philip, 80–81

Floyd, Edward, case of, 228, 230

Fontaine, M. de la, letter of, 270n

Fortescue, Sir John, chancellor of the duchy of Lancaster, election case, 56–59, 69, 82, 99, 104n; fails to influence election, 77; negligible role in commons, 83; commons told not to fear, 206. *See also* Goodwin vs. Fortescue

Fotherley, Thomas, 190n, 191n, 203n

France, 49, 66, 79, 168, 258, 259, 266, 286

Franklin, Sir John, 190n; elections of, 72–73

Freeman, Sir Ralph, master of requests, 190n, 203n

Fuller, Nicholas, leader of opposition, 121; reproved in conference, 227; objects to judges as assistants in lords, 230

Fullerton, Sir James, connections of, 185–86; not in commons in *1628*, 202

Fyvie, Lord, letter of, 26n

Gawdy, Sir Francis, chief justice of the common pleas, 299

Gawdy, Philip, 143n

Gee, William, letter of, 106n

Genoa, 266

Germany and German affairs, 18, 147, 266

Gerrard, Sir Gilbert, elections of, 71–73

Gewen, Thomas, auditor of the duchy of Cornwall, 167n, 191n

Gibbs, Thomas, 143n

Gifford, Emanuel, 156n, 191n

Glanville, John, 188, 303; calms house, 222; on types of conferences, 234n; clash with Edmondes, 241–42; on supply, 277; criticizes messages, 292–93, 301

Glass, patent for, 184n, 310

Glemham, Sir Charles, 167n, 190n

Godfrey, Thomas, 144n, 203n

Gold and silver thread, patent for, 292

Goldsmith, Henry, 90, 309

Gondomar, Count, *see* Sarmiento de Acuña, Diego

Goodere, Sir Henry, letters of, 166n, 283n

Goodwin, Sir Francis, 144n; elections of, 57, 109n; meets privately with Salisbury, 118

Goodwin vs. Fortescue, 56–58, 82, 206, 227–28, 293

Gorges, Sir Ferdinand, letter of, 195

Goring, Sir George, 156n, 167n, 190n, 191n, 203n; agent of Buckingham in parliament, 148–49; lobbying by, 154, 158, 191–93; defends Buckingham, 172; protests against suspicion of courtiers, 213n; warns Buckingham, 195; a peer, 62n

Grandison, Viscount, *see* St. John, Oliver

Great Contract, 26–29, 121, 125–27, 133, 228, 235

Grenville, Sir Richard, 203n

Greville, Sir Fulke, Lord Brooke, speech in council, 37; influence in elections, 70, 99; retains seat in commons, 61; position in commons, 92; a peer, 59n, 61, 65; message by, 292; sent to king, 311; comment on Sir John Coke, 96; letter of, 189n; letters to, 48, 173–74

Greville, Sir Fulke, lobbying by, 191–92

Grievances, 24–25, 49n, 167n, 169, 237n, 246; petitions of, 26–27; commons weigh value of, 28–29; debated in council, 29, 34–40; judges debate in *1620*, 41–42; deplored by Edmondes, 92; Cranfield on, 248–49; Sir Edward Coke chairman for, 89; Bacon on, 132, 135; attempt of government to reform, 45–48; dropped as result of message from king, 293n; lists of, 28, 31, 41–42. *See also* Baronets; Courts of justice; Gold and silver thread; Impositions; Ireland; Musters; Ordnance; Surrounded grounds

Griffith, John, secretary to Northampton, 108

Grimstone, Sir Harbottle, 263

Gunpowder Plot, 261, 269